Team Development with Microsoft® Visual Studio® Team Foundation Server

patterns & practices

J.D. Meier

Jason Taylor

Alex Mackman

Prashant Bansode

Kevin Jones

ISBN 978-0-7356-2571-6

Contents

Chapter 4
Structuring Projects and Solutions in Team Foundation Source Control 27

Chapter 5
Defining Your Branching and Merging Strategy 37

Chapter 6

Managing Source Control Dependencies in Visual Studio Team System 49

Part III: Builds 67

Chapter 7

Team Build Explained 69

Foreword by Jeff Beehler

Foreword

Before we released Microsoft® Visual Studio® 2005 Team Foundation Server (TFS), we first used it to develop TFS. For the final 18 months of the project, we used it extensively to manage the development life cycle of our project, a practice commonly known as "dogfooding." Through this dogfooding, we learned a lot about the powerful system that we were creating. We certainly found and fixed many quality issues so that the resulting product was much more stable and performed better than we could have achieved otherwise. But perhaps more importantly, we learned about ways to best use (and not use) the tools we were creating. This experience, in conjunction with feedback from our customers on their practices, forms the basis for this guide.

At first glance, one might expect this information to be included with or to replace the product documentation. In fact, at one time, I held that belief as well. However, as I've worked closely with J.D. Meier and the other authors of this guide, it's become clear to me that this split is both natural and important. I think the best way to describe it is to compare the two guides to your car's owner's manual and a driver's guide you need both, but for different reasons. Traditionally, the product team has focused on product documentation and left the guidance aspect to others. While we still depend on others to help us out here, we're starting to invest more of our time and energy in the guidance portion because we realize how important it is to the successful adoption of our product and its role in increasing overall customer satisfaction.

Like a car, TFS is a powerful tool that can take you and your team nearly anywhere you want to go; this guide can help you get there. Every team approaches TFS somewhat differently depending on its particular needs and history. For this reason, we've written this guide in such a way as to allow you either to read it from cover to cover if you want the full picture, or to dive into specific topics as your needs dictate.

Customer feedback led us to write this guide in the first place, and it continues to play an important role in helping set our direction and how we achieve our objectives. We're convinced that close community involvement in projects such as these helps make the content more useful and ultimately more successful than if we wrote it in a vacuum. With this in mind, real users helped us determine what to write about, what best practices to recommend, and how to organize the content. However, our collective job is not finished. Please help us continue to improve this guide, and let us know what else needs to be covered. The surface area of TFS is so broad that sometimes it's overwhelming even for us. With your input, we can help our customers make the best use of the tools we've developed.

We designed TFS to bring teams together to deliver great software. By dogfooding TFS, we brought our teams together and I hope you'll agree that the result is a great product. This guide can help you and your team to also realize this vision with your next project.

All the best!

Jeff Beehler

Chief of Staff, Visual Studio Team System

July, 2007

Jeff Beehler is the Team System Chief of Staff. After graduating from the University of Colorado, he began his career at Microsoft in 1990, working on early versions of Visual C++. In 1996, he left Microsoft to pursue other interests including consulting, teaching elementary school and starting a family. He returned to Microsoft in 2003 to work on Visual Studio Team System where he is involved with many aspects of the project from planning to execution to release. He's an avid dogfooder of all parts of Team System to help him do his job better. Outside of work, Jeff enjoys spending time with his family, taking pictures and playing outdoors in the great Northwest.

Foreword by Brian Harry

Foreword

Developing software can be a very complex process. A software-development project can range from a very small team to a team of thousands of people with a multitude of specialized roles. When setting out to build Microsoft® Visual Studio® Team System, we intended to create tools that help developers conceive, organize, design, schedule, build, test, deploy, and manage software applications. Team Foundation Server (TFS) is the centerpiece of Team System that helps to tie together all of the people and activities involved in the application life cycle.

As a result, Team System is broad in scope, designed for many different people with many different roles. We have endeavored to make the product as simple as possible while keeping it flexible enough to adapt to the needs of widely varying development teams. These are competing goals. Over the past year or so, it has become clear that we've been missing a key component for users of Team System. While we have lots of documentation and help on "how to" do things, we have lacked good information on how things "should" be done. The process guidance in Team System fills part of this gap but focuses primarily on people, roles, and workflow. What has been missing is really solid information on software development process implementation strategies.

This new patterns & practices TFS Guide does a terrific job of filling that gap. It covers a wide array of topics ranging from "How should I organize my Team Projects?" and "What kind of branching and merging structure should I use?" to "How many builds should I have and how often?" and "How do I use Team System to manage my project?" It explains things both in terms of best practices and how they map to your team, and in terms of how you can implement them in TFS.

Much of this guidance is rooted in the software-development practices we have learned and established at Microsoft over the past 30 years. Further, we are able to base this guidance on real-life experience with TFS, as we have been using it for much of our development process in the Developer Division for more than two years. I sincerely hope that you will benefit from the lessons we've learned and the best practices we've established.

Brian Harry

Technical Fellow, Visual Studio Team System

July, 2007

Brian Harry is the Product Unit Manager for Team Foundation Server. Brian has always had a passion for software development tools, dating all the way back to his college years in the mid '80s at North Carolina State University where he did research on compilers, linkers, assemblers, processor simulation systems and the like. After joining Microsoft, Brian worked in what was then the Tools and Databases division. For a couple of years he worked on SourceSafe and then the Microsoft Repository. Next he worked on the .NET Framework, where he was the Development manager for the Common Language Runtime and then served as the Product Unit Manager. At the end of 2002, he moved back to North Carolina to help open a development center to build tools for developers. Brian has built a team of about 50-60 people in NC who work on the Team Foundation Server and Visual Studio Team System for Testers products.

Foreword by Rob Caron

Foreword

Ever since the early days of Visual Studio Team System, we knew software development teams would need more content than we could possibly provide prior to shipping. In particular, we knew they would need proven guidance and best practices; however, that knowledge wouldn't be known until the product was put through its paces by a variety of teams in a diverse array of environments, projects and scenarios to prove what works, and what doesn't.

Unfortunately, the identification and development of proven guidance and best practices takes time. Over the last few years, we have learned a great deal about the use of Team System in general, and Team Foundation Server in particular. But that knowledge wasn't always easy to find and digest. It would take the dedicated and methodical work of patterns & practices veteran J.D. Meier and his team months to make sense of it all.

Finally, the wait is over! Team Development with Microsoft Visual Studio Team Foundation Server represents the collective wisdom of innumerable people who contributed directly, and indirectly, to this project. The team that assembled this content didn't ignore the experience of those who went before them. They culled through a scattered collection of blog posts, forum threads, articles, and more to better understand how teams are adopting and using Team System "in the wild."

Along the way, they examined the key areas that impact software development teams, and identified which practices were responsible for predictable and repeatable success. Some of the most informative content explains a number of Team Foundation Server feature areas, such as work item tracking, reporting, and process templates.

In retrospect, I am thankful that as a documentation team we had the presence of mind to defer this work instead of trying to provide best-guess filler content. I apologize to all of those who suffered without this content, and I thank those who persevered and pioneered the use of Team System.

Rob Caron

Lead Product Manager

Microsoft Corporation

July, 2007

Rob Caron is the Lead Product Manager for Developer Content Strategy at Microsoft. Rob started at Microsoft in 1999 as a writer for Visual Studio product documentation. Over the years, he contributed content for Visual Studio .NET 2002, Visual Studio .NET 2003, and Visual Studio Team System. In mid-2004, he started a blog that became the nexus for information on Team System. After seven years of creating content, Rob moved to the Developer Marketing team in the fall of 2006. He now leads a group that is focused on the increasingly complex developer story at Microsoft with a goal of making it simpler.

Introduction

This guide shows you how to get the most out of Visual Studio 2005 Team Foundation Server to help improve the effectiveness of your team-based software development. Whether you are already using Team Foundation Server or adopting from scratch, you'll find guidance and insights you can tailor for your specific scenarios.

The information in this guide is based on practices learned from customer feedback and product support, as well as experience from the field and in the trenches. The guidance is task-based and presented in the following parts.

- **Part I, "Fundamentals,"** gives you a quick overview of team development with Team Foundation Server. You'll see the big picture in terms of your software development environment, including the development and test environment. You'll also learn the basic architecture of Team Foundation Server.
- **Part II, "Source Control,"** shows you how to structure your source code and manage dependencies. It also shows you how to determine a branching and merging strategy if you need isolation for your development efforts.
- **Part III, "Builds,"** shows you how to set up team builds, how to produce continuous integration builds for your development team, and how to drop scheduled builds to your test team. It also discusses common problems and how to work around them.
- **Part IV, "Large Project Considerations,"** show you additional considerations you need to deal with when working with large projects.
- **Part V, "Project Management,"** shows you how to use Team Foundation Server work items, areas and iterations to streamline your development process regardless of what project management approach you use.
- **Part VI, "Process Templates,"** shows you how to get the most out of the process templates and process guidance that is supplied with Team Foundation Server out of the box. It also shows how you can customize the process templates, and make modifications to work items and workflow to map to the software engineering process your team is already using.
- **Part VII, "Reporting,"** shows you how all of the other Team Foundation Server components integrate their data store into a common reporting mechanism. You'll learn how to use the default reports as well as how to build your own custom reports.

- **Part VIII, "Setting Up and Maintaining the Team Environment,"** removes the mystery from Team Foundation Server deployment. You'll learn how to choose between a single server and multiple server deployment. You'll also learn how to support remote development teams and how to maximize Team Foundation Server performance.
- **Part IX, "Visual Studio Team System 2008 Team Foundation Server",** shows the changes that are coming in the next version of Team Foundation Server. You'll learn what new features are planned as well as what features are going to be significantly improved. Some of the changes impact the guidance we give elsewhere in this guide, so use this section to improve your Team Foundation Server upgrade planning.
- **Guidelines** provide concise recommendations for Team Server Build, Project Management, Reporting and Source Control. Each guideline tells you what to do, why and how to follow the guideline.
- **Practices** provide a set of best practices based on the lessons development teams have learned when using Team Foundation Server in the field and within Microsoft. Each practice focuses on how to accomplish a task that is important for team effectiveness with Team Foundation Server.
- **Questions and Answers** provide answers to common questions on Team Foundation Source Control.
- **How Tos** give step-by-step in depth guidance on how to accomplish specific tasks with Team Foundation Server.
- **Resources** are a compendium of web sites, service providers, forums and blogs that you can use to learn more about Team Foundation Server and stay on top of latest developments in the toolset.

Team Development

There are many elements, processes, and roles that combine to enable successful team-based software development projects. This guide focuses on:

- The development process
- The build process
- The project management process

The following diagram illustrates the relationship between typical software development processes relating to team development and how Team Foundation Server can be leveraged to provide horizontal foundational support for these initiatives.

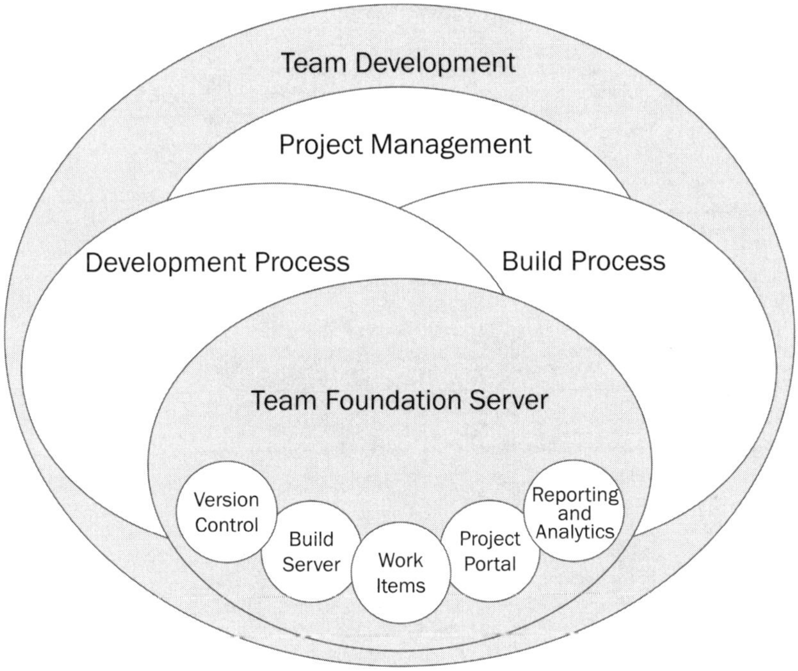

Figure 0.1

Scope of This Guide

This guide is focused on deploying Team Foundation Server and using it effectively for source control, build automation, work item management, and process management.

The diagram on the next page outlines a sample logical implementation of Team Foundation Server as it relates to the roles most common to the software engineering and development lifecycle.

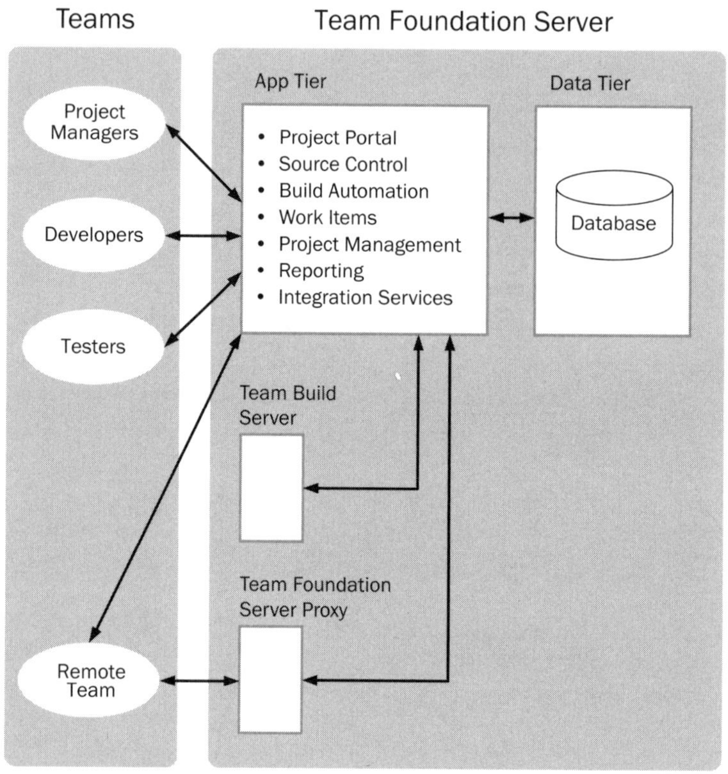

Figure 0.2

Why We Wrote This Guide

From our own experience with Team Foundation Server and through conversations with customers and Microsoft employees who work in the field, we determined there was demand for a guide that would show how to use Team Foundation in the real world. While there is information in the product documentation, in blog posts and in forums, there has been no single place to find proven practices for the effective use of Team Foundation Server in the context of a development project under real world constraints.

Who Should Read This Guide

This guide is targeted at providing individuals involved in the software development process with the resources, patterns and practices for creating an effective team development environment. The following are examples of roles that would benefit from this guidance:

- A development team that wants to adopt Team Foundation.
- A project manager looking to get the most out of Team Foundation, with regard to managing projects and development efforts, providing status of software development initiatives and providing feedback to business stakeholders.
- Interested parties investigating the use of Team Foundation but don't know how well it would work for their development scenarios and team constraints.
- Individuals tasked with planning a deployment and installing Team Foundation.

How to Use This Guide

The guide is divided into parts based on the order we see most teams think about and adopt Team Foundation. If you are in the process of adopting Team Foundation you'll probably want to read the entire guide from start to finish. If you are interested in using Team Foundation for a particular use, such as Source Control or Team Build, you can restrict your reading to just those sections. Use the main chapters to learn concepts and guiding principles. Use the appendix of "Guidelines", "Practices", "How To" articles and "Questions and Answers" to dive into implementation details. This separation allows you to understand the topics first and then dive into details as you see fit.

Organization of This Guide

You can read this guide from end to end, or you can read the chapters you need for your job.

Parts

The guide is divided into nine parts:

- Part I, Fundamentals
- Part II, Source Control
- Part III, Builds
- Part IV, Large Project Considerations
- Part V, Project Management
- Part VI, Process Templates

- Part VII, Reporting
- Part VIII, Setting Up and Maintaining the Team Environment
- Part IX, Visual Studio Team System 2008 Team Foundation Server

Part I, Fundamentals

- Ch 01—Introducing the Team Environment
- Ch 02—Team Foundation Server Architecture

Part II, Source Control

- Ch 03—Structuring Projects and Solutions in Source Control
- Ch 04—Structuring Projects and Solutions in Team Foundation Source Control
- Ch 05—Defining Your Branching and Merging Strategy
- Ch 06—Managing Source Control Dependencies in Visual Studio Team System

Part III, Builds

- Ch 07—Team Build Explained
- Ch 08—Setting Up Continuous Integration with Team Build
- Ch 09—Setting Up Scheduled Builds with Team Build

Part IV, Large Project Considerations

- Ch 10—Large Project Considerations

Part V, Project Management

- Ch 11—Project Management Explained
- Ch 12—Work Items Explained

Part VI, Process Templates

- Ch 13—Process Templates Explained
- Ch 14—MSF for Agile Software Development Projects

Part VII, Reporting

- Ch 15—Reporting Explained

Part VIII, Setting Up and Maintaining the Team Environment

- Ch 16—Team Foundation Server Deployment
- Ch 17—Providing Internet Access to Team Foundation Server

Part IX, Visual Studio Team System 2008 Team Foundation Server

- Ch 18—What's New in Visual Studio Team System 2008 Team Foundation Server

Guidelines

- Guidelines: Team Build
- Guidelines: Source Control
- Guidelines: Reporting
- Guidelines: Project Management

Practices

- Practices at a Glance: Team Build
- Practices at a Glance: Source Control
- Practices at a Glance: Reporting
- Practices at a Glance: Project Management

Questions and Answers

- Questions and Answers: Source Control

"How To" Articles

- How To: Add a New Developer to Your Project in Visual Studio Team Foundation Server
- How To: Automatically Run Code Analysis with Team Build in Visual Studio Team Foundation Server
- How To: Create a Custom Report for Visual Studio Team Foundation Server
- How To: Create a Risk Over Time Report for Visual Studio Team Foundation Server
- How To: Create Custom Check-in Policies in Visual Studio Team Foundation Server
- How To: Create Your Source Tree in Visual Studio Team Foundation Server
- How To: Customize a Process Template in Visual Studio Team Foundation Server
- How To: Customize a Report in Visual Studio Team Foundation Server
- How To: Manage Projects in Visual Studio Team Foundation Server
- How To: Migrate Source code to Team Foundation Server from Visual Source Safe
- How To: Perform a Baseless Merge in Visual Studio Team Foundation Server
- How To: Set Up a Continuous Integration Build in Visual Studio Team Foundation Server
- How To: Set Up a Scheduled Build in Visual Studio Team Foundation Server
- How To: Structure ASP.NET Applications in Visual Studio Team Foundation Server

- How To: Structure Windows Applications in Visual Studio Team Foundation Server
- How To: Structure Your Source Control Folders in Visual Studio Team Foundation Server

Resources

- Team Foundation Server Resources

Feedback and Support

We have made every effort to ensure the accuracy of this guide and its companion content.

Feedback on the Guide

If you have comments on this guide, send e-mail to *TFSguide@microsoft.com*.

We are particularly interested in feedback regarding the following:

- Technical issues specific to recommendations
- Usefulness and usability issues

Technical Support

Technical support for the Microsoft products and technologies referenced in this guide is provided by Microsoft Product Support Services (PSS). For product support information, please visit the Microsoft Product Support Web site at *http://support.microsoft.com*.

Community Support

MSDN Newsgroups:
http://forums.microsoft.com/MSDN/default.aspx?ForumGroupID=5&SiteID=1

Forum	Address
Team Foundation Server - General	http://forums.microsoft.com/MSDN/ShowForum.aspx?ForumID=22&SiteID=1
Team Foundation Server - Setup	http://forums.microsoft.com/MSDN/ShowForum.aspx?ForumID=68&SiteID=1
Team Foundation Server - Administration	http://forums.microsoft.com/MSDN/ShowForum.aspx?ForumID=477&SiteID=1
Team Foundation Server - Build Automation	http://forums.microsoft.com/MSDN/ShowForum.aspx?ForumID=481&SiteID=1

Forum	Address
Team Foundation Server - Power Toys	http://forums.microsoft.com/MSDN/ShowForum.aspx?ForumID=930&SiteID=1
Team Foundation Server - Process Templates	http://forums.microsoft.com/MSDN/ShowForum.aspx?ForumID=482&SiteID=1
Team Foundation Server - Reporting & Warehouse	http://forums.microsoft.com/MSDN/ShowForum.aspx?ForumID=480&SiteID=1
Team Foundation Server - Team System Web Access	http://forums.microsoft.com/MSDN/ShowForum.aspx?ForumID=1466&SiteID=1
Team Foundation Server - Version Control	http://forums.microsoft.com/MSDN/ShowForum.aspx?ForumID=478&SiteID=1
Team Foundation Server - Work Item Tracking	http://forums.microsoft.com/MSDN/ShowForum.aspx?ForumID=479&SiteID=1

The Team Who Brought You This Guide

This guide was created by the following team members:

- J.D. Meier
- Jason Taylor
- Alex Mackman
- Prashant Bansode
- Kevin Jones

Contributors and Reviewers

- **External Contributors/Reviewers.** David P. Romig, Sr; Dennis Rea; Eugene Zakhareyev; Leon Langleyben; Martin Woodward; Michael Rummier; Miguel Mendoza ; Mike Fourie; Quang Tran; Sarit Tamir; Tushar More; Vaughn Hughes
- **Microsoft Contributors / Reviewers.** Aaron Hallberg; Ahmed Salijee; Ajay Sudan; Ajoy Krishnamoorthy; Alan Ridlehoover; Alik Levin; Ameya Bhatawdekar; Bijan Javidi; Bill Essary; Brett Keown; Brian Harry; Brian Moore; Brian Keller; Buck Hodges; Burt Harris; Conor Morrison; David Caufield; David Lemphers; Doug Neumann; Edward Jezierski; Eric Blanchet; Eric Charran; Graham Barry; Gregg Boer; Grigori Melnik; Janet Williams Hepler; Jeff Beehler; Jose Parra; Julie MacAller; Ken Perilman; Lenny Fenster; Marc Kuperstein; Mario Rodriguez; Matthew Mitrik; Michael Puleio; Nobuyuki Akama; Paul Goring; Pete Coupland; Peter Provost; Granville (Randy) Miller; Richard Berg, Rob Caron; Robert Horvick; Rohit Sharma; Ryley Taketa; Sajee Mathew; Siddharth Bhatia; Tom Hollander; Tom Marsh; Venky Veeraraghavan

Tell Us About Your Success

If this guide helps you, we would like to know. Tell us by writing a short summary of the problems you faced and how this guide helped you out. Submit your summary to: *MyStory@Microsoft.com* .

Part I
Fundamentals

In this part:

- Introducing the Team Environment
- Team Foundation Server Architecture

1

Introducing the Team Environment

Objectives

- Describe how Microsoft® Visual Studio® Team Foundation Server supports the software development lifecycle.
- Describe how a typical development team uses Team Foundation Server.
- Describe how a typical test team uses Team Foundation Server.
- Describe the development and test team's physical environment.

Overview

This chapter describes how Team Foundation Server (TFS) and Microsoft Visual Studio Team System (VSTS) are used in a team-based software development environment. It introduces the core features of TFS and VSTS and describes the workflow between development and test teams during a software development project. Because TFS integrates source control, work tracking, reporting, project management and an automated build process, it enables a development team to work together more effectively.

A successful team-based software development project has many processes that must work together smoothly to ensure an efficient working environment. The core processes include:

- Development
- Test
- Build
- Deployment
- Release

This chapter introduces you to typical functions that the development and test teams can perform with TFS and describes how you can use TFS to manage the workflow to support efficient collaboration across teams.

How to Use This Chapter

Use this chapter to learn how TFS is designed to support the software development lifecycle. By reading this chapter, you will also learn about the TFS workflow and how TFS enables you to improve team collaboration.

For more detailed information about TFS architecture and the TFS core components, see Chapter 2, "Team Foundation Server Architecture."

Logical Workflow of Team Foundation Server

TFS enables a development team to store code in a centrally managed source code repository. You can create builds from this repository by using the build server and you can then distribute these builds to your test team.

Figure 1.1 shows the logical workflow of TFS and how the development and test environments are connected.

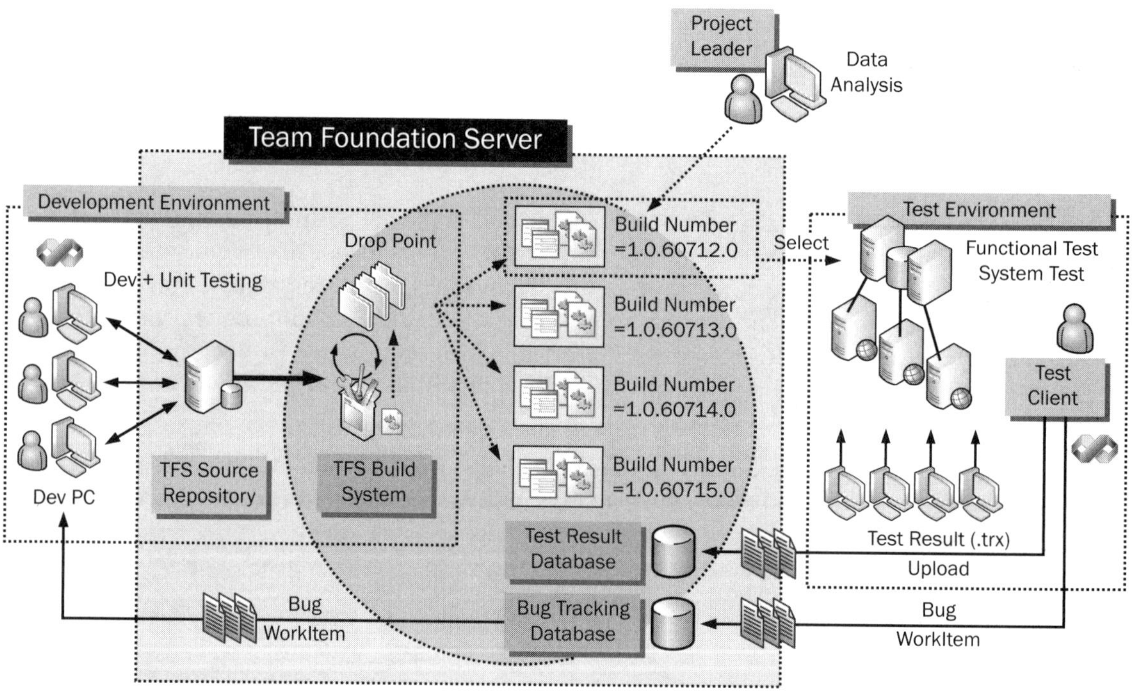

Figure 1.1 *Team Foundation Server Logical Workflow*

The test team picks up builds from a drop location and runs them through its testing environment by performing a combination of manual and automated tests. Test results are stored by TFS and are used to provide feedback on the build quality. The test team can also create work items and bugs (a specific type of work item) on which the development team needs to take action. These work items allow the test team to track the work of the development team.

Logical Workflow of Development, Test, and Production Environments

In larger organizations with multiple development teams, each development team maintains a separate TFS including separate source code repositories and team build servers. Figure 1.2 shows an example of the logical workflow that results from two development teams delivering application builds to an integration test team.

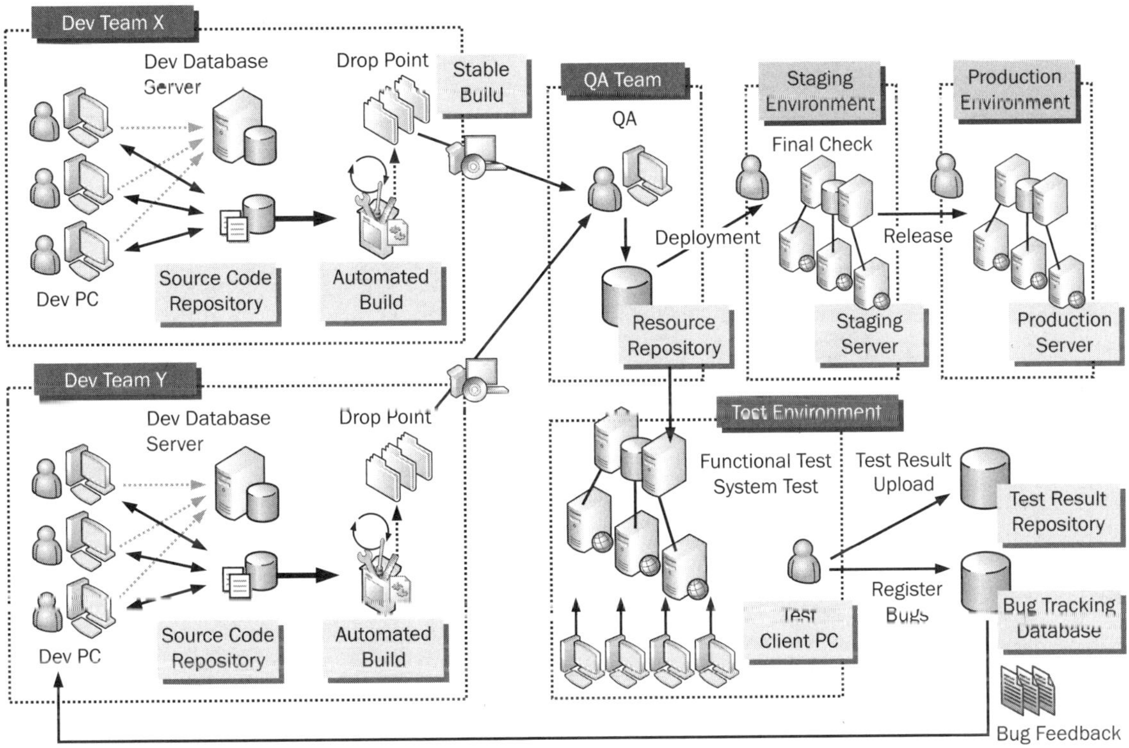

Figure 1.2 *Logical Workflow Showing Two Development Teams and an Integration Test Team*

Each development team delivers scheduled builds to a drop point such as a network share. These builds are picked up by the test team and tested to measure the quality of the build. When test quality gates are passed the applications are deployed to a staging server for final checks and user acceptance before ultimately being deployed to a production server.

Development Processes

Developers perform a number of key interactions with TFS throughout the duration of a software development project. For example, as a developer you interact with TFS in the following ways:

- You access bugs and task work items from TFS to determine what work you need to do. For example, work items might have been assigned by your project manager, by another developer, or by the test team.
- You use the VSTS Source Control Explorer to access the TFS source control repository and pull the latest source code into a local workspace or your development computer.
- After performing the work identified by the work item, you check your code back into the source control database.
- The check-in event might trigger a continuous integration build that uses Team Build.
- If the build fails a new work item is created to track the build break.

Test Processes

As a member of a test team, you might interact with TFS in the following ways:

- You pick up the output of a scheduled build from a specific drop location.
- You perform manual and automated testing including security testing, performance testing, and Web testing by using various VSTS tools.
- You upload the results from the tests to the TFS Test Result database for future reference.
- You log bugs identified by your testing into TFS as new work items.
- You resolve existing bugs, if the latest build fixes previously logged bugs.

Development and Test Physical Environments

The size and number of computers associated with your development and test environments varies depending upon the size of your teams and projects. Figure 1.3 shows a typical development and test physical environment.

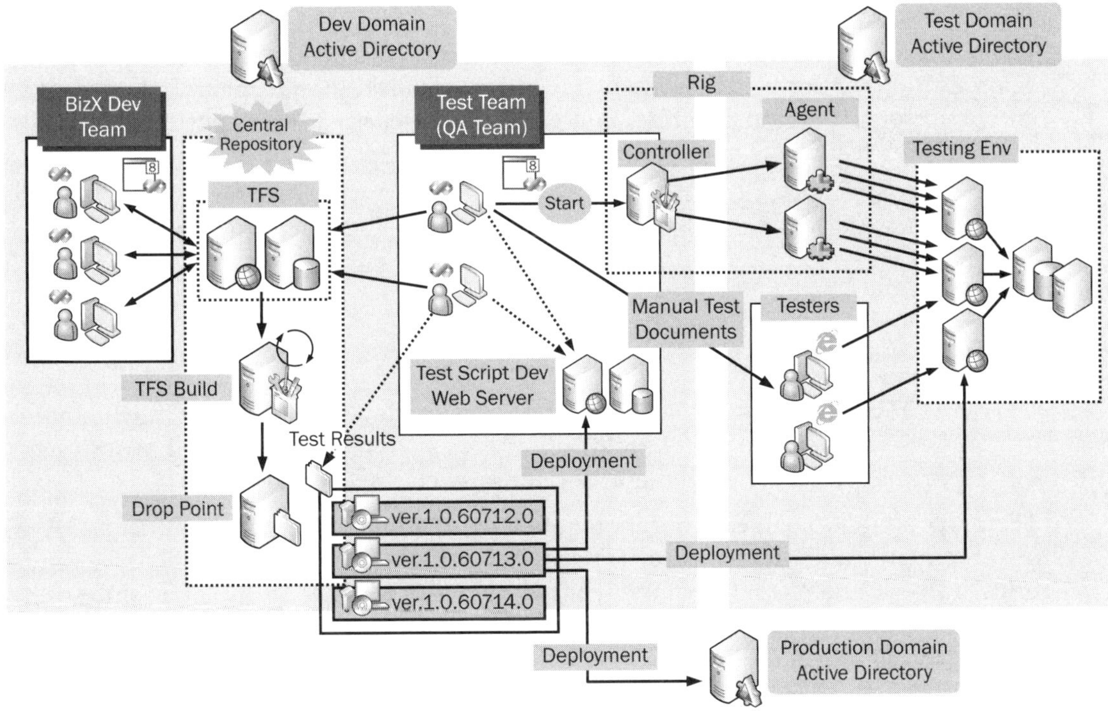

Figure 1.3 *Development and Test Physical Environment*

Development Environment

The development environment supports your development and build processes. The development environment contains the following computers:

- A Team Foundation Server
- A build server
- A server to store the drops from the build server
- Developer workstations

If your development team accesses TFS remotely, or you have a particularly large team that causes performance issues on your central TFS server, you can also set up a TFS proxy to help improve performance.

Test Environment

The test environment consists of one or more test workstations with Visual Studio Team Edition for Software Testers installed. This is used to manage the test life cycle and to perform functional testing, system testing, security testing, performance testing, and Web testing. Team members use TFS to manage work items, bugs, and test results.

The test environment might also include Visual Studio Team Test Load for performance testing.

Summary

VSTS and TFS are designed to support the software development life cycle by integrating various aspects of software development such as source control, work tracking, reporting, project management, and automated build process.

TFS plays a vital role in collaboration between the test and development teams. A development team interacts with TFS throughout the development cycle, accessing bugs and work items to determine what work needs to be done and accessing source control to enable development. A test team interacts with TFS to run tests, upload test results, and log bugs.

Additional Resources

- For more information on TFS fundamentals, see "Team Foundation Server Fundamentals: A Look at the Capabilities and Architecture" at *http://msdn2.microsoft.com/en-us/library/ms364062(vs.80).aspx*
- For an overview of Team Foundation, see the Team Foundation production documentation on the Microsoft MSDN® Web site at *http://msdn2.microsoft.com/en-us/library/ms181232(vs.80).aspx*

2

Team Foundation Server Architecture

Objectives

- Describe Microsoft® Visual Studio® Team System (VSTS) and Team Foundation Server (TFS) architecture.
- Identify the components that make up the client, application and data tiers.
- Highlight the differences between a single-server and multi-server deployment.

Overview

This chapter introduces you to TFS architecture and basic deployment topologies. TFS has a logical three-tiered architecture that includes a client tier, an application tier, and a data tier. TFS clients interact with the application tier through various Web services, and the application tier uses various Microsoft SQL Server™ databases in the data tier.

You can choose to install the application tier and data tier on the same physical server or on separate servers. Your choice depends largely on the size of your team. A single-server deployment works best for teams with fewer than 50 team members, but with a sufficiently powerful server can support up to 400 users. A dual-server deployment can scale up to around 2000 users.

How to Use This Chapter

Use this chapter to learn about the core TFS components and how they interact with one another. By reading this chapter, you will also learn the purpose of each of these components and how they are most commonly deployed.

If you are new to TFS, you should first read Chapter 1, "Introducing the Team Environment," to learn how development and test teams interact with TFS and use it to improve collaboration and the overall efficiency of their software development efforts.

Team Foundation Server Architecture

TFS employs a logical three-tiered architecture, including *client*, *application*, and *data* tiers. TFS clients interact with the application tier through various Web services; the application tier is in turn supported by various databases in the data tier. Figure 2.1 shows the components of each TFS tier as well as their interactions.

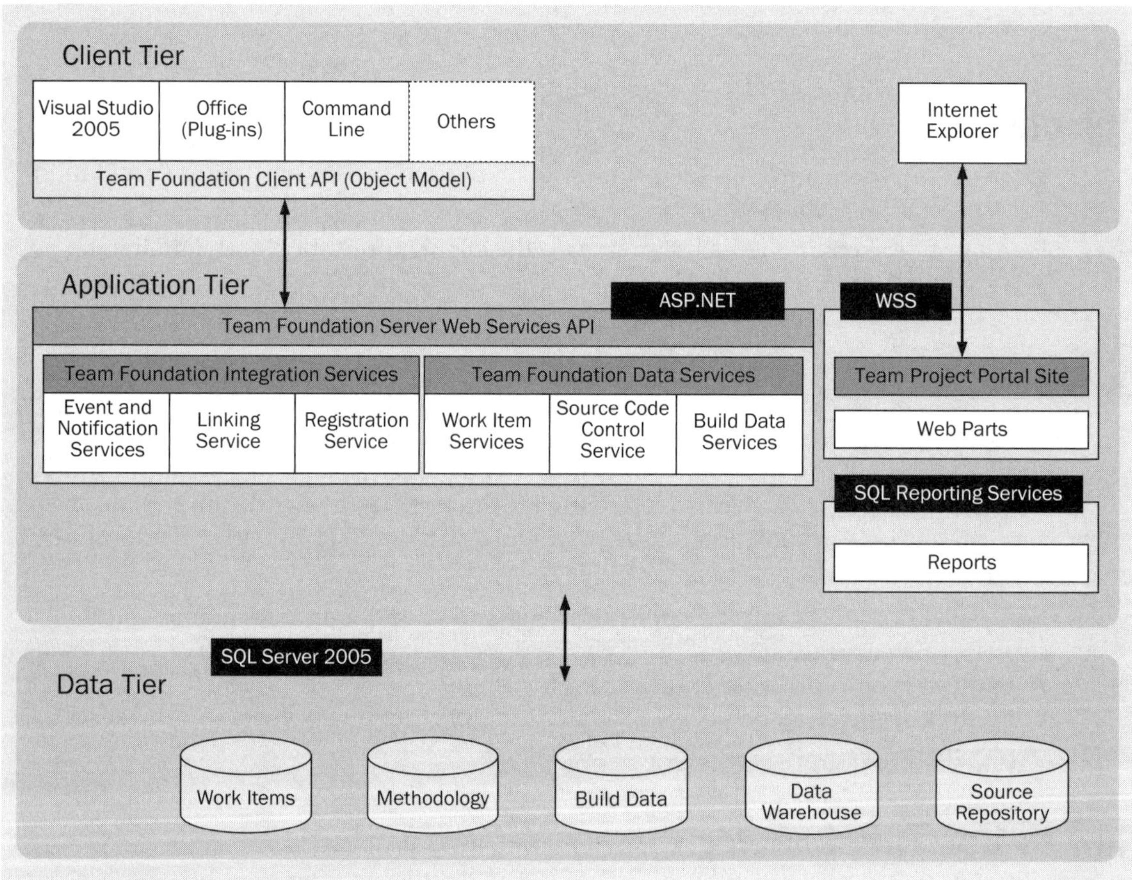

Figure 2.1 *TFS Components and Tiers*

Client Tier

The client tier contains the following important components:

- **Team Foundation Server object model.** This is the public API used to interact with TFS. You can use the object model to create your own client-side applications that interact with TFS.
- **Visual Studio Industry Partners (VSIP) components.** These are third-party tools, add-ins and languages for use within Visual Studio.
- **Microsoft Office integration.** This consists of a set of add-ins for Microsoft Office Excel® and Microsoft Office Project that enables you to query and update work items in the TFS Work Item Tracking database. This is particularly useful for project managers who already use these tools extensively.
- **Command-line tools.** These are the tools that enable you to interact with TFS from the command line. The majority of these tools provide source control functionality and they are useful for automating repetitive tasks and for scheduling tasks.
- **Check-in policy framework.** This supports the check-in policy feature, which is an extensible mechanism that enables you to validate code during the check-in process.

Application Tier

The application tier exposes the following ASP.NET Web services accessed by the client tier. These Web services are not intended for third-party integrators to program against, but are described here for completeness. Web services are grouped into the following collections:

- Team Foundation Data Services
- Team Foundation Integration Services

Team Foundation Data Services

This set of Web services is primarily concerned with manipulating data in the data tier. These services include:

- **Version Control Web service.** The client tier uses this Web service to execute various TFS source control features and to interact with the source control database.
- **Work Item Tracking Web service.** The client tier uses this Web service to create, update and query work items in the Work Item Tracking database.
- **Team Foundation Build Web service.** The client tier and the MSBuild framework use this Web service to execute build processes.

Team Foundation Integration Services

This set of Web services provides integration and automation functionality. These services do not interact with the data tier. The Team Foundation Integration services include:

- **Registration Web service.** This service is used to register various other TFS services. It maintains information in a registration database. The information is used by the services to discover and determine how to interact with one another.
- **Security Web service.** This service consists of the Group Security Service and the Authorization Service. The Group Security Service is used to manage all TFS users and groups. The Authorization Service provides an access control system for TFS.
- **Linking Web service.** This service enables tools to establish loosely coupled relationships (or "links") between the data elements they hold. For example, the relationship between a defect work item and the source code that was changed to fix the defect is held by TFS using a link.
- **Eventing Web service.** This service enables a tool or service to register event types. Users can subscribe to those events and receive notification through e-mail or by invocation of a Web service. For example, you can use a check-in event to trigger a continuous integration build.
- **Classification Web service.** This service works together with the Linking Web service to enable TFS artifacts to be classified according to predefined taxonomies. This helps support cross-tool reporting even for artifacts that do not share a common taxonomy to organize their data. For example, if work items are normally organized by team, while tests are normally organized by component, you can also organize tests by team so that they can be reported alongside work items.

Data Tier

TFS does not support direct access to data stored on the data tier from client applications. Instead, all requests for data must be made through the Web services on the application tier. The TFS data tier consists of the following data stores corresponding to data services on **the** application tier.

- **Work item tracking.** This stores all the data related to work items.
- **Version control.** This stores all the data related to source control.
- **Team Foundation Build.** This stores all the information related to the TFS Team Build feature.
- **Reporting warehouse.** This stores information related to all the TFS tools and features. The reporting warehouse simplifies the creation of reports that combine data from multiple tools.

Deployment Topology

You can deploy TFS by using a variety of different topologies ranging from single-server installations to more complex multiple-server topologies. Regardless of which topology you use, you need to be aware of a number of key requirements.

Key Requirements

Regardless of your selected deployment topology:

- You must install the application tier and the data tier in the same domain, although they can be on the same or separate server nodes.
- You must install TFS computers with Microsoft Windows Server™ 2003 with Service Pack 1 (SP1) or later.
- You must install all TFS application-tier Web services to the same server.
- You must install single TFS instances on a single physical computer.
- You cannot install more than one instance of TFS per physical server.
- You cannot distribute TFS databases across multiple database servers. All projects must reside on one Team Foundation server group, and cannot be deployed across groups.
- You cannot use an existing Microsoft SharePoint® Portal Server infrastructure to host the team project portal. Consider using a dedicated server to host TFS SharePoint portals.
- You should not install TFS on a server configured as a domain controller because this is not supported.
- For dual-server deployments, you must prepare some domain accounts to use when running TFS services. For example, you need to create accounts such as DOMAIN\TFSSERVICE and DOMAIN\TFSREPORTS.

Single-Server Deployment

A single-server deployment is the simplest topology and is appropriate for development teams or pilot projects with up to 400 users. With this approach, you install all of the application tier and data tier components on a single server and access them from the same domain.

If you need to install test rig components for performance testing, you can install them on the server node or on one or more clients. Figure 2.2 on the next page shows the single-server topology.

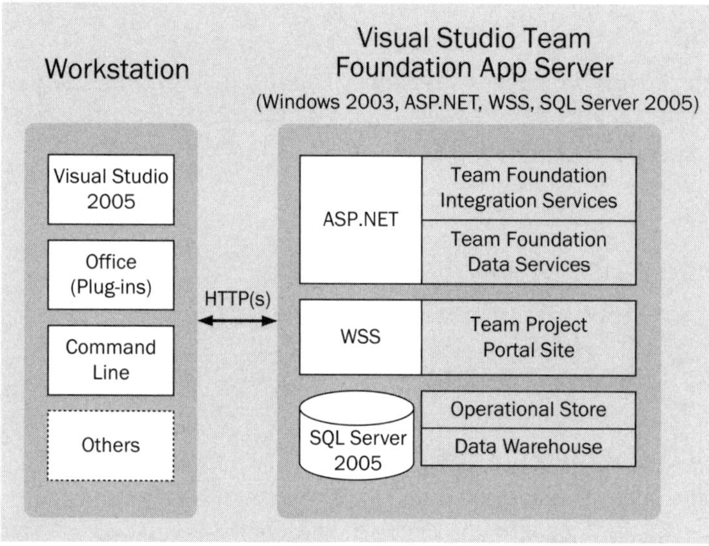

Figure 2.2 *Single Server Topology*

Dual-Server Deployment

The dual-server deployment topology is useful for large development teams in the range of 2000 users. In this deployment topology you install the application tier on a separate server node from the data tier.

You can install Team Foundation Build Services on the application tier, but you are recommended to set up one or more dedicated build servers for large teams. If your project needs performance testing, you can deploy the test rig (controller and agents) to additional sever nodes. Figure 2.3 shows the dual-server topology.

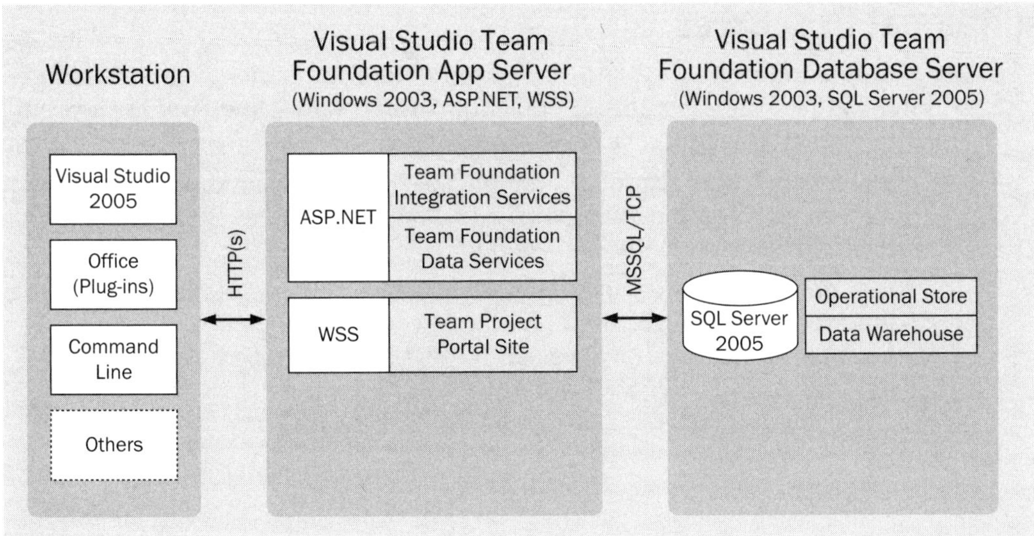

Figure 2.3 *Dual Server Topology*

Summary

Team Foundation Server architecture consists of three tiers: a client-tier, an application-tier and a data-tier.

- The client-tier contains client components such as Team Explorer in Visual Studio 2005, Microsoft Office integration, and command-line tools.
- The application-tier contains components such as Team Foundation version control services, work item tracking services, and build services.
- The data-tier contains the databases to store data necessary for work item tracking, version control, team build, and the reporting warehouse.

TFS supports single-server and dual-server deployment topologies. In a single-server deployment the application-tier and data-tier are installed on the same machine. A single-server deployment is useful for smaller teams or when conducting pilot projects. In a dual-server deployment, the application-tier and data-tier are installed on separate servers. A dual-server deployment is useful for larger teams that need to scale to a large number of users.

Additional Resources

- For more information about Team Foundation fundamentals, see "Team Foundation Server Fundamentals: A Look at the Capabilities and Architecture" at *http://msdn2.microsoft.com/en-us/library/ms364062(vs.80).aspx*
- For an overview of Team Foundation, see the Team Foundation production documentation on the Microsoft MSDN® Web site at *http://msdn2.microsoft.com/en-us/library/ms181232(vs.80).aspx*
- For more information about Team Foundation Server scalability limits, see "Team Foundation Server Capacity Planning" at *http://blogs.msdn.com/bharry/archive/2006/01/04/509314.aspx*

Part II

Source Control

In this part:

- Structuring Projects and Solutions in Source Control
- Structuring Projects and Solutions in Team Foundation Source Control
- Defining Your Branching and Merging Strategy
- Managing Source Control Dependencies in Visual Studio Team System

3

Structuring Projects and Solutions in Source Control

Objectives

- Structure your Microsoft® Visual Studio® Team System solutions and projects appropriately.
- Know when to use multiple solutions and when to use a single solution.
- Identify appropriate structures for small, medium-size and very large teams.

Overview

This chapter explains various options for structuring Visual Studio solution and project files in a manner appropriate for team development. Visual Studio uses solution (.sln) files to group together related Visual Studio project (.csproj and .vbproj) files. Deciding how to structure your projects and solutions is an important decision because the pattern you choose has a number of consequences. For example, it impacts how easily members of your development teams can push and pull solutions and projects to and from source control, the mechanism you use to reference dependencies, and also your build processes.

If you are working on a small project you can use a single solution to contain all of your project files. If you are working on a software development project with a large number of project files, you should use multiple solution files to group related projects that correspond to subsets of functionality within your overall team project. Depending on your specific scenario you may also need a single solution file to group together all of your project files.

How to Use This Chapter

Use this chapter to select an approach for structuring your Visual Studio solutions and projects. To gain the greatest benefits from this chapter, you should:

- **Use the strategies list.** Use the initial list of strategies: single solution, partitioned solution, and multiple solutions to quickly evaluate the best approach for your scenario.
- **Read the scenario section that is most relevant to your needs.** Read the section describing how to implement the option you have chosen.
- **Read Chapter 4, "Structuring Projects and Solutions in Team Foundation Source Control" next.** Chapter 4 introduces you to important considerations to keep in mind when storing your code in Team Foundation Server (TFS) source control.
- **Read Chapter 6, "Managing Source Control Dependencies in Visual Studio Team System."** Project structure impacts the strategies available to you when managing dependencies across projects and solutions. For more information about how to manage dependencies, read Chapter 6.
- **Read the companion How To articles.** Read the following companion How To articles for a step-by-step walkthroughs of various procedures discussed in this chapter.
  - How To: Structure ASP.NET Applications in Visual Studio Team Foundation Server.
  - How To: Structure Windows Applications in Visual Studio Team Foundation Server.
  - How To: Structure Your Source Control Folders in Visual Studio Team Foundation Server.

Strategies for Solution and Project Structure

The three most common strategies used to structure solution and project files are:

- **Single solution.** If you work on a small system, create a single solution and place all of your projects within it.
- **Partitioned solution.** If you work on a large system, use multiple solutions to group related projects together. Create solutions to logically group subsets of projects that a developer would be most likely to modify as a set, and then create one master solution to contain all of your projects. This approach reduces the amount of data that needs to be pulled from source control when you only need to work on specific projects.
- **Multiple solutions.** If you are working on a very large system that requires dozens of projects or more, use multiple solutions to work on sub-systems but for dependency mapping and performance reasons do not create a master solution that contains all projects.

In general you should:

- Use a single solution strategy unless the resulting solution is too large to load into Visual Studio.
- Use multiple solutions to create specific views on sub-systems of your application.
- Use multiple solutions to reduce the time it takes to load a solution and to reduce build time for developers.

Keep the following considerations in mind when designing a project and solution structure:

- Each project generates an assembly at build time. Start by determining what assemblies you want to create and then use this to decide what projects you need. Use this to determine how to factor your codebase into projects.
- Start with the simplest single solution structure. Only add complexity to your structure when it is really necessary.
- When designing a multi-solution structure:
  - Consider project dependencies. Try to group those projects that have dependencies on one another as part of the same solution. This enables you to use project references within your solution. By using project references instead of file references, you enable Visual Studio to keep build configurations (debug/release) synchronized, and to track versioning to determine when projects need to be rebuilt. Try to minimize the number of cross-solution project references.
  - Consider source sharing. Place projects that share the same source in the same solution.
  - Consider team structure. Structure your solutions to make it easy for teams to work on a set of related projects together.
- Keep a flat project structure so that it is easy for you to group projects into solutions without needing to make file system or source control folder structure changes.

Single Solution

If you work on a small system, consider using a single Visual Studio solution to contain all of your projects. This structure simplifies development because all of the code is available when you open the solution. This strategy also makes it easy to set up references, because all references are between projects in your solution. You might still need to use file references to reference third-party assemblies, such as purchased components, that are outside your solution. Figure 3.1 on the next page shows the single solution approach.

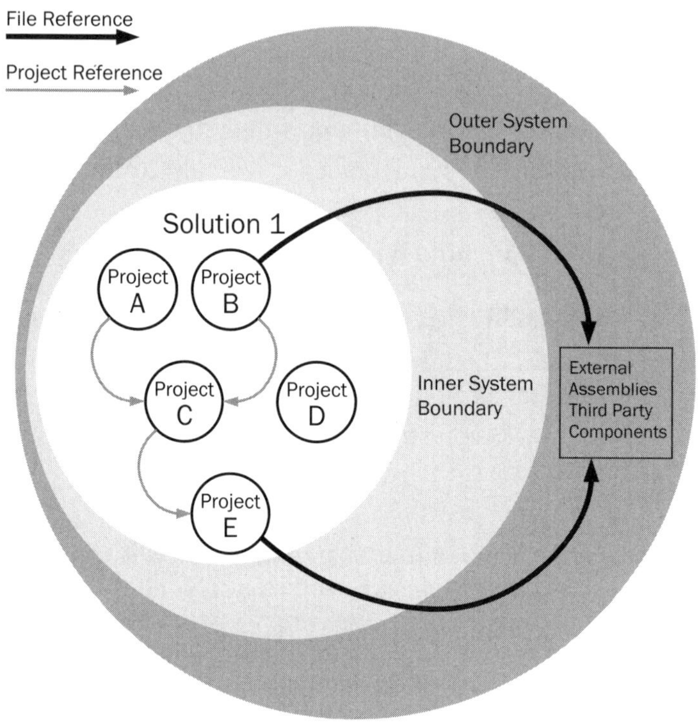

Figure 3.1 *Single Solution Approach*

The main reasons to choose this structure include:

- You can keep build scripts simple.
- You can easily map dependencies across projects within the solution.

You should use this structure if all developers use the same solution and have the same set of projects. This could be a problem for large systems where you want to organize projects by sub-system or feature.

Partitioned Solution

If you work on a large system, consider using multiple solutions, each representing a sub-system in your application. These solutions can be used by developers in order to work on smaller parts of the system without having to load all code across all projects. Design your solution structure so any projects that have dependencies are grouped together. This enables you to use project references rather than file references. Also consider creating a master solution file that contains all of the projects. You can use this to build your entire application.

Note: Unlike previous versions of Visual Studio, Visual Studio 2005 relies upon MSBuild. It is now possible to create solution structures that do not include all referenced projects and still build without errors. As long as the master solution has been built first, generating the binary output from each project, MSBuild is able to follow project references outside the bounds of your solution and build successfully. This only works if you use project references, not file references. You can successfully build solutions created this way from the Visual Studio build command line and from the IDE, but not with Team Build by default. In order to build successfully with Team Build use the master solution that includes all of the projects and dependencies.

Figure 3.2 shows the partitioned solution approach.

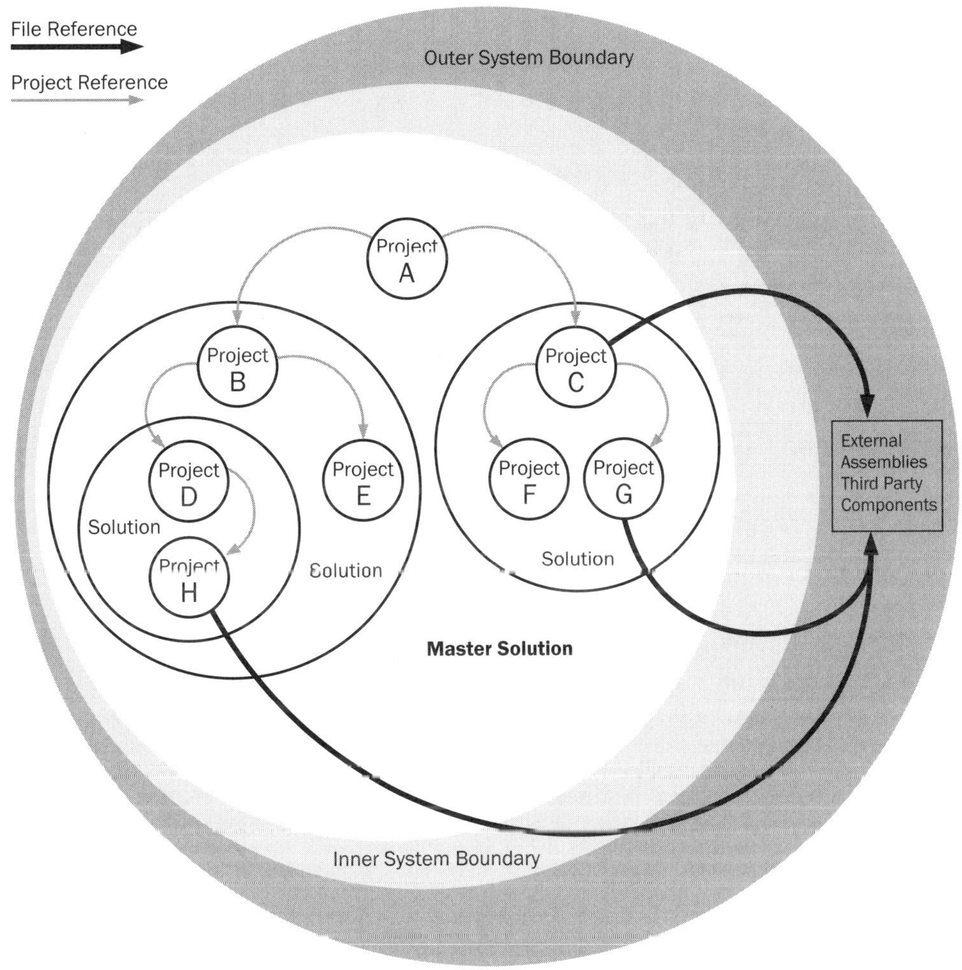

Figure 3.2 *Partitioned Solution Approach*

When working with multiple solutions, use a flat file structure for all of your projects.

A typical example is an application that has a Microsoft Windows® Forms project, an ASP.NET project, a Windows service, and a set of class library projects shared by some or all of those projects.

You can use the following flat structure for all projects:

- /Source
  - /WinFormsProject
  - /WebProject
  - /WindowsServiceProject
  - /ClassLibrary1
  - /ClassLibrary2
  - /ClassLibrary3
  - Web.sln
  - Service.sln
  - All.sln

Keeping the structure flat provides a lot of flexibility and the ability to use solutions for presenting different views on the projects. The physical folder structure around solution files is very hard to change, especially if you realize that you need to reuse a class library from another solution.

Reasons to use this structure include:

- Performance is improved when loading and building application sub-solutions.
- Sub-solutions can be used to create views on sets of projects based on development sub-teams or boundaries of code sharing.
- You can use the master solution to build the entire application.
- You can easily map dependencies across projects in each sub-solution.
- It reduces overall complexity if the solutions are broken up logically. For example breaking up the solution along technology or feature lines makes it easier for new developers to understand which solution to work on.

The main reason not to use this structure is:

- Increased solution maintenance costs. Adding a new project might require multiple solution file changes.

Multiple Solutions

If you work on a very large solution requiring many dozens of projects, you may encounter solution scalability limits. In this scenario, break your application into multiple solutions but do not create a master solution for the entire application because all references inside each solution are project references. References to projects outside of each solution (for example to third-party libraries or projects in another sub-solution) are file references. This means that there can be no "master" solution.

Instead, you must use a script that understands the order in which the solutions need to be built. One of the maintenance tasks associated with a multiple-solution structure is ensuring that developers do not inadvertently create circular references between solutions. This structure requires complex build scripts and explicit mapping of dependency relationships. In this structure it is not possible to build the application in its entirety within Visual Studio. Instead, you can use TFS Team Build or MSBuild directly.

Figure 3.3 shows the multiple solutions approach.

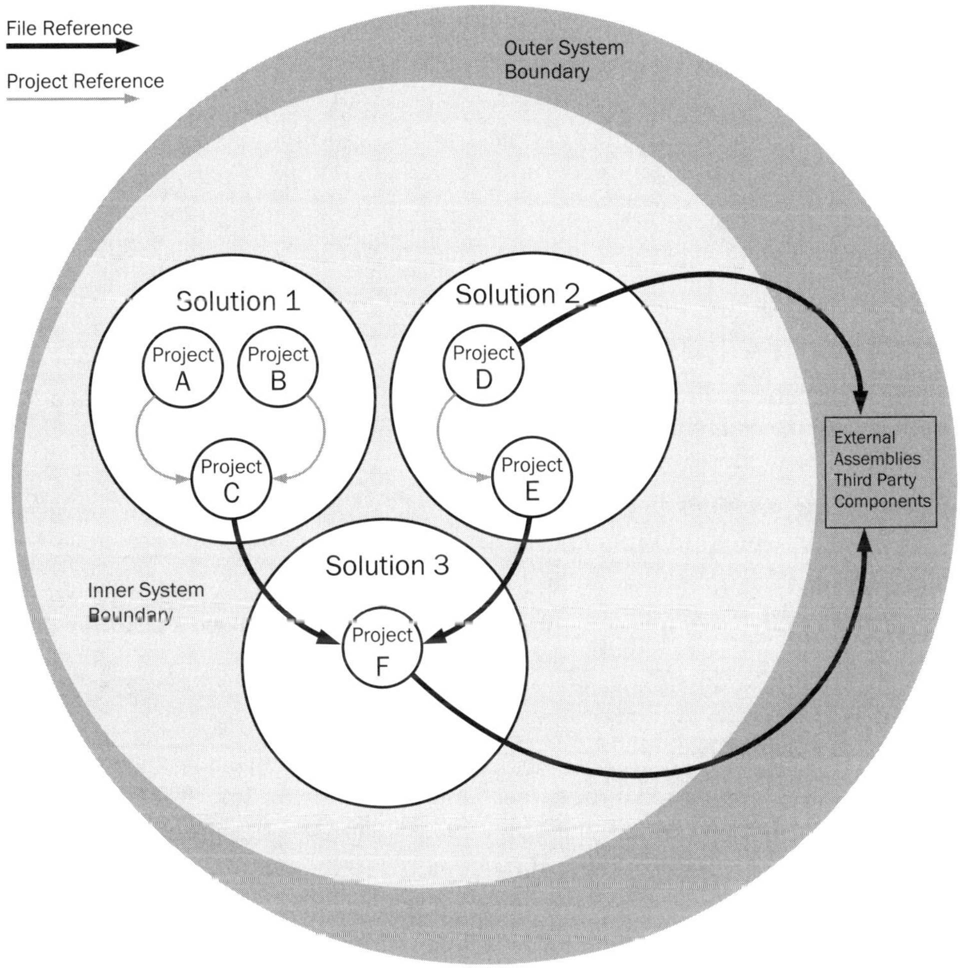

Figure 3.3 *Multiple Solution Approach*

You should use this structure to work around Visual Studio IDE performance and scalability limits for very large applications.

One reason not to use this structure is that it requires a complex build script to handle dependencies across the sub-solutions by building solutions in the right order.

Large Project Considerations

Large development teams are likely to distinguish themselves from smaller teams in the following ways:

- They require a more complex branching and merging structure.
- They are more likely to manage dependencies across solutions and team projects.
- They are more likely to maintain multiple builds for components and teams.

A partitioned solution approach works well for most large projects because it provides solution flexibility while maintaining a single solution that you can use to build the application. If your application is large enough that you hit solution scalability limits, use the multiple solutions approach.

Summary

Use a single solution for small projects in which it is not necessary to partition your source into separate sub-solutions.

Use a partitioned solution for logically grouping subsets of projects that a developer would be most likely to modify as a set, and then create one master solution that contains all of your projects.

Use multiple solutions to create specific views on subsystems and to reduce the load and build time of your application.

A partitioned solution works well for most large projects because it provides solution flexibility while maintaining a single solution that can be used to build the application.

Additional Resources

- For more information about project and solution structure (though not directly applied to Team Foundation Server), see "Team Development with Visual Studio .NET and Visual SourceSafe" at *http://msdn2.microsoft.com/en-us/library/ms998208.aspx*

4

Structuring Projects and Solutions in Team Foundation Source Control

Objectives

- Structure projects for effective team development in Microsoft® Visual Studio® Team Foundation Server (TFS) source control.
- Keep server-side and client-side folder structures synchronized.
- Choose a strategy for unit test structure.
- Create a folder structure that supports various branching scenarios.
- Learn what a workspace is and how it maps local files to source control.
- Understand what files are added to source control.

Overview

Many of the default folder conventions used by Visual Studio when creating new solutions and projects are not optimized for team development and for use with TFS source control. Rather than accepting the defaults when you create new Visual Studio projects and solutions, you should give careful consideration to your local and server-based folder structure.

This chapter starts by explaining how you should structure solutions and projects on your development computer (the client-side) and how you should structure your folders within TFS source control (the server-side). It provides example folder structures for a variety of application types including Microsoft Windows® Forms, smart clients, and Web applications. The chapter then explains how workspaces are used to manage the mappings between client and server folder structures.

How to Use This Chapter

Use this chapter to learn about sample folder structures suitable for team development projects of various sizes and complexity. To gain the greatest benefits from this chapter, you should:

- **Use the server-side structure suggestions.** Use the suggested server-side folder structures to organize your project source code within TFS source control.
- **Use the client-side structure suggestions.** Use the suggested client-side folder structures to organize your project source code in your local development workspace.
- **Read the companion How To articles.** These articles provide a step-by-step walkthroughs of some of the processes discussed in this chapter:
  - How To: Create Your Source Tree in Visual Studio Team Foundation Server.
  - How To: Structure ASP.NET Applications in Visual Studio Team Foundation Server.
  - How To: Structure Windows Applications in Visual Studio Team Foundation Server.
  - How To: Structure Your Source Control Folders in Visual Studio Team Foundation Server.

Server-Side Structure

Most team projects contain one or more Visual Studio solutions, each of which contains one or more Visual Studio projects. When you require branching to support isolated development paths, you use a root level folder named **Main** (on both client and server) to group together your Visual Studio projects. The following is a sample folder structure within TFS source control:

```
$MyTeamProject1
  /Main                                  Can contain solution (.sln) files
      /Source
          /MyApp1                        Contains MyApp1.sln file
              /Source                    Contain folder for all source
                  /ClassLibrary1         Contains ClassLibrary1.csproj
                  /MyApp1Web             Contains Default.aspx
              /UnitTests                 Container folder for unit tests
                  /ClassLibrary1Tests    Contains test project and code
                  /MyApp1WebTests        Contains test project and code
          /SharedBinaries                Shared binaries e.g. libraries
          /SharedSource                  Shared source code
      /Docs                              Contains product documentation
      /Tests                             Container for tests
```

/FunctionalTests	
/PerformanceTests	
/SecurityTests	
/TeamBuildTypes	Created automatically by Team Build.
/BuildType1	
/BuildType2	

Main is a container folder for the source files and other related artifacts such as build output, design documentation, and test cases. An application folder (such as **MyApp1** in the preceding example) contains the Visual Studio solution (.sln) file used to group together a related set of Visual Studio projects. Each project file (.vcproj or .vbproj) is contained in a dedicated project folder, located beneath /Main/Source/MyApp1/Source. Unit tests that accompany each source project are located beneath the **UnitTests** folder. You can place additional Visual Studio solution (.sln) files in the **Main** folder to allow you to work with multiple different groupings of projects.

The **Docs** and **Test** folders are used to hold additional artifacts associated with the team project including product documentation and automated tests.

The **TeamBuildTypes** folder is automatically created for you when you generate your first Team Build. If you want to manually check in a team build type you can create this folder by hand, add your Team Build files, and TFS recognizes this folder for you automatically.

For more information about project groupings and solution structure, see Chapter 3, "Structuring Projects and Solutions in Source Control."

Storing Unit Tests

You can store unit tests beneath a folder named **UnitTests** at the same level as **Source** as shown here.

/MyApp1	Contains MyApp1.sln file
/Source	Contain folder for all source
/ClassLibrary1	Contains ClassLibrary1.csproj
/MyApp1Web	Contains Default.aspx
/UnitTests	Container folder for unit tests
/ClassLibrary1Tests	Contains test project and code
/MyApp1WebTests	Contains test project and code

This scenario treats unit tests as first-class citizens. However, it does so at the expense of project level branching compatibility. An alternate structure is shown here:

/MyApp1
/Source
/ClassLibrary1
/ClassLibrary1Tests
/MyApp1Web
/MyApp1WebTests

The following pros and cons apply to each approach:

UnitTests As a Peer to the Source folder

- Pro: You can find unit tests in one place.
- Pro: You separate shipping code from non-shipping code.
- Pro: Your build process can easily run all unit tests across all projects.
- Con: It is harder for developers to run unit tests for their project only.
- Con: When you branch source, it will not include unit tests.

UnitTests in Each Project

- Pro: Developers can easily run unit tests on a single project.
- Pro: When you branch, your branched folders include unit tests, so they can stay tightly bound to the source in each branch.
- Con: You mix shipping with non-shipping code in the source folder.
- Con: It is generally harder to run all unit tests at once at build time across all projects.

Storing Documents

The **Documentation** folder is for product related documentation. To help determine what documents to store in TFS source control and what to store in a document library on your Microsoft Windows SharePoint® team site, consider the following:

- Use SharePoint for internal team documents such as use cases, scenario and requirements documentation, and design documentation.
- Use TFS source control for product-related documentation that you ship to your customers. This could include installation and deployment guides, operations guides, and Help files.

Most documents are binary files, so consider using exclusive locks to avoid manual merges. By doing so, you get notified when a file is in use and you help avoid having to perform manual merges.

Use caution when using SharePoint because strict management of document versions is required. It is easier to overwrite changes in SharePoint compared to TFS source control. By default, SharePoint enables the "overwrite existing file" option selected when files are uploaded.

Client-Side Structure

The local folder structure on your development workstations should be identical to the server folder structure. Keep source artifacts well organized on your workstations by placing all source from all team projects together beneath a single root folder, such as C:\DevProjects. Create one sub-folder for each team project as shown in this example:

C:\DevProjects	Root container folder for all team projects
\MyTeamProject1	Container folder for TeamProject1
\MyTeamProject2	Container folder for TeamProject2

Beneath each team project folder, use a copy of the application folder structure used on the source control server as shown in the following example:

\MyTeamProject1	Container folder for TeamProject1
\Main	Contains .sln files that span projects
\Source	
\MyApp 1	Contains MyApp1.sln
\Source	
\ClassLibrary1	Contains ClassLibrary1.csproj
\MyApp1Web	Contains Default.aspx
\UnitTests	Contains unit test projects and source
\ClassLibrary1Tests	
\MyWinApp1Tests	
\SharedBinaries	Shared binaries e.g. libraries
\SharedSource	Shared source code
\Docs	Contains product documentation
\Tests	Container for tests
\FunctionalTests	
\PerformanceTests	
\SecurityTests	

Note: The client-side structure automatically mirrors the server-side structure if you create a workspace mapping from the application root to your local computer. However, in very large projects this can result in slow workspace load times. To optimize your approach for very large projects, create workspace mappings below the root to only retrieve the files you need for development.

Branched Folders

To support development isolation with branches, create additional folders as siblings of **Main**. You can also place additional Visual Studio solution (.sln) files in **Main** to enable developers to work with various groupings of projects. Branches created from the **Main** source folders can be used to support ongoing maintenance of product releases or parallel streams of development.

In the following sample structure, in addition to the **Main** root folder, a **Development** folder (branched from **Main**) is used to provide isolation for features or for teams. A **Releases** folder which is a container for release branches (again branched from **Main**) provides isolation for released builds that require ongoing maintenance and current release lockdown.

```
$MyTeamProject1
    /Development
        /FeatureBranch1
            /Source
                /MyApp
        /FeatureBranch2
            /Source
                /MyApp
/Main
        /Source
/Releases
        /Release1 – Maintenance
            /Source
                /MyApp
        /Release2 – Maintenance
            /Source
                /MyApp
        /Release3 – Current release lockdown
            /Source
                /MyApp
```

Note: Do not branch unless you need to. If required, you can label a release and branch at a later time.

For more information about project groupings and solution structure, see Chapter 03, "Structuring Projects and Solutions in Source Control."

For more information about branching scenarios and related folder structures, see Chapter 5, "Defining Your Branching and Merging Strategy."

Workspaces Explained

A TFS workspace is a client-side copy of the files and folders in TFS source control. A workspace maps source control folders to local file system directories. When you make changes to files within the workspace on your local computer, the local changes, referred to as *pending changes,* are isolated in your workspace until you check them into the server as an atomic unit. The collective set of changes, checked in as a batch is referred to as a *changeset.*

A single workspace can contain references to multiple team projects. You can also use multiple workspaces to isolate files or versions for your use only. Workspaces are per computer, per user account. Therefore, you can have different workspace definitions for each computer you use. Also, as a single user, you can have multiple workspaces on a single computer.

Note: You can only map each physical location on the local file system by using a single workspace. However, you can map each server directory to entirely different local directories by using different workspaces.

Creating a New Workspace Mapping

Because mappings are recursive, when you create a new workspace mapping and you perform a **Get Latest Version** operation at the root of that workspace, the entire local folder structure is created automatically. The newly created local folder structure matches the server structure.

Keep the following recommendations in mind when you create new workspace mappings:

- The project owner must ensure that the correct folder structure is used locally prior to adding the solution to source control for the first time.
- When establishing a workspace mapping for a team project for the first time and performing a **Get Latest** operation, be sure to map the root team project folder into an appropriate local folder such as C:\DevProjects\TeamProject1.

Where Are Workspace Mappings Stored?

Workspace information is maintained on both the client and the server. On the client, workspace information is held in VersionControl.config which is located in the following folder:

```
\Documents and Settings\[user]\Local Settings\Application Data\Microsoft
\Team Foundation\1.0\Cache.
```

The VersionControl.config file maps the name of the workspace to a local directory on your computer. It does not hold the mapping between individual source control folders and your local directories. That information is held on the server in several tables (including tbl_Workspace and tbl_workingfolder) in the TfsVersionControl database.

Cloaking

You can use cloaking as a performance optimization when you want to prevent a part of the source control tree from being retrieved. The following are typical scenarios for using cloaking:

- You want to build the project locally and a folder is not needed for the build, for example a documentation folder.
- You are part of a large team project and you only want to retrieve part of the project.

For either of the above scenarios you can cloak folders to stop the client retrieving those folders. You cloak folders on the client by editing the workspace and changing the status of the working folder from active to cloak.

Keep the following recommendations in mind when you cloak:

- Do not cloak individual files. This is likely lead to maintenance problems later in the project.
- For a large project, map out the root folder and cloak sub folders rather than creating multiple workspaces for the project.

What Files Should Be Version Controlled?

The following list identifies the key file types that you should add to source control. These are the file types that are added when you click **Add Solution to Source Control**.

- **Solution files (*.sln).** Solution files maintain a list of constituent projects, dependencies information, build configuration details, and source control provider details.
- **Project files (*.csproj or *.vbproj).** Project files include assembly build settings, referenced assemblies (by name and path), and a file inventory.
- **Visual Studio Source Control Project Metadata (*.vspscc).** These files maintain project bindings, exclusion lists, source control provider names and other source control metadata.
- **Application configuration files (*.config).** Extensible Markup Language (XML) configuration files contain project and application specific details used to control your application's run-time behavior. Web applications use files named Web.config. Non-Web applications use files named App.config.

Note: At run time, the Visual Studio build system copies App.config to your project's Bin folder and renames it as <YourAppName>.exe.config. For non-web applications, a configuration file is not automatically added to a new project. If you require one, add it manually. Make sure you name it App.config and locate it within the project folder.

- **Source files (*.aspx, *.asmx, *.cs, *.vb, …).** These are source code files, depending on application type and language.
- **Binary dependencies (*.dll).** If your project relies on binary dependencies such as third–party dynamic-link libraries (DLLs), you should also add these to your project within source control. For more information about managing dependencies, see Chapter 6, "Managing Source Control Dependencies in Visual Studio Team System."

What Files Should Not Be Source Controlled?

The following files are specific to each developer and therefore should not be added to version control:

- **Solution user option files (*.suo).** These contain personalized customizations made to the Visual Studio IDE by an individual developer.
- **Project user option files (*.csproj.user or *.vbproj.user).** These files contain developer specific project options and an optional reference path that is used by Visual Studio to locate referenced assemblies.
- **WebInfo files (*.csproj.webinfo or *.vbproj.webinfo).** This file keeps track of a project's virtual root location. This is not added to source control, to allow individual developers to specify different virtual roots for their own working copy of the project. While this capability exists, it is recommended that all team members use a consistent (local) virtual root location when developing Web applications.
- **Build outputs.** These include assembly DLLs, interop assembly DLLs and executable files (EXEs). (However, note that assemblies such as third-party binaries that are not built as part of the build process should be placed under version control as described above).

Summary

Structure projects in TFS source control for effective team development. Use a root-level folder called **Main** to group together your Visual Studio projects. The **Main** folder should contain child folders to store various project assets such as source code, tests, documents, and team build types.

Use SharePoint for internal team documents such as use cases and design documentation. Use TFS source control for product-related documentation that you plan to ship to your customers. This might include installation and deployment guides, operations guides, and Help files.

Keep the server-side and client-side folder structures synchronized in order to reduce confusion caused by differences in folder organization. To optimize your approach for very large projects, create workspace mappings below the root to ensure that you only retrieve the files you need for development.

Additional Resources

- For more information about Team Foundation Source Control, see "Using Source Code Control in Team Foundation" at *http://msdn2.microsoft.com/en-us/library/ms364074(VS.80).aspx*
- For more information about creating a workspace, see "How to: Create a Workspace" at *http://msdn2.microsoft.com/en-us/library/ms181384(VS.80).aspx*

5

Defining Your Branching and Merging Strategy

Objectives

- Know when and when not to branch.
- Choose a branching and merging strategy for your project.
- Describe how normal branching strategy needs to be adapted to support very large teams.
- Identify appropriate folder structures for different branching scenarios.

Overview

This chapter introduces branching and merging strategies for a range of common scenarios. Usually, you need branches to support either releases or parallel development.

For many simple scenarios, you do not need to branch and labeling your builds is sufficient. For example, by using labels you can re-create a build at any point in the future or find out which versions of a source file were used to create a particular build. You should consider branching if you need isolation for parallel teams, either to work on separate but overlapping features or to support a release.

How to Use This Chapter

Use this chapter to learn when and when not to branch. If you decide that branching is appropriate for your situation, use this chapter to learn how to branch and merge effectively.

If you want an overview of branching and merging, then read the chapter from start to finish to learn about the different strategies for branching and the different scenarios where branching is appropriate. If you are interested in a particular scenario, go directly to the relevant section. To gain the greatest benefits from this chapter, you should:

- **Use the scenarios list.** Use the scenarios list to locate the scenario closest to your own. Read the recommendations to create a branched folder structure appropriate for your needs.
- **Use the companion guidance.** Refer to the branching and merging guidelines in "Source Control Guidelines" in this guide for a summary of branching and merging guidelines.

Scenarios for Branching and Merging

The following are examples of scenarios where you might need to create branches and perform merges:

- If you are having regular problems with broken builds, you should create a development branch to isolate parallel development efforts.
- If you have features that are causing stability issues, or teams causing stability issues among each other, create separate feature or team branches beneath a development container folder in source control.

Do not branch unless it becomes necessary for your development team. Branching introduces additional source tree maintenance and merging tasks. Most development teams such as those building line of business applications, working on short release cycles do not need to branch. Development teams working on longer release cycles such as Independent Software Vendors (ISVs) building packaged applications are more likely to need branching as part of the development process.

If you have one stream of development, or are performing incremental and continuous releases, you might not need to create branches unless you frequently experience breaking changes that are destabilizing your development efforts.

Common Scenarios in Practice

The following are the most common branching scenarios:

- **Scenario 1 – No Branches.** Your team works only from the main source tree. In this case, you do not create branches and you do not need isolation. This scenario is generally for small or medium size teams that do not require isolation for teams or for features, and do not need the isolation for releases.

- **Scenario 2 – Branch for Release.** Your team creates branches to support an ongoing release. This is the next most common case where you need to create a branch to stabilize for a release. In this case, your team creates a branch before release time to stabilize the release and then merges changes from the release branch back into the main source tree after the software is released.
- **Scenario 3 – Branch for Maintenance.** Your team creates a branch to maintain an old build. In this case, you create a branch for your maintenance efforts, so that you do not destabilize your current production builds. You may or may not merge changes from the maintenance branch back into the main tree. For example, you might work on a quick fix for a subset of customers that you do not want to include in the main build.
- **Scenario 4 – Branch for Feature.** Your team creates branches based on features. In this case, you create a development branch, perform work in the development branch, and then merge back into your main source tree. You can create separate branches for work on specific features to be completed in parallel.
- **Scenario 5 – Branch for Team.** You branch to isolate sub-teams so they can work without being subject to breaking changes, or can work in parallel towards unique milestones.

You may encounter one or more of these scenarios. Use these scenarios as a reference point to see what guidance may or may not apply to you.

Example Folders and Their Purpose

The following folders are examples of folders you might create in Microsoft® Visual Studio® Team Foundation Server (TFS) source control when structuring your source tree for branching and merging scenarios.

- **Development** is branched from **Main** and used to isolate active development. Development branches may be temporary, in order to develop risky changes without impacting **Main**.
- **Main** contains your main source tree. Changes from other branches are integrated here.
- **Releases** contains branches you have already shipped but now need to maintain for customers. This provides isolation from the active development occurring in your development branch. It also contains a current release branch which is branched from **Main** and contains the version you are currently locking down prior to release. You work in this branch to prepare your software for release, while others continue to work in the **Development** branch working on new features.

The following sections show the use of branching in each of the preceding scenarios with concrete examples.

Scenario 1 — No Branches

This scenario generally applies to smaller teams for whom isolated development is not a concern. By labeling builds, you are able to retrieve the source corresponding to a particular build. There is no need to introduce branching complexity because you can work directly from **Main** folder. The following is a view depicting the no-branch scenario:

```
My Team Project
    Main
        Source
```

Scenario 2 — Branch for Release

In this scenario your team creates a branch to stabilize the release and then merges the release branch back into the main source tree after the software is released. The following is a view showing branching for releases:

```
My Team Project
    Main                        Main integration branch
        Source
    Releases
        Release 1               Release branch
            Source
```

Scenario 3 — Branch for Maintenance

In this scenario, you create a branch for your maintenance efforts, so that you do not destabilize your current production builds. The following is a view showing maintenance branches. This is very similar to branch for release, however at this point the branch is maintained over time in order to support the release:

```
My Team Project
    Main                                Main integration branch
        Source
    Releases                            Maintenance branch container
        Release 1                       Maintenance branch
            Source
            Other Asset Folders
        Release 2                       Maintenance branch
            Source
            Other Asset Folders
```

Scenario 4 — Branch for Feature

In this scenario, you create a development branch, perform work in that branch, and then merge your work back into your main source tree. You organize your development branches based on product features. The following is a physical view showing branching for feature development:

```
My Team Project
    Development                         Isolated development branch container
        Feature A                       Feature branch
            Source
        Feature B                       Feature branch
            Source
        Feature C                       Feature branch
            Source
    Main                                Main Integration branch
        Source
```

Scenario 5 — Branch for Team

This scenario is similar to the preceding branch-by-feature scenario, except that you organize your development branches according to sub-team rather than product feature. There might be a one-to-one correspondence between team and feature, but in some cases a team might work on multiple features. The following is a physical view showing branching for sub-team development:

```
My Team Project
    Development                         Isolated development branch container
        Team 1                          Team branch
            Feature A                   Isolated branch for development
                Source
            Feature B                   Isolated branch for development
                Source
        Team 2                          Team branch
            Feature A                   Isolated branch for development
                Source
            Feature B                   Isolated branch for development
                Source
    Main                                Main Integration branch
        Source
```

Logical Structure

The logical structure consists of the parent/child relationships for each branch. This may be different from the physical structure you can see in the Source Control Explorer. For example, in the preceding physical structure, **Development** and **Main** appear to be peers, when **Development** is actually a child of **Main**.

Figure 5.1 shows an example of a logical relationship and how branches and merges flow through the structure.

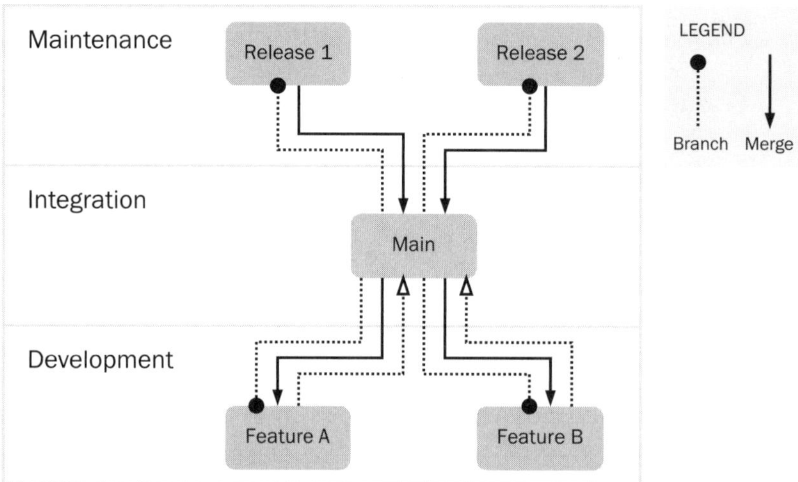

Figure 5.1 *Logical Relationship Showing Branch and Merge Flow*

Release Scenario

Figure 5.2 shows a typical timeline when branching for a release:

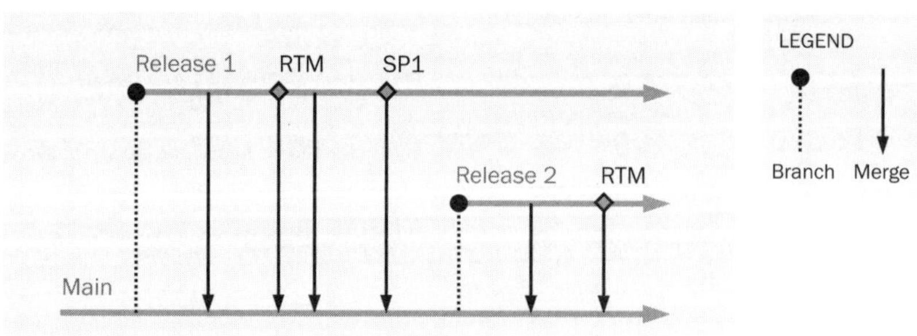

Figure 5.2 *Branching for Release Timeline*

The sequence of events is as follows:

1. The **Release 1** branch is created from **Main** once the release is ready to be locked down.
2. Periodic merges into **Main** ensure bug fixes from the release are moved into the main integration branch.
3. The release build is labeled in the **RTM** branch and merged back into **Main**.
4. A service pack, SP1, is released. The build is labeled and changes are merged into **Main**.
5. The **Release 1** branch lives on in support of SP1 and to enable future service packs.

This process repeats for future releases.

Note: Successful use of release branches requires you to identify which branch the fix should be applied to before implementing it. If you release a fix as a hotfix or service pack, you should make the change first on the appropriate **Release** branch, and then merge it into **Main** to ensure it gets applied to future releases.

Isolated Development Scenario

Figure 5.3 shows a typical timeline when branching for development isolation.

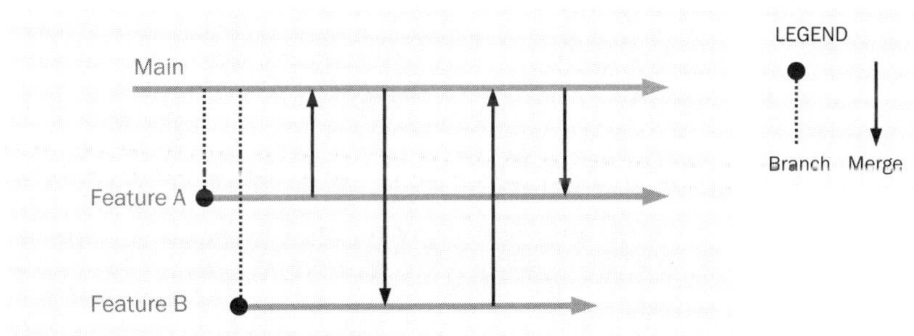

Figure 5.3 *Branching for Development Isolation TimeLine*

The sequence of events is as follows:

1. A feature branch is created to isolate development for Feature A.
2. A feature branch is created to isolate development for Feature B.
3. Each team merges its changes into **Main** as feature milestones are completed, so that they can be integrated into the main build and picked up by other teams.

4. On a periodic schedule, each team merges the latest changes from **Main** in order to remain synchronized with the work of other teams and to reduce the number of conflicts per merge.
5. When the feature is complete, the changes are fully merged back to **Main** and the feature branch is removed.

Branching Considerations

When branching, consider the following:

- Do not branch unless your development team needs to work on the same set of files concurrently. If you are unsure about this, you can label a build and create a branch from that build at a later point. Merging branches can be time consuming and complex, especially if there are significant changes between them.
- Structure your branch trees so that you only need to merge along the hierarchy (up and down the branch tree) rather than across the hierarchy. Branching across the hierarchy requires that you use a baseless merge, which requires more manual conflict resolution.
- The branch hierarchy is based on the branch parent and branch child, which may be different than the physical structure of the source code on disk. When planning your merges, keep in mind the logical branch structure rather than the physical structure on disk.
- Do not branch too deeply. Because it takes time to execute each merge and resolve conflicts, a deep branching structure can mean that changes in a child branch may take a very long time to propagate to the main branch. This can negatively impact project schedules and increase the time to fix bugs.
- Branch at a high-level and include configuration and source files.
- Evolve your branching structure over time.
- Merging requires one or more developers to execute the merge and resolve conflicts. The merged source must be thoroughly tested because it is not uncommon to make bad merge decisions that can destabilize the build.
- Merging across the branch hierarchy is especially difficult and requires you to manually handle many conflicts that could otherwise be handled automatically.

The decision whether to create a branch can be reduced to whether the cost of merging conflicts in real time is higher than the overhead cost of merging conflicts between branches.

Large Project Considerations

Large development teams with long development cycles are likely to distinguish themselves from smaller teams in the following ways:

- They require a more complex branching and merging structure.
- They are more likely to manage dependencies across solutions and team projects.
- They are more likely to maintain multiple builds for components and teams.

Large teams are likely to branch both by team and by feature and are also more likely to have one or more branches designed to integrate external dependencies. Because the branching structure is deeper there is more lag between a change in a development branch and merging that change into the main integration branch. For this reason, you should carefully consider your merging strategy when creating branches.

For example, consider the following when determining whether your merges will be scheduled or event driven:

- Reverse integration, such as merging from the development branch to the main branch, may be based on an event, such as a feature milestone being completed, or scheduled in order to integrate code from multiple branches at particular points in time. Use care when promoting code from a child branch to a parent branch through a reverse integration since any resulting destabilization will impact a larger portion of the development team.
- Forward integration, such as merging from the main branch to a development branch, occurs when a child branch is ready to accept the latest code that has been integrated into a parent branch. Frequent forward integrations into development branches are a best practice. Keeping the code base more closely synchronized across branches will help you discover bugs that occur when components are integrated together.

Rationalize your branch/merge strategy with the frequency with which you want to produce builds. A deeper branching structure results in more time to merge from child branches to the main integration branch. Symptoms of this causing a problem for your development team include:

- Broken builds where the fix takes too long to propagate up to the main integration branch.
- Missed milestones because features take too long to propagate up to the main branch.
- Large amounts of time are spent merging changes between various branches.

If this becomes a problem for your team, consider reducing the depth of your branching structure.

The following is an example of a complex branching structure:

- **My Team Project**
  - **Development**—Container to isolate active development branches
    - **Feature A**—Isolated branch for development
      - **Source**
    - **Feature B**—Isolated branch for development
      - **Source**
  - **Main**—Main integration and build branch. All changes come together here.
    - **Source**
    - **Other Asset Folders**
  - **Releases**—Container for current release and maintenance branches
    - **Release 2**—Active maintenance branch
      - **Source**
      - **Other Asset Folders**
    - **Release 3**—Active maintenance branch
      - **Source**
      - **Other Asset Folders**
    - **Release 4**—Branch containing the code currently being locked down to release
      - **Source**
      - **Other Asset Folders**
  - **Safe Keeping**
    - **Release 1**—Old release in safe keeping
      - **Source**
      - **Other Asset Folders**

This structure includes:

- Feature branches for multiple teams to work in isolation.
- A main branch to gather changes by all teams as well as bug fixes from the release branches.
- A release branch used to lockdown the current release.
- A maintenance branch for an old release that is being actively maintained and supported.
- Safekeeping branches for older releases that are no longer being maintained.

Summary

Branches are usually created to lock down a release, to maintain a previous release, or to support isolated parallel development. You should not branch unless you have good reason to do so.

When creating branches, you should logically structure your branch trees so that you only need to merge along the hierarchy (up and down the branch tree) rather than across the hierarchy. Merging across the hierarchy is time-consuming and error-prone.

For large teams, the branching structure is deeper, so you should be prepared for more lag time between a change occurring in a development branch and that change being merged back into the main integration branch.

Additional Resources

- For an introduction to branching and merging, see "Branching and Merging Primer" at *http://msdn2.microsoft.com/en-us/library/aa730834(VS.80).aspx*
- For more information about branching, see "How to: Branch Files and Folders" at *http://msdn2.microsoft.com/en-us/library/ms181425(VS.80).aspx*
- For more information about merging, see "How to: Merge Files and Folders" at *http://msdn2.microsoft.com/en-us/library/ms181428(VS.80).aspx*
- For additional descriptions of how to branch and merge in Visual Studio 2005, see "Branching and Merging Team Foundation Source Control" at *http://msdn2.microsoft.com/en-us/library/ms181423(VS.80).aspx*

6

Managing Source Control Dependencies in Visual Studio Team System

Objectives

- Manage source control dependencies in Microsoft® Visual Studio Team System.
- Reference projects and assemblies from different solutions in the same team project.
- Reference projects and assemblies from other team projects.
- Reference third-party assemblies.
- Manage Web service references in a team environment.
- Manage database references in a team environment.

Overview

This chapter explains how you should handle source control dependencies both within and across Visual Studio solutions. A consistent approach to managing dependencies in a team environment is necessary in order to reduce build instability and ongoing source control maintenance costs.

Dependencies include other projects, external assemblies, Web services, and databases. Dependencies inevitably change over time and as a result they impact the build process and the build order of your application. A good dependency management approach improves the integration process while making builds as seamless as possible.

How to Use This Chapter

Use this chapter to learn about managing dependencies in a team environment. You can either read this chapter from start to finish or read the section that addresses your specific dependency management requirement. Use the "Scenarios and Solutions" section to understand the general dependency management scenarios in a team environment. This section serves as a jumping-off point to following sections that describe each dependency scenario in detail.

- **Use the "Referencing Projects" section** to learn how to manage dependencies on other projects both inside and outside of your current team project.
- **Use the "Referencing Third-Party Assemblies" section** to learn how to manage dependencies on third-party assemblies for which you do not own the source.
- **Use the "Referencing Web Services" section** to learn how to reference shared Web services in a team environment.
- **Use the "Referencing Databases" section** to learn how to reference and connect to shared databases in a team environment.

Scenarios and Solutions

The following scenarios are common when managing dependencies:

1. You want to reference an assembly generated by another project in the same solution.
2. You want to reference an assembly generated by another project in a separate solution.
3. You want to reference an assembly contained in another team project.
4. You want to reference a third-party assembly.

Referencing Assemblies Generated by another Project in the Same Solution

If you need to reference another assembly in the same Visual Studio solution, use a Visual Studio project reference. By using project references, you enable Visual Studio to do a few things automatically for you, such as keeping build configuration (debug/release) synchronized and tracking versioning and rebuilding of components as necessary when assembly versions change.

Referencing Assemblies Generated by Projects in a Separate Solution

If you need to reference an assembly generated by a project in a different Visual Studio solution, you have two choices:

- Use a file reference to point to the binary assembly.
- Add the Visual Studio project (project and source files) to your solution and then use a project reference.

File references are more fragile than project references, do not adhere to your build configuration, and are not tracked by Visual Studio build dependencies. Therefore, if the assemblies that you have referenced changes, the Visual Studio build system does not automatically know that a rebuild is required.

Alternatively you can branch the external project into your solution, build the binary and then use a project reference. The reference will be more robust, although you need to merge from the source branch regularly in order to pick up changes.

Referencing an Assembly from another Team Project

If you share source or binaries across team projects, you have two options:

- **Branching.** With this approach, you branch the source from the other team project into your current solution. This creates a configuration that unifies the source from the shared location and your project on the server-side.
- **Workspace Mapping.** With this approach, you map the source from the other team project into a workspace on your development computer. This creates a configuration that unifies the source from the other team project and your project on the client-side.

Branching is the preferred approach because it stores the dependency relationship on the source control server. Workspace mapping is a client-side-only approach, which means that you and every developer must create the mapping on your own computers and also on the build server in order to successfully build the application.

Branching adds additional merge overhead but it enables you to make the decision to pick up updated binaries or source more explicitly.

Referencing a Third-Party Assembly

This scenario is very similar to referencing across team projects except that you only share binaries, not source code. The choice between branching and workspaces is very similar, with the added caveat that the overhead is likely to be lower because third-party assemblies are less likely to change as frequently.

Referencing Projects

If you have a Visual Studio project, for example a team project containing shared library code that is used by multiple team projects, you can either manage the project within the owning team's project or you can create a separate team project specifically for the shared project.

If you choose the latter approach and use a common shared project, the folder structure in Microsoft Visual Studio Team Foundation Server (TFS) source control looks like Figure 6.1 on the next page.

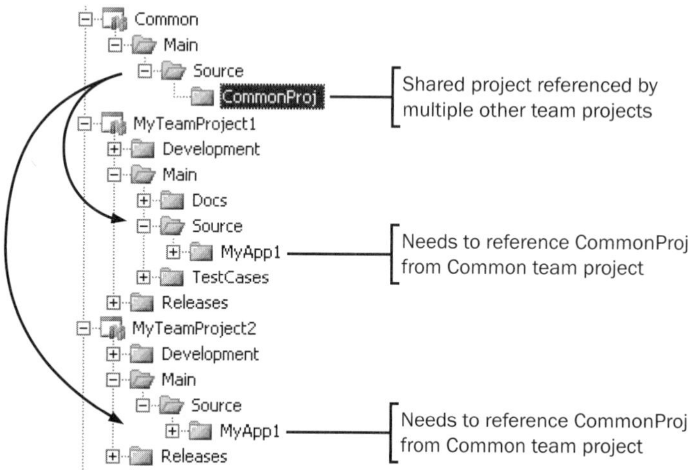

Figure 6.1 *Using a Common, Shared Project Folder Structure*

To consume the common shared project from your own team project you have two options:

- Branching
- Workspace mapping

Branching

Branching is the preferred method for most shared-source scenarios. It enables you to pull the shared source into your project and check it into your team project's source control. In this scenario, you branch the source from the common shared location into your team project. This creates a configuration that unifies the source from the shared location and your project on the server-side.

Shared source changes are picked up as part of a merge process between the branches. This makes the decision to pick up changes in the shared source more explicit and easier to test, but it also adds some overhead. Additionally, this process makes the use of Team Build much simpler because the mapping is done on the server side; there is no client-side mapping that needs to be duplicated on the build server.

For example, if you have two team projects named $TeamProject1 and $Common, and Common is the shared project source, you create a branch from the shared location to the project that references it. The TFS folder structure should resemble the one shown in Figure 6.2.

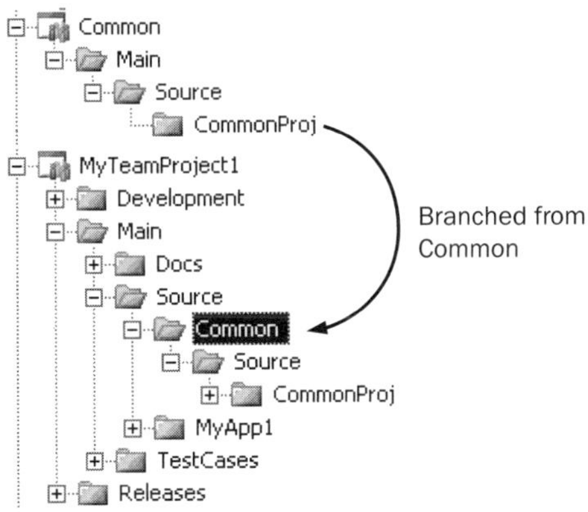

Figure 6.2 *Using Branches*

Your workspace mapping should resemble the following:

Source Control Folder	Local Folder
$/MyTeamProject1/Main/Source/	C:\MyTeamProject1\Main\Source

The client side workspace folder structure should resemble the one shown in Figure 6.3.

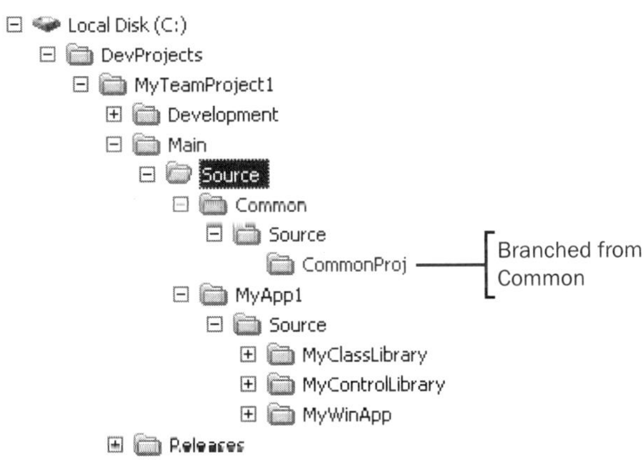

Figure 6.3 *Client Side Workspace Mapping*

Workspace Mapping

If you want your developers to instantly pick up any code changes from the shared source without incurring the overhead of branching and merging, you can map the shared source from the common project into the workspace on your development computer. This creates a configuration that unifies the source from the shared location and your project on the client-side.

The advantage of this approach is that shared project changes are picked up every time you retrieve the latest source into your workspace. However, this makes the use of Team Build more complex since the workspace mapping is a client-side construct.

For example if you have two team projects named $MyTeamProject2 and $Common, and Common is the shared project source, for referencing the code from the shared location, these projects share a common path on the client's hard drive. The client side workspace folder structure should resemble the one shown in Figure 6.4.

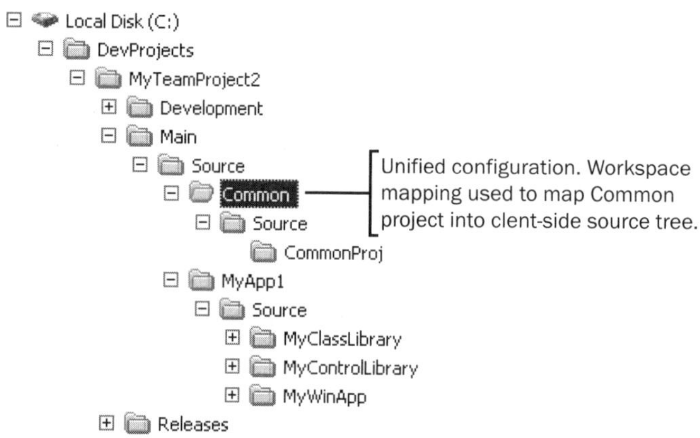

Figure 6.4 *Using Workspace Mapping*

The workspace mappings should resemble the following:

Source Control Folder	Local Folder
$/MyTeamProject2/Main/Source/	C:\DevProjects\MyTeamProject2\Main\Source\
$/Common	C:\DevProjects\MyTeamProject2\Main\Source\ Common

For more information, see "Working with multiple team projects in Team Build" at *http://blogs.msdn.com/manishagarwal/archive/2005/12/22/506635.aspx*

Referencing Third-Party Assemblies

If you cannot use a project reference and you need to reference an assembly outside of your current solution's project set, such as a third-party library, and you do not want to or cannot create a branch from the originating project into your project, you must set a file reference.

Managing shared binaries is similar to managing shared project source, and you must decide where you want to store the binaries and how you want your team to access the binaries. If you have binaries that are used by multiple team projects, you can either manage the binaries within the team project of the owning team or create a team project specifically for the shared binaries.

For the teams consuming the shared binaries, the same two options available for referencing projects are available for binaries.

- Branching
- Workspace Mapping

Branching

In this scenario, you branch the binaries from the common shared location into your team project. This creates a configuration that unifies the binaries from the shared location and their project on the server-side.

The difference is that any changes to the binaries, such as new versions are picked up as part of a merge process between the branches. This makes the decision to pick up changed shared binaries much more explicit.

For example if you have two team projects named $TeamProject1 and $Common, and Common contains the shared binaries, you create a branch from the shared location to the project that references it. The TFS folder structure should resemble the one shown in Figure 6.5.

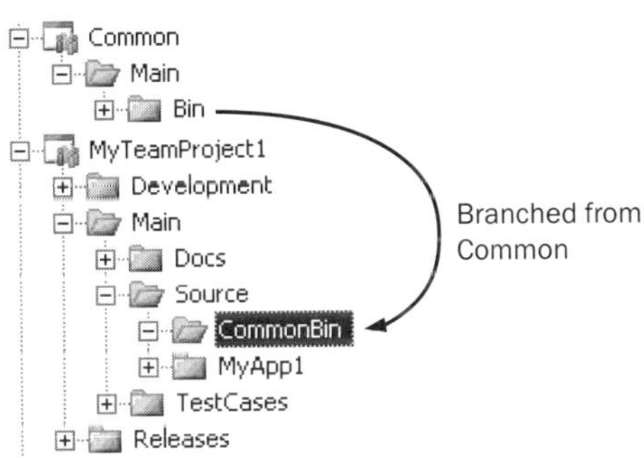

Figure 6.5 *Branching from Common*

Your workspace mapping should resemble the following:

Source Control Folder	Local Folder
$/MyTeamProject1/Main	C:\MyTeamProject1\Main

The client side workspace folder structure should resemble the one shown in Figure 6.6.

Figure 6.6 *Client-Side Workspace Folder Structure*

Workspace Mapping

In your team project that consumes the shared binaries, you reference the binaries from the shared location into your workspace on your development computer. This creates a configuration that unifies the binaries from the shared location and your project on the client-side.

The advantage of this approach is that changes to shared binaries are picked up every time you retrieve the latest source into your workspace.

For example if you have two team projects named $TeamProject2and $Common, and TeamProject2 references the binaries available in Common, then the client side workspace folder structure should resemble the one shown in Figure 6.7.

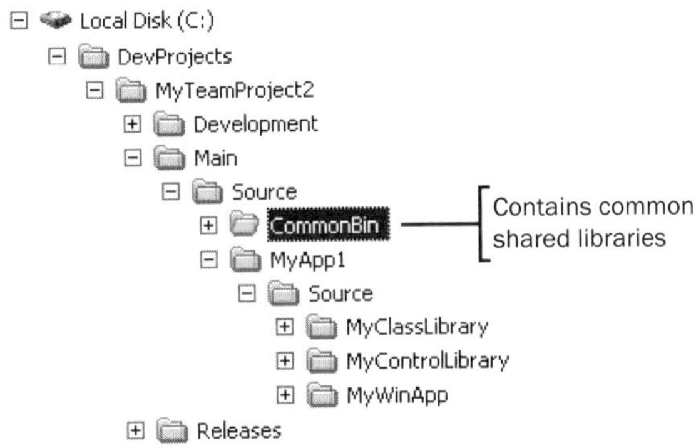

Figure 6.7 *Storing Common Shared Libraries*

The workspace mappings should resemble the following:

Source Control Folder	Local Folder
$/MyTeamProject2/Main/	C:\DevProjects\MyTeamProject2\Main\
$/Common/Main/Bin	C:\DevProjects\MyTeamProject2\Main\Source\CommonBin

For more information, see "Working with multiple team projects in Team Build" at *http://blogs.msdn.com/manishagarwal/archive/2005/12/22/506635.aspx*

Guidelines for Referencing Projects and Assemblies

You can set a file reference in one of two ways:

- To reference a .NET Framework assembly, you select the assembly from the list displayed on the **.NET** tab of the **Add References** dialog box.
- You can use the **Browse** button in the **Add Reference** dialog box.

Assemblies such as System.XML.dll are located in the Global Assembly Cache (GAC). However, you never directly refer to an assembly within the GAC. Instead, when you select an assembly on the **.NET** tab of the **Add References** dialog box, you actually reference a copy of the assembly, located within the %windir%\Microsoft.NET\Framework\<version>\ folder.

Project references are preferable to file references. Keep the following guidelines in mind when managing assembly references:

- Use project references whenever possible.
- Use file references only where necessary.
- Use **Copy Local = True** for project and file references.

For more information, see "Source Control Guidelines" in this guide.

Automated Dependency Tracking

Each time you build your local project, the build system compares the date and time of the referenced assembly file with the working copy on your development workstation. If the referenced assembly is more recent, the new version is copied to the local folder. One of the benefits of this approach is that a project reference established by a developer does not lock the assembly dynamic-link library (DLL) on the server and does not interfere in any way with the build process.

Referencing Web Services

In simpler systems where all of the projects for the system are contained within the same team project, all developers end up with local working copies of all Web services because they are defined by Visual Studio projects within the team project. When you open a solution from source control for the first time, all projects (including any Web services) are installed locally. Similarly, if a Web service is added to the solution by another developer, you install the Web service the next time you refresh your solution from source control. In this scenario, there is no need to publish Web services on a central Web server within your team environment.

For larger systems, Web services can be published through Internet Information Server (IIS) on a centrally accessed Web server and not all developers need to locally install the Web service. Instead developers can access the Web service from their client projects, although you need to reference the Web service appropriately as discussed below.

For more information, see "Source Control Guidelines" and "Source Control Practices" in this guide.

Use Dynamic URLs When Referencing Web Services

If you want to call a Web service, you must first add a Web reference to your project. This generates a proxy class through which you interact with the Web service. The proxy code initially contains a static Uniform Resource Locator (URL) for the Web service, for example http://localhost or http://SomeWebServer.

Important: For Web services in your current solution that execute on your computer, always use http://localhost rather than http://MyComputerName to ensure the reference remains valid on all computers.

The static URL that is embedded within the proxy is usually not the URL that you require in either the production or test environment. Typically, the required URL varies as your application moves from development to test to production. You have three options to address this issue:

- You can programmatically set the Web service URL when you create an instance of the proxy class.
- A more flexible approach that avoids a hard coded URL in the proxy is to set the **URL Behavior** property of the Web service reference to **Dynamic**. This is the preferred approach. When you set the property to **Dynamic**, code is added to the proxy class to retrieve the Web service URL from a custom configuration section of the application configuration file, Web.config for a Web application or SomeApp.exe.config for a Windows application.
- You can also generate the proxy by using the WSDL.exe command line tool and specifying the /urlkey switch. This works in a similar way to setting the **URL Behavior** property in that it adds code to the proxy to retrieve the Web service URL, but in this case the URL is stored in the <applicationSettings> section of the application configuration file.

The dynamic URL approach also lets you provide a user configuration file, which can override the main application configuration file. This enables separate developers and members of the test team to temporarily redirect a Web service reference to an alternate location.

How to Use Dynamic URLs and a User Configuration File

Set the **URL Behavior** property of your Web service reference to **Dynamic** to gain maximum configuration flexibility within both the development and production environments. By default, Visual Studio sets the value of this property to **Dynamic** when you add a Web reference. To check that this value is still set to **Dynamic**:

1. In the Solution Explorer, expand the list of Web references.
2. Select each Web reference in the list.
3. For each Web reference, check that the value of the **URL Behavior** property is set to **Dynamic**.

To specify a Web Service URL in a user configuration file

- When you first add a Web reference, Visual Studio automatically generates the App.config file for you. This file contains the Web service reference and the configuration setting in the App.config file looks like the following:

```
<configuration>
    <configSections>
        <sectionGroup name="applicationSettings" type="System.Configuration.
ApplicationSettingsGroup, System, Version=2.0.0.0, Culture=neutral, PublicKeyTo
ken=b77a5c561934e089" >
            <section name=" YourProject.Properties.Settings" type="System.
Configuration.ClientSettingsSection, System, Version=2.0.0.0, Culture=neutral,
PublicKeyToken=b77a5c561934e089" requirePermission="false" />
        </sectionGroup>
    </configSections>
    <applicationSettings>
        <YourProject.Properties.Settings>
            <setting name="SomeService_ localhost _Service"
serializeAs="String">
                <value>http://localhost/someservice/Service.asmx</value>
            </setting>
        </ YourProject.Properties.Settings>
    </applicationSettings>
</configuration>
```

This file contains a new configuration section that is used by the generated proxy. This configuration section contains the address of the Web service that Visual Studio found when generating this proxy.

Visual Studio also places the default value of the URL into the code generated for this proxy. This value lives in a file named Settings.Designer.cs. To see this file,

1. In the **Solution Explorer**, right-click on the Web service.
2. Select **View in Object Browser**. In the Object Browser look for the entry that says **YourProject.Properties** entry, where YourProject is the project name that contains Web service reference.
3. Expand **YourProject.Properties** and you then double-click **Settings.** This opens the Settings.Designer.cs file that contains a line similar to the following:

```
[global::System.Configuration.DefaultSettingValueAttribute("http://localhost:/
webservice/Service.asmx")]
```

This is the default value used for the URL of the Web service if no configuration information is found.

You often need to change the URL of the Web service you are calling. For example you might want to test against the Web service running locally on your computer or against a version of the Web service running in a test environment. It is also highly likely that the URL of the production Web service is not the same as the URL used during development. To manage each of these URLs the URL value should be specified in a user configuration file, which is referenced from the main App.config file. The name of the user configuration file is arbitrary. The following example uses User.config as the file name to make clear that this is where the user's configuration would go.

To create a User.config file perform the following steps:

1. In Solution Explorer, right-click the project that contains the Web service reference, point to **Add** and then click **New Item**.
2. Select **Application Configuration File**, change the name to User.config and then click **Add**.
3. Copy the *<YourProject.Properties.Settings>* element setting from your application configuration file (App.config) to the User.config file. This file should contain only the element for which the runtime is redirected. Delete the <?xml> directive and the <configuration> element if present, as shown in the following example

```
<YourProject.Properties.Settings>
    <setting name="SomeService_localhost_Service" serializeAs="String">
       <value>http://localhost/someservice/Service.asmx</value>
    </setting>
</YourProject.Properties.Settings>
```

Individual developers should set the contents of their User.config file as needed to reference the appropriate URL. You now need to specify that the configuration system should use this User.config file for this configuration data rather than the App.config file. To do this you must update the App.config file as follows:

1. Add a **configSource="user.config"** attribute to the *<YourProject.Properties.Settings>* element of your main application configuration file. This silently redirects the runtime to the named user configuration file when it accesses information from this section.
2. Delete the content of the *<YourProject.Properties.Settings>* element.

Your App.config should now look like the following:

```
<?xml version="1.0" encoding="utf-8" ?>
<configuration>
    <configSections>
        <sectionGroup name="applicationSettings" type="System.Configuration.Appli-
cationSettingsGroup, System, Version=2.0.0.0, Culture=neutral, PublicKeyToken=b77
a5c561934e089" >
            <section name="YourProject.Properties.Settings" type="System.Configura-
tion.ClientSettingsSection, System, Version=2.0.0.0, Culture=neutral, PublicKeyTok
en=b77a5c561934e089" requirePermission="false" />
        </sectionGroup>
    </configSections>
  <applicationSettings>
    <yourProject.Properties.Settings  configSource="user.config">
    </YourProject.Properties.Settings>
   </applicationSettings>
</configuration>
```

In the preceding example, *YourProject* is the name of the project that contains the Web service reference.

Important: If you use the **configSource** attribute, then the user configuration file must be present, with only the *<YourProject.Properties.Service>* element. You must also ensure that when you add the **configSource="user.config"** attribute you remove the Extensible Markup Language (XML) content from the *<YourProject.Properties.Service>* element.

When you use the User.config approach:

- Make sure that you deploy your User.config file along with the application code. To do this in Solution Explorer, right click the User.config file, click **Properties** option and then set the **Copy To Output Directory** property to **Copy if newer**.
- Do not add your User.config file to source control. In this way, each developer and the test team can explicitly bind to specific URLs by using their own User.config files. Source control may contain other User.config files, for example, for testing and for production. These files should be managed by the users responsible for managing the testing and production environments. These test and production User.config files should not be stored as part of the Web service projects but should be in different areas of the source control system.
- Store a global User.config file in source control. This could either contain only the root element (no <setting> element) or it could specify the default location of the Web service. The User.config file must be present for the configuration system to work.

Tip: By default, the user configuration file is automatically added to source control when you add the solution. To prevent this, when you first check in the file, clear the User.config file check box. You can then right-click on the file in Solution Explorer and select the **Undo Pending Changes** option to ensure that the file is subject to source control.

Important: If the User.config file that specifies the URL only contains the root element and there is no setting element in the User.config, then the Web service proxy uses its default value for the URL. This default value is hard coded into the proxy in a file named Settings.Designer.cs. The value is specified as a **DefaultValueSettings** attribute and looks like the following:

```
[global::System.Configuration.DefaultSettingValueAttribute("http://localhost/web-
service/Service.asmx")]
```

Important: For Web applications that use a user configuration file, any changes made to the file result in the Web application being automatically recycled by default. If you do not want to recycle the application when a value changes, add the **restartOnExternalChanges**="**false**" attribute to the configuration section definition as follows:

```
<configSections>
      <sectionGroup name="applicationSettings" type="System.Configuration.Appli-
cationSettingsGroup, System, Version=2.0.0.0, Culture=neutral, PublicKeyToken=b77a
5c561934e089">
            <section name="Test.Properties.Settings" type="System.Configuration.
ClientSettingsSection, System, Version=2.0.0.0, Culture=neutral, PublicKeyToken=b7
7a5c561934e089" requirePermission="false" restartOnExternalChanges="true"/>
      </sectionGroup>
</configSections>
```

If you add this attribute to the configuration section in the Web.config file then changes to the external User.config configuration file do not cause the Web application to recycle. However, those changes are still visible to the application.

It is important to understand that if you are using this mechanism then the User.config file must be present. Somebody must be responsible for ensuring the environment is correct when creating builds for production releases and for any test environments. As part of this build setup, the appropriate User.confg file must be retrieved from the source control system and copied into the correct location for MSBuild to be able to find it.

Referencing Databases

Database references in the form of connection strings can also be managed by using an external configuration file. The advantage of this approach is that each developer can easily specify his or her own connection string in their own private User.config file. Any changes made by one developer, such as redirecting the connection to a local database for unit testing purposes, do not affect other developers.

User configuration files can also be used to control environment-specific settings, such as those required by a test environment. The test environment can also use a User.config file that references the test database.

The procedure is similar to the preceding Web references example, except that in that example the Web service proxy contains the code to retrieve the Web service URL from the configuration file. For database connection strings, you must provide the code to read the connection string.

How to Use User Configuration Files for Database Connection Strings

The following procedure explains how to store and then reference a database connection string within a user configuration file.

To use a user configuration file to store database connection strings:

1. Add a **configSource="user.config"** attribute to the <connectionStrings> element of your main application configuration file.

```
<configuration>
   <connectionStrings configSource="user.config"/>
</configuration>
```

2. To override the main application configuration file, create a User.config file (located in the same folder as the application configuration file), and then add a similar <connectionStrings> entry to the file. Notice that the following connection string references a local database.

```
<connectionStrings>
      <add name="DBConnStr"
     connectionString="server=localhost;Integrated Security=SSPI;database=Acco
unts"/>
   </connectionStrings>
</configuration>
```

3. Within your project, use the following code to obtain the connection string from the user configuration file. This code uses the static **ConnectionStrings** property of the **System.Configuration.ConfigurationManager class.** In the WinForm application, you must add a reference to **System.Configuration.dll** explicitly.

```
using System.Configuration;
private string GetDBaseConnectionString()
{
  return ConfigurationManager.ConnectionStrings["DBConnStr"].ConnectionString;
}
```

4. Ensure that the User.config file is deployed along with the application code. To do so in Solution Explorer right click the User.config file, click the **Properties** and then in the Properties pane, set the **Copy To Output Directory** property to **Copy if newer**.

Do not add the User.config file to source control. In this way, each developer and the test team can explicitly specify the connection string through their own User.config file. Source control may contain other User.config files, for example for testing and for production. These files should be managed by the users responsible for managing the testing and production environments. These test and production User.config files should not be stored as part of the database projects but should be in different areas of the source control system.

In source control you should have a User.config file for each of the environments that you use, such as production and test. These configuration files should specify the connection string for the database. The User.config file must be present for the configuration system to work.

Note: By default, the user configuration file is automatically added to source control when you add the solution. To prevent this, when you first check in the files, clear the User.config file check box. You can then right-click on the file in Solution Explorer and select Undo Pending Changes to ensure that the file never comes under source control.

It is important to understand that if you are using this mechanism, the User.config file must be present. Somebody needs to be responsible for ensuring the environment is correct when creating builds for production releases and for any test environments. As part of this build setup, the appropriate User.confg file will need to be retrieved from the source control system and copied into the correct location for MSBuild to be able to find it.

Summary

When managing projects or third-party assemblies, you can use either branching or workspace mapping. Branching is the preferred approach because it stores the dependency relationship on the source control server. Using branches enables you to make a conscious decision to pick up updated binaries or source.

Workspace mapping is a client-side-only approach, which means each team member needs to create the mapping on their own computer as well as on the build server in order to be able to build the application. This approach is most commonly used when you want to instantly pick up updated binaries or source at the time of your build.

Use dynamic URLs when referencing Web services and use an external configuration file to manage Web services. The advantage of this approach is that each developer can easily specify his or her own Web services reference in a private User.config file. You can also manage database references in the form of connection strings by using an external configuration file. The advantage of this approach is that each developer can easily specify his or her own connection string in a private User.config file.

Additional Resources

- For more information about project references, see "Project References" at *http://msdn2.microsoft.com/en-us/library/ez524kew(VS.80).aspx*
- For more information about branching, see "How to: Branch Files and Folders" at *http://msdn2.microsoft.com/en-us/library/ms181425(VS.80).aspx*
- For more information about workspaces, see "Working with Source Control Workspaces" at *http://msdn2.microsoft.com/en-us/library/ms181383(VS.80).aspx*

Part III

Builds

In this part:

- Team Build Explained
- Setting Up Continuous Integration with Team Build
- Setting Up Scheduled Builds with Team Build

7

Team Build Explained

Objectives

- Understand Microsoft® Visual Studio® Team System Team Build architecture.
- Learn the components that make up Team Build.
- Understand the functionality Team Build provides.
- Select an appropriate build strategy.
- Identify ways in which your build strategy may need to be changed if you work on a large project.

Overview

This chapter explains how you can use Team Build to automate the build process. It outlines a number of common build-related stumbling blocks and compares various approaches to builds ranging from daily scheduled builds to continuous integration builds.

Team Build is built on top of the Microsoft Build Engine (MSBuild) and you can use it to retrieve the necessary source code for a build, compile solutions and (if required) execute unit tests and static code analysis tools as part of the build process. You can also release build output to a specified shared location.

Team Build labels the source code used for a particular build with build numbers so that you can retrieve the source used to create a specific build at some point in the future. In case of failures, you can configure Team Build to create work items and to notify the users about the build failures it encountered.

How to Use This Chapter

Use this chapter to learn about the functionality that Team Build provides for automating and managing the build process, and to understand the different strategies for scheduling builds. To gain the greatest benefit from this chapter, you should:

- **Read Chapter 8, "Setting up Continuous Integration with Team Build"** to learn more about using continuous integration with Team Foundation Server (TFS).
- **Read Chapter 9, "Setting up Scheduled Builds with Team Build"** to learn more about using scheduled builds.
- **Read the companion How To articles** to help perform build-related tasks:
  - How To: Automatically Run Code Analysis with Team Build in Visual Studio Team Foundation Server.
  - How To: Set Up a Continuous Integration Build in Visual Studio Team Foundation Server.
  - How To: Set Up a Scheduled Build in Visual Studio Team Foundation Server.

Architecture

This section introduces the architecture of Team Build through a description of its physical architecture and logical workflow.

Physical Architecture

The physical architecture of Team Build consists of the following components:

- **New Team Build Type Creation Wizard**—This client-side component accessed from Team Explorer, enables you to create new build types.
- **Team Build Browser**—This client-side component accessed from Team Explorer, enables you to view the Team Build reports and build progress information in Team Explorer.
- **Source Control Web Service**—This application-tier component is used by the build service to access source code.
- **Team Foundation Build Web Service**—This application-tier component accepts requests from the client and coordinates the execution of build steps.
- **Build Service**—This service runs the build steps in response to instructions from the Team Build Web service. You can locate the build service on a separate build server or on the application-tier server.
- **Team Foundation Build Store**—This data-tier component is used to hold records related to Team Build processes.
- **Source Code database**—This data-tier component is used to store the source code which is accessed by Build Service during the build process.

Logical Workflow

Figure 7.1 shows the Team Build logical workflow.

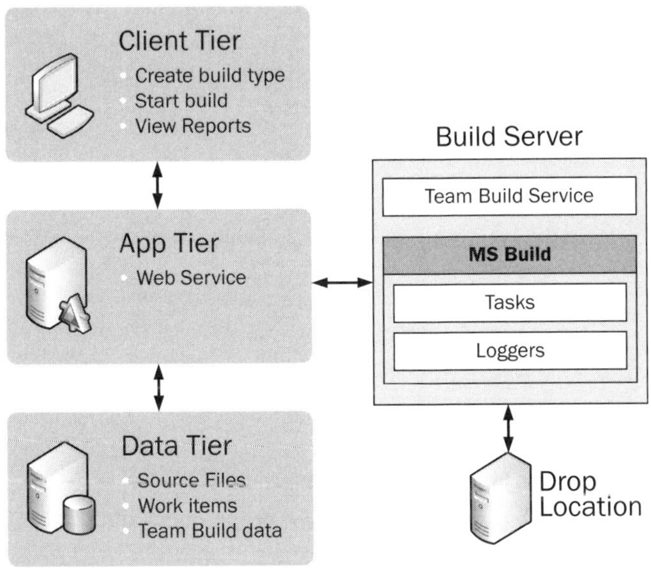

Figure 7.1 *Team Build logical workflow*

Team Build integrates with TFS through the application-tier and interacts with work items, code coverage, code analysis, test cases and reporting.

The TFSBuild.proj file controls the build, including what projects to build, configurations, drop locations, code analysis, and tests to be run. This file is generated by the **Team Build Type Creation Wizard**, when the build is first created. You can edit it directly.

Team Build uses the eventing system in TFS. You can use events fired by Team Build to create custom build steps, or to generate notifications of build status changes or build completion.

Key Points

Keep in mind the following key points related to Team Build physical architecture:

- Team Foundation Build is built on top of MSBuild
- The TFSBuild.proj file contains all of the build settings. You generate this file by using Team Build Type Creation Wizard. You can then edit the file directly.
- The TFSBuild.rsp file contains command-line options for MSBuild. You can modify this file to further customize the build
- Event notification enables custom build steps or notifications through the **BuildStatusChangeEvent** and **BuildCompletionEvent** events.
- Team Build integrates with work items, code coverage, code analysis, and test cases.

How Team Build Works

Team Build consists of the Team Build Service layered on top of the MSBuild build system. MSBuild is responsible for the build itself, while the Team Build Service is responsible for communicating with the TFS application-tier. Team Builds are created from the Visual Studio client and you can start them from the client, by an event on the build server, or from the command-line, for example as a scheduled task. Once started, the build process consists of the following steps:

1. Get sources from source control into the build directory.
2. Compile the source and generate binaries.
3. Run code analysis (Optional).
4. Create a work item if there is a build failure.
5. Run tests (Optional).
6. Calculate code coverage (Optional).
7. Log build details.
8. Copy the build to the drop location.

After the build is complete, the following are available:

- **Build details.** You can view details from any client or from reports.
- **Build binaries.** Binaries are placed in the drop location.
- **Build Log.** You can review the log for errors and warnings.
- **Work item.** If the build fails, a work item is created to track the build break.

How to Determine Your Build Strategy

Use the following steps to determine your build strategy:

1. Consider your build consumers.
2. Review solution scenarios.
3. Understand common stumbling blocks.

Consider Your Build Consumers

Most development teams have one or more of the following build consumers:

- Development team
- Test team
- Internal build adopters
- External beta adopters
- Customers

Each consumer has different needs in terms of build quality and frequency. In general, build consumers can be divided into two groups; those who need predictable, scheduled builds and those who need rapid, event-driven builds. Scheduled builds are most commonly daily builds but can occur more or less frequently. Event-driven builds are usually initiated by a check-in and are designed to give the development team rapid feedback. If your development team has problems with breaking builds, consider using a gated check-in model, where check-ins are tested before they are allowed into the source tree and are rejected if the tests fail.

Review Solution Scenarios

Choose solution scenarios based on how closely their purpose and build consumers match your team's situation. When in doubt, use the simplest build scenario possible, such as a scheduled build, and add more complex scenarios only if necessary.

Build Scenarios

The following are the most common Team Build scenarios:

- **Team with single daily builds.** Most teams rely on a scheduled build in order to provide consistent binaries to their test team and other users.
- **Team with daily builds and continuous integration builds.** Some teams choose to use continuous integration builds in order to provide rapid feedback to their developers upon every check-in. Although a pure continuous integration build works well for small teams, larger teams are likely to overload their build server due to high-frequency check-ins and longer build times. When this happens, a rolling build can be used to build less frequently without giving up too much time between check-in and build feedback.
- **Team with multiple build labs, each performing daily build and continuous integration builds.** Very large teams are likely to require more complex solutions to improve build quality and timeliness. You can use gated check-ins to reduce build breaks by rejecting bad check-ins before they make it into source control. Teams that branch can use multiple build servers, one per branch, to keep the builds focused on each branch's purpose. For example, integration branches create integration builds, while development branches create development builds.

Scheduled Builds

A *scheduled build* is a time-based build based on a fixed time frequency. The purpose of a scheduled build is to produce consistently reliable builds that can be used to gain feedback on the quality of the build. Scheduled builds are usually daily builds, but they could occur more or less frequently depending upon your needs.

The consumers of a scheduled build are most often:

- Test team
- Internal build adopters
- External adopters

Use the following steps to create a scheduled build:

1. Create a batch file with a command line build.
2. Use Windows Scheduled Tasks to execute the batch file on a schedule.

For more information, see Chapter 9, "Setting Up Scheduled Builds with Team Build."

Continuous Integration Build

A *continuous integration build* is triggered any time a check-in occurs. The purpose of a continuous integration build is to gain rapid feedback about build quality as soon after a check-in as possible. Development teams are typically the consumers of a continuous integration builds.

Depending on the size of your team, the length of your build, and the number of check-ins, choose one of the following strategies:

1. Continuous integration build immediately following each check-in.
2. Rolling build after a specified number of check-ins, or a specified time period (whichever comes first).

For more information, see Chapter 8, "Setting Up Continuous Integration with Team Build."

Gated Check-ins

Gated check-ins is a process that requires each check-in to meet some quality standard before it can be added to the source tree. The purpose of a gated check-in is to reduce the number of build breaks and improve the quality of the build by requiring that each check-in be run through a set of tests before it can be admitted.

Understand Common Stumbling Blocks

There are several common scenarios that Team Build does not fully support by default. Review the following scenarios and consider whether your team is likely to face any of them:

- **Building a project with external dependencies**. If you use branching to bring external dependencies into your team project, you can use project references and the build will work on the build server without any additional steps. If you use client-side workspace mapping to reference external dependencies, you need to maintain the mapping on the build server in order for the build to complete successfully. For more information, see Chapter 6, "Managing Source Control Dependencies in Visual Studio Team System."
- **Building a setup project.** Team Build does not support setup projects by default. Use a custom post-build step to compile the setup project and copy the binaries to the build drop location. For more information, see "Walkthrough: Configuring Team Foundation Build to Build a Visual Studio Setup Project" at *http://msdn2.microsoft.com/en-us/library/ms404859(VS.80).aspx*

- **Building .NET 1.1 Applications.** Team Build does not support .NET 1.1 applications by default. The MSBuild Extras – Toolkit for .NET 1.1 (MSBee) supports .NET 1.1 builds but requires that your projects and solutions be upgraded to Visual Studio 2005. If you cannot upgrade to Visual Studio 2005 projects and solutions, you can use a custom post-build step to compile your .NET 1.1 applications. To download MSBee, go to *http://www.codeplex.com/MSBee*. For more information about creating a custom build step to compile a .NET 1.1 applications, see Nagaraju's blog entry at *http://blogs.msdn.com/nagarajp/archive/2005/10/26/485368.aspx* or see "Microsoft SDC DevEnv task" at *http://www.codeplex.com/sdctasks*.
- **Building Microsoft Visual Basic® 6.0 applications.** Team Build does not support Visual Basic 6.0 applications by default. Use a custom post-build step to compile the Visual Basic 6.0 application. To see a similar post build step that can be used to compile a .NET 1.1 applications, see Nagaraju's blog entry at *http://blogs.msdn.com/nagarajp/archive/2005/10/26/485368.aspx* or see "MSBuild task to build VB6" at *http://freetodev.spaces.live.com/blog/cns!EC3C8F2028D842D5!261.entry*.

Considerations for Large Project

If you work on a large development team, there are additional considerations to keep in mind. Large development teams typically differ from smaller teams in the following ways:

- They require a more complex branching and merging structure.
- They are more likely to manage dependencies across solutions and team projects.
- They are more likely to maintain multiple builds for components and teams.

Keep the following considerations in mind when working with large development teams:

- Large teams are likely to have longer build times. The frequency of continuous integration builds should be less than the build time to avoid too much queuing and loading of the build server.
- If your team branches, you can set up a build server per branch. This enables each build to be focused on the purpose of the branch, for example integration or development.
- Integration branches are likely to have scheduled builds only. Development branches may have continuous integration and scheduled builds.

Build Customization

To modify information about the build, such as the build server, drops location or build directory you can edit the TFSBuild.proj file.

The TFSBuild.proj file contains much of the information needed to execute a team build. This information includes the build locations and whether the build should perform static code analysis and run unit tests. To modify the build you edit the TFSBuild.proj file. To edit the file you:

1. Check the file out of source control.
2. Update the build information in the file.
3. Check the file back in, committing the changes.

The next time the build is executed it will use the amended build data.

For more information about customizing the build, see the "Customization" section in "Build Guidelines" and "Build Practices" in this guide.

Summary

Team Build is built on top of MSBuild. It integrates with TFS through the application-tier and interacts with work items, code coverage, code analysis, test cases, and reporting features.

When determining your build strategy you need to consider your build consumers and build requirements. Common build strategies include using scheduled builds for consistent, reliable builds that can be used by the test team and others to give feedback on the quality of the build, and using a continuous integration build to gain rapid feedback on build quality for the development team.

Additional Resources

- For more information about Team Build, see "Overview of Team Foundation Build" at *http://msdn2.microsoft.com/en-us/library/ms181710(vs.80).aspx*

8

Setting Up Continuous Integration with Team Build

Objectives

- Understand the purpose of a continuous integration build.
- Set up continuous integration by using Microsoft® Visual Studio® Team System Team Build.
- Optimize your continuous integration build to reduce bottlenecks.

Overview

This chapter explains how you can set up continuous integration builds with Team Build and Microsoft Visual Studio Team Foundation Server (TFS). You use continuous integration builds to gain rapid feedback on build quality as soon after a check-in as possible. During team development, it is important to get rapid feedback on the quality of check-ins, especially if they combine with other developer's changes and break the build. A continuous integration build gives you the chance to fix code quickly in order to unblock other team members, thereby improving the consistency and quality of your build.

Team Foundation Server does not support continuous integration builds by default. It is possible, with the help of a Microsoft-supplied extension, to extend the build engine to support continuous integration.

How to Use This Chapter

Use this chapter to learn strategies for continuous integration and to learn how to set up and configure continuous integration builds with Team Build. For a step-by-step walkthrough to help you set up continuous integration build see "How To: Set Up a Continuous Integration Build."

If you are new to TFS and Team Build, or if you want to learn more about the options available for automating and scheduling builds, read Chapter 7, "Team Build Explained" before reading this chapter.

Strategies for Continuous Integration Builds

Continuous integration (CI) is the process of creating builds whenever a developer checks code into source control. The following list identifies various strategies used for continuous integration builds:

- Build on each check-in
- Rolling build after a specific number of check-ins
- Rolling build after a specific time interval
- Rolling build after a specific number of check-ins or time interval

Build on Each Check-In

Building immediately after every check-in is the simplest continuous integration strategy and generally gives you the most rapid feedback. However, if check-ins occurs rapidly enough to overwhelm the build server, you should use a rolling build approach where you build after a specified number of check-ins or after a specified time period. To decide if you need to use a rolling build, determine the following:

- Length of your team build in minutes
- Average frequency of check-ins in minutes
- Time window during which frequent check-ins occur

If the length of the build is longer than the average frequency of check-ins, your builds start to queue up because first build does not complete before the next check-in occurs which initiates another build. If the build queue grows long enough, this can impact the performance of the build server and blocks other builds from being started, such as scheduled builds. Review the time window during which frequent check-ins occur and determine if the queue has time to clear itself after the busiest check-in period is over.

For more information, see "How To: Set Up a Continuous Integration Build in Visual Studio Team Foundation Server."

Rolling Build After a Specific Number of Check-ins

If your build server is overloaded as a result of creating builds after each check-in, you can choose to only build after a specified number of check-ins have completed. While this is the simplest rolling build solution it has a significant drawback. Because the build server must see a specific number of check-ins before a build is started, the last check-in of the day is virtually guaranteed not to get a build and therefore build feedback is delayed.

Rolling Build After a Specific Time Interval

Producing a build only after a specific time interval elapses after each check-in is an improvement over building after a specific number of check-ins. This approach is guaranteed to produce a build within a specific timeframe around each check-in that is made. Keep in mind that each build may have a varying number of associated check-ins – some builds may only have one check-in, while others may have more. The more check-ins in each build, the more difficult it is to determine which check-in created the breaking change.

Rolling Build After a Specific Number of Check-Ins or Time Interval

Producing a build after a specific time interval or number of check-ins (whichever occurs first) results in the most consistency in your rolling builds while still reducing build server load. Use a rolling build if your continuous integration build creates a very long build queue and results in builds that occur a significant time after the check-in. Use a check-in interval to specify the number of check-ins between each build. Use the time-out period to ensure a build occurs even if there is no additional check-ins.

Determining Your Rolling Build Interval

To determine the ideal rolling build interval, divide the average frequency of check-ins by the length of your build. For example, if you have a build that takes 10 minutes and you average a check-in every 5 minutes you could set a check-in interval of two check-ins and a time-out period of 10 minutes. This helps ensure that the build is complete before the next build is initiated. If you notice excessive load on your build server, you can increase these values.

Continuous Integration Build in Team Foundation Server

Team Foundation Server 2005 does not provide a continuous integration solution out of box, but it does provide the framework for you to implement your own continuous integration build solution.

For more information about setting up a continuous integration build with TFS, see "How To: Setup a Continuous Integration Build in Visual Studio Team Foundation Server." This How To article uses the solution provided by the Visual Studio Team System development team. The solution installs a Web service that runs under an account which has access to the TFS server. Team Foundation Server is able to send an e-mail message or call a Web service when specific events occur. This event mechanism is used by the continuous integration solution to register a Web service with the **CheckinEvent,** so that whenever a check in occurs, the Web service initiates a Team Build.

Summary

Use continuous integration builds to kick off a build whenever a developer checks code into source control. Although Team Build does not provide a continuous integration solution out of the box, you can customize the build and implement your own continuous integration build solution.

Depending on your specific project requirements, you can set continuous integration builds as follows:

- Continuous Integration build on each check-in
- Rolling build after a specific number of check-ins or specific time interval (whichever occurs earlier) in order to reduce build server load

Additional Resources

- For more information about how to use the Visual Studio Team System continuous integration solution, see "Continuous Integration Using Team Foundation Build" at *http://msdn2.microsoft.com/en-us/library/ms364045(VS.80).aspx*
- To download the Visual Studio Team System continuous integration solution MSI, go to *http://download.microsoft.com/download/6/5/e/65e300ce-22fc-4988-97de-0e81d3de2482/ci.msi*
- For more information about agile development and continuous integration in Team Foundation Server, see "Extend Team Foundation Server To Enable Continuous Integration" at *http://msdn.microsoft.com/msdnmag/issues/06/03/TeamSystem/default.aspx*

9

Setting Up Scheduled Builds with Team Build

Objectives

- Understand the purpose of a scheduled build.
- Setup a scheduled build with Microsoft® Visual Studio® Team System Team Build.

Overview

This chapter explains how you can set up scheduled builds by using Team Build and Microsoft Visual Studio Team Foundation Server (TFS). The purpose of a scheduled build is to automate the process of creating a reliable build on a consistent schedule. This is the type of build most often used by test teams, internal adopters, and external beta users.

Scheduled builds are the simplest form of build automation. You can configure scheduled builds to run hourly, daily, weekly, or at any time interval that works best for your team.

How to Use This Chapter

Use this chapter to learn strategies for scheduled builds and to learn how to set up and configure scheduled builds by using Team Build. For a step-by-step walkthrough to help you set up a scheduled build see, "How To: Set Up a Scheduled Build."

If you are new to TFS and Team Build, or if you want to learn more about the options available for automating and scheduling builds, read Chapter 7, "Team Build Explained" before reading this chapter.

If you are concerned about build instability caused by the quality of the code that your development team checks in, you should consider using continuous integration builds. For more information about continuous integration, see Chapter 8, "Setting Up Continuous Integration with Team Build."

Strategy for Scheduled Build Frequency

The frequency of your builds is one of the most important decisions to make, when creating a scheduled build. You can choose to schedule your builds at an hourly, nightly, or weekly basis.

Hourly Builds

If you are working on a project that has enough check-ins to cause significant changes within an hour, and you do not employ continuous integration builds you can choose an hourly build frequency. Hourly builds to provide rapid feedback to developers and can also be made available to testers and other team members to solicit their feedback.

Nightly Builds

This is the most common scheduled build frequency because it gives your test and development team a new build every morning incorporating the changes from the previous day, ready to be tested.

Weekly Builds

If you are working on a large, complex project, where the build time can last for days, you should opt for weekly builds. This ensures that your test team has a build at the start of each week incorporating the changes from the previous week, ready to be tested.

Scheduled Build in Team Foundation Server

The Team Build feature in TFS does not support scheduled builds from the user interface. Instead, you can use the Microsoft Windows® Task Scheduler to run the TFSBuild command utility to start builds at predetermined time.

Use the following steps to create a scheduled build:

1. Create a TFSBuild command line.

   ```
   TfsBuild start <<TeamFoundationServer>> <<TeamProject>> <<BuildTypeName>>
   ```

2. Place the command line in a batch file. Note that you must specify the full path to the TFSBuild.exe file so that it can run from windows command prompt. An example of the command used in the batch file is shown here:

   ```
   "C:\Program Files\Microsoft Visual Studio 8\Common7\IDE\TFSBuild" start
   <<TeamFoundationServer>> <<TeamProject>> <<BuildTypeName>>
   ```

3. Create a Windows Scheduled Task that runs the batch file at your desired interval.

For more information see "How To: Set Up a Scheduled Build in Visual Studio Team Foundation Server."

Summary

Use a scheduled build to produce consistent builds that you can give to your test team or other build consumers who can provide feedback on the quality of the build. Team Foundation Server does not support scheduled builds from its user interface. Instead you can use the Windows Task Scheduler to run the TFSBuild command utility to start your builds at a predetermined time.

You can configure scheduled builds to run hourly, daily, weekly, or at any time interval that suits the requirements of your project.

Additional Resources

- For more information about setting up a scheduled build see, "How To – Configure a Scheduled Build (Command Line)" at *http://msdn2.microsoft.com/en-us/library/ms181727(VS.80).aspx*

Part IV
Large Project Considerations

In this part:

10

Large Project Considerations

Objectives

- Understand large project workflow in Microsoft® Visual Studio® Team System Team Foundation Server (TFS).
- Learn how to optimize source control and builds for large teams.
- Learn how source control is impacted by large projects.
- Learn how your branching and merging strategy may need to change if you are involved in a large project.
- Learn how build strategy is influenced by large projects.

Overview

This chapter describes additional considerations for large-scale development efforts with TFS. A large project typically differs from a smaller project in the following ways:

- They require a more complex branching and merging structure.
- They must deal with a greater number of dependencies across solutions and team projects.
- They are more likely to maintain multiple builds for components and teams.

For example, in a large project you might need to support multiple branches in order to support the parallel development efforts of multiple feature teams. In this scenario, you are likely to need to manage dependencies across solutions and team projects and to share common Web services and databases. Each sub-team may need to maintain its own build server and output builds to a specific drop point.

How to Use This Chapter

Use this chapter if you need to manage, support or participate in large-scale development project. Chapters 3, 5, and 7 also provide specific "Large Project Considerations" sections. Use this chapter to review all of the large project considerations in a single place.

Logical Workflow for Large Projects

Figure 10.1 outlines a common scenario of multiple sub-teams working together to produce a complex application.

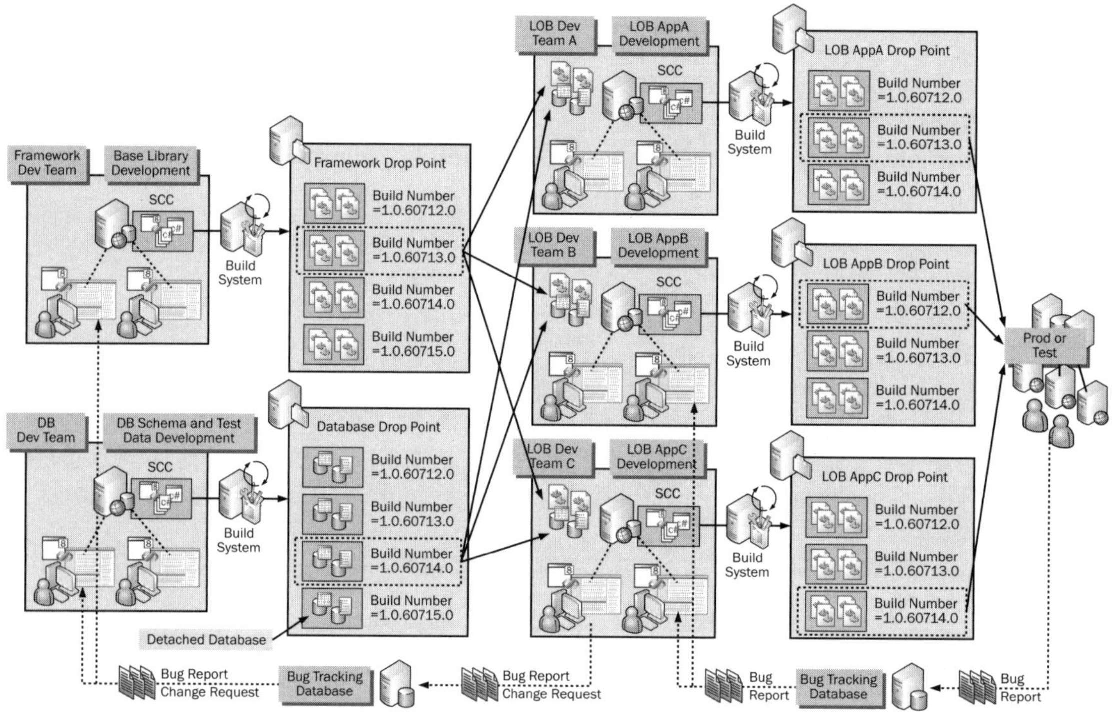

Figure 10.1 *Large Project Scenario*

Figure 10.1 highlights a number of key points about the way in which a large team project operates:

- Each sub-team maintains its own build server and output builds to a drop point.
- Application teams pick up builds from the component teams, reuse them as part of their solutions, and include them in their builds.
- Component and integration testing occurs on each build. Bugs are filed in the appropriate bug database.

Source Control Considerations

If you work on a very large solution requiring many dozens of projects, you may encounter Visual Studio solution (.sln) scalability limits. For this reason, you should organize your source control structure by sub-systems or sub-applications and use multiple solution files. Divide your application into multiple solutions, but do not create a master solution for the entire application. Figure 10.2 on the next page shows the multiple solutions approach commonly used by large teams.

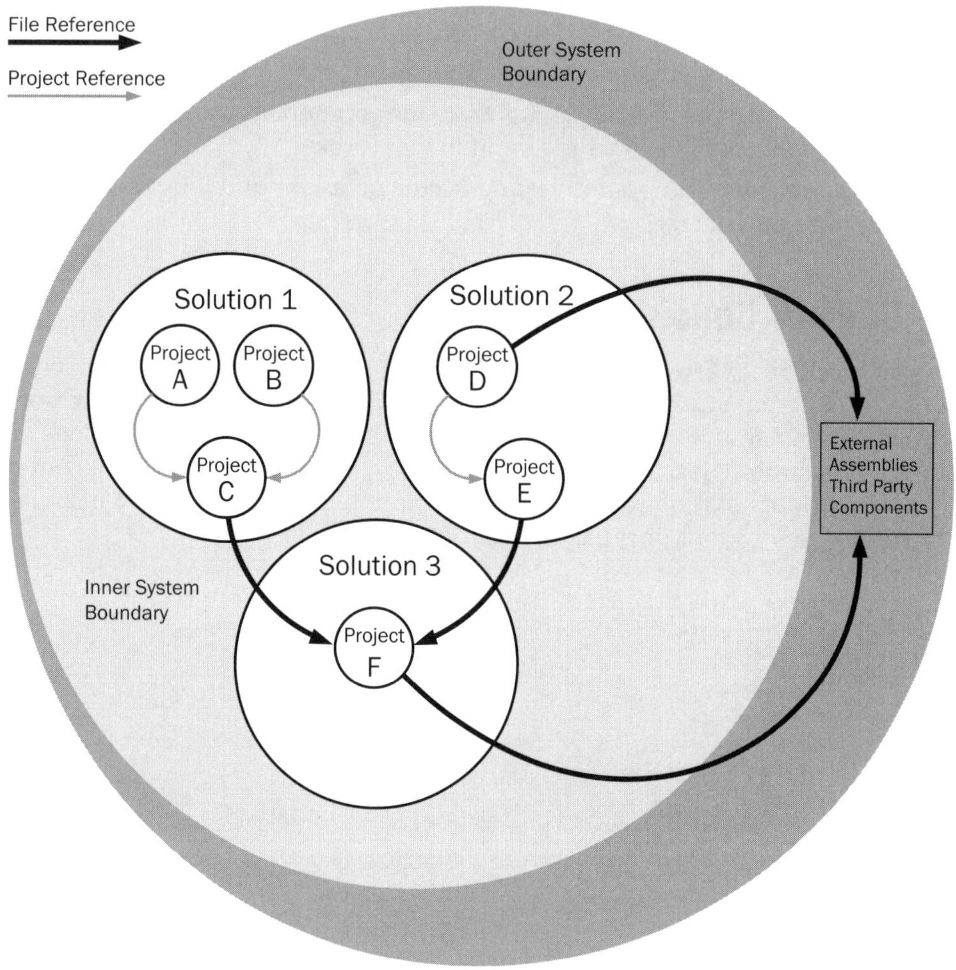

Figure 10.2 *Multiple Solution Approach*

In this scenario, all references inside each solution are project references. References to projects outside of each solution (for example to third-party libraries or projects in another sub-solution) are file references. This means that there can be no "master" solution. Instead, you must use a script that understands the order in which the solutions must be built.

One of the maintenance tasks associated with a multiple-solution structure is ensuring that developers do not inadvertently create circular references between solutions. This structure requires complex build scripts and explicit mapping of dependency relationships. In this structure it is not possible to build the application in its entirety within Visual Studio. Instead, you use TFS Team Build.

For more information about this multiple solution approach, see Chapter 3, "Structuring Projects and Solutions in Source Control."

Branching and Merging Considerations

Large teams are likely to branch both by team and by feature and are also more likely to have one or more branches designed to integrate external dependencies. Since the branching structure is deeper, there is more lag between a change in a development branch and getting that change into the main integration branch. For this reason it pays to careful consider your merging strategy when creating branches.

For example, consider the following when deciding whether your merges will be scheduled or event-driven:

- Reverse integration, such as merging from the development branch to the main branch, may be based on an event, such as a feature milestone being completed, or scheduled in order to integrate code from multiple branches at particular points in time. Use care when promoting code from a child branch to a parent branch through a reverse integration since any resulting destabilization will impact a larger portion of the development team.
- Forward integration, such as merging from the main branch to a development branch, occurs when a child branch is ready to accept the latest code that has been integrated into a parent branch. Frequent forward integrations into development branches are a best practice. Keeping the code base more closely synchronized across branches will help you discover bugs that occur when components are integrated together.

Rationalize your branching / merging strategy according to the frequency with which you want to produce builds. A deeper branching structure results in more time to merge from child branches to the main integration branch. Symptoms of this causing a problem for your development team include:

- Broken builds where the fix takes too long to propagate up to the main integration branch.
- Missed milestones because features take too long to propagate up to the main branch.
- Large amounts of time spent merging changes between various branches.

If this becomes a problem for your team, consider reducing the depth of your branching structure.

The following is an example of a branching structure for a large team:

My Project
- **Development**—Container to isolate active development branches
  - **Team 1**
    - **Feature A**—Isolated branch for development
      - **Source**
    - **Feature B**—Isolated branch for development
      - **Source**
  - **Team 2**
    - **Feature A**—Isolated branch for development
      - **Source**
    - **Feature B**—Isolated branch for development
      - **Source**
- **Main**—Main integration and build branch. All changes come together here.
  - **Source**
  - **Other Asset Folders**
- **Releases**—Container for release branches
  - **Release 4**—Branch containing the code currently being locked down to release
    - **Source**
  - **Release 2**—Active maintenance branch
    - **Source**
  - **Release 3**—Active maintenance branch
    - **Source**
- **Safe Keeping**
  - **Release 1**—Old release in safe keeping
    - **Source**

This structure includes:

- Feature branches for multiple teams to work in isolation from each other.
- A main branch to gather changes by all teams, as well as bug fixes from the release branches.
- A release branch used to lock down the current release.
- A maintenance branch for an old release that is being actively maintained and supported.
- Safekeeping branches for older releases that are no longer being maintained.

Build Considerations

Larger teams are likely to have longer build times. The frequency of continuous integration builds should be less than the build time to avoid excessive queuing and loading of the build server. A build system for a large team is typically organized as follows:

- If the team uses multiple team or feature branches, a build server is dedicated to each branch. This enables the team to focus each build on the purpose of the branch, for example integration or development.
- Build frequency is determined based on team's needs. The build infrastructure is designed and built to support these needs.
- Build frequency is chosen first, and based on that goal, the merge frequency is determined.
- Scheduled builds are generally used for integration branches.
- A combination of continuous integration and scheduled builds is used for development branches. Integration builds are distributed to the integration test team. The output from the development branch scheduled build goes to the associated test team and the development branch continuous integration build provides feedback specific to the particular development team.

Another key question is whether you should have build, testing, and quality gates at each integration point. Alternatively, you could save that for your main integration branch. Ideally, you would have a build server for each branch, and quality gates along with a supporting development and test team. You should be pragmatic though, and if that option does not exist, you might want to remove quality gates or remove branches to simplify your structure.

Summary

When working on very large solutions requiring many dozens of projects, you may encounter Visual Studio solution (.sln) scalability limits. If you do, organize your source control structure by subsystems or sub-applications and use multiple solution files.

For large teams, the branching structure is deeper, so you should expect a greater time lag between a change in a development branch and the merging of that change into the main integration branch.

Large teams are likely to have longer build times. The frequency of continuous integration builds should be less than the build time to avoid too much queuing and loading of the build server. If you are still having problems with build server performance, consider using a build server for each branch in your source control structure.

Additional Resources

- For more information about Team Foundation Source Control, see "Using Source Code Control in Team Foundation" at *http://msdn2.microsoft.com/en-us/library/ms364074(VS.80).aspx*
- For more information about creating a workspace, see "How To - Create a Workspace" at *http://msdn2.microsoft.com/en-us/library/ms181384(VS.80).aspx*
- For an introduction to branching and merging, see "Branching and Merging Primer" at *http://msdn2.microsoft.com/en-us/library/aa730834(VS.80).aspx*
- For more information about branching, see "How To - Branch Files and Folders" at *http://msdn2.microsoft.com/en-us/library/ms181425(VS.80).aspx*
- For more information about merging, see "How To - Merge Files and Folders" at *http://msdn2.microsoft.com/en-us/library/ms181428(VS.80).aspx*
- For additional descriptions of how to branch and merge in Visual Studio 2005, see "Branching and Merging Team Foundation Source Control" at *http://msdn2.microsoft.com/en-us/library/ms181423(VS.80).aspx*
- For more information about Team Build, see "Overview of Team Foundation Build" at *http://msdn2.microsoft.com/en-us/library/ms181710(vs.80).aspx*

Part V
Project Management

In this part:

- Project Management Explained
- Work Items Explained

11

Project Management Explained

Objectives

- Learn what functionality Microsoft® Visual Studio® Team System (VSTS) provides for project managers.
- Choose a strategy for team project creation.
- Create and manage projects with Visual Studio Team System

Overview

This chapter introduces you to the project management features provided by Visual Studio Team System and how they help you to overcome many of the common problems and challenges associated with managing software development projects.

Visual Studio Team System and Team Foundation Server (TFS) provide tools, templates and reports to help you monitor and support your software development processes. As a result team communication is made easier, handoffs required between team members are automated, work items such as tasks are more easily assigned and tracked, and metrics that indicate project health and progress are more easily monitored.

How to Use This Chapter

Use this chapter to learn about the specific features of TFS and VSTS that are specifically relevant to project managers.

- Read the "Project Management Summary" and "Traditional Project Management Issues" sections to understand the problems that TFS project management is attempting to solve.
- Read the "Strategies for Team Projects" section to identify your strategy for team project creation and organization.
- Use the remaining sections to better understand process templates, work items, and other project management features.

Project Management Summary

Planning a project generally consists of some variation of the following steps:

1. **Generating a vision statement.** This step involves creating view of the desired end result of your project, shared by all project stakeholders.
2. **Generating scenarios.** This step includes determining the initial set of usage scenarios for the software. This involves using customer inputs. It also involves validating the scenarios to make sure that they are of value to your customer.
3. **Generating set of features to support those scenarios.** This step includes breaking the scenarios down into specific items of value to your customers, so that you can talk to the customers about their expectations regarding these items.
4. **Generating a set of work items.** This step involves breaking the scenarios and features down into specific tasks. Put another way, when the work items are completed, the relevant feature or scenario is implemented.
5. **Breaking tasks into areas.** This step involves breaking tasks down into areas. These areas could either be functional or based on how specific team is organized.
6. **Scheduling the work.** This step could involve scheduling all the work up front, or breaking the work into iterations.

Traditional Project Management Issues

Most project managers today use a variety of different tools to manage the software development process and these tools usually have little if any integration with the tools used by software developers to do their job. This lack of integration and cohesion across tools and teams leads to significant challenges for the project manager. Typical issues include:

- **Dealing with disparate information sources.** Project management tools are usually used in isolation, leading to separate sources of information that are not easily integrated. Also, it is usually difficult to integrate the data maintained by project management tools with the data maintained by other team members such as bugs tracked within a separate bug tracking system, in order to generate meaningful metrics.
- **Difficultly capturing project-related metrics.** Obtaining project related metrics is critical to tracking status, making well-informed decisions and answering fundamental questions such as "Will the project be delivered on time and to budget?" To answer these key questions, project managers typically rely on data obtained from Microsoft Office Project or the bug-tracking system used by the development and test teams. Consolidating data from these disparate systems is difficult, time-consuming and error-prone. Most of the metrics generated by tools are not stored or accessed in a uniform manner. Creating reports is usually an intensive manual effort that requires much copying and pasting of information between different tools.

- **Difficultly ensuring that requirements are met.** There is often a gap between the work planed for the development team and customer requirements and key non-functional requirements identified for your system. There is another gap between scheduled work and actual work. Vital information gets lost in these gaps which results in requirements not being met.
- **Managing processes and process changes.** Communicating the processes that your team should follow can be a challenging task. Implementing changes to address systematic problems without impacting team productivity can be even more difficult.
- **Lack of auditable communication and task tracking.** Collaboration and team cohesion are normally addressed by holding team meetings and by allocating task lists to developers to help them focus on the right priorities. Tracking the progress of individual tasks can be challenging. Also, project managers often spend a lot of valuable time gathering status information from different plans and lists. Team members also spend time completing status reports and updating a variety of different documents and forms.
- **Quality assurance.** Predicting the number and severity of bugs in the software you are producing is difficult and as a result schedule estimates and costs are usually "best guesses". These estimates traditionally take into account contingency measures, the amount of which usually depends on how confident the project manager is about the current health of the project.

VSTS is designed to help address many of these traditional problems faced by project managers. It does so by providing a set of integrated tools to help teams improve their software development activities and to help project managers better support the software development processes.

Project Management Features in Team Foundation Server

The key project management features provided by Visual Studio Team System include:

- **Process management.** Team Foundation Server process management includes Microsoft Solution Framework (MSF) process guidance as well as process templates that set up new team projects with work item types, reports, a project SharePoint portal, and source control settings.
- **Security and permissions.** New projects contain default groups and permissions that map to common development team roles.
- **Centralized work item management.** Work items including bugs, risks, tasks, scenarios and quality of service (QoS) requirements are centrally recorded, managed, and maintained in the TFS work item database. Centralizing their storage makes it easy for all team members to view and access them.

- **Microsoft Office Excel® and Microsoft Office Project integration.** By using the Office Excel and Office Project integration features, project managers can continue to access the work item repository and schedule information by using tools they already know.
- **Metrics and reporting.** TFS provides a reporting service which transforms operational data such as work items, build results, and test results into metrics stored within TFS data warehouse. Predefined reports allow you to query a variety of project health and quality metrics.
- **Project portals.** For every team project, TFS creates an associated project portal that uses Microsoft Windows SharePoint® Services. You use the portal to manage project-related documentation, and to quickly view key reports and assess project's current status.

Benefits

The project management features of TFS provide the following benefits:

- Centralized management
- High traceability
- Integrated project planning and scheduling
- Improved process control
- Improved team communication and cohesiveness
- Accurate progress reporting

Creating and Managing Projects with Team Foundation Server

The following steps summarize the general approach for creating team projects in Team Foundation Server:

1. **Choose a process template.** You can either use a default template out of the box or you can customize your own.
2. **Create a team project.** Your team project will be based on your process template.
3. **Add appropriate groups and members to your team project.**
4. **Decide on your iteration cycle duration for the project.** This includes creating iterations in your team project.
5. **Capture your scenarios as work items in TFS.**
6. **Determine which scenarios need to be completed for each iteration.**
7. **Define the quality of service (QoS) requirements.** Link the quality of service requirements to your scenarios.
8. **Break your scenarios down into stories to provide manageable work items for developers.** Obtain estimates from the developers for each work item.

9. **Create a project schedule.** Create a project schedule (by using Microsoft Project) and adds it to the Team Project.
10. **Define acceptance criteria.** Define acceptance criteria for the work items (correlated to the QoS requirements).
11. **Define reporting requirements.** Define your project's key performance indicators and identify reporting requirements.

For more information on creating and managing a team project see, "How To: Manage Projects in Visual Studio Team Foundation Server."

Strategies for Team Projects

You need at least one team project to start working with TFS. When a project manager creates a new team project, an associated team project Web site is created containing document libraries with document templates and stock reports. A work item database is created for tracking all effort on the project, and a methodology template is installed that determines rules, policies, security groups, and queries for all work efforts. Additionally, a source code branch is created for source control.

The structure you choose for your team project should be guided by your requirements and might change as your software development process evolves. There are three common strategies for creating new team projects. You might use one of these strategies or a combination of several. The three common strategies are:

- Team Project per application
- Team Project per release
- Team Project per team

Team Project per Application

This is the most common strategy for creating team projects. This approach is useful for both large and small applications, as well as multiple releases of applications being developed in parallel. With this approach, you create one project for each application under development.

Team Project per Release

This approach is useful for large teams who are working on long-running projects. After every major release, you create a new project and have a clean start. With this approach you don't have to worry about carrying the previous release's baggage forward, including work items. Also, this approach provides you with the opportunity either to improve the process templates or use new ones based on your newly acquired experience and learning.

Team Project per Team

This approach is useful for large projects that span multiple teams, where central control and activity monitoring is important. With this approach, you create a project for each team. This approach closely aligns a team with the workflows defined in TFS work item types and provides a unit of reporting that spans the entire team.

Process Management

With VSTS, the software development lifecycle has been made an integral part of the tooling to support software project development efforts. By integrating the lifecycle processes into VSTS, the process and handoffs for development team interaction are fully supported by the tooling and can be automated in many areas.

Process Templates

VSTS uses process templates to define the set of instructions and artifacts like process guidance documents, document templates, default work items etc, for setting up a new project. A process template is a self-contained set of instructions that provide development teams with the methodology for a software development initiative. A process template contains the following elements:

- **Process guidance.** This is supplied for each template and provides contextual information, help, and direction for team members who need assistance following or understanding a particular activity. Process guidance is integrated into the Visual Studio Help System.
- **Document templates.** These templates enable team members to create new documents such as specifications, risks assessment and project plans in a consistent manner.
- **Work items and workflow.** Work items have their own set of fields and rules that determine the workflow of the work item and how team members can assign and perform work.
- **Security groups.** These groups are used to define who can control and manipulate reports, work products such as source code and documentation, and work items. Project managers can administer security groups without needing to be Windows administrators.
- **Check-in policies.** These policies can be used to enforce rules and quality gates for all code checked into source control. For example, you can enforce that checked-in code meets specific criteria, such as conforming to your corporate coding standards, or passing unit tests. For more information about how to create and configure custom check-in policies, see "How To: Create Custom Check-in Policies in Visual Studio Team Foundation Server."

- **Reports.** These are used to monitor the ongoing performance and status of the project. VSTS ships with many predefined reports including code quality reports, schedule progress reports, test effectiveness reports and many others. You can create your own report and customize existing reports.

MSF for Agile Software Development and MSF for CMMI Process Improvement Process Templates

The following two process templates are available out-of-the box.

- **MSF for Agile Software Development.** This lightweight process template for small, agile, or informal software projects is based on scenarios and context driven actions and is project and people centric.
- **MSF for CMMI® Process Improvement.** This process template is designed for more mature software projects. It extends MSF for Agile Software Development process template by providing support for auditing, verification, and formal processes. It relies on process and conformance to process and is organization centric.

If the provided templates do not match your specific process requirements and methodology closely enough, you can add new process templates to the system, and you can customize the supplied templates to fit the needs of your organization. For more information about customizing existing templates, see "How To: Customize a Process Template in Visual Studio Team Foundation Server."

Security and Permissions

When you create a project in TFS, four default groups are created for that project regardless of your choice of process template. By default, each of these groups has a set of permissions defined for it that govern what members of those groups are authorized to do.

- Project Administrator
- Contributor
- Reader
- Build Services

You can create security groups for your team project to better meet the security requirements of your organization. Creating a security group is an efficient way to grant a specific set of permissions to a group of users on your team project. Make sure that you allow only the minimum permissions necessary for the group, and add only those users or groups who must belong to this new team project group

After you have created a team project group, you must add the new group, give the group the appropriate permissions, and add members to the group. By default, a team project group is created without any permission granted.

Work Item Management

Work items are used as units of work for communication and collaboration between the team. Your selected process template provides an initial set of work item types and project managers then create and manage additional work items that need to be completed on a development project. A work item might define a task, risk, scenario, bug, or quality of service (QoS) requirement. You can link work items together to provide better traceability. For example, you could associate a specific work item task with the related scenario or QoS requirement to which that work item relates.

The process template provides the definitions for the work item types, including the set of fields defined for each work item type. Therefore selection of the process template is important, because it can't be modified during the project. If required, you should customize the process template to include any additional work item types other than those provided by the base templates.

A number of pre-defined work-items are generated in both the MSF for Agile Software Development and MSF for CMMI Process Improvement process templates when you create a new team project. These work items can be used to jumpstart your use of the process, as they contain tasks that are necessary to complete in order to begin the software development process.

MSF for Agile Software Development Process Template

The work item types provided by this process template include:

- **Scenario**—Used to represent a user interaction with the application system. It records the specific steps necessary to reach a goal. When writing scenarios, be sure to be specific as there may be many possible paths.
- **Task**—Used to represent a unit of work that needs to be performed. Each role has its own requirements for a task. For example, a developer uses development tasks to assign work.
- **Quality of Service Requirement**—Used to document the system characteristics such as performance, load, availability, stress, accessibility, and serviceability
- **Bug**—Used to communicate a potential problem in the system.
- **Risk**—Used to identify and manage the inherent risks of a project.

MSF for CMMI® Process Improvement Process Template

The work item types provided by this process template include:

- **Requirement**—Used to capture the requirements defined during the requirements gathering phase.
- **Change Request**—Used to capture any change requests subsequent to the gathering of requirements.
- **Issue**—Used to capture issues to be tracked in the projects.

- **Task**—Used to represent a unit of work that needs to be performed. Each role has its own requirements for a task. For example, a developer uses development tasks to assign work.
- **Review**—Used to represent the review work units with in the projects, like code review, design review etc.
- **Bug**—Used to communicate a potential problem in the system.
- **Risk**—Used to identify and manage the inherent risks of a project.

Microsoft Project Integration

Installing VSTS or the Team Explorer application provides extensions for Microsoft Project. For large projects that involve a large number of resources, you can use Microsoft Office Project, to manipulate schedule data within TFS.

For example, you can use Microsoft Project to manage and plan, assign, balance and track work, and then publish the updates back to the work item database when they are ready to be used by other team members.

For more information, see "Working with Work Items in Microsoft Project" at *http://msdn2.microsoft.com/en-us/library/ms244368(VS.80).aspx*

Microsoft Excel Integration

Installing VSTS or the Team Explorer application provides extensions for Microsoft Excel. For projects that involve a very large number of work items, you can use the Excel integration feature to create work items in an Excel spreadsheet and upload it to the work item database for use by other team members.

For more information, see "Working with Work Item Lists in Microsoft Excel" at *http://msdn2.microsoft.com/en-us/library/ms181694(VS.80).aspx*

Progress and Reporting

The reports provided with TFS help you quickly assess the status of your team project, the quality of the software under development, and the progress made toward project completion. These reports are generated from data maintained within the TFS data warehouse, and they summarize metrics derived from work items, source control, test results, and builds.

For example, you can use reports to find out how fast your team is working from week-to-week, based on a team's actual activities. The goal of the TFS reporting system is to provide integrated data from across VSTS components, to enable project managers and team members to understand the state of the software development project, and take appropriate action to ensure its success.

The process template you use to create your team project determines which reports are available by default, but you can also add your own custom reports. The content and use of each report created by the process template is explained in the process guidance for that template. Team Foundation Server is built on Microsoft SQL Server™ 2005 and uses SQL Server to store all data related to work items, quality attributes, testing, test results, and build results. TFS then uses SQL Server Analysis Services to aggregate and analyze the data and drive the reports. The reports that are created by the process template, or by individual team members by using Microsoft Office Excel or Visual Studio 2005 Report Designer, are made available through SQL Server 2005 Reporting Services and the team SharePoint portal site.

For more information about customizing reports, see "How To: Create a Custom Report for Visual Studio Team Foundation Server."

Summary

Team Foundation Server provides project management features such as centralized work item management, process management, security and permissions management, project metrics, and reporting to improve your ability to manage development projects in Visual Studio.

The software-development lifecycle has been made an integral part of the tooling to support software project development efforts. TFS provides the MSF Agile and MSF CMMI process templates, which support two very different development methodologies. You can modify the supplied process templates or create one from scratch in order to meet your team's development process needs.

Additional Resources

- For more information on software project management using VSTS, see "Visual Studio 2005 Team System: Software Project Management" at *http://msdn2.microsoft.com/en-us/library/aa302181.aspx*
- For more information on using Microsoft Office Excel for project-management tasks, see "Working with Work Item Lists in Microsoft Excel" at *http://msdn2.microsoft.com/en-us/library/ms181694(VS.80).aspx*
- For more information on using Microsoft Office Project for project-management tasks, see "Working with Work Items in Microsoft Project" at *http://msdn2.microsoft.com/en-us/library/ms244368(VS.80).aspx*

12

Work Items Explained

Objectives

- Learn about the purpose and structure of work items.
- Describe work item workflow.
- Customize work items to meet your team's specific needs.

Overview

This chapter introduces you to work items and explains how you can use them to help manage your software development projects. Each work item represents a unit of work to be carried out by your development team. A set of work item types is defined in the process template you choose when creating a new team project.

After your project has started, you can create any of the available work item types to track work efforts. While default work item types and behaviour are defined in the process templates, any aspect of a work item type can be modified to better fit the way your team works.

How to Use This Chapter

To gain the greatest benefits from this chapter, you should:

- Read the "Work Item Structure" section to learn about predefined work item types and how work item workflow is defined.
- Read the "Customizing Work Items" section to learn how and why you would customize a work item type.

Scenarios and Solutions

Work items are the primary way that project managers and team leaders track the work that remains to be done on a project, as well as the work that has been already been completed. Team members use work items to track their personal work queue and assign work to each other for example, in the form of bugs or tasks.

The following are common uses of work items in team projects:

- Create user requirements or Quality of Service (QoS) requirements for an application.
- Track development and testing against requirements.
- Create development tasks to represent the work that must be completed in order to implement application components and features.
- Create bugs to represent defects in the implementation of application components and features.
- Triage bugs and tasks so that they are appropriately prioritized and balanced across the team.
- Track development tasks to determine progress toward code complete status.
- Track bugs, along with other quality metrics, to determine the quality of the application and its readiness to be shipped.

How you use work items depends on the work item types that are defined for your project. The work item definitions are stored in the process template you choose when the team project is first created. You can choose one of the two default templates - Microsoft® Solution Framework (MSF) for Agile Software Development (MSF Agile) or MSF for CMMI® Process Improvement (MSF CMMI) or you can customize work items to meet your team's specific needs and process.

Work Item Structure

Each work item type can be defined as follows:

- It has a purpose and intended use. For instance, bugs are used to track quality defects, tasks are used to track scheduled work, QoS requirements are used to capture critical non-functional aspects such as security and performance requirements, and so on
- It has a workflow defined by states and transitions. For example, the steps from "Opened" to "Resolved" to "Closed" status.
- It has a set of fields that can be set, queried, and reported on. For example, Priority, Status and, Iteration.

Work Item Types

The MSF Agile and MSF CMMI process templates each define a set of work items that map to the roles and activities defined in the process guidance.

MSF Agile Work Item Types

MSF Agile contains the following work item types:

- **Bug.** Represents a problem or potential problem in your application.
- **Risk.** Represents a possible event or condition that would have a negative impact on your project.
- **Scenario.** Represents a single path of user interaction through the system.
- **Task.** Represents the need for a member of the team to do some work.
- **Quality of Service Requirement.** Represents a requirement constraining how the system should work.

MSF CMMI Work Item Types

MSF CMMI contains the following work item types:

- **Bug.** Represents a problem or potential problem in your application.
- **Change Request.** Represents a proposed change to your application.
- **Issue.** Represents a situation that may block work or is currently blocking work.
- **Requirement.** Represents a description of what your application should do to solve a customer problem.
- **Review.** Represents the results of a code, design, or deployment review.
- **Risk.** Represents a possible event or condition that would have a negative impact on the project.
- **Task.** Represents the need for a member of the team to do some work.

Work Item Workflow

Each work item has a pre-defined workflow representing each state the work item can be in as well as transitions between states. Each state is naturally associated with a role in TFS. For example when a tester opens a new bug in MSF Agile the state is **Active**. When a developer fixes the bug the state is changed to **Resolved**. When the tester verifies the fix the bug state is changed to **Closed**.

Workflow Examples

The following examples show workflow for two common work item types.

MSF CMMI Task

An MSF CMMI task has the following possible states:

- **Proposed.** For example, proposed by a developer, tester, or architect.
- **Active.** For example, accepted by a lead or manager.
- **Resolved.** For example, resolved by a developer.
- **Closed.** For example, tested and closed by a tester.

Figure 12.1 shows each state along with the possible transitions between the states.

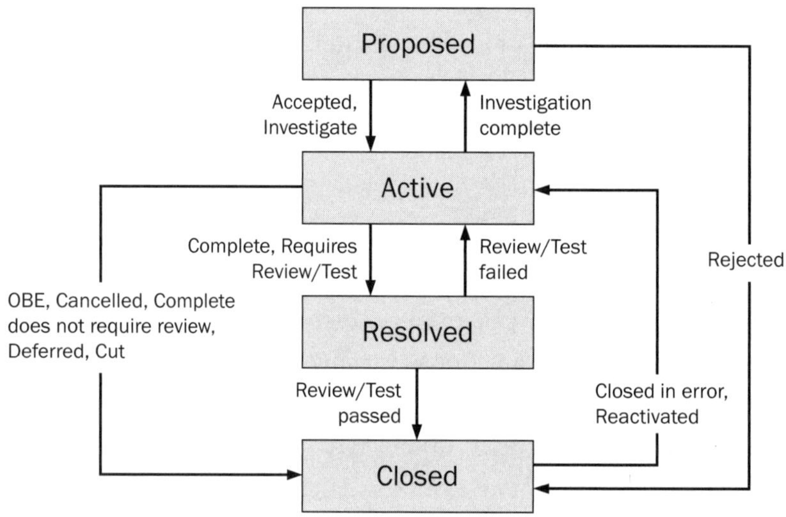

Figure 12.1 *Transition States for MSF CMMI*

MSF Agile Bug

An MSF Agile Bug has the following possible states:

- **Active.** For example, opened by a tester.
- **Resolved.** For example, resolved by a developer.
- **Closed.** For example, tested and closed by a tester.

Figure 12.2 shows each state along with the possible transitions between the states.

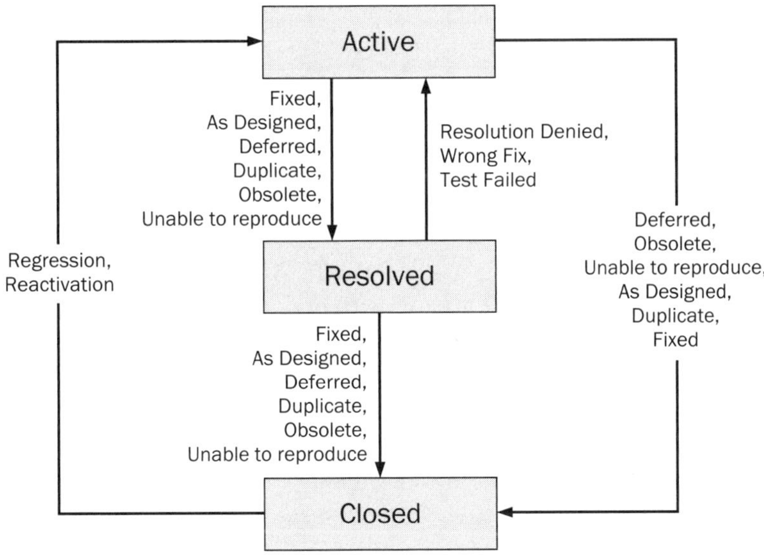

Figure 12.2 *Transition States for MSF Agile*

Customizing Work Items

There are a few scenarios in which you may want to modify the work item types defined in MSF Agile or MSF CMMI:

- A work item is missing a field that is important for your development process.
- A work item workflow does not match how your team works.
- You need a new work item type.

To support these scenarios, you can do the following in TFS:

- Add/remove work item types.
- Modify fields in existing work items.
- Modify states and transitions in existing work items.

For more information about customizing work items, see "How To: Customize a Process Template in Visual Studio Team Foundation Server."

Summary

Work items are used by project managers and team leaders to track the work to be done on a project. They are used to create development tasks to represent the work that must be completed, create bugs to represent defects in the implementation and create user requirements or Quality of Service (QoS) requirements. Additionally they can be used to track development and testing against requirements, and to determine the quality of the application and its readiness to be shipped.

The MSF Agile and MSF CMMI process templates provide a set of default work item types. You can customize these or create new work item types to meet your process requirements.

Additional Resources

- For more information on work items, see "Managing Team Foundation Work Items" at *http://msdn2.microsoft.com/en-us/library/ms181314(VS.80).aspx*
- To download the MSF CMMI process template and review available work item types, go to *http://www.microsoft.com/downloads/details.aspx?FamilyID=12A8D806-BB98-4EB4-BF6B-FB5B266171EB&displaylang=en*
- To download the MSF Agile process template and review available work item types, go to *http://www.microsoft.com/downloads/details.aspx?FamilyID=EA75784E-3A3F-48FB-824E-828BF593C34D&displaylang=en*

Part VI

Process Templates

In this part:

- Process Templates Explained
- MSF for Agile Software Development Projects

13

Process Templates Explained

Objectives

- Understand the purpose, content and structure of process templates.
- Learn the key differences between the Microsoft® Solution Framework (MSF) for Agile Software Development (MSF Agile) and MSF for CMMI® Process Improvements (MSF CMMI) process templates.
- Customize process templates to meet your team's specific needs.

Overview

This chapter explains the role of process templates in Microsoft Visual Studio® 2005 Team Foundation Server (TFS). It identifies the main features and main differences between the two supplied process templates: MSF Agile and MSF CMMI.

Software-development processes are complex, involving many levels of interdependent activities. These processes are generally available to development team in the form of documentation but are usually not enforced by tools. This lack of tool support makes it difficult for development teams to learn and follow the processes consistently. Project managers might use a variety of different tools for project management, requirement management, bug tracking, or review management and they are often not well integrated. This lack of integration makes it more difficult to enforce a consistent methodology across multiple projects and to generate consistent reports to drive common team understanding of project progress and health. This lack of consistency can server to make process analysis unreliable, which makes it more difficult to identify and implement process improvements over time.

Visual Studio Team System (VSTS) and TFS provide an integrated environment that supports most of the process activities involved in a software-development project. TFS implements its life-cycle methodologies through the use of process templates. A process template is a set of Extensible Markup Language (XML) files that provides specifications for processes and artifacts that make up a development methodology. This chapter explains the architecture of a process template and its components to give you a better understanding of how to utilize and customize the supplied process templates.

If existing process templates are not a good match for your team's development process you can create a new process template, modify the existing templates, or choose from process templates offered by Microsoft Partners. To review process templates offered by Microsoft Partners, see:
http://msdn2.microsoft.com/en-us/teamsystem/aa718801

How to Use This Chapter

Use this chapter to understand process template architecture, structure, and customization. To gain the greatest benefits from this chapter, you should:

- **Read the "MSF Agile and MSF CMMI Process Templates" section.** To learn about the default process templates and how to choose the template that best fits your team's needs.
- **Read the "Customizing Process Guidance" section.** To learn how to customize the existing process templates to better suit your team's needs.

MSF Agile and MSF CMMI Process Templates

Team Foundation Server comes with two process templates: MSF Agile and MSF CMMI. These two process templates are aimed at two different styles of software development. You should use MSF Agile if you are employing an agile methodology to build your software. MSF Agile encourages test-driven development and other agile practices. You should use MSF CMMI if you are following the Software Engineering Institute (SEI) Capability Maturity Model® Integration methodology. This is a formal process aimed at improving existing development processes.

The templates differ in what they provide. For example, they create different types of default reports and work item types. These templates can easily be edited to suit your project's needs.

Customizing Process Guidance

The project you are creating may not fit the process templates provided with VSTS. You might need a different work item type or you are using an entirely different process methodology. For example, if you are using SCRUM there is no mention of sprints in the current process template. In this case you need to amend or replace the existing process template to fit the methodology your team uses.

Process Template Architecture

There are three key pieces to the process template architecture:

- Process template plug-ins
- XML process definition files
- New Team Project Wizard

Process Template Plug-ins

Process template plug-ins are components that run when a new team project is created. A plug-in sets up required files and configures data for a specific area of the template. The following plug-ins are available out-of-box with TFS.

- **Classification**—Defines a team project's initial iteration and areas.
- **Groups and Permissions**—Defines a team project's initial security groups and their permissions.
- **Windows SharePoint Services**—Defines the project portal for the team based on a Microsoft Windows SharePoint® site template. It also defines template files and process guidance.
- **Work Item Tracking**—Defines a team project's initial work item types, queries, and work item instances.
- **Reports**—Defines a team project's initial reports and sets up the report site.
- **Version Control**—Defines a team project's initial version control security permissions, and check-in notes.

You can modify each plug-in definition file to customize a process template. Except for the classification plug-in, you can also delete plug-in definition files to customize a process template.

XML Process Definition Files

The *XML process definition* files are a set of XML files that define a set of tasks that must run in order to correctly configure a new team project for the process. When you use the **New Team Project** Wizard to create a team project, it runs the required plug-ins. Each plug-in reads its corresponding XML process definition file to obtain the list of tasks it must run. By using the XML process definition files, you specify what configurations and settings the plug-ins must implement. The following are the details about the XML files:

- **Work Item Tracking XML**—This process definition file is named Workitems.xml and is located in the Work Item Tracking folder in the process template folder hierarchy. There are three key types of tasks to specify: work item types, work item queries, and work item instances.
  - **Work Item Types**—Defines the rules, fields, states, and transitions for an item of work that will be tracked on a team project such as tasks, bugs, and requirements.
  - **Work Item Queries**—Used to find specific groupings of work items, such as tasks or active bugs. Work item queries are specified in work item query (WIQ) files in the Queries folder under the Work Item Tracking folder in the process template folder hierarchy.
  - **Work Item Instances**—The initial set of work item instances that are created by default when you create the team project.
- **Classification XML**—This process definition file is named Classification.xml and is located in the Classification folder in the process template folder hierarchy. It consists of two parts: Iterations and Areas.
  - **Iterations**—Used to define how many times the team will repeat a particular set of major activities (such as plan, develop, test). Iterations affect work item queries and reports because iterations are used to group work items.
  - **Areas**—Used to organize work in the team project. For example, a team could organize the work based on product or feature, such as UI area, Application area, and Database area. Areas are used to group work items for queries and reports.
- **Windows SharePoint Services XML**—This process definition file is named WssTasks.xml and is located in the Windows SharePoint Services folder in the process template folder hierarchy. There are three key tasks to specify: Site Template (which site template to use), Document Libraries (which document libraries to create), and Folders and Files (which folders and files to copy into the document libraries).
  - **Site Template**—You must specify a site template on which the project portal is based on. This site template also must be available on the TFS SharePoint Portal. Site templates are not included in the process template.

- **Document Libraries**—After the project portal is created, you can specify that additional document libraries be created.
- **Folders and Files**—After the project portal is created, you can specify additional folders to create. You can also specify files to copy such as template files.

- **Version Control XML**—This process definition file is named VersionControl.xml and is located in the Version Control folder in the process template folder hierarchy. It defines a team project's initial version control security permissions, check-in notes, and whether exclusive check-out is required.
  - **Check-in Notes**—Specify whether to include check-in notes or not. Check-in notes are provided by the developer when code is checked in to describe how, or if, the code changes are related to team processes. For example, a check-in note can indicate if the change was part of a security review, and can include details about the changes relative to the security review.
  - **Exclusive Check-out**—Used to control whether multiple users can check out a file at the same time.
  - **Permissions**—Defines what actions security groups and individuals can perform on items under version control.
- **Reports XML**—This process definition file is named ReportsTasks.xml and is located in the Reports folder in the process template folder hierarchy. It defines the team project's initial reports.
  - **Reports Site**—The reporting site has a link to it, labeled Reports, on the project portal home page.
  - **Folders**—You can create folders on the reporting site. The folder(s) you create will appear on the project site and under the Reports folder in Team Explorer.
  - **Reports**—Used to add reports by using the .rdl files
- **Groups and Permissions XML**—This process definition file is named GroupsandPermissions.xml and is located in the Groups and Permissions folder in the process template folder hierarchy. It is used to define the team project's initial security groups.
  - **Groups**—Used to specify a new TFS security group.
  - **Permissions**—Used to define permissions for each group you specify.

New Team Project Wizard

You use the **New Team Project** Wizard to create new team projects. The wizard uses the plug-ins and the XML process definition files to create the project.

Customization Approach

To customize a process template, perform the following steps:

1. Review the process templates provided by TFS and choose the one that most closely matches your organizational process.
2. Download the chosen process template.
3. Customize various components of the process template.
4. Upload the customized template to TFS.
5. Verify that the changes suit your process requirements.

This core approach is used as part of the following solutions for customizing the process templates:

- **Manually customize the XML files.** Manual customization is error-prone but nevertheless gives fine grained control over the customization of process templates. For more information, see "Customizing Process Templates" at *http://msdn2.microsoft.com/en-us/library/ms243782(VS.80).aspx*
- **Process Template Editor Tool available with Power tools.** The latest version the Visual Studio 2005 Team Foundation Server Power Tool   a set of enhancements, tools, and command-line utilities that improve the TFS experience   provides a graphical tool for viewing and customizing process templates. When connected to TFS, you can use this tool to customize work item type definitions and global lists on an active project. For more information, see "How To: Customize a Process Template in Visual Studio Team Foundation Server"

Common Customizations

The following are descriptions of the set of the components that you generally will customize to create your own custom process:

- **Groups and Permissions.** The out-of-box process templates have a set of groups with various permissions assigned to them. If the default groups and permissions associated with these templates are not adequate or appropriate for your process requirements, you can update those groups or create new groups. You can also add individual users to a group, remove users from a group, or grant and revoke permissions for a group.
- **Source Control Check-In Notes and Policies.** The out-of-box process templates have a set of Source Control Check-In notes and Policies. If the default check-in notes are not adequate or appropriate for your process requirements, you can add or remove check-in note fields, or make some fields required and others not. If the default check-in policies are not adequate or appropriate, you can add, update, or delete individual check-in policies.

- **Areas and Iterations.** The out-of-box process templates do not provide a classification structure for either areas or iterations. You can customize the areas and iterations according to your specific process requirements. The recommended approach is to carve out the areas based on the component or features of the project. Iterations can be time-based cycles for which you will repeat particular set of major activities (such as plan, develop, and test).
- **Team Portal.** The out-of-box process templates provide a default team portal, which can be the central hub for communication among team members and others in the organization. You can modify the team portal to change its appearance, behavior, and content to suit your process requirements.
- **Process Guidance.** The out-of-box process templates provide relevant process guidance that explains the roles, forms, reports, and workflow used in the team project. When customizing the process template to meet your requirement, you must edit the process guidance to reflect the changes for various components.
- **Reports.** The out-of-box process templates provide a set of default reports. If the default reports are not appropriate or adequate, you can create your own custom reports based on your requirements.
- **Work Item Types and Queries.** The out-of-box process templates have a set of Work item types, default work item instances and queries. If the default Work item types, work item instances and queries are not adequate or appropriate for your process requirements, you can customize work item types to fit your workflow or different types of work items that you want to track. For example, you can:
    - Add new work item types.
    - Remove existing work item types.
    - Add default work item type instances.
    - Remove default work item type instances.
    - Create your own public or private queries.

  You can also modify an existing work item type; for example:
    - Add fields.
    - Rename fields.
    - Restrict the list of allowed values for fields.
    - Change the states and supported state transitions.
    - Make fields required or read-only.
    - Make one field dependent on another.
    - Automatically populate field values.
    - Rearrange the appearance of information on the form.
    - Change the Microsoft Office Project column to which a certain field is mapped.

How Does the Customization Process Work?

Customizing a process template involves the following steps:

1. The user launches the **New Team Project** Wizard.
2. The wizard asks for:
   - The name of the team project.
   - The process template to be used when creating the team project.

   The screens displayed in the wizard are determined by the plug-ins used. For example, if a process template does not include the Windows SharePoint Services plug-in, there is no screen presented to ask information about the project portal.
3. After the user provides the information the wizard requests and clicks **Finish**, the wizard makes calls to the plug-ins to perform the work of creating the team project. The order in which the plug-ins are called is determined by the XML process definition files.
4. The wizard reads the instructions contained in the process template and then creates and configures the specified items.
5. The user does not need to specify any details about the various types of work items to be created because the instructions are already provided by the process template.

Note: If the wizard encounters a problem while creating the new team project, you will see an error message describing the problem and suggesting corrective action.

Summary

Use MSF Agile process template if you are employing an agile methodology to build your software. Use the MSF CMMI if you are following the Software Engineering Institute (SEI) Capability Maturity Model Integration methodology.

The key components of the process template architecture are process template plug-ins, XML process definition files, and the **New Team Project** wizard.

If the default process templates do not satisfy your process requirements, you can customize the template by manually customizing the XML process definition files, or you can use the Process Editor Tool to customize the process templates.

The most common areas of customization are groups and permissions, source control check-in notes and policy, areas and iteration, reports, and work item type definitions.

Additional Resources

- For information about choosing a process template, see "Choosing a Process Template" at *http://msdn2.microsoft.com/en-us/library/ms400752(vs.80).aspx*
- To download the MSF CMMI process template, go to *http://www.microsoft.com/downloads/details.aspx?FamilyID=12A8D806-BB98-4EB4-BF6B-FB5B266171EB&displaylang=en*
- To download the MSF Agile process template, go to *http://www.microsoft.com/downloads/details.aspx?FamilyID=EA75784E-3A3F-48FB-824E-828BF593C34D&displaylang=en*
- For more information about process template customization, see "Process Template Customization Overview" at *http://msdn2.microsoft.com/en-us/library/ms194945(VS.80).aspx*
- To download the Team Foundation Server Power Tools including the Process Template Editor, go to *http://msdn2.microsoft.com/en-us/vstudio/aa718351.aspx*
- To review process templates offered by Microsoft Partners, see *http://msdn2.microsoft.com/en-us/teamsystem/aa718801*

14

MSF for Agile Software Development Projects

Objectives

- Learn when to use the Microsoft® Solution Framework (MSF) for Agile Software Development (MSF Agile) process template.
- Identify how teams typically use the MSF Agile process template.
- Customize the MSF Agile process template to meet your team's specific needs.

Overview

The process defined by the MSF Agile process template incorporates key ideas from the Agile software movement, along with principles and practices from MSF. The process supports an agile software engineering strategy that uses multiple iterations and a scenario based approach for building applications. The template provides the automation and guidance necessary to support your team development, including configuration management, project management, work item tracking, and a project portal for communication.

This chapter explains the workflow of a typical MSF Agile software development project, shows examples of teams using MSF Agile process, and describes the default template settings and what options you have to customize in the supplied template.

How to Use This Chapter

Read this chapter if you want to gain a better understanding of how the MSF Agile process template and process guidance works as well as how it is has been used successfully by various teams. To gain the greatest benefits from this chapter, you should:

- **Read "MSF for Agile Software Development Defaults" section.** To understand the details of the MSF Agile process template including default reports, work items, and permissions.
- **Read through the "Examples of MSF for Agile Software Development in Practice" section.** To see how real teams have successfully used MSF Agile to develop and release applications.
- **Read Chapter 13, "Process Templates Explained."** If you would like to learn more about process templates in general, read Chapter 13, "Process Templates Explained."

Workflow for MSF for Agile Software Development

The MSF Agile process template defines a set of tasks to be performed during iterations by the various roles involved in a software-development lifecycle including business analysts, architects, project managers, developers, and testers. Figure 14.1 shows the key activities associated with each of the defined task.

Task	Key Activities
Create a project backlog	Capture project vision
Create a solution architecture	Create an architectural prototype Determine interfaces Create an infrastructure architecture
Create customer usage scenarios	Break into scenarios Capture scenarios into TFS Prioritize the scenarios list
Create a quality of service requirement	Identify security objectives Identify performance objectives Capture requirements in TFS Prioritize the requirements
Plan for iteration	Divide scenarios and requirements into development and test tasks Create estimates for the development and test tasks Schedule and assign development and test tasks
Development for Iteration	Write code for development tasks Create/update unit test for the development task Run unit tests and perform code analysis
Testing for Iteration	Write validation tests for the test tasks Run the test cases and conduct exploratory testing Open bugs for the issues found
Review progress for the iteration	Assess progress of the tasks for the iteration Triage bugs identified in the iteration Evaluate test metric thresholds

Figure 14.1 *MSF Agile Tasks and Key Activities*

MSF for Agile Software Development Defaults

When you create a new team project by using the MSF Agile process template, a concepts page outlining the process guidance is displayed in the main window of Microsoft Visual Studio®. This is your initial viewpoint into the MSF Agile process. You can also access this information from the project portal home page.

The configuration of the tooling goes well beyond the description of the process and includes work items (such as scenarios, quality of service requirements, tasks, bugs, and risks), project reports, roles (groups and permissions), and a project portal. Key items supplied by the MSF Agile template include:

- Work items
- Groups and permissions
- Source control
- Areas and iterations
- Reports
- Portal

The following sections detail the important defaults available to you when using the MSF Agile process template.

Work Items

The MSF Agile process template contains the following work item types:

- **Bug.** Represents a problem or potential problem in your application.
- **Risk.** Represents a possible event or condition that would have a negative impact on your project.
- **Scenario.** Represents a single path of user interaction through the system you are building.
- **Task.** Identifies a specific item of work for a team member to perform.
- **Quality of Service Requirement.** Represents a non-functional requirement such as a security, performance or manageability requirement.

When you create a new team project based on the MSF Agile process template, the following work items are created for you. This saves you work by providing you with a common set of tasks that you need to perform at project initiation.

- **Set up: Set Permissions.** The purpose of this task is to add team members to one of the four security groups: Build Services, Project Administrators, Contributors, or Readers.
- **Set up: Migration of Source Code.** The purpose of this task is to migrate your existing source code from Microsoft Visual SourceSafe®, if you are moving an existing project to Microsoft Visual Studio Team Foundation Server (TFS). You should

complete migration of source code before you grant team members access to the team project.

- **Set up: Migration of Work Items.** If you are bringing an existing project into TFS, you can migrate work items such as bugs and tasks from Clearquest or a comma-separated value (CSV) file. You should complete this migration of work items before you grant team members access to the team project.
- **Set up: Set Check-in Policies.** The purpose of this task is to setup the business rules or policies that surround source code check-ins.
- **Set up: Configure Build.** The purpose of this task is to create an initial source tree and set up the build to run on a periodic (usually daily) basis.
- **Set up: Send Mail to Users for Installation and Getting Started.** The purpose of his task is to send an e-mail to team members that provides information about which TFS they should connect to, and which team project they should use to get started working on the team project.
- **Create Vision Statement.** The purpose of his task is to create a vision statement for the project—a view of the desired end result of your project, shared by all project stakeholders.
- **Set up: Create Project Description on Team Project Portal.** The purpose of this task is to change the default project description to better describe the new team project, for example describing project's purpose, goals, or vision.
- **Create Personas.** The purpose of this task is to create personas that represent users interacting with the system. You can use the personas when thinking through application design as they are the target users for the system.
- **Define Iteration Length.** The purpose of this task is to define the iteration cycle to be used by the project. This depends upon the size and complexity of the project.
- **Create Test Approach Worksheet including Test Thresholds.** The purpose of this task is to understand your test strategy from the very start of the project iteration. Understanding your test approach can help you schedule your testing tasks more efficiently and will allow your developers to implement with the test considerations in mind.
- **Brainstorm and Prioritize Scenarios List.** The purpose of this task is to identify and prioritize key usage scenarios.
- **Brainstorm and Prioritize Quality of Service Requirements List.** The purpose of this task is to identify non-functional QoS requirements such as security, performance and manageability scenarios.
- **Set up: Create Project Structure.** The purpose of this task is to create the project structure that captures the areas in which the development team will be working in.
- **Create Iteration Plan.** The purpose of this task is to decide how to divide your development efforts into iterations.

Reports

The following reports are available by default with the MSF Agile process template:

- **Bugs by Priority.** Are the correct bugs being found? This report shows you the rate of high-priority versus low–priority bugs being found.
- **Bug Rates.** How effectively are bugs being found, fixed, and closed? This chart shows trends over time for new bugs, bug backlogs, and bug resolution.
- **Builds.** What is the quality of a build? This report provides a list of available builds including build quality and other detailed information.
- **Project Velocity.** How quickly is the team completing its work? This report shows how quickly the team is completing planned work and shows rates of change from day to day.
- **Quality Indicators.** What is the quality of the software? This report collects test results, bugs, code coverage, and code churn into a single report in order to track project health.
- **Load Test Summary.** This report shows test results for load testing on your application.
- **Regressions.** This report shows a list of all the tests that previously passed but are now failing.
- **Reactivations.** How many work items are being reactivated? This report shows work items that have been resolved or closed prematurely.
- **Related Work Items.** What work items are dependent on other work items? This report shows a list of work items that are linked to other work items so you can trace dependencies.
- **Remaining Work.** How much work is left to be done and when will it be completed? This report shows the amount of work that is remaining, resolved and closed over time. Projecting remaining work trends forward can enable you to predict the point at which you will be code complete.
- **Unplanned Work.** How much unplanned work is there? This report charts total work versus remaining work and distinguishes planned from unplanned activities.
- **Triage.** What work items need to be triaged? This report shows every work item that is still in the proposed state.
- **Work Items.** What are the active work items? This report lists every active work item.
- **Work Items by Owner.** How much work is assigned to each member of the team? This report shows work items per team member.
- **Work Items by State.** How many active, resolved and closed work items are there? This report shows lists every active, resolved, and closed work item.

Groups and Permissions

The following groups are available by default in the MSF Agile process template:

- **Readers.** Members of this group have read-only access to the team project.
- **Contributors.** Members of this group can add, modify, and delete items within the team project.
- **Build Services.** Members of this group have build service permissions for the team project. This group is used for service accounts only.
- **Project Administrators.** Members of this group can perform all operations in the team project.

Source Control

MSF Agile uses the following default source control settings:

- **Multiple Checkout.** By default MSF Agile allows multiple checkouts to enable multiple team members to work on the same file at the same time. Any resulting conflicts must be resolved at check-in time.
- **Permissions.** The default permissions on the source control are as follows:
  - **Project Administrators.** Have all available rights.
  - **Build Services.** Have rights to read, pend changes, check-in, label, start build, and edit build.
  - **Contributors**. Have rights to read, pend changes, check-in, check-out, label, and start build.
  - **Readers.** Has only read-only access to source control

Areas and Iterations

The out-of-box MSF Agile process template does not provide a classification structure for either areas or iterations. The recommended approach is to carve out the areas based on the component or features of the project. Iterations can be time-based cycles for which you will repeat a particular set of major activities such as plan, develop, and test.

Examples of MSF for Agile Software Development in Practice

The following examples show how the MSF for Agile Software Development process has been adopted and used by the *patterns & practices* team within Microsoft as well as by a development team outside of Microsoft.

Example 1: patterns & practices Teams

The following example shows how a typical *patterns & practices* project is executed by using the MSF Agile process.

New Project Through Iteration 0

- The product manager:
  1. Interacts with customers and stake holders to gather project requirements. These are captured in a Microsoft Office Word document named the Project Back Log.
  2. Creates a vision statement for the project by using Microsoft Office PowerPoint®.
  3. Brainstorms with customers and various stakeholders and defines the scenarios that will address the project's requirements and vision.
  4. Works with the project manager and other stakeholders to prioritize the scenarios.
- The project manager:
  1. Captures the scenarios as work items in TFS.
  2. Decides the iteration cycle duration, depending on the project size, and delivery capabilities.

Pre-Iteration Planning

- The project manager decides which scenarios should be worked on during the iterations, depending on their priority.
- The product manager together with the project manager creates Quality of Service (QoS) Requirements for the scenario. The QoS is then linked to the scenarios.

Iteration Planning

- The project manager:
  1. Breaks the scenarios into development tasks, in collaboration with developers and other team members.
  2. Captures the development tasks in TFS and links them to the scenarios.
  3. Defines the acceptance criteria for each of the development tasks.
  4. Breaks the QoS requirements into test tasks.
  5. Captures the test tasks in TFS and links them to the QoS.
  6. Defines the acceptance criteria for each of the test tasks.
  7. Schedules and assigns the tasks.

- The developer estimates each development task.

Important: If it looks like the tasks (developer stories) might take longer than a day or two to implement, then you should break these down into sub-stories.

- The tester provides an estimation for each of the test tasks.

During the Iteration

- The project manager guides the iteration.
- The developer writes code for the development task, and then closes the tasks once the acceptance criteria have been met.
- The tester executes the test tasks that he or she is assigned and then creates new bugs (work items) for any issues identified.

After the Iteration

- The project manager:
  1. Assesses the project progress and reprioritizes any scenarios that are incomplete from the current iteration.
  2. Provide a status report to stakeholders.
  3. Decides which scenarios should be worked on during next iteration based on their priority.
- The product manager:
  1. Adds any newly discovered scenarios.
  2. Reprioritizes scenarios (where necessary).
  3. Together with the project manager, creates QoS requirements for the project. The QoS is linked to the scenarios.

Example 2: Field Customer Engagement

The following example shows how the MSF Agile process is used by a field customer engagement.

New Project Through Iteration 0

- The business analyst:
  1. Creates a short (one-page) vision statement
  2. Identifies an on-site customer who can be used to provide input and creates personas for the system.
  3. Brainstorms scenarios (names only) with the customer.
  4. Prioritizes scenarios with the customer.
  5. Writes scenarios for the upcoming iteration.

- The project manager:
  1. Gathers the developers together and obtains their estimates. The estimates are rough-order-of-magnitude estimates.
  2. Checks if priorities change as a result of costs.
  3. Schedules scenarios for the upcoming iteration.
- The architect divides scenarios into architecture tasks.
- The developer:
  1. Divides scenarios into development tasks.
  2. Defines an appropriate build strategy (Continuous Integration, if possible).
- The tester divides scenario into test tasks.

During the Iteration

- The project manager:
  1. Guides the iteration.
  2. Guides the project.
- The architect defines the solution architecture.
- The developer implements a development task.
- The tester tests a scenario.

After Iteration 0

The tasks change slightly at this point.

- The business analyst:
  1. Updates personas (where necessary).
  2. Adds any newly discovered scenarios.
  3. Reprioritizes scenarios (where necessary).
  4. Writes scenarios for the upcoming iteration.
- The project manager:
  1. Estimates any new scenarios.
  2. Schedules scenarios for the upcoming iteration.
- The architect divides the scenarios into architecture tasks.
- The developer:
  1. Divides scenarios into development tasks.
  2. Updates the build process (Continuous Integration, if possible).
- The tester divides the scenarios into test tasks.

Customizing the MSF Agile Process Template

You can use two methods to customize the MSF Agile process template to suit your specific organizational requirements:

- **Manually customize the XML files.** Manual customization is error-prone but nevertheless gives you fine grained control on the customization of the process templates. For more information, see "Customizing Process Templates" at *http://msdn2.microsoft.com/en-us/library/ms243782(VS.80).aspx*
- **Process Template Editor.** The latest version of the Visual Studio 2005 Team Foundation Server Power Tool—a set of enhancements, tools, and command-line utilities that improve the TFS experience—provides you with a user interface-based tool, that you can use to view and customize process templates. When connected to TFS, you can use this tool to customize work item type definitions and global lists on an active project. For more information, see "How To: Customize a Process Template in Visual Studio Team Foundation Server."

Summary

The MSF Agile process template defines a set of tasks to be performed by the various roles involved in a software-development lifecycle. The MSF Agile process template defines work items, groups and permissions, source control, areas and iterations, reports and a team portal in order to support the agile process.

If the default process template does not satisfy your process requirements, you can customize the template by manually customizing the XML process definition files or by using the Process Editor Tool that ships with TFS Power Tools.

Additional Resources

- To download the MSF Agile process template, go to *http://www.microsoft.com/downloads/details.aspx?FamilyID=EA75784E-3A3F-48FB-824E-828BF593C34D&displaylang=en*
- To download the Team Foundation Server Power Tool including the Process Template Editor, go to *http://msdn2.microsoft.com/en-us/vstudio/aa718351.aspx*
- For more information on process template customization, see "Process Template Customization Overview" at *http://msdn2.microsoft.com/en-us/library/ms194945(VS.80).aspx*
- For more information about how to manually customize process templates, see "Customizing Process Templates" at *http://msdn2.microsoft.com/en-us/library/ms243782(VS.80).aspx*

Part VII
Reporting

In this part:

- Reporting Explained

15

Reporting Explained

Objectives

- Describe Microsoft® Visual Studio® Team Foundation Server (TFS) reporting architecture.
- Identify the components that make up TFS reporting.
- Describe the purpose of each available report.
- Know which process template contains which report.
- Customize and create new reports.

Overview

This chapter describes TFS reporting architecture and the common reports that you can use with new team projects. It also connects common reporting scenarios with reports available in TFS, and describes common reasons to customize existing reports or create new reports. TFS reporting enables you to view aggregated data over many aspects of your team project. You can use this information to analyze project progress, project health, and the effectiveness of your development and test teams.

TFS reporting uses Microsoft SQL Server™ 2005 Reporting Services to create, manage, and run reports. Each process template contains a set of predefined reports which are deployed to the project's report folder when the project is created. By using Reporting Services you can also amend these reports and create custom reports for your project. You can add new reports to an existing process template so that they are available for other team projects.

How to Use This Chapter

Use this chapter to understand how TFS reporting works and how it can help you assess project health and status. To gain the greatest benefits from this chapter, you should:

- **Read the "Scenarios and Solutions" section.** Understand common reasons to use TFS reporting and learn the purpose of each standard report.
- **Read the "Physical Architecture" section.** Learn what components make up the reporting system and how they interrelate.
- **Read the "Customizing Reports" section.** Learn the mechanisms available for report customization and creation.
- **Read the companion How To articles.** Read the following companion How To articles for a step-by-step walk through of various procedures discussed in this chapter.
  - How To: Customize a Report with Visual Studio 2005 Team Foundation Server"
  - How To: Create a Custom Report in Visual Studio 2005 Team Foundation Server
  - How To: Create a Risk Over Time Report with Visual Studio 2005 Team Foundation Server

Scenarios and Solutions

Reports are the primary way project managers and team leaders keep up to date with an ongoing project. After you create a new team project, a set of reports is generated for you based on the process template you chose. These reports are available to you from the project's Microsoft Office SharePoint® portal site or from the reports node in Team Explorer inside Visual Studio.

The following are common questions that can be answered by using TFS reports:

- When will my application be ready to ship?
- Is work proceeding according to plan?
- What is the quality of the build?
- What is the status of development against defined scenarios?
- How quickly is development work getting completed?
- Are bugs getting fixed?
- Are bugs regressing?

Team Foundation Server Reports

Both the Microsoft Solution Framework (MSF) for Agile Software Development (MSF Agile) and MSF for CMMI® Process Improvement (MSF CMMI) process templates each include a set of reports by default.

Bugs

The bug-related reports in the process templates enable you to see what types of bugs are being generated and fixed and to identify trends. The following bug related reports are available:

- **Bugs by Priority.** Are the correct bugs being found? This report shows you the rate of high-priority bugs found versus low priority bugs. This report is available in both of the supplied process templates.
- **Bug Rates.** How effectively are bugs being found, fixed, and closed? This report shows trends over time for new bugs, bug backlogs, and bug resolution. This report is available in both of the supplied process templates.

Release Management

Release management reports enable you to judge how close your software is to being fit for release. The following release management reports are available:

- **Actual Quality versus Planned Velocity.** How many scenarios can be completed before quality is unacceptable? This report presents the relationship for each iteration, of estimated size to overall quality. This report is available in both process templates.
- **Builds.** What is the quality of a build? This report provides a list of available builds including build quality and other detailed information. This report is available in MSF for CMMI Process Improvement.
- **Quality Indicators.** What is the quality of the software? This report collects test results, bugs, code coverage and code churn into a single report to track project health. This report is available in MSF Agile and MSF CMMI.
- **Velocity.** How quickly is the team completing work? This report shows how quickly the team is completing planned work and show rates of change from day to day. This report is available in MSF Agile and MSF CMMI.
- **Scenario Details.** What scenarios are we building the application against? This report provides information on each scenario including completion status, risks and testing progress. This report is available in MSF CMMI.

Testing

Testing reports enable you to monitor the effectiveness and progress of your testing. The following test reports are available:

- **Regressions.** What tests passed at one point but are now failing? This report shows a list of all the tests that passed previously and now are failing. This report is available in MSF CMMI.
- **Requirements Test History.** How well tested are my scenarios and requirements? This report shows the progress of testing against defined scenarios and requirements. This report is available in MSF CMMI.
- **Test Failure Without Active Bug.** Are there bugs to track every known defect? This report shows any tests that have failed and are not associated with an open bug. This report is available in MSF CMMI.
- **Test Passing With Open Bug.** Is the bug list up to date and consistent with application quality? This report shows stale bugs for which tests are now passing. This report is available in MSF CMMI.
- **Load Test Summary.** What are the results of load testing on application performance? This report shows test results for load testing on your application. This report is available in MSF Agile.

Work Items

Work item reports enable you to assess the current state of your project and current project progress. The following work item reports are available.

- **Open Issues and Blocked Work Items Trend.** How many open issues remain? This report shows the remaining open issues as well as the trend toward resolving them. This report is available in MSF CMMI.
- **Reactivations.** How many work items are being reactivated? This report shows work items that have been resolved or closed prematurely. This report is available in MSF Agile and MSF CMMI.
- **Related Work Items.** What work items are dependent on other work items? This report shows a list of work items that are linked to other work items so you trace dependencies. This report is available in MSF CMMI.
- **Remaining Work.** How much work is left to be done and when will it be completed? This report shows work remaining, resolved and closed over time. Projecting remaining work trends forward can enable you to predict the point at which you will be code complete. This report is available in MSF Agile and MSF CMMI.
- **Triage.** What work items need to be triaged? This report shows every work item that is still in the proposed state. This report is available in MSF CMMI.

- **Unplanned Work.** How much unplanned work is there? This report charts total work versus remaining work and distinguishes planned from unplanned tasks. This report is available in MSF Agile and MSF CMMI.
- **Work Items.** What are the active work items? This report lists every active work item. This report is available in MSF CMMI.
- **Work Items by Owner.** How much work is assigned to each member of the team? This report shows work items per team member. This report is available in MSF CMMI.
- **Work Items by State.** How many active, resolved and closed work items are there? This report lists work items organized by state. This report is available in MSF CMMI.

Customizing Reports

You might want a report that does not exist in either of the MSF process templates. You can customize reports in one of three ways:

- **Use a filter on an existing report.** Many reports provide parameters that you can use to filter the report. For example date, area, iteration, and priority filters are available. Use these filters to review a subset of the data provided in the report. Note that these filters are temporary and are lost when you browse away from the report.
- **Customize an existing report.** If a report you want is similar to an existing report, it is often easiest to make a copy of the existing report and then modify it. For example, you might want to plot risks over time to analyze how well your team is working with project risks.
- **Create a new report.** You can create a new report from scratch.

If you modify an existing report or create a new report from scratch you can publish it to the Report Server so that it is available to the rest of your team. If you want to modify an existing report or create a new report, you can use one of the following methods:

- Use Microsoft Office Excel® to create pivot tables from data in the reporting databases.
- Create a new Report Server project in Visual Studio and then create new reports or import existing reports.

Creating a Report Server project in Visual Studio is the most powerful and flexible method for report creation and modification.

Note: It is possible to use the Report Builder, available from the team reporting site; however this tool is not well supported for Visual Studio reporting scenarios and is not recommended.

More Information

- For more information about customizing an existing report, see "How To: Customize a Report with Visual Studio Team Foundation Server."
- For more information about creating a custom report, see "How To: Create a Custom Report in Visual Studio Team Foundation Server."
- For a step-by-step guide to creating a Risk over Time report, see "How To: Create a Risk over Time Report with Visual Studio Team Foundation Server."

Physical Architecture

Team Foundation Server is built on SQL Server 2005 and uses SQL Server Analysis Services to aggregate data and drive reports. You can create new reports by using Microsoft Excel or Visual Studio 2005 Report Designer. Reports are hosted on SQL Server 2005 Reporting Services and can be viewed from the report server Web site, team SharePoint project portal or from the Reports node in Team Explorer. Figure 15.1 shows the physical reporting architecture.

Each TFS component maintains its own set of transaction databases. This includes work items, source control, tests, bugs, and Team Build. This data is aggregated into a relational database. The data is then placed in an Online Analytical Processing (OLAP) cube to support trend-based reporting and more advanced data analysis.

The TfsWarehouse relational database is a data warehouse designed to be used for data querying rather than transactions. Data is transferred from the various TFS databases, which are optimized for transaction processing, into this warehouse for reporting purposes. The warehouse is not the primary reporting store, but you can use it to build reports. The TfsReportDS data source points to the relational database. The Team System Data Warehouse OLAP Cube is an OLAP database that is accessed through SQL Server Analysis Services. The cube is useful for reports that provide data analysis of trends such as 'how many bugs closed this month versus last month?' The TfsOlapReportDS data source points to the Team System Data Warehouse OLAP cube in the analysis services database.

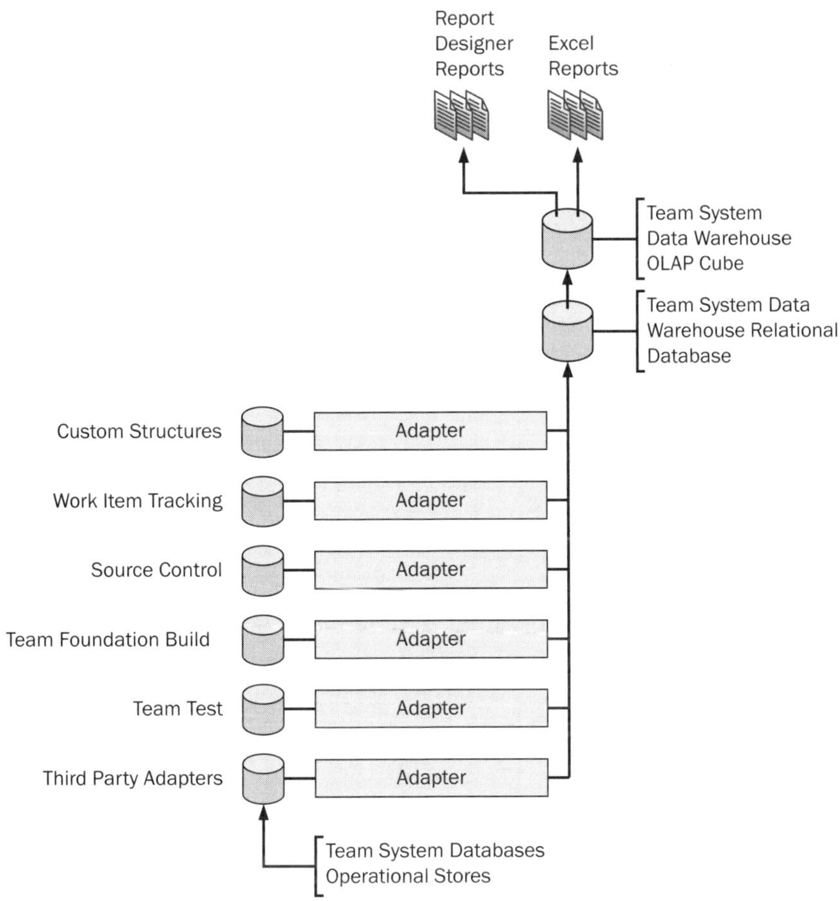

Figure 15.1 *Physical Reporting Architecture*

Components of the Reporting System

The reporting system consists of the following server-side and client-side components.

Server-Side Components

Server-side components include:

- **Report server databases.** These databases contain the report definitions, historical reports, and configuration data.
- **Report server Web service.** This Web service provides programmatic access to the Report Server.
- **Report Manager Web site.** This site provides user access to Report Server through a Web browser.
- **Windows service.** This service provides the scheduling and delivery of report snapshots.

Client-Side Components

Client-side components include:

- **Browser.** This component provides access to the Report Manager Web site.
- **Team Explorer.** This component provides access to reports through Visual Studio.

Report Development Tools

Development tools include:

- **Business Intelligence Designer Studio (BIDS).** This component enables developers to design and deploy reports from within Visual Studio 2005.
- **Excel.** Excel can be used to generate pivot tables from the reporting store.
- **Report Builder.** This component allows end users to design ad-hoc reports. It is not well supported for Team Foundation reporting scenarios and is not recommended.

Summary

The MSF Agile and MSF CMMI process templates each provide a set of default reports for bugs, release management, testing, and work item tracking:

- Bug-related reports in the process templates enable you to see what types of bugs are being generated to help identify bug trends.
- Release management reports help you judge if your application is fit for release.
- Testing reports enable you to monitor the effectiveness and progress of your testing efforts.
- Work item reports enable you to assess the current state of your project and current project progress.

If you want to modify an existing report or create a new report, you can use the Report Builder available from the team reporting site, use Excel to create pivot tables from data in the reporting databases, or create a new Report Server project in Visual Studio.

Additional Resources

- For more information about Team Foundation Server Reporting, see *http://msdn2.microsoft.com/en-us/library/ms194922(VS.80).aspx*

Part VIII

Setting Up and Maintaining the Team Enviornment

In this part:

- Team Foundation Server Deployment
- Providing Internet Access to Team Foundation Server

16

Team Foundation Server Deployment

Objectives

- Learn about the advantages and disadvantages of single-server and multiple-server deployments.
- Select a deployment topology to suit your organization's requirements.

Overview

This chapter outlines the main approaches to deploying Microsoft® Visual Studio® 2005 Team Foundation Server (TFS) and describes key decision points you will face when deploying TFS in your organization. The chapter explains the two deployment options and describes how to choose between these options.

There are two TFS deployment options, single-server or dual-server installation. A single-server installation places the data-tier and application-tier on a single server. A dual server installation splits the application and data tiers onto separate servers. Additionally, you can install the build server and the source control proxy on separate servers. Each client requires access to the servers and the appropriate client-side tools must be installed.

How to Use This Chapter

Use this chapter to determine your TFS deployment strategy. To gain the greatest benefits from this chapter, you should:

- **Understand TFS Architecture.** Make sure that you fully understand TFS architecture. If you are unfamiliar with the Team Foundation Server architecture read the "TFS Architecture" section, or read Chapter 2, "Team Foundation Server Architecture" for more information.

- **Choose a deployment strategy.** Choose the deployment strategy that best suits your organization's needs. If you have not already done so, read the "Deployment Scenarios" section to determine which deployment strategy will work best for your team.

TFS Architecture

Figure 16.1 shows TFS architecture.

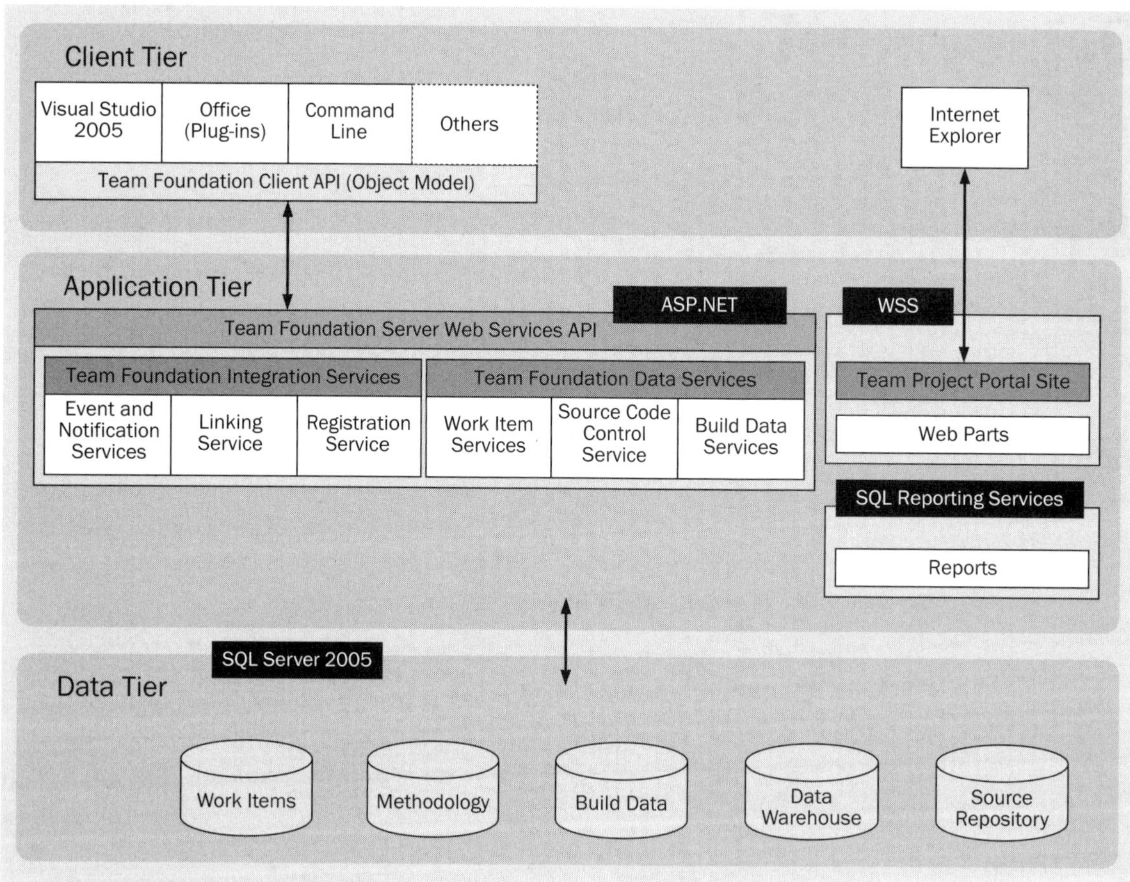

Figure 16.1 *TFS Architecture*

TFS architecture is made up of three tiers, the data tier, the application tier and the client tier. These are logical separations, and all three tiers can be installed onto the same computer.

The Team Foundation data tier consists of Microsoft SQL Server™ 2005. A number of databases are installed that store the work items, the version control system, test results and any reports.

The application tier contains a Web-based front end integrated into Internet Information Services (IIS), the Team Foundation Web services, and Microsoft Office SharePoint® services. The application tier also contains any build servers and source control proxy servers.

The client tier contains the applications that access TFS. Developers use Team Explorer to connect to Team Server, installed either as a stand-alone tool or as part of Visual Studio 2005. Project Managers use Microsoft Office Excel® or Microsoft Office Project. You can also use third-party tools to connect to the server.

For more information, see Chapter 2, "Team Foundation Server Architecture."

Deployment Scenarios

You can deploy TFS in the following ways:

- Single-server deployment
  - Within a workgroup.
  - Using Microsoft Active Directory ® directory service.
- Dual-server deployment

Single-Server Deployment with Workgroup

With this deployment approach, you create a workgroup where you have no Active Directory domain controller. You use this installation mode when you have a small team. If you use this installation mode, each user requires a local account on the server to enable them to log on to the server. For this type of deployment you can only install onto a single-server, and dual-server installation is not supported.

Single-Server Deployment with Active Directory

If you have an Active Directory, then you have two deployment choices. You can install both the data tier and the application tier on the same server, or you can install the data tier and the application tier on separate servers.

What Is the Right Type of Deployment for My Organization?

To decide whether a single-server or dual-server install is the right choice for your organization, consider the following questions:

- **How many users do I need to support?** If you plan to have more than 400 users, consider whether a dual-server deployment might better suit your needs.
- **How many projects will I be supporting with TFS?** If you are supporting a large number of projects, consider whether a dual-server TFS deployment might better suit your business needs. Each TFS instance can support up 5000 projects. If you need to support more than 5000 projects then consider setting up more than one Team Foundation Server instance.
- **Do I have a server I can dedicate to TFS?** The server in a single-server Team Foundation Server deployment should be dedicated to TFS functionality. The TFS should not serve any other purpose, such as being a mail server, file server, or database server for other applications.

Advantages of Single-Server Deployments

Consider the following advantages when deciding whether to implement a single-server deployment:

- **Simplicity**
  - You can manage all aspects of TFS deployment on a single-server.
  - You can configure all access rights and permissions for users and groups on one server.
  - You only have one server to schedule for backup and maintenance.
- **Availability.** Because both the application tier and the data tier are present on a single server, you do not have to consider network restrictions or network latency between the application tier and data tier when planning your deployment.

Advantages of Dual-Server Deployments

Consider the following advantages when deciding whether to implement a dual-server deployment:

- **Scalability.** Single-server deployments are designed for up to 400 users, while a dual-server deployment will allow you to scale beyond this limit up to 2000 users.
- **Fail-over.** You can redirect the application-tier server to a different data-tier server in case of maintenance or repairs, and you cannot configure and deploy an additional server that can act as a standby or fail-over application-tier server.

Single-Server Deployment

Figure 16.2 shows a typical single server deployment. Installed on the server are the TFS application and data tiers, along with SharePoint Services and SQL Server 2005.

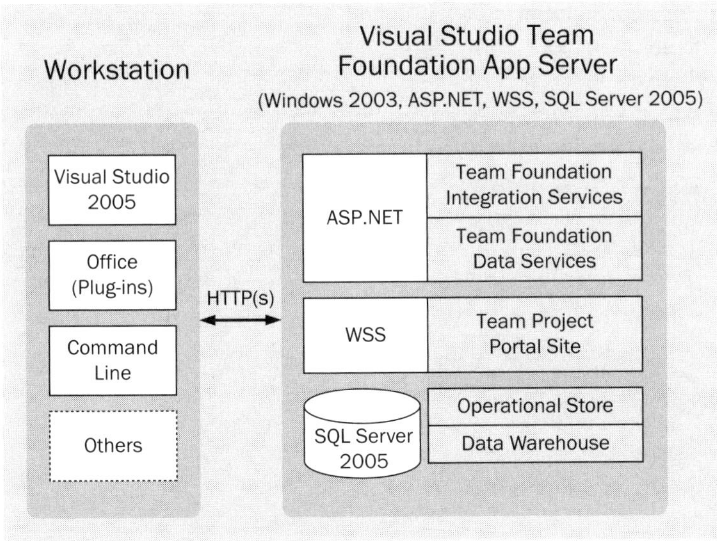

Figure 16.2 *Typical Single-Server Installation*

Dual-Server Deployment

Figure 16.3 shows a typical dual server installation. The TFS application tier is installed along with SharePoint Services on one tier. The TFS data tier is installed alongside SQL Server 2005 on another server.

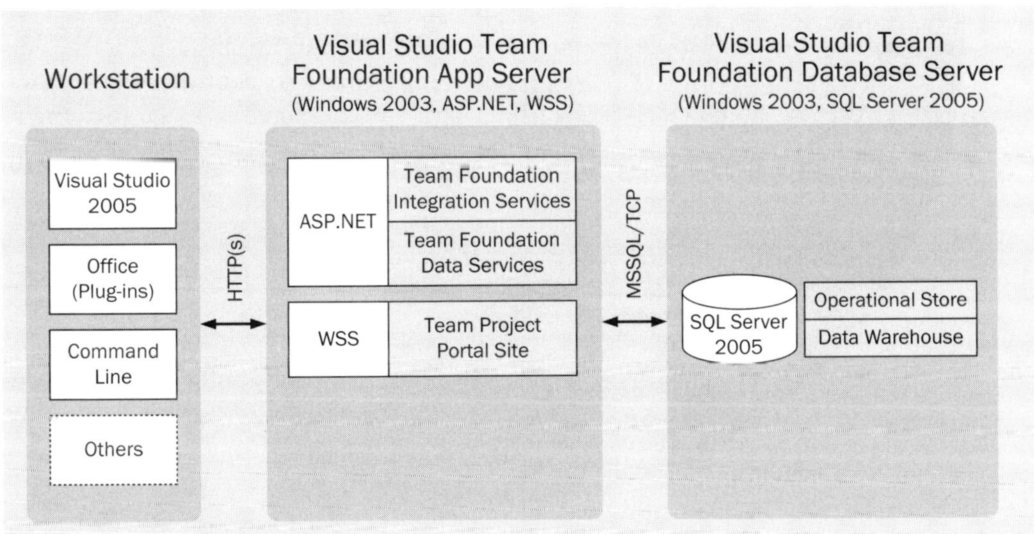

Figure 16.3 *Typical Dual-Server Installation*

Other Servers

In either the single-server or dual-server installation, you can install a separate build server as well as a proxy server. These can be installed onto the same server as the application-tier or on different servers.

Build Server Installation

You can locate your build services on a separate server to improve build performance and reduce the load on your application tier. For example, if your application tier server performance is impacted by frequent builds, consider moving the build services to a separate server.

Team Foundation Proxy Server

The Team Foundation proxy server caches copies of source control files. You should use the proxy server if you are accessing the source control server over a network and there is high latency.

Team Foundation Server Topologies

After you have decided on either single-server or dual-server installation, there are several topologies you can use. Topologies range from simple to complex. Each topology is designed for teams of certain sizes.

Simple Topology

Figure 16.4 shows a simple topology where the TFS application-tier and data-tier components are deployed to a single server. The TFS proxy server is deployed to a separate server. The server can be accessed from client workstations in the same domain.

This configuration is appropriate for development teams or pilot projects with up to 400 users.

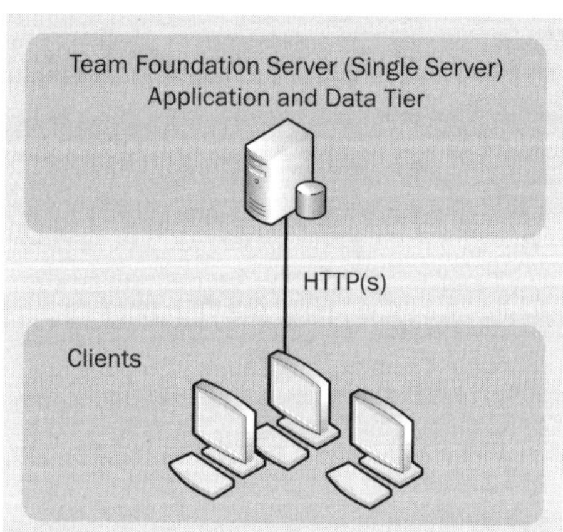

Figure 16.4 *Simple Team Foundation Server Topology*

Moderate Topology

Figure 16.5 shows TFS installed onto different tiers. The application services are deployed onto one application-tier node and the databases onto a separate data-tier node.

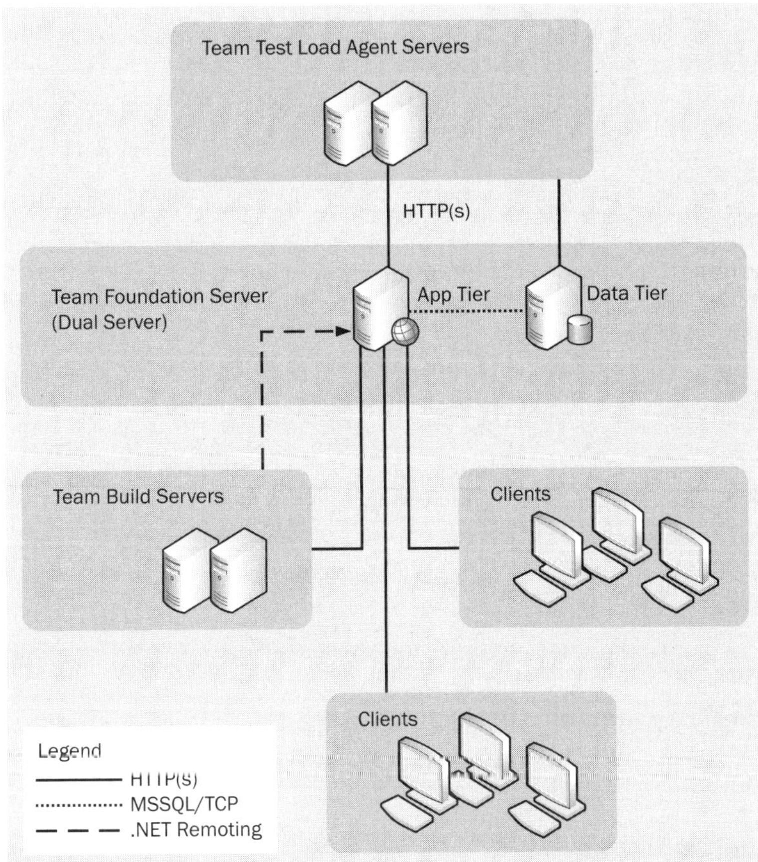

Figure 16.5 *Moderate Team Foundation Server Topology*

Figure 16.5 also shows a test rig and some build servers deployed to separate nodes. The client nodes are either in the same domain as the servers or in a domain that has a trust relationship with the servers. Topologies of this complexity are targets for larger development teams in the range of 400 to 2000 users.

Complex Topology

The complex topology shown in Figure 16.6 on the next page is similar to the moderate topology. However, in this topology fail-over components have been added with an application-tier standby server and a data tier with SQL clustering technologies.

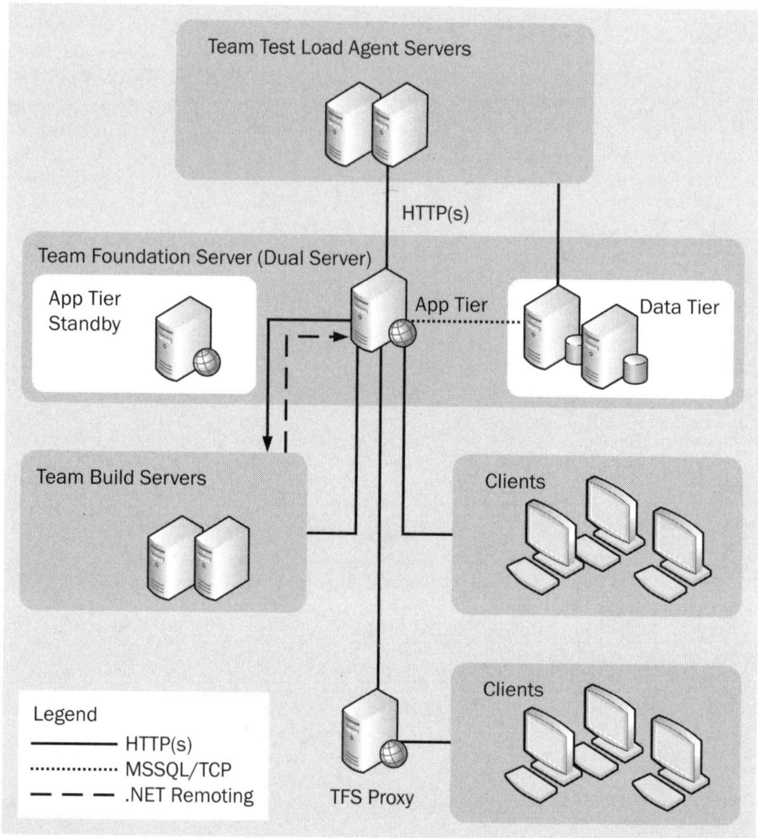

Figure 16.6 *Complex Team Foundation Server Topology*

Figure 16.6 also shows a geographically distant child domain that uses a limited-bandwidth connection. These clients use the TFS proxy server to improve access times to source control.

Additional Considerations

When deploying TFS consider the following:

- If you already have a SharePoint server set up and want to use this to host your Team Foundation Server SharePoint site you can move the TFS SharePoint site to another server. For more information, see *http://blogs.msdn.com/bharry/archive/2006/10/30/moving-your-tfs-sharepoint-site.aspx*
- Moving the OLAP engine and cube to a third machine has proved beneficial for larger teams. You can setup SQL clustering on the data tier, and have an active/active configuration with SQL on one node, and OLAP on the other, each acting as failover for its twin. For more information, see: *http://msdn2.microsoft.com/en-us/library/aa721760(vs.80).aspx* and *http://msdn2.microsoft.com/en-us/library/ms252505(VS.80).aspx*

Team Foundation Server Scaling and Backup Strategy

As part of your installation and deployment of Team Foundation Server you must decide how you are going to manage the backup and failover of your servers. The backup and failover strategies you choose depend on the size of the installation and the facilities and resources available to your organization. Because the data-tier is built on SQL Server 2005 the strategies you adopt are based on the approach you currently take to SQL Server backup.

If you currently mirror or cluster SQL Server 2005 installations then you can take the same approach to the TFS data-tier. You also need to decide how to manage failure of the application-tier server. If you want to support application-tier failover, you will need a backup application-tier server in place and must be able to fail over to that server quickly.

Choose the Appropriate Installation and Backup/Recovery Strategies for Your Company.

When installing TFS you need to make several choices about the installation and backup/recovery strategies. Take the following things into consideration when deciding on your installation strategy:

- Size of teams
- Number of projects
- Size of projects
- Location of teams
- Failover needs
- Backup needs

Recommended Team Foundation Server Hardware

Generally, smaller teams with fewer projects can run on a single tier installation, while larger teams require dual tiers and faster hardware. The choice of single-tier versus dual-tier installation also impacts your backup and failover mechanisms.

Use Table 16.1 to help decide on a single-tier or dual-tier installation and to identify the hardware needed to support your team.

Table 16.1 Required hardware for TFS deployment

Configuration	Tiers	CPU	Hard Disk Drive	Memory
One server, fewer than 20 users	Application-tier and data tier server	Single processor, 2.2 gigahertz (GHz)	8 gigabytes (GB)	1 GB
One server; 20 to 100 users	Application-tier and data tier server	Dual processors, 2.2 GHz	30 GB	2 GB
Two servers; 100 to 250 users	Application-tier server	Single processor, 2.2 GHz	20 GB	1 GB
	Data-tier server	Dual processors, 2.2 GHz	80 GB	2 GB
Two servers; 250 to 2000 users	Application-tier server	Dual processors, 2.8 GHz	40 GB	4 GB
	Data-tier server	Quadruple processors, 2.7 GHz	Direct attach storage, 14,000 – 15,000 RPM RAID 0 spindles	16 GB

Backup and Failover Strategy

When considering your backup and failover strategy you need to take into account the impact of losing a server on your team's productivity.

Backup

You should plan your backup strategy as part of the deployment of you TFS installation. You must consider:

- The frequency of your backup.
- The frequency of full and incremental backups.
- The storage requirements for the backup, such as on-site and off-site backup.

You can use the same standard backup practices that you use for any SQL Server 2005 database.

You can use backups to restore TFS in the following three scenarios:

- Data-only recovery
- Single-server deployment full recovery
- Dual-server deployment full recovery

Data-only recovery is used if the data tier becomes corrupted. You can use the backup data and logs to recover the full database.

Server recovery is used when the servers fail. In this case, you can restore the full database to a second computer.

Application-Tier Standby Server

Although there is no data to backup on your application-tier servers, the servers can still fail. To mitigate the cost of this failure you should consider a warm standby server to enable failover over the application tier.

Failover

When considering whether to provide a failover solution for your TFS, you should consider the cost of the hardware needed to provide the failover servers against the cost of lost productivity for your company if the TFS is unavailable.

Failover adds extra complexity to your installation with an added maintenance overhead. You must factor the cost of this maintenance into your cost considerations when deciding on your strategy.

Clustering has a high cost in terms of resources and maintenance and is recommended if your organization already provides the resources to manage a clustered server.

Mirroring has a cost, but it is not as high as clustering. Mirroring has the advantage of enabling you to take the principal server offline for maintenance. You should consider mirroring if your organization is able to set up and maintain a second data-tier server.

The Data Tier

Clustering the Data-Tier Servers

If your organization has the necessary resources, you should consider setting up dedicated servers in a cluster. The cluster will provide uninterrupted access to the data-tier. Note, however, that hardware requirements for a cluster are exacting. The cost in terms of resources of setting up and maintaining a cluster is high.

When clustering, TFS supports a configuration with a passive node, an active node and a single quorum device server. When the data tier fails over to the passive node, this node takes ownership of the quorum and the data tier.

You must prepare the cluster for installation before installing TFS in a cluster. For more information on SQL Server 2005 clustering, download the "SQL Server 2005 Failover Clustering White Paper" at *http://www.microsoft.com/downloads/details.aspx?familyid=818234dc-a17b-4f09-b282-c6830fead499&displaylang=en*

Mirroring the Data-Tier Servers

Mirroring a server involves synchronizing the data on one server with a copy of that data on another server. The data-tier server is the primary server, and the server with the mirrored data is the backup or mirroring server. If your data-tier server fails you can manually switch to the mirrored server.

Having a mirrored server enables you to take the main server offline for maintenance and repair, and also provides a fast recovery mechanism if your main data-tier server fails.

Mirroring can either be synchronous or asynchronous. You can exchange servers from the main server to the mirror server in a move known as *role switching*. When a role switch occurs, the mirror takes over the role of the principal server. If the former principal is still available, it can take over the role of the mirror. In principle, the roles can switch back and forth.

For TFS, automatic switching is not supported and instead you must use manual switching.

► To configure SQL mirroring for the data tier

1. Make a full backup of the databases and transaction log.
2. Backup the Reporting Services encryption key.
3. Install SQL Server 2005 on the mirror server.
4. Restore the data from the data-tier onto the mirror server.
5. For each database on the data-tier principal server run the **Configure Database Mirroring Security Wizard** to configure its mirror server.
6. Start mirroring.

Failing over a Mirrored Server

You have to fail over the mirrored server manually by performing the following steps:

1. On the TFS application-tier
   a. Reconfigure the Report Service to use the new server.
   b. Stop the default Web site.
   c. Stop the SharePoint Web site.
   d. Stop the SharePoint Timer service.
   e. Stop the TfsServerScheduler service.
   f. Stop the ReportServer application pool.
   g. Stop the TFS App Pool application pool.
2. On the mirror data-tier server ensures that the correct service accounts have been added.

3. Fail over each database from the principal server to the mirroring server.
4. Build the data warehouse on the new server.
5. Configure the application-tier server to use the mirror tier server as follows:
   a. From a command prompt, run TFSAdminUtil RenameDT MirrorDataTierServer.
   b. Restart IIS.
   c. Change the Reporting Services connection strings to reference the mirror data-tier server.
   d. Change the SharePoint server to use the mirror data-tier server
   e. Start the SharePoint timer service.
   f. Start the TfsServerScheduler service.
   g. Start the ReportServer application pool.
   h. Start the TFS App Pool application pool.
   i. Start Reporting Services.
   j. Invoke the StampWorkItemCache Web service.

The Application Tier

Failover the Application Tier

After setting up the primary application-tier server, you can add a warm standby computer to allow a warm failover of the application tier.

Standby Hardware and Software

The standby server does not need to be identical to the primary server, but it must match the hardware requirements for the application tier. You install the TFS application-tier software onto the warm standby server.

You must ensure that both servers have the same configuration, including the same user accounts, permission changes, and software updates. Any updates on the primary computer must also be applied to the warm standby server.

To minimize any problems with the failover, you must configure the network adapters to use the same host name from both the primary and standby computers. There are many ways to do this.

Failing over the Application Tier Server

You fail over the application tier server manually. When the primary server fails, you have to complete the steps to manually activate the warm standby server. You can run the **TFSAdminUtil** utility passing the **ActivateAT** command, on the standby server, to help fail over the primary server.

► **To warm fail over the server**

1. Take the original server offline when the standby application-tier server is activated.
2. On the standby server:
   a. Log as administrator.
   b. Run **TFSAdminUtil** passing **ActivateAT**
   c. Start the Web services on the standby server.

   This command will

   - Register the warm standby server name in the TFS integration database.
   - Connect the warm standby application-tier server to the active data-tier server.

Verify that the correct application-tier server is connected to the correct data-tier server.

For more information about how to activate an application-tier failover server, see "How to: Activate a Fail-Over Application-Tier Server" at *http://msdn2.microsoft.com/en-us/library/ms252501(VS.80).aspx*

Summary

The TFS architecture has three tiers: an application-tier, a data-tier, and a client-tier. When you install the server, you can choose to install the application and data tiers on the same server or on separate servers. Your choice of TFS deployment depends primarily on the number of users you want to support. After you have chosen a topology that supports your team's needs, you can decide what level of backup and failover support you need.

For the data-tier, you can use the same backup mechanism that your organization uses for your other SQL Server 2005 backups. For failover support, you can choose to mirror or cluster the data-tier servers.

The application-tier does not support automatic failover. If you need to support rapid failover, you can provide a warm failover server that you can fail over manually.

Additional Resources

- For more information about installing TFS, see the Visual Studio 2005 Team Foundation Installation Guide at *http://go.microsoft.com/fwlink/?linkid=40042*
- For more information about TFS scalability limits, see "Team Foundation Server Capacity Planning" at *http://blogs.msdn.com/bharry/archive/2006/01/04/509314.aspx*
- For more information about how to move the OLAP cube and analysis engine to a separate server, see "How To: Move the Data Warehouse SQL Server Analysis Services Database to a Separate Server" at *http://msdn2.microsoft.com/en-us/library/aa721760(vs.80).aspx*
- For more information about SQL Server 2005 clustering download the "SQL Server 2005 Failover Clustering White Paper" at *http://www.microsoft.com/downloads/details.aspx?familyid=818234dc-a17b-4f09-b282-c6830fead499&displaylang=en*
- For more information about creating a SQL Server failover cluster see "How To: Create a New SQL Server 2005 Failover Cluster (Setup)" at *http://uat.technet.microsoft.com/en-us/library/ms179530(SQL.90).aspx*
- For more information about how to set up a SQL Server cluster for your data-tier, see "Clustering the Data-Tier Server" at *http://msdn2.microsoft.com/en-us/library/ms252505(VS.80).aspx*
- For more information about how to move your TFS SharePoint site to another server, see "Moving your TFS SharePoint site" at *http://blogs.msdn.com/bharry/archive/2006/10/30/moving-your-tfs-sharepoint-site.aspx*
- For more information about Team Foundation Server Scalability, see Brian Harry's blog at *http://blogs.msdn.com/bharry/archive/2005/12/09/502190.aspx*
- For more information about planning for disaster recovery see "Visual Studio Team System User Education" at *http://www.microsoft.com/technet/itshowcase/content/vs05teamsystemnote.mspx*
- For more information about backup failure and recovery of a Team Foundation Server, see "Ensuring Team Foundation Server Availability" at *http://msdn2.microsoft.com/en-gb/library/ms253159(VS.80).aspx*
- For more information about clustering the data-tier servers, see "Clustering the Data-Tier Server" at *http://msdn2.microsoft.com/en-gb/library/ms252505(VS.80).aspx*
- For more information about mirroring the Team Foundation Server data tier, see "Mirroring the Team Foundation Data-Tier Server" at *http://msdn2.microsoft.com/en-gb/library/aa980644(VS.80).aspx*
- For more information about configuring SQL Server mirroring for the data-tier, see "How to: Configure SQL Server Mirroring for the Team Foundation Data-Tier Server" at *http://msdn2.microsoft.com/en-us/library/aa980629(VS.80).aspx*

- For more information about failing over the data tier, see "How To: Fail Over to a Mirrored Data-Tier Server" at *http://msdn2.microsoft.com/en-gb/library/aa980627(VS.80).aspx*
- For more information about failing over the data tier if the principle server is unavailable, see "How To: Fail Over to a Mirrored Data-Tier Server if the Principal Data-Tier Server is Unavailable" at *http://msdn2.microsoft.com/en-gb/library/aa980528(VS.80).aspx*
- For more information about how to activate an application tier fail over server, see "How To: Activate a Fail-Over Application-Tier Server" at *http://msdn2.microsoft.com/en-us/library/ms252501(VS.80).aspx*
- For more information about activating an application tier fail over server, see "Activating a Fail-Over Application-Tier Server" at *http://msdn2.microsoft.com/en-us/library/ms252486(VS.80).aspx*

17

Providing Internet Access to Team Foundation Server

Objectives

- Learn key remote access scenarios and when to apply them.
- Provide remote access to your Microsoft® Visual Studio® 2005 Team Foundation Server (TFS) over the Internet.
- Improve remote access performance by using the Team Foundation Server Proxy.

Overview

This chapter explains how to provide remote access to TFS over the Internet. You can choose from one of the following three options in order to provide remote access:

- You can provide access to TFS over a virtual private network (VPN).
- You can provide access to TFS through a reverse proxy such as Microsoft Internet Security and Acceleration (ISA) Server.
- You can host your TFS server on an extranet.

Versions of TFS prior to Service Pack 1 (SP1) support only VPN access. TFS SP1 adds support for Basic authentication. This enables the extranet and reverse proxy solutions as well as VPN.

How to Use This Chapter

Use this chapter to set up your TFS server for remote access over the Internet. To gain the greatest benefits from this chapter, you should:

- **Use the scenarios list.** Consult the scenarios list to determine quickly which approach you should adopt to provide external Internet access to your server.

- **Use the referenced walkthroughs.** Use the walkthroughs in this chapter for step-by-step guidance on installing and configuring the certificates and Secure Sockets Layer (SSL) access to be used with Basic and Digest authentication.
- **Use the "Improving Remote Access Performance" section.** Read the "Improving Remote Access Performance" section to identify ways to reduce the amount of traffic that needs to be sent over the Internet.

Key Strategies

The following are solution strategies for providing remote access to a TFS server:

- **Use a VPN connection.** Your TFS sits inside the internal network, and external users access it over a VPN. Internal users access a TFS directly.
- **Publish your TFS through a reverse proxy.** Your TFS sits inside the internal network, and one or more reverse proxy machines, such as ISA Server, bring in client requests from the Internet to your TFS.
- **Locate your TFS in the extranet ("hosted scenario").** Only external clients access your TFS, and it is located outside of the firewall on an extranet.

Common Scenarios

- **Remote office.** If you are supporting remote users with VPN access, use the VPN solution. This is the easiest solution to enable, provides well-understood security, allows remote access to all TFS features, and allows you to use the TFS Proxy to improve performance.
- **Offshore team.** If you are supporting remote users without VPN access or without access to the domain, use the reverse proxy scenario. This solution is more difficult to set up, but it enables remote users to access an internally located TFS without the need for VPN.
- **Hosted community.** If you are supporting a set of remote users who will be using a TFS installation dedicated to their use, such as a community development site, use the extranet scenario. This solution gives you the most separation between the remote users and your internal network resources.

Using a VPN connection

Figure 17.1 shows architecture for exposing TFS over a VPN.

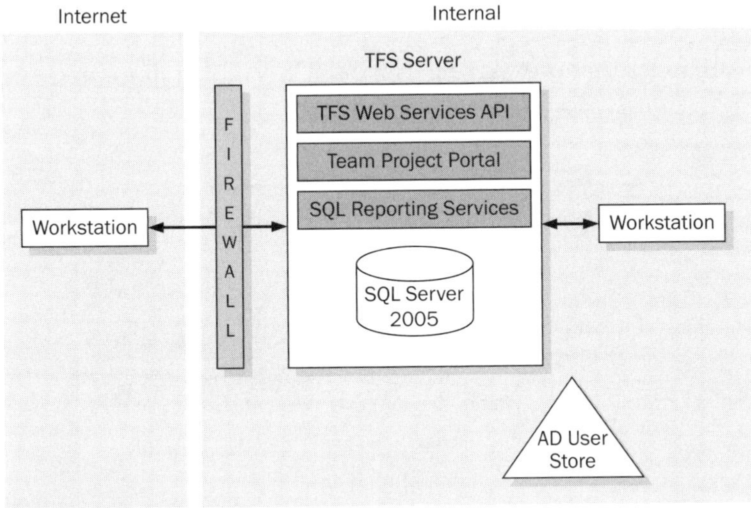

Figure 17.1 *TFS over VPN Architecture*

With this approach, your remote development team uses a direct VPN connection to your TFS on your internal network. If you have TFS without SP1, or if you require Integrated Windows authentication, then using a VPN connection is your only option. TFS is designed to work in low-bandwidth situations, such as VPN access, and provides acceptable performance when used in this scenario.

Advantages

- All TFS features work, including the TFS Proxy.
- This approach supports the use of Integrated Windows authentication and enables you to leverage existing enterprise infrastructure.
- If you already have a VPN set up, this is the easiest solution to adopt.

Disadvantages

- A VPN solution might not be set up for your infrastructure, or might not be available to your remote users.

For more information about creating a VPN, see *http://support.microsoft.com/kb/324747*.

Publishing TFS Through a Reverse Proxy

With this approach, you install a TFS server on your internal network and use the ISA Server Web publishing functionality to expose it to the external network. Remote users access TFS over SSL and use Basic authentication. This option will not work unless you have TFS SP1 installed.

Networks without a domain controller on the perimeter

Figure 17.2 shows architecture for exposing TFS over ISA with a domain controller on the internal network.

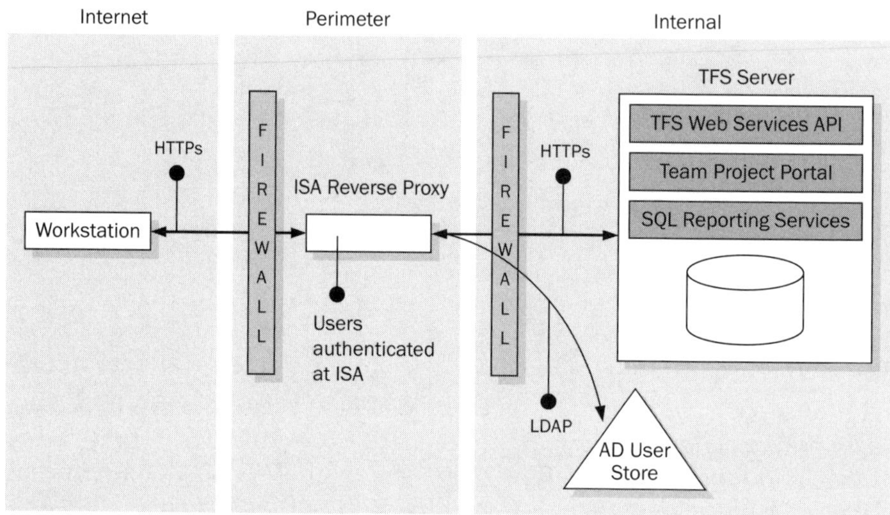

Figure 17.2 *TFS over ISA, Domain Controller on Internal Network Architecture*

If you do not have a domain controller on your perimeter network, you can open a port on the firewall to allow a Lightweight Directory Access Protocol (LDAP) connection from the ISA Server to your internal domain controller, specifically to authenticate external TFS users.

Networks with a domain controller on the perimeter

Figure 17.3 shows architecture for exposing TFS over ISA with a domain controller in the perimeter network.

If you do have a domain controller on your perimeter network, remote users can authenticate directly against the perimeter domain controller. One-way trust between the internal and perimeter domain controllers allows external users to access the TFS server. Internal users access the TFS server directly, using Integrated Windows authentication.

Advantages

- Reverse proxies, such as ISA Server, authenticate users and inspect traffic.
- Your remote users do not need access to the domain.
- Your remote users do not need VPN access.

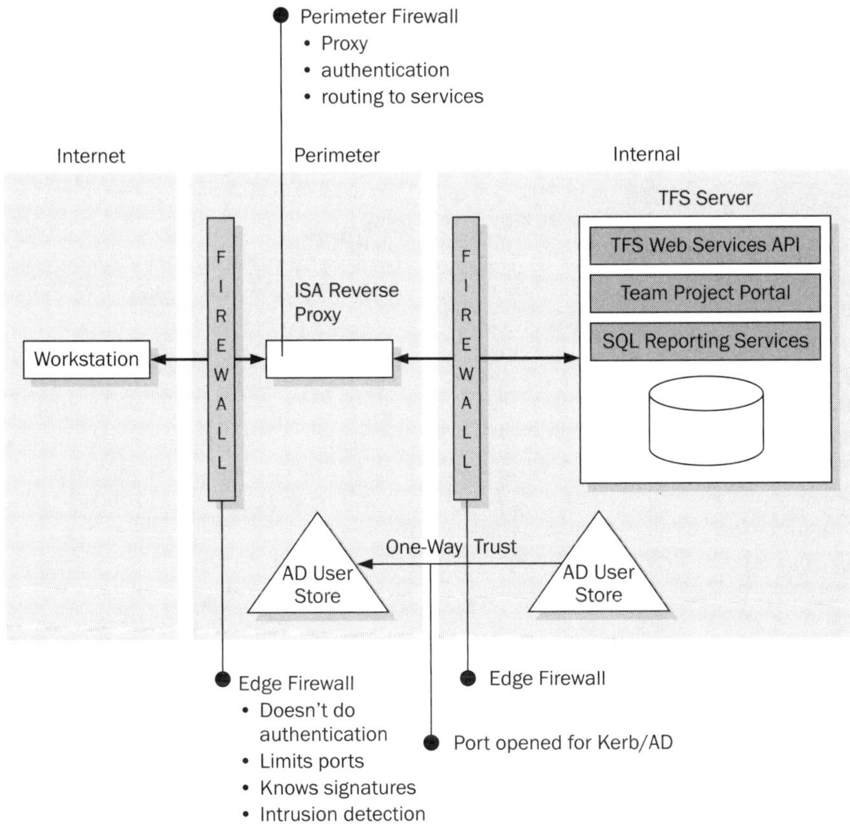

Figure 17.3 *TFS over ISA, Domain Controller on Perimeter Network Architecture*

Disadvantages

- You cannot use the TFS Proxy at the remote location.
- Your remote users cannot add users to TFS groups.
- Your remote users cannot add Microsoft Active Directory® groups to folders in source control.
- Your remote users will not be able to initiate or manage builds remotely.
- Your remote users cannot create new team projects.
- Your remote users cannot publish test results to your TFS.

Note: Whenever you use Basic authentication, use SSL. Basic authentication transmits credentials in clear text. Use SSL to protect this information.

Locating TFS in an Extranet ("Hosted Scenario")

Figure 17.4 shows architecture for hosting TFS in an extranet.

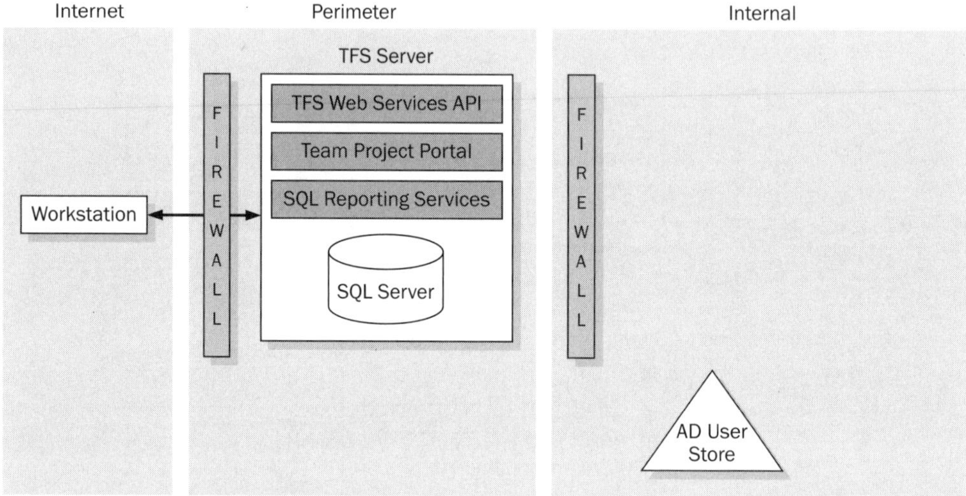

Figure 17.4 *TFS Hosted in an Extranet Architecture*

With this approach, you install your complete TFS infrastructure both application tier and data tier inside your perimeter network, off of your internal intranet. All connections to your TFS come over the Internet, whether they are from external or internal users. TFS can work with or without a domain controller (DC). If your perimeter network does not have access to a DC, the Active Directory service features of TFS will not work. For example, adding users to TFS groups, or adding an Active Directory group to folders in source control, will not work without a DC. This option will not work unless you have TFS SP1 installed.

Advantages

- Your TFS users are cleanly segregated from your internal network.
- Your remote users do not need access to the domain.

Disadvantages

- You cannot use the TFS Proxy at the remote location.
- Your remote users cannot initiate or manage builds.
- Your remote users cannot create new team projects.
- Your remote users cannot publish test results to the TFS.
- Internal users must connect to the extranet TFS over SSL just like external users.

Note: Whenever you use Basic authentication, use SSL. Basic authentication transmits credentials in clear text. Use SSL to protect this information.

Basic Authentication / SSL

If you are using TFS SP1 and want to support the extranet or reverse proxy scenario, you need to enable Basic authentication over SSL by configuring IIS on your TFS application tier. With Basic authentication, logon credentials are passed over the Internet using an unprotected Base64 encoded format. To protect your client's credentials, use only Basic authentication over a Secure HTTP (HTTPS) connection that uses SSL.

Use an Internet Server API (ISAPI) filter so that remote clients connect using Basic authentication over SSL, while local clients still connect using Integrated Windows authentication. The ISAPI filter looks for clients that you have configured as "external/Internet" and strips out NTLM authentication on the 401 response to force these clients to use other authentication methods, such as Basic authentication.

More information

- For more information about how to configure your TFS server to require Basic authentication and HTTPS over remote connections, see "Walkthrough: Setting up Team Foundation Server to Require HTTPS and Secure Sockets Layer (SSL)" at *http://msdn2.microsoft.com/en-us/library/aa833873(VS.80).aspx*
- For more information about setting up the ISAPI filter, see "Walkthrough: Setting up Team Foundation Server with Secure Sockets Layer (SSL) and an ISAPI Filter" at *http://msdn2.microsoft.com/en-us/library/aa833872(VS.80).aspx*
- For more information about ISAPI filters for TFS, see James Manning's blog post "The TFS extranet ISAPI filter mechanics" at *http://blogs.msdn.com/jmanning/archive/2006/10/27/the-tfs-quot-extranet-quot-isapi-filter-mechanics.aspx*

Team Foundation Server Proxy

Figure 17.5 on the next page shows architecture for the use of the Team Foundation Server Proxy.

The TFS Proxy is not required to enable remote access but is an optional cache for source control files. To help improve the performance that your remote team experiences, you can install a TFS Proxy in remote offices that connect to your TFS through a VPN. This improves performance by caching source control files on the remote office's proxy server. Whenever the remote client needs access to source code in the source control repository, it will request the source from the TFS Proxy. The proxy will then return a local version from its cache if it is available. If the source is not in the cache, the proxy will request the source from the remote TFS server. This reduces network traffic and improves source control responsiveness at the remote location.

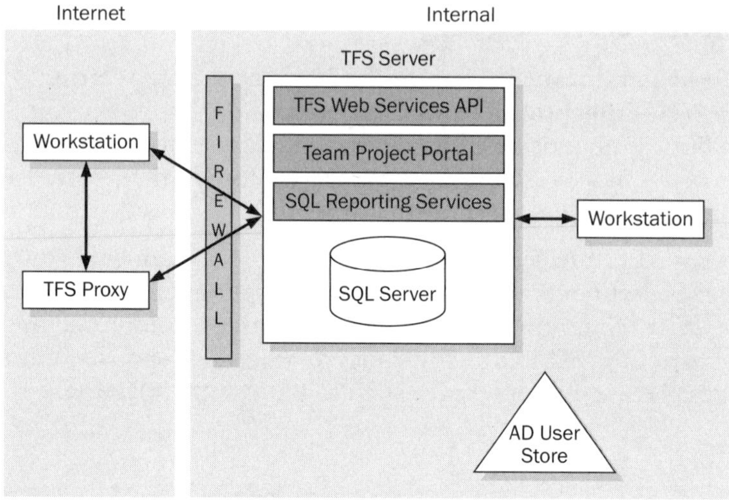

Figure 17.5 *TFS Proxy Architecture*

Tips to improve proxy performance

Consider the following recommendations for improving proxy performance:

- Ensure that caching is enabled, and monitor the performance of your cache. Monitor the performance counters (installed by default) and event logs (for errors and warnings) on your proxy server regularly, to see how your proxy is performing. Note that the TFS Proxy saves cache performance statistics to an Extensible Markup Language (XML) file named ProxyStatistics.xml, and that you can change the interval for saving these statistics. The ProxyStatistics.xml file is located in the App_Data folder in the proxy installation directory.
- Run a scheduled task regularly to retrieve the latest files to the proxy server. This helps to ensure that the latest versions of the files are available in the proxy cache, and that subsequent client requests for these files result in a cache hit.
- If you know that large files are going to be downloaded over a low-bandwidth (< 3 megabits per second [Mbps]) network, set the **executionTimeout** configuration to an appropriate value in Web.config. The default value is one hour <httpRuntime executionTimeout="3600"/>.
- If the proxy is going to be down for an extended time, disable the proxy on the clients to prevent fruitless reconnections. By default, reconnections are attempted every five minutes.

- Consider using workspace cloaking to hide specific workspaces from being viewed and to prevent unnecessary file transfers. Cloaking hides specified workspace folders from view, increases performance bandwidth, and conserves local disk space by preventing folders and files that you do not currently need from being copied to your local workspace. Although you can cloak an existing folder mapping in your workspace, a better approach is to create a new folder mapping that is specifically intended to be cloaked.

For more information about these performance optimization guidelines, see "Distributed / Remote Development" in "Guidelines: Source Control Guidelines" in this guide.

Mirrored Accounts

The TFS Proxy is supported in remote offices only over a VPN connection. However, if you have deployed your TFS using the extranet or reverse proxy scenario for a small remote team that requires the TFS Proxy, you can use mirrored accounts to enable the proxy.

To enable the proxy, you can use workgroup accounts with matching usernames and passwords on the TFS, the TFS Proxy, and each of the remote client computers. The fact that you need to maintain the exact username/password match for all users in three different locations increases administration time and restricts this workaround to small remote teams.

More information

- To learn more about the TFS Proxy, see "Team Foundation Server Proxy and Source Control" at *http://msdn2.microsoft.com/en-us/library/ms252490(VS.80).aspx*
- For more information about managing the TFS Proxy, see "Managing Remote Connections to TFS Proxy" at *http://msdn2.microsoft.com/en-us/library/ms253156(VS.80).aspx*
- For more information about troubleshooting the TFS Proxy, see "Troubleshooting TFS Server Proxy" at *http://msdn2.microsoft.com/en-us/library/ms400681(VS.80).aspx*

Remote Build Server

Figure 17.6 shows architecture for the use of a remote build server.

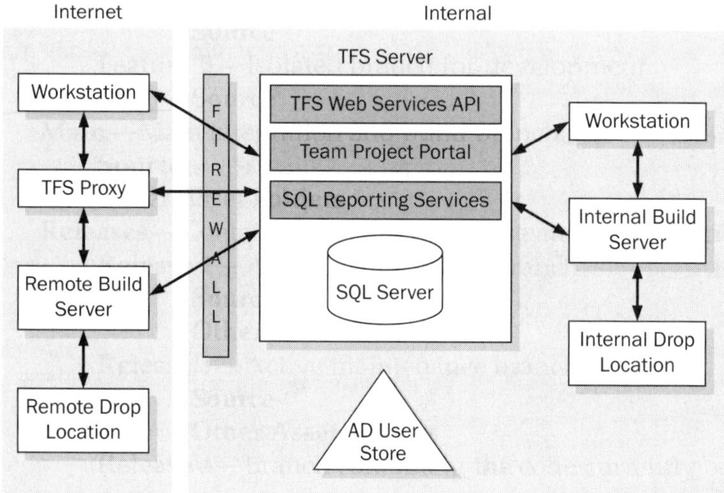

Figure 17.6 *Remote Build Server Architecture*

To improve remote team performance further, you can set up a build server in the remote office. If you have a TFS Proxy installed in the remote office, it will act like any other source control client and get code from the proxy before each build. A remote build server has the following advantages:

- Team builds from the remote team impact that team's build server, rather than increasing load on the internal build server.
- Remote builds provide binaries to the remote team, without the need to transmit the binaries over the network.

Don't use the remote build server as a complete replacement for builds generated on the internal build server. Even if the remote build is generated from the same source code version as the internal build, you might see different behavior because of build or source configuration differences between the servers. As a guideline, base important testing on the internal build, especially when you're nearing a release.

Note: The application tier communicates with the build server on port 9191. If you have a remote build server, set up your firewall so that the application tier can connect on this port.

Summary

If you are using TFS without SP1, use a VPN to provide remote access. If you are using TFS SP1, then you can use Basic authentication over SSL to locate your TFS in your extranet, or you can give access through a reverse proxy.

If you want to improve remote access performance, especially in the VPN scenario, you can install and configure the TFS Proxy to cache source control files in the remote location.

Additional Resources

- For more information about setting up TFS for remote development, see "Walkthrough: Setting up TFS for a Remote Development Location" at *http://msdn2.microsoft.com/en-us/library/ms242919(VS.80).aspx*
- For more information about setting up TFS with SSL, see "Walkthrough: Setting up Team Foundation Server with Secure Sockets Layer (SSL)" at *http://msdn2.microsoft.com/en-us/library/ms242875(VS.80).aspx*
- For more information about TFS Basic and Digest authentication, see "Team Foundation Server, Basic Authentication, and Digest Authentication" at *http://msdn2.microsoft.com/en-us/library/aa833874(VS.80).aspx*
- For more information about the TFS Proxy, see "Team Foundation Server Proxy and Source Control" at *http://msdn2.microsoft.com/en-us/library/ms252490(VS.80).aspx*
- For more information about managing the TFS Proxy, see "Managing Remote Connections to TFS Proxy" at *http://msdn2.microsoft.com/en-us/library/ms253156(VS.80).aspx*
- For more information about troubleshooting the TFS Proxy, see "Troubleshooting TFS Server Proxy" at *http://msdn2.microsoft.com/en-us/library/ms400681(VS.80).aspx*
- For more information about examining TFS Proxy performance, see *http://msdn2.microsoft.com/en-us/library/ms252455(VS.80).aspx*

Part IX

Visual Studio Team System 2008 Team Foundation Server

In this part:

18

What's New in Visual Studio Team System 2008 Team Foundation Server

Microsoft® Visual Studio® Team System 2008 Team Foundation Server introduces a number of new features and capabilities. The primary changes have been:

- **Administration, Operations & Setup.** Installation has been simplified to reduce setup time and improved to support more deployment scenarios.
- **Build.** Build includes Continuous Integration, scheduled builds, and build queuing solutions out of the box. Build management and extensibility has been simplified with more functionality available from the UI.
- **Version Control.** Version control includes much better support for offline work and has improved performance.
- **Work Item Tracking.** Work item tracking includes an improved query builder and improved support for work item attachments.

These product changes are listed and briefly described below, followed by a table explaining how the changes will impact the guidance in this guide. Use this chapter to aid in your Microsoft Visual Studio Team Foundation Server upgrade planning.

Administration, Operations & Setup

- **Simplified installation**—Installation is made easier and quicker compared to Visual Studio 2005 TFS. Improvements include the elimination of the separate data-tier installation as well as the elimination of the domain account requirement. Team Foundation Server 2008 supports built-in machine accounts (such as Network Service) wherever possible
- **Support for SharePoint 2007**—Adds support for SharePoint 2007 and Windows SharePoint Services 3.0. Team Foundation Server 2008 will support SharePoint on a separate server from the Team Foundation Application Tier Server.

- **Support for Windows Server 2008**—Supports the next version of Microsoft Windows Server™; for example Microsoft Windows Server 2008 and Internet Information Services (IIS) 7.0.
- **Support for X.509 Client Certificates**—Supports the use of X.509 client certificates to improve authentication security.
- **Large group synchronization**—Improves performance and robustness and will be able to support large numbers of users — approximately 30,000 or more users in a single instance of TFS.
- **Support for SQL named instances**—Allows sharing of a SQL Server between multiple TFS instances, or with other applications. This allows different instances of TFS to use the same installation of SQL Server 2005.
- **Support for non-default ports**—Improves configurability to support alternate Web sites and ports.

Build

- **Continuous Integration builds** — Supports the creation of build triggers that allows you to configure exactly when Continuous Integration builds should be started. For example, you can set a trigger so that every check-in starts a build, or you can set up a rolling build so that builds will start no more often than every X minutes.
- **Support for build queuing**—Supports build queuing and queue management. This is especially useful for Continuous Integration as multiple check-ins may queue up multiple builds.
- **Scheduled builds**—Supports scheduled builds, which can be configured to start at specified times based on your organization's requirements.
- **Drop management**—Supports drop management, which gives you the ability to set policies for when builds should be automatically deleted.
- **Specify build properties**—Allows you to specify what source and versions of source should be built along with other build properties for a build type. There are many more exposed properties for customizing a build. Additionally, MSBuild command-line parameters can be passed when queuing builds.
- **Extensibility of build targets**—Improves extensibility of the build targets. For example, you now have the ability to easily execute targets before and after each Visual Studio solution or project is built.
- **Build management** — Allows you to stop and delete builds from within Visual Studio.
- **Build configuration**—Simplifies the ability to specify what tests get run as part of a build.
- **Build project file location flexibility**—Provides the ability to store the MSBuild project file (and its associated rsp file) anywhere in the version control hierarchy instead of forcing the use of the **TeamBuildTypes** folder.

- **Support for GUI tests**—Allows running graphical user interface (GUI) tests as part of the build.
- **Check-in Policy**—Supports a new check-in policy, which prevents users from checking-in code when a Continuous Integration build is broken.
- **Managing build server**—Improves ability to manage multiple build machines.
- **Workspace mapping**—Build definition can be associated with a "real" workspace, meaning code from multiple team projects can be retrieved, client mappings can be specified, etc. Working folder mappings will be managed in the GUI instead of in workspacemapping.xml

Version Control

- **Annotate**—Supports an annotation feature that allows your developers to inspect a source code file and see line-by-line-level detail about who last changed each section of code.
- **Folder Diff**—Supports comparing of folders where the contents of the folder are recursively compared in order to identify files that differ. Folder Diff can compare local folders to local folders, local folders to server folders, and server folders to server folders.
- **Destroy**—Supports the Destroy feature with the ability to remove files and folders from the version control system. The destroyed files and folders cannot be recovered after they have been destroyed.
- **Get Latest On Checkout**—Includes an option for downloading the latest version of the file while checking it out.
- **Workspace wild card mappings**—Allows mapping of a folder or file under a cloaked folder and wildcard mappings so that you can map all files in a folder without mapping sub folders.
- **Performance improvements**—A variety of version control performance enhancements have been made, improving all aspects of version-control performance. Although the gains for smaller servers/projects (< 10,000 files) will be modest, the gains for larger projects (particularly where the file count approaches hundreds of thousands) will be substantial.
- **Team Foundation Server 2008 command line Help**—Supports the ability to get command line Help for the *tf* tool. You get the Help by running "*tf help*" and obtain Help for individual commands by running "*tf command /help*"
- **Offline improvements**—Improves the experience of going offline and has integrated the *tfpt* online capability into the Visual Studio Integrated Development Environment (IDE) for going back online.
- **Check-in override information captured**—Supports adding check-in policy overrides to the warehouse.

Work Item Tracking

- **Attachments improvements**—Supports drag-and-drop support for adding an attachment and allows multi-select for attaching files.
- **Query Builder**—Query Builder usability has improved in the following ways:
  - Drop-down filtering is now based on the current project
  - Improved MRU lists
  - Column drag-and-drop
  - SHIFT + click mouse-based multi-column sorting

Compatibility Issues with Visual Studio 2005 Team System

The Visual Studio 2008 Team Foundation Server client is able to work with a Visual Studio 2005 Team Foundation Server and a Visual Studio 2005 client is able to work with a Visual Studio 2008 Team Foundation Server, except for the following compatibility issues.

- **Visual Studio add-ins**—Client-side Visual Studio add-ins will need to be recompiled (or have their policy changed) because the Team Foundation Server Object Model (TFSOM) assembly versions will change and add-ins will need to bind to the new assemblies.
- **Team builds**—Most build operations—such as listing build definitions, starting and stopping builds and examining build reports will work with the combination of Visual Studio 2005 TFS and Visual Studio 2008 clients and server. The following are the known issues:
  - A Visual Studio 2008 Team Foundation Server instance will only work with a Visual Studio 2008 Team Foundation Server build server.
  - For a Visual Studio 2005 client to start a build on an Visual Studio 2008 Team Foundation Server instance, the build definition needs to be stored at $/<TeamProject>/TeamBuildTypes/<name>.
  - Changes made to properties in the tfsbuild.proj file that are in the database in Team Foundation Server 2008 will not be updated in the database and will no longer be in sync.
  - When working with the Continuous Integration feature in Team Foundation Server 2008, the Visual Studio 2005 client will be able to start a build, but it will not be able to queue a build, see the list of builds in the queue, see the list of build agents, etc.
  - A new build type cannot be created on a Visual Studio 2005 TFS server, using a Visual Studio 2008 Team Foundation Server client.
  - Parameters in the dialog for starting a build on Visual Studio 2005 Team Foundation Server cannot be changed when using a Visual Studio 2008 Team Foundation Server client.

Impact on the Guidance

Guidance for Visual Studio 2005 Team Foundation Server	Guidance for Visual Studio 2008 Team Foundation Server
Dual server deployment will support up to 2000 users.	You can use dual server deployment to support up to 30,000 users.
Users need correct domain accounts as part of deployment.	Domain accounts are no longer required, instead you can use the built in machine accounts, such as Network Service account.
Use a custom solution to create Continuous Integration builds.	You can use Visual Studio build triggers to create and configure Continuous Integration builds or Rolling builds.
Use automated tests as part of your build to measure the quality of the build.	It's easier to build test lists and specify what tests get run as part of a build step. It's possible to run GUI tests as part of your automated build tests.
Build types must be placed in a specific folder in order for them to be recognized by Team Build.	Build definition project files (tfsbuild.proj) can be stored anywhere in the version control hierarchy.
Use a custom solution to create Scheduled Builds.	You can create Visual Studio scheduled builds without the need for a custom solution.
There are a set of check-in policies available out-of-box.	A new check-in policy is available for broken CI builds. This prevents check-in of code while the CI build is broken.
Use the tool converter.exe to migrate from VSS to Team Foundation Server.	Use the Visual Studio toolkit for building conversion and mirroring solutions between Team Foundation Server and other source control systems – including VSS.
Use workspace mapping to define the set of files you want synchronized to your local machine.	Team Foundation Server 2008 now allows mapping of a folder or file under a cloaked folder, and wildcard mappings so that you can map all files in a folder without mapping sub-folders.
Use workspacemapping.xml file to modify workspace mapping.	The Team Foundation Server 2008 GUI is used to manage workspace mapping, workspacemapping.xml is no longer used.
Use the TFS Power Tool to work offline.	Use the Visual Studio IDE for working offline.
Getting the latest version of a file and checking it out for edit are two separate source control operations.	You can use an option, to automatically get the latest version of a file when you check it out for edit.

Guidance for Visual Studio 2005 Team Foundation Server	Guidance for Visual Studio 2008 Team Foundation Server
Customize pre-build steps to get dependencies when referencing project assemblies from a different team project	The build definition workspace template is managed in the VS GUI and has the full flexibility of a standard workspace, including mapping paths from multiple team projects.
Use the TFSBuild command line tool to delete builds.	Use the Visual Studio IDE to stop and delete builds.

Additional Resources

- For more information on Visual Studio 2008 Team Foundation Server, see "An Overview of Microsoft Visual Studio Code Name "Orcas" White Paper" at *http://go.microsoft.com/?linkid=6625887*

Guidelines: Team Build

Index

Strategy

- *Use a scheduled build to produce regular builds.*
- *Use a Continuous Integration (CI) build to get rapid feedback on check-ins.*
- *Use a rolling build if CI builds are adversely impacting build server performance.*
- *Use branching to reduce build breaks.*
- *Use check-in policies to improve check-in quality.*
- *Use build notification alerts to learn when the build has completed.*

Branching

- *Use new Team Build Types when creating a partial branch.*
- *Modify the paths to solutions in the TFSBuild.proj files, when creating a complete branch.*

Check-in Policies

- *Use check-in policies to improve check-in quality.*
- *Use check-in policies to associate work items with the build.*

Continuous Integration Builds

- *Use a CI build to get rapid feedback on check-ins.*
- *Use a rolling build if CI builds are adversely impacting build server performance.*
- *Ensure that the frequency of your rolling builds is less often than the build times.*

Customization

- *Use a custom post-build step to build an installer project.*
- *Use MS Build Toolkit Extras to build Microsoft .NET 1.1 applications.*
- *Use TFSBuild.proj to modify your build.*
- *Use a custom pre-build step to build a project that has dependencies to another team project.*

Deployment

- *On larger teams, install the build services on a separate server.*

Performance

- *Use incremental builds to improve performance.*
- *Avoid synchronizing redundant folders in your build.*
- *Use workspaces to avoid checking out unwanted files and projects when doing a Team Build.*
- *Consider using multiple build machines to improve performance.*

Projects

- *Avoid dependencies across team projects.*
- *Use project references instead of file references.*
- *Use Web Deployment Project for Web applications.*
- *Use a single-solution strategy if you are working on a small team project.*
- *Use a partitioned-solution strategy if you are working on a large team project with multiple independent sub-projects.*
- *Use a multiple-solution strategy if you are working on a very large team project that requires many dozens of independent sub-projects.*

Scheduled Builds

- *Use a scheduled build to produce regular builds.*

Test-Driven Development

- *Run code analysis on each build.*
- *Run automated tests on each build.*
- *Consider setting builds to fail when automated tests fail.*

Work Items

- *Use work items to track build breaks.*

Strategy

- **Use a scheduled build to produce regular builds.**
- **Use CI build to get rapid feedback on check-ins.**
- **Use a rolling build if CI builds are adversely impacting build server performance.**
- **Use branching to reduce build breaks.**
- **Use check-in policies to improve check-in quality.**
- **Use build notification alerts to learn when the build has completed.**

Use a Scheduled Build to Produce Regular Builds

Use a scheduled build to produce builds at regular, predictable intervals.

Generally, builds provided to your test team and to others need to be reliable and should be made available at a fixed time frequency, so that feedback on the build can be collected in a timely fashion.

The Team Build feature in Microsoft® Visual Studio® 2005 Team Foundation Server (TFS) does not support scheduled builds from the user interface. Instead, you can use the Microsoft Windows® Task Scheduler to run the TFSBuild command-line utility to start builds at a predetermined time.

► **To create a scheduled build**

1. Create a TFSBuild command line as follows:

   TfsBuild start <<TeamFoundationServer>> <<TeamProject>> <<BuildTypeName>>

2. Place the command line in a batch file.
3. Create a Windows Scheduled Task that runs the batch file at your desired interval.

Additional Resources

- For more information about setting up scheduled builds with Team Build, see Chapter 9, "Setting Up a Scheduled Build with Team Build" in this guide.
- For more information about setting up scheduled build with TFS, see "How To: Set Up a Scheduled Build in Visual Studio Team Foundation Server" in this guide.

Use a Continuous Integration Build to Get Rapid Feedback on Check-ins

You should use CI builds to provide your development team with rapid feedback on any breaking changes and on the quality of the build after each check-in. This helps the development team to fix the build issues quickly and can be used as a tool to improve the quality of your code.

Although Team Foundation Server 2005 does not provide a CI solution out of box, it does provide the framework for you to implement your own CI build solution.

For more information on setting up a CI build with TFS, see "How To: Set Up a Continuous Integration Build in Visual Studio Team Foundation Server." This How To article uses the solution provided by the Microsoft Visual Studio Team System (VSTS) development team. The solution installs a Web service that runs under an account that has access to the TFS server. Team Foundation Server is able to send an e-mail message or call a Web service when specific events occur. This event mechanism is used by the CI solution to register a Web service with the **CheckinEvent** event, so that whenever a check-in occurs, the Web service initiates a Team Build.

Additional Resources

- For more information, see Chapter 8, "Setting Up a Continuous Integration Build with Team Build" in this guide.
- For more information about setting up a CI build, see "How To: Set Up a Scheduled Build with Visual Studio Team Foundation Server" in this guide.
- For more information about how to use the VSTS CI solution, see "Continuous Integration Using Team Foundation Build" at *http://msdn2.microsoft.com/en-us/library/ms364045(VS.80).aspx*
- To download the VSTS CI solution MSI, go to *http://download.microsoft.com/download/6/5/e/65e300ce-22fc-4988-97de-0e81d3de2482/ci.msi*
- For more information about agile development and CI in TFS, see "Extend Team Foundation Server To Enable Continuous Integration" at *http://msdn.microsoft.com/msdnmag/issues/06/03/TeamSystem/default.aspx*

Use a Rolling Build if CI Builds Are Adversely Impacting Build Server Performance

Building immediately after every check-in is the simplest CI strategy and generally provides you with the most rapid feedback. However, if check-ins occurs rapidly enough to overwhelm your build server, you should use a rolling build approach where you build after a specified number of check-ins or after a specified time period. To decide if you need to use a rolling build, determine the following:

- Length of your Team Build in minutes
- Average frequency of check-ins in minutes
- Time window during which frequent check-ins occur

If the length of the build is longer than the average frequency of check-ins, your builds will run continuously because the first build will not complete before the next check-in occurs, which will start another build. If check-ins continue to occur before each build is complete, this impacts the performance of the build server and will block other builds (such as scheduled builds) from being started. Review the time window during which frequent check-ins occur and determine if CI builds will impact the delivery of scheduled builds or other important Team Builds.

Additional Resources

For more information, see Chapter 8, "Setting Up a Continuous Integration Build with Team Build" in this guide.

Use Branching to Reduce Build Breaks

To help avoid build breaks, you should use a **Development** branch for active development and a **Main** branch for your integration build.

The following is an example of what your branch structure might look like after you have created a **Development** branch:

- **Development**—Development Branch
  - **Source**
- **Main**—Integration Branch
  - **Source**
  - **Other Assets folders**

Keep the following recommendations in mind when working with a release branch:

- **When to branch.** If you are creating daily builds and are having problems with build stabilization and integration, you should create both a main and a development branch to ensure greater predictability of your daily builds. You may also want to consider more stringent check-in policies to improve check-in quality.
- **When not to branch.** If you are only creating CI builds, or your daily builds are already predictably stable, you might not need the extra overhead of an integration branch.
- **Permissions on branch:**
  - The **Main** branch permissions should be read/write for developers responsible for merging and integration, but read-only for everyone else.
  - The **Dev** branch permissions should be read/write for everyone.
- **Build frequency in branch:**
  - Daily builds on the **Main** branch.
  - CI builds on the **Dev** branch.
- **Testing focus on branch:**
  - Perform integration, performance, and security testing on the **Main** branch.
  - Perform feature and quick feedback testing on the **Dev** branch.

Use the **Main** branch as a staging area for integrating changes that have been checked into the development branch. Perform all active development in the **Dev** branch, and integrate non-breaking changes into the **Main** branch.

Additional Resources

- For more information on defining a branching and merging strategy, see Chapter 5, "Defining Your Branching and Merging Strategy" in this guide.
- For an introduction to branching and merging, see "Branching and Merging Primer" at *http://msdn2.microsoft.com/en-us/library/aa730834(VS.80).aspx*

- For more information about branching, see "How to: Branch Files and Folders" at *http://msdn2.microsoft.com/en-us/library/ms181425(VS.80).aspx*
- For more information about merging, see "How to: Merge Files and Folders" at *http://msdn2.microsoft.com/en-us/library/ms181428(VS.80).aspx*
- For additional descriptions of how to branch and merge in Visual Studio 2005, see "Branching and Merging Team Foundation Source Control" at *http://msdn2.microsoft.com/en-us/library/ms181423(VS.80).aspx*

Use Check-in Policies to Improve Check-in Quality

You should use a combination of code analysis and testing policies to improve check-in quality. For example, use the supplied testing policy to ensure that specific tests are executed and passed prior to allowing source to be checked into TFS source control. You can also configure a code analysis policy to help ensure that your code meets certain quality standards by ensuring that security, performance, portability, maintainability, and reliability rules are passed.

By enforcing this type of check-in policy in addition to policies that enforce coding standards and guidelines, you can test your code against specific code quality issues.

To enforce a code analysis check-in policy for a team project, you right-click your team project in **Team Explorer**, point to **Team Project Settings**, and then click **Source Control**. Click the **Check-in Policy** tab, click **Add**, and then select and configure the appropriate policy.

Additional Resources

- For more information about creating and using a custom check-in policy, see "How To: Step Through Creating Custom Check-in Policies for TFS" in this guide.
- To learn how to customize a check-in policy, see "Walkthrough: Customizing Check-in Policies and Notes" at *http://msdn2.microsoft.com/en-us/library/ms181281(VS.80).aspx*
- To see sample code that will disallow selected patterns on check-in, see "Checkin Policy to Disallow Certain Patterns" at *http://blogs.msdn.com/jmanning/archive/2006/02/02/523125.aspx*
- To see sample code that will enforce comments on check-in, see "Sample Checkin Policy: Make Sure the Comment Isn't Empty" at *http://blogs.msdn.com/jmanning/archive/2006/01/21/515858.aspx*
- To learn how to register a new check-in policy, see "I've Made a New Check-In Policy! How Do I Add It?" at *http://blogs.msdn.com/jmanning/archive/2006/02/07/526778.aspx*

Use Build Notification Alerts to Learn When the Build Has Completed

To keep track of your build process, you can create alerts that send e-mail messages to you or to others when a build has completed.

This is important because it provides quick turnaround among teams. For example, if the test team is notified by e-mail of a completed build, they can start their test pass without having to wait for manual instructions.

Additional Resources

- For more information about build notifications, see "How to: Receive Build Notification E-Mail" at *http://msdn2.microsoft.com/en-us/library/ms181725(VS.80).aspx*
- For further information about build notifications, see "How to: Add or Edit Alerts" at *http://msdn2.microsoft.com/en-us/library/ms181335(VS.80).aspx*

Branching

- **Use new Team Build Types when creating a partial branch.**
- **Modify the paths to solutions in the TFSBuild.proj files, when creating a complete branch.**

Use New Team Build Types When Creating a Partial Branch

When you create a branch that contains a subset of the solutions in your team project, you might need to create new build types in order to build successfully.

There are two types of partial branches:

1. **A partial branch that does not include branching of any build types.** This would occur within a team project, and would simply branch solution and source files but would not branch any of the TeamBuildTypes folders into new folders.
2. **A partial branch that includes branching of build types.** This would occur within a team project, and would branch some of the TeamBuildTypes subfolders (that is, build types) in addition to other folders containing the relevant solution and source files.

If you create a partial branch that does not include Team Build Types all of the existing Team Builds will continue to work, but you will need to create a new Team Build Type if you want to build the branch. Create new build types by using the Team Build Wizard in order to build the code in the new branch. These new build types will point to the new branch location and may also point to the parent location for any solutions that must be included in the build but that were not branched.

If you create a partial branch that includes Team Build Types, the build types that are copied over with the branch will point to the original, parent branch locations and therefore will not allow you to build the new branch. Modify the branched build types so that they point to the new branched code locations.

Additional Resources

- For more information about how to update your build type, see "How to: Update Build Types on Branched Team Projects" at *http://msdn2.microsoft.com/en-us/library/ms252500(VS.80).aspx*

Modify the Paths to Solutions in the TFSBuild.proj Files, When Creating a Complete Branch

When you create a new branch, including the Team Build Types, the paths in the build types still point to the previous location. In order for the build to work on the new branch, you must update the paths in the build type project files so that they reference the new path locations created after the branching operation.

When you create a full branch, you also branch the build types. The build types contain references to folders from the original source control tree. To have these build types refer to the branch folders, you must edit the folder references in these files.

To perform the update, check out the build types from the branch you want to modify, apply the updates, and then commit the changes to the branch.

Additional Resources

- For more information about how to update your build types, see "How to: Update Build Types on Branched Team Projects" at *http://msdn2.microsoft.com/en-us/library/ms252500(VS.80).aspx*

Check-in Policies

- **Use check-in policies to improve check-in quality.**
- **Use check-in policies to associate work items with the build.**

Use Check-in Policies to Improve Check-in Quality

Use a combination of code analysis and testing policies to improve check-in quality. For example, use the supplied testing policy to ensure that specific tests are executed and passed prior to allowing source to be checked into TFS source control. You can also configure a code analysis policy to help ensure that your code meets certain quality standards by ensuring that security, performance, portability, maintainability, and reliability rules are passed.

By enforcing this type of check-in policy in addition to policies that enforce coding standards and guidelines, you can test your code against specific code quality issues.

Additional Resources

- For more information about creating and using a custom check-in policy, see "How To: Step Through Creating Custom Check-in Policies for TFS" in this guide.
- To learn how to customize a check-in policy, see "Walkthrough: Customizing Check-in Policies and Notes" at *http://msdn2.microsoft.com/en-us/library/ms181281(VS.80).aspx*
- To see sample code that will disallow selected patterns on check-in, see "Check-in Policy to Disallow Certain Patterns" at *http://blogs.msdn.com/jmanning/archive/2006/02/02/523125.aspx*
- To see sample code that will enforce comments on check-in, see "Sample Check-in Policy: Make Sure the Comment Isn't Empty" at *http://blogs.msdn.com/jmanning/archive/2006/01/21/515858.aspx*
- To learn how to register a new check-in policy, see "I've Made a New Check-In Policy! How Do I Add It?" at *http://blogs.msdn.com/jmanning/archive/2006/02/07/526778.aspx*

Use Check-in Policies to Associate Work Items with the Build

Set the Work Items check-in policy to force developers to associate their check-in with a work item.

If a build breaks, it is important that you know what change sets are associated with this build and what work items those change sets are associated with. With this knowledge, you can identify the developer responsible for checking in the changed code and the area of the project on which he or she is working.

For a build to be associated with a set of completed work items, each check-in must be associated with a work item. These check-ins are represented as change sets associated with the build, and it is possible to trace from build to change set to work item.

Additional Resources

- For more information about creating and using a custom check-in policy, see "How To: Step Through Creating Custom Check-in Policies for TFS" in this guide.
- To learn how to customize a check-in policy, see "Walkthrough: Customizing Check-in Policies and Notes" at *http://msdn2.microsoft.com/en-us/library/ms181281(VS.80).aspx*

Continuous Integration Builds

- **Use a CI build to get rapid feedback on check-ins.**
- **Use a rolling build if CI builds are adversely impacting build server performance.**
- **Ensure that the frequency of your rolling builds is less often than the build times.**

Use a CI Build to Get Rapid Feedback on Check-ins

You should use Continuous Integration builds to provide your development team with rapid feedback on any breaking changes and quality of the build after each check-in. This helps the development team to fix the build issues in a timely manner and can be used as a tool to improve the quality of your code.

Although Visual Studio 2005 Team Foundation Server does not provide a CI solution out of the box, it does provide the framework for you to implement your own CI build solution.

For more information on setting up a CI build with TFS, see "How To: Set Up a Continuous Integration Build in Visual Studio Team Foundation Server." This How To article uses the solution provided by the VSTS development team. The solution installs a Web service that runs under an account that has access to the TFS server. Team Foundation Server is able to send an e-mail message or call a Web service when specific events occur. This event mechanism is used by the CI solution to register a Web service with the **CheckinEvent** event, so that whenever a check-in occurs, the Web service initiates a Team Build.

Additional Resources

- For more information about CI builds, see Chapter 8, "Setting Up a Continuous Integration Build with Team Build" in this guide.
- For more information about setting up a CI build, see "How To: Set Up a Continuous Integration Build with Visual Studio Team Foundation Server" in this guide.
- For more information about how to use the VSTS CI solution, see "Continuous Integration Using Team Foundation Build" at *http://msdn2.microsoft.com/en-us/library/ms364045(VS.80).aspx*
- To download the Visual Studio Team System CI solution MSI, go to *http://download.microsoft.com/download/6/5/e/65e300ce-22fc-4988-97de-0e81d3de2482/ci.msi*
- For more information about agile development and CI in TFS, see "Extend Team Foundation Server to Enable Continuous Integration" at *http://msdn.microsoft.com/msdnmag/issues/06/03/TeamSystem/default.aspx*

Use a Rolling Build if CI Builds Are Adversely Impacting Build Server Performance

Building immediately after every check-in is the simplest CI strategy and will generally give you the most rapid feedback. However, if check-ins occurs rapidly enough to overwhelm your build server, you should use a rolling build approach where you build after a specified number of check-ins or after a specified time period. To decide if you need to use a rolling build, determine the following:

- Length of your Team Build in minutes
- Average frequency of check-ins in minutes
- Time window during which frequent check-ins occur

If the length of the build is longer than the average frequency of check-ins, your builds will run continuously because the first build will not complete before the next check-in occurs, which will start another build. If check-ins continue to occur before each build is complete, it will impact the performance of your build server and will delay other builds, such as scheduled builds. Review the time window during which frequent check-ins occur and determine if CI builds will impact the delivery of scheduled builds or other important Team Builds.

Additional Resources

- For more information about setting up CI builds, see Chapter 8, "Setting Up an Continuous Integration Build with Team Build" in this guide.

Ensure That the Frequency of Your Rolling Builds Is Less Often than the Build Times

It is important to determine the rolling build time interval to ensure an efficient build process. If the frequency of the rolling build is less than the time it takes to complete a build, it ensures that your build machine will be available for other build types between your rolling build intervals.

To determine the ideal rolling build interval, divide the average frequency of check-ins by the length of your build. For instance, if you have a build that takes 10 minutes and you average a check-in every 5 minutes, you could set a check-in interval of two check-ins and a timeout period of 10 minutes. This would help ensure that the build is complete before the next build kicks off. If you notice excessive load on your build server, you can increase these values.

Additional Resources

- For more information about CI builds, see Chapter 8, "Setting Up a Continuous Integration Build with Team Build" in this guide.

Customization

- **Use a custom post-build step to build an installer project.**
- **Use MS Build Toolkit Extras to build Microsoft .NET 1.1 applications.**
- **Use TFSBuild.proj to modify your build.**
- **Use a custom pre-build step to build a project that has dependencies to another team project.**

Use a Custom Post-Build Step to Build an Installer Project

Because Team Build does not support setup projects by default, you should use a custom post-build step to compile the setup project and copy the binaries to the build drop location.

Additional Resources

- For more information, see "Walkthrough: Configuring Team Foundation Build to Build a Visual Studio Setup Project" at *http://msdn2.microsoft.com/en-us/library/ms404859(VS.80).aspx*

Use MS Build Toolkit Extras to Build Microsoft .NET 1.1 Applications

Team Build does not support .NET 1.1 applications by default. The MSBuild Extras – Toolkit for .NET 1.1 (MSBee) allows .NET 1.1 builds but requires that your projects and solutions be upgraded to Visual Studio 2005. If you cannot upgrade to Visual Studio 2005 projects and solutions, you can use a custom post-build step to compile the .NET 1.1 applications.

Additional Resources

- To download MSBee, go to *http://www.codeplex.com/MSBee*
- For more information about creating a custom post-build step to compile a .NET 1.1 application, see Nagaraju's blog entry at *http://blogs.msdn.com/nagarajp/archive/2005/10/26/485368.aspx*

Use TFSBuild.proj to Modify Your Build

To modify information about the build—such as the build server, drops location, or build directory—you edit the TFSBuild.proj file.

The TFSBuild.proj file contains much of the information needed to execute a Team Build. This information includes the build locations and whether the build should perform static code analysis and unit tests. To modify the build, you edit the TFS-Build.proj file.

To edit the TFSBuild.proj file

1. Check out the file from source control.
2. Update the build information in the file.
3. Check the file back in, committing the changes.

The next time the build is executed, it will use the amended build data.

Additional Resources

- For more information about customizing Team Foundation Build, see "Customizing Team Foundation Build" at *http://msdn2.microsoft.com/en-us/library/ms400688(VS.80).aspx*

Use a Custom Pre-build Step to Build a Project That Has Dependencies to Another Team Project

Team Build does not support building solutions that cross team projects. To enable this, you must customize the TFSBuild.proj file to check out the code you need from the other projects on which your build depends.

Additional Resources

- For more information, see "Working with multiple team projects in Team Build" at *http://blogs.msdn.com/manishagarwal/archive/2005/12/22/506635.aspx*
- For more information about customizing Team Foundation Build, see "Customizing Team Foundation Build" at *http://msdn2.microsoft.com/en-us/library/ms400688(VS.80).aspx*

Deployment

- **On larger teams, install the build services on a separate server.**

On Larger Teams, Install the Build Services on a Separate Server

Large Team Builds can take a long time and use up significant server resources. If you run your builds on your Team TFS server, this impacts the reliability, performance, and scalability of the server.

To improve the performance of your build and reduce load on your application tier, it is recommended that you run builds on a dedicated build server.

Additional Resources

- To download the Team Foundation Installation Guide, or for more information about installing TFS and Team Build, go to *http://www.microsoft.com/downloads/details.aspx?FamilyId=E54BF6FF-026B-43A4-ADE4-A690388F310E&displaylang=en*

Performance

- **Use incremental builds to improve performance.**
- **Avoid synchronizing redundant folders in your build.**
- **Use workspaces to avoid checking out unwanted files and projects when doing a Team Build.**
- **Consider using multiple build machines to improve performance.**

Use Incremental Builds to Improve Performance

By default, Team Build cleans out the directory it uses to perform the build before it checks out the complete source code tree needed for the build. Team Build also removes and re-initializes the workspace used to check out the sources for the build. To improve performance, you can set Team Build to only get sources that have changed since the last Team Build.

If the amount of source needed for a build is large and the build server is remote from the TFS server, the source code checkout could take a long time to execute. In such a case, you should consider using an incremental build. To perform the incremental build, you need to set several values in your TFSBuild.proj file should be true. You need to:

- Stop Team Build from cleaning the local build folder and sources folder.
- Stop Team Build from re-creating the workspace used for the build.
- Configure the Team Build to only get the changed sources from source control.

► **To perform an incremental build**

1. Create a new build type to represent the incremental build.
2. Check out for edit the TFSBuild.proj file associated with the incremental build type you just created.
3. Add the following <PropertyGroup> section just before the closing </project> element in TFSBuild.proj:

```
<PropertyGroup>
    <SkipClean>true</SkipClean>
    <SkipInitializeWorkspace>true</SkipInitializeWorkspace>
    <ForceGet>false</ForceGet>
</ PropertyGroup>
```

These settings accomplish the following:

- **SkipClean.** Setting **SkipClean** to **true** ensures that the build will not clean out the local build and sources folder.
- **SkipInitializeWorkspace.** Setting **SkipInitializeWorkspace** to **true** ensures that the build will leave the existing workspace in-place for the build machine.
- **ForceGet.** Setting **ForceGet** to **false** ensures that the build will only get updated source, rather than getting all source for the workspace.

Additional Resources

- For more information, see "Practices at a Glance: Team Build" in this guide.
- For more information about configuring an incremental build, see "How to: Configure Team Foundation Build for an Incremental Build" at *http://msdn2.microsoft.com/en-us/library/aa833876(VS.80).aspx*

Avoid Synchronizing Redundant Folders in Your Build

You should scale down your workspace mapping or cloak folders that are not needed as part of the build.

When you execute a Team Build, the server retrieves all of the files it needs from source control. The files that are retrieved are defined by the workspace that is used to create the Team Build Type. Some of the files that are mapped into the workspace may not be needed. You can change your workspace definition to reduce the folders included, or you can cloak unnecessary files so that they are not retrieved as part of the build.

For example, the default mapping for a new project is $/TeamProject. If all your source files are under $/TeamProject/foo/bar/foobar/sources, you should map only that directory.

To cloak files beneath your workspace mapping, you can edit the WorkspaceMapping.xml file that is created when the Team Build Type is created and is used to define the folders that are retrieved when performing the build. You can cloak files and folders that are not needed as part of the build. Folder cloaking is preferred because individual file cloaking can introduce maintenance overhead.

► **To cloak folders**

1. Check out WorkspaceMapping.xml from source control.
2. Add the appropriate cloak entries to this file.
3. Check in WorkspaceMapping.xml.

The following example ensures that the documentation folder will not be retrieved from source control during a Team Build:

```
<Mappings>
  <InternalMapping ServerItem="$/MyTeamProject" LocalItem="c:\projects\teampro-
ject" Type="Map" />
  <InternalMapping ServerItem="$/MyTeamProject/documentation" Type="Cloak" />
</Mappings>
```

Additional Resources

- For more information about cloaking folders in a workspace, see "How To: Cloak and Decloak Folders in a Workspace" at *http://msdn2.microsoft.com/en-us/library/ms181378(VS.80).aspx*

- For more information about making Team Build ignore folders, see "How to make 'Team Build' skip getting certain folders?" at *http://blogs.msdn.com/manishagarwal/archive/2005/10/13/480584.aspx*
- For more information about the WorkspaceMapping schema, see "Schema for the WorkspaceMapping.xml file" at *http://blogs.msdn.com/buckh/archive/2007/02/28/schema-for-the-workspacemapping xml-file.aspx*

Use Workspaces to Avoid Checking Out Unwanted Files and Projects When Doing a Team Build

Team Build checks out your sources in order to execute the build. If you have a large source tree for a project, checking out the sources can be very time-consuming. If you are only building part of the team project, you should ensure that only the necessary sources are checked out.

If you have a large team project, it will contain multiple Visual Studio solutions, each of which is used to build a separate part of the team project. When you create a Team Build Type, you specify the solution that Team Build will use. If you specify a solution file without specifying a workspace, Team Build will check out all of the sources in the team project before performing a build.

To check out only the sources you need, you must first define a workspace. Before creating the Team Build Type, you first define a workspace and only map the solution you want to build to that workspace. When you define the Team Build Type, select the workspace you have defined and then select the solution. In this way, only the sources defined in that workspace will be checked out.

Additional Resources

- For more information about creating a Team Build Type, see "Walkthrough: Creating a Build Type in Team Foundation Build" at *http://msdn2.microsoft.com/en-us/library/ms181286(VS.80).aspx*
- For more information about why Team Build checks out all the source code in a workspace, see "Why does Team Build sync all sources in spite of my selecting only a subset of solutions?" at *http://blogs.msdn.com/anutthara/archive/2005/12/07/500923.aspx*

Consider Using Multiple Build Machines to Improve Performance

If you have multiple build types all executing on a single build server, the server could become overwhelmed. In such a situation, you should consider executing different build types on different build servers.

A build can take a long time to execute, especially if the build is for a large project. If you are using CI or frequent scheduled builds, the build server might not be able to keep up with the volume of builds being generated.

You can install multiple build servers to distribute the load among different servers. Assign different build types to each server to even out the build load.

Additional Resources

- For more information, see Chapter 7, "Team Build Explained" in this guide.

Projects

- **Avoid dependencies across team projects.**
- **Use project references instead of file references.**
- **Use Web Deployment Project for Web applications.**
- **Use a single-solution strategy if you are working on a small team project.**
- **Use a partitioned-solution strategy if you are working on a large team project with multiple independent sub-projects.**
- **Use a multiple-solution strategy if you are working on a very large team project that requires many dozens of independent sub-projects.**

Avoid Dependencies Across Team Projects

In general, you should avoid dependencies that cross team projects and instead try to keep all related/dependent solutions/projects under same team project. This reduces the need for build script customization. If you have a dependency, use project references to define it, or branch the dependency from a shared project into your project. You should avoid file references because they are more difficult to manage.

Additional Resources

- For more information about creating a workspace, see "How to: Create a Workspace" at *http://msdn2.microsoft.com/en-us/library/ms181384(VS.80).aspx*
- For more information about editing a workspace, see "How to: Edit a Workspace" at *http://msdn2.microsoft.com/en-us/library/ms245466(VS.80).aspx*
- For more information about branching, see "How to: Branch Files and Folders" at *http://msdn2.microsoft.com/en-us/library/ms181425(VS.80).aspx*

Use Project References Instead of File References

If you need to reference another assembly in the same Visual Studio solution, you should use a Visual Studio project reference. By using project references, you enable Visual Studio to do a few things automatically for you, such as keeping build configuration synchronized (debug/release) and tracking versioning and rebuilding of components as necessary when assembly versions change.

Additional Resources

- For more information about project references, see "Project References" at *http://msdn2.microsoft.com/en-us/library/ez524kew(VS.80).aspx*

Use Web Deployment Project for Web Applications

Web deployment projects are associated with a Visual Studio Web Site project or Web Application project. They allow you to manage build settings as well as a variety of other settings common to ASP.NET Web applications. For instance, the deployment project gives you easy access to Web.config, connection strings, and virtual directories, and allows you to more easily deploy the compiled Web application to the hosting server.

Additional Resources

- For more information, see "Visual Studio 2005 Web Deployment Projects" at *http://msdn2.microsoft.com/en-us/asp.net/aa336619.aspx*

Use a Single-Solution Strategy if You Are Working on a Small Team Project

If you work on a small team, consider using a single Visual Studio solution to contain all of your projects. This structure simplifies development because all of the code is available when you open the solution. This strategy also makes it easy to set up references, because all references are between projects in your solution. You may still need to use file references to reference third-party assemblies, such as purchased components, that are outside your solution.

Additional Resources

- For more information, see Chapter 3, "Structuring Projects and Solutions in Source Control" in this guide.

Use a Partitioned-Solution Strategy if You Are Working on a Large Team Project with Multiple Independent Sub-Projects

If you work on a large team, consider using multiple solutions, each representing a subsystem in your application. Developers can use these solutions to work on smaller parts of the system without having to load all code across all projects. You should design your solution structure so that any projects that have dependencies are grouped together. This enables you to use project references rather than file references. Consider creating a master solution file that contains all of the projects, if you want to use this to build the entire application.

Note: If you are building with Team Build (which relies upon MSBuild), it is possible to create solution structures that do not include all referenced projects. As long as the entire solution has been built first, generating the binary output from each solution, MSBuild will be able to follow project references outside the bounds of your solution and build successfully. Solutions created in this way will not build from the Visual Studio build command, but will only work with Team Build and MSBuild.

Additional Resources

- For more information, see Chapter 3, "Structuring Projects and Solutions in Source Control" in this guide.

Use a Multiple-Solution Strategy if You Are Working on a Very Large Team Project That Requires Many Dozens of Independent Sub-Projects

If you work on a very large solution requiring many dozens of projects, you may run up against solution scalability limits. In this scenario, break your application into multiple solutions but do not create a master solution for the entire application because all references inside each solution are project references. References to projects outside of each solution (for example, to third-party libraries or projects in another sub-solution) are file references. This means that there can be no "master" solution. Instead, a script must be used that understands the order in which the solutions must be built. One of the maintenance tasks associated with a multiple-solution structure is ensuring that developers do not inadvertently create circular references between solutions. This structure requires complex build scripts and explicit mapping of dependency relationships. In this structure, it is not possible to build the application in its entirety within Visual Studio. Instead, you can use TFS Team Build or MSBuild directly.

Additional Resources

- For more information, see Chapter 3, "Structuring Projects and Solutions in Source Control" in this guide.

Scheduled Builds

- **Use a scheduled build to produce regular builds.**

Use a Scheduled Build to Produce Regular Builds

You should use a scheduled build to produce builds at regular, predictable intervals.

In general, builds provided to test teams and others need to be reliable and should be made available at a fixed time frequency, so that feedback on the build can be collected in a timely fashion.

Although the Team Build feature in TFS does not support scheduled builds from the user interface, you can use the Microsoft Windows Task Scheduler to run the TFS-Build command utility to start builds at a predetermined time.

► To create a scheduled build

1. Create a TFSBuild command line as follows:

   ```
   TfsBuild start <<TeamFoundationServer>> <<TeamProject>> <<BuildTypeName>>
   ```
2. Place the command line in a batch file.
3. Create a Windows Scheduled Task that runs the batch file at your desired interval.

Additional Resources

- For more information, see Chapter 9, "Setting Up Scheduled Build with Team Build" in this guide.
- For more information about setting up scheduled build, see "How To: Set Up a Scheduled Build with Visual Studio Team Foundation Server" in this guide.

Test-Driven Development

- **Run code analysis on each build.**
- **Run automated tests on each build.**
- **Consider setting builds to fail when automated tests fail.**

Run Code Analysis on Each Build

Use code analysis as part of the build to improve build quality. You can configure a code analysis step in the build to help ensure that your code meets certain quality standards, ensuring that security, performance, portability, maintainability, and reliability rules are passed.

To turn on code analysis for a build type, you can either select the **code analysis** check box in the Team Build Type wizard when you create the new Team Build Type, or you can modify the TFSBuild.proj file after the build type has been created.

► To enable code analysis in the TFSBuild.proj file

- If you want all projects to run code analysis, regardless of project settings, change the **<RunCodeAnalysis>** tag to **Always**.
- If you want to run code analysis on each project based on project settings, change the **<RunCodeAnalysis>** tag to **Default**.

Additional Resources

- For more information about automatic code analysis as part of a build, see "How To: Automatically Run Code Analysis with Team Build in Visual Studio Team Foundation Server" in this guide.

- For more information about code analysis tools, see "Guidelines for Using Code Analysis Tools" at *http://msdn2.microsoft.com/en-us/library/ms182023(VS.80).aspx*

Run Automated Tests on Each Build

Run automated tests to automatically gain feedback on build quality after every build. In order to create a test list to associate with the build you must have either Visual Studio Test Edition or Visual Studio Team Suite installed. In order to run automated tests on the build server you must have either Visual Studio Developer Edition, Visual Studio Test Edition, or Visual Studio Team Suite installed on the build server.

► To run automated tests as part of the Team Build process

1. Create one or more automated tests that you want to run with the build.
2. Use the Test Manager to create a Test List.
3. Use the Test Manager to group tests into the new Test List by dragging and dropping the tests from the Test View to the Test List in the Test Manager.
4. Create a new Team Build Type.
5. Select the check box to run automated tests.
6. Select the test project within which your tests and test list were created.
7. Select the test list you want to run.

Additional Resources

- For more information about automatically running build verification tests, see "How to: Configure and Run Build Verification Tests (BVTs)" at *http://msdn2.microsoft.com/en-us/library/ms182465(VS.80).aspx*
- For more information about how to run automated build tests without Visual Studio Test Edition or a VSMDI file, see "How to run tests in a build without test metadata files and test lists (.vsmdi files)" at *http://blogs.msdn.com/buckh/archive/2006/11/04/how-to-run-tests-without-test-metadata-files-and-test-lists-vsmdi-files.aspx*

Consider Setting Builds to Fail When Automated Tests Fail

When a build fails because of compilation errors, a work item is created to track the failure and the build is marked as failed. When an automated test fails, however, the build does not fail. The test failure is converted into a warning and the build continues.

You may want to fail the build if an associated automated test fails. You may also want to generate a work item automatically to track the test failure.

► To fail the build upon test failure

1. Open the Microsoft.TeamFoundation.Build.targets file from Program Files\MSBuild\Microsoft\VisualStudio\v8.0\TeamBuild.
2. Check out for edit and open the TFSBuild.proj file for the Team Build Type you want to have failed upon test failure.
3. Copy the **RunTestWithConfiguration** target from Microsoft.TeamFoundation.Build.targets to the end of the TFSBuild.proj file, just before the closing **</Project>** tag.
4. Modify the **ContinueOnError** attribute from **true** to **false**.

> **Note:** There will be two test tool tasks. Modify the end-to-end task in order to only modify the behavior of builds on the build server. The desktop build task is used when building on a developer's desktop.

5. If you want to create a work item when the build fails, modify the **RunTestWithConfiguration** by adding an **OnError** element just before the closing **</Target>** tag The **OnError** element should look like the following:

```
<OnError ExecuteTargets="CreateWorkItem;"/>
```

Alternatively, if you want all Team Build Types to fail upon test failure, you can modify Microsoft.TeamFoundation.Build.targets directly. This change will modify behavior for all Team Build Types.

The solution recommended above is straightforward to implement but is not guaranteed to continue working for future versions of Visual Studio. If you would like to implement a solution that is guaranteed to continue working after upgrade, see Aaron Hallberg's blog entry, "Determining Whether Tests Passed in Team Build," at *http://blogs.msdn.com/aaronhallberg/archive/2006/09/21/determining-whether-tests-passed-in-team-build.aspx*

Additional Resources

- For more information about setting up a build to create a work item upon test failure, see "Create Workitems for Test Failures in TeamBuild" at *http://blogs.msdn.com/nagarajp/archive/2005/10/14/481290.aspx*
- For more information about a solution that is guaranteed to continue working after a Visual Studio upgrade, see "Determining Whether Tests Passed in Team Build" at *http://blogs.msdn.com/aaronhallberg/archive/2006/09/21/determining-whether-tests-passed-in-team-build.aspx*

Work Items

- **Use work items to track build breaks.**

Use Work Items to Track Build Breaks

If Team Build fails, it automatically creates a work item to track that failure. By default, the work item will be assigned to 'Active' and the title will inform you that there has been a build failure. You should assign this work item to the responsible developer or build manager in order to fix the build and resolve the problem.

The build task in TFSBuild.proj that defines this work item looks like the following:

```
<!-- Create WorkItem for build failure -->
    <CreateNewWorkItem
          BuildId="$(BuildNumber)"
          Description="$(WorkItemDescription)"
          TeamProject="$(TeamProject)"
          TeamFoundationServerUrl="$(TeamFoundationServerUrl)"
          Title="$(WorkItemTitle)"
          WorkItemFieldValues="$(WorkItemFieldValues)"
          WorkItemType="$(WorkItemType)"
          ContinueOnError="true" />
```

If you would like to customize the work item that is created (for instance, to assign it to a specific developer or to set severity and priority), you can modify the WorkItem-FieldValues field.

Additional Resources

- For more information about customizing the build failure work item, see "Team Foundation Build Tasks" at *http://msdn2.microsoft.com/en-us/library/ms243778(vs.80).aspx*

Build Resources

- For more information about Team Builds in general, see "Overview of Team Foundation Build" at *http://msdn2.microsoft.com/en-us/library/ms181710(VS.80).aspx*

Guidelines: Source Control

Index

Accessing Version Control

- *Consider using command-line tools.*
- *Use Microsoft® Visual Studio® 2005 Team Foundation Power Tools (TFPT) to unshelve a change.*
- *Use Team Foundation Power Tools to roll back a change.*
- *Use Team Foundation Power Tools to work offline.*
- *Use Team Foundation Power Tools to get a changeset.*
- *Use Team Foundation Power Tools to remove pending edits.*

Administration

- *Turn off inherited permissions on maintenance branches.*
- *Deny check-in permissions to developers you do not yet trust to make changes to your source.*

Branch / Label / Merge

- *Use labels to mark builds you might need to return to.*
- *Use branches to isolate supported releases.*
- *Plan your branching structure along merge paths.*
- *Branch at a high level, including configuration and source files.*
- *Do not branch too deeply.*
- *Do not branch unless you need to.*
- *Avoid baseless merges where possible.*
- *Prefer full merges to "cherry-pick" merges.*
- *Merge frequently*
- *Always create a top-level folder for a new team project to serve as a main branch.*
- *Consider using the candidate or preview switch to double-check before merging.*
- *When renames are part of the merge, pay close attention to the path that the tool recommends.*
- *Be careful when resolving merge conflicts.*
- *Check in the results of one merge at a time.*
- *Build and run tests after the merge and prior to check-in.*

Check-ins and Check-in Policies

- *Only check in your code when you are ready to share it.*
- *Use shelvesets to back up or share pending changes.*
- *Resolve one work item per check-in.*
- *Use check-in policies to enforce coding standards.*
- *Use check-in policies to enforce a code quality gate.*
- *Detect when a policy has been overridden.*
- *Plan to avoid conflicts.*

Checkout, Get, and Lock

- *Get the latest source before making changes.*
- *Use the **lock** command with discretion.*
- *Communicate with your teammates when locking files.*

Dependencies

- *Use project references whenever possible.*
- *Use file references only where necessary.*
- *Use **copy local = true** for project and file references.*
- *Use dynamic URLs when referencing Web services.*

Distributed / Remote Development

- *Make sure that you get an appropriately sized disk drive for your proxy.*
- *Create a scheduled task to pull the latest files on a periodic basis.*
- *Periodically monitor proxy performance counters and the event log.*
- *Configure executionTimeout based on file sizes and bandwidth.*
- *Disable the proxy if it is going to be down for an extended time period.*
- *Consider workspace cloaking to reduce unnecessary file transfers.*

Migration

- *Use the VSS converter to migrate to Team Foundation Server Source Control.*
- *Migrate from other source-control systems to Team Foundation Server Source Control.*

Project / Workspace Management

- *Isolate a single developer using workspaces rather than branches.*
- *Delete and rename files by using source control, not Microsoft Windows® Explorer.*
- *Only delete and rename with your solution open.*

- *Create one team project per application if you want to move your assets between application versions.*
- *Create one team project per version if you want to start fresh with each application version.*
- *Use branching to share code and binaries that require integration testing.*
- *Avoid workspace mapping to support cross-project dependencies.*
- *Create workspace mappings at the team project root level.*
- *Use a unique local folder path on shared computers.*
- *Consider mapping only part of the source tree.*
- *Structure your source tree to support branching.*

Shelving

- *Use shelving to share pending changes for review or handoff.*
- *Use shelving to back up pending changes to the server.*
- *Use shelving if interrupted by higher-priority work.*

Accessing Version Control

- **Consider using command-line tools.**
- **Use Team Foundation Power Tools to unshelve a change.**
- **Use Team Foundation Power Tools to roll back a change.**
- **Use Team Foundation Power Tools to work offline.**
- **Use Team Foundation Power Tools to get a changeset.**
- **Use Team Foundation Power Tools to remove pending edits.**

Consider Using Command-Line Tools

For operations not available from Visual Studio, or if you need to schedule operations, consider using command-line tools such as the Team Foundation Power Tools (Tfpt.exe) that are provided with Team Foundation Server (TFS). The Tfpt.exe tools are available as a separate download. You can use these command-line tools to schedule operations by using the Windows Task Scheduler.

To ensure that the appropriate path and other environment variables are set up, run Tf.exe from the Visual Studio 2005 Command Prompt window, or run the Vsvars32 batch file, which is normally located in *DriveLetter*:\Program Files\Microsoft Visual Studio 8\Common7\Tools. The Tf.exe tool supports most source control commands including **Checkin**, **Checkout**, **Get**, **History**, **Shelve**, **Branch**, **Merge**, **Label**, **Status**, **Undelete**, and **Undo**.

The following are common operations you might want to execute from the command line by using Tf.exe:

- Synchronize files from the server to your local machine – **tf get**
- Add a file to the server – **tf add**
- Check out a file for editing – **tf checkout**
- Check in pending changes – **tf checkin**
- Retrieve a particular changeset from the server – **tf get /version**

There are certain operations that you can only be perform from the command line:

- Delete another user's workspace – **tf workspace /delete**
- Undo another user's check-in – **tf undo**
- Unlock another user's lock – **tf lock**
- Define label scope – **tf label**
- Perform a baseless merge – **tf merge**

Additional Resources

- For more information, see "Walkthrough: Working with Team Foundation Source Control from Command Line" on the Microsoft MSDN® Web site at *http://msdn2.microsoft.com/en-us/library/zthc5x3f.aspx*
- For more information about commands that are only available from the command line, see "Operations Available Only From the Command-Line (Team Foundation Source Control)" at *http://msdn2.microsoft.com/en-us/library/ms194957(VS.80).aspx*

Use Team Foundation Power Tools to Unshelve a Change

The Team Foundation Power Tools (TFPT) provides version-control functionality that is not available from Visual Studio. For example, you can use TFPT to help support offline working or to perform rollback operations in order to undo check-ins of a changeset. Consider using TFPT if you need to unshelve a change.

The **unshelve** operation supported by TFS does not allow shelved changes and local changes to be merged together. By using TFPT to unshelve a change from a changeset, if an item in your local workspace has a pending change that is an edit, and the shelved change is also an edit, then TFPT can merge the changes with a three-way merge.

You run this command from the command line by using Tfpt.exe.

Additional Resources

- To download Team Foundation Power Tools, go to *http://www.microsoft.com/downloads/details.aspx?familyid=7324C3DB-658D-441B-8522-689C557D0A79&displaylang=en*
- To view a forum discussing Team Foundation Power Tools, see *http://forums.microsoft.com/MSDN/ShowForum.aspx?ForumID=930&SiteID=1*

Use Team Foundation Power Tools to Roll Back a Change

Consider using TFPT if you need to roll back a change. The ability to undo a check-in of a changeset is not directly supported by TFS. By using the TFPT **rollback** command, you can attempt to undo any changes made in a specified changeset. Not all changes can be rolled back, but the rollback works for most scenarios.

You run this command from the command line by using Tfpt.exe.

Additional Resources

- To download Team Foundation Power Tools, go to *http://www.microsoft.com/downloads/details.aspx?familyid=7324C3DB-658D-441B-8522-689C557D0A79&displaylang=en*
- To view a forum discussing Team Foundation Power Tools, see *http://forums.microsoft.com/MSDN/ShowForum.aspx?ForumID=930&SiteID=1*

Use Team Foundation Power Tools to Work Offline

Offline working is not supported natively by TFS. If you want to work offline, you must adhere to the following strict workflow:

1. Manually remove read-only flags.
2. Edit files.
3. Add or delete files
4. Run the TFPT online command.

Each of these steps is described in detail below.

Important: You must not rename any files while you are offline.

---

1. **Manually remove read-only flags.**

   By default, all files in the workspace that have not been checked out are marked as read-only. When you work without a server connection, you must manually remove the read-only flags from files before editing or deleting them. To do this, right-click the file in Windows Explorer, click **Properties**, clear the **Read-only** check box, and then click **OK**. Alternatively, you can use the DOS command **attrib -r**.

2. **Edit files.**

   You can now edit any files for which you have removed the read-only flag.

3. **Add or delete files.**

   You can add or delete files for which you have removed the read-only flag. Do not rename files, because the TFPT **online** tool cannot distinguish a rename operation from a deletion paired with an add operation.

   Note: You must specify an option to the **Tfpt online** command to get it to look for deletions, as this is a more time-consuming operation.

   ---

4. **Run the TFPT online command.**

   When you are back online, run the TFPT online command by typing TFPT online at the command line. This command scans your workspace for writable files and determines what changes should be pended on the server. If you have deleted any files, use the /delete switch. This tells the tool to scan for deleted files in your local workspace as well. The tool then displays the online window from which you can choose which changes to pend into the workspace.

Additional Resources

- To download Team Foundation Power Tools, go to *http://www.microsoft.com/downloads/details.aspx?familyid=7324C3DB-658D-441B-8522-689C557D0A79&displaylang=en*
- To view a forum discussing Team Foundation Power Tools, see *http://forums.microsoft.com/MSDN/ShowForum.aspx?ForumID=930&SiteID=1*

Use Team Foundation Power Tools to Get a Changeset

Consider using TFPT if you need to get a changeset. The TFPT **GetCS** command enables you to get all the items listed in a changeset at the time of that changeset version. This is useful if a colleague has checked in a change that you need to have in your workspace, but you cannot update your entire workspace to the latest version.

You run this command from the command line by using Tfpt.exe.

Additional Resources

- To download Team Foundation Power Tools, go to *http://www.microsoft.com/downloads/details.aspx?familyid=7324C3DB-658D-441B-8522-689C557D0A79&displaylang=en*
- To view a forum discussing Team Foundation Power Tools, see *http://forums.microsoft.com/MSDN/ShowForum.aspx?ForumID=930&SiteID=1*

Use Team Foundation Power Tools to Remove Pending Edits

Consider using TFPT if you need to remove pending edits from files. The TFPT **Undo Unchanged** command removes pending edits from files that have not actually been edited. This is useful in a scenario where you check out a large number of files for editing, but only actually make changes to a small number of the files. You can undo your edits on the unchanged files by running the TFPT UU tool, which compares hashes of the files in the local workspace to hashes on the server in order to determine whether or not the file has actually been edited.

You run this command from the command line by using Tfpt.exe.

Additional Resources

- To download Team Foundation Power Tools, go to *http://www.microsoft.com/downloads/details.aspx?familyid=7324C3DB-658D-441B-8522-689C557D0A79&displaylang=en*
- To view a forum discussing Team Foundation Power Tools, see *http://forums.microsoft.com/MSDN/ShowForum.aspx?ForumID=930&SiteID=1*

Administration

- **Turn off inherited permissions on maintenance branches.**
- **Deny check-in permissions to developers you do not yet trust to make changes to your source.**

Turn Off Inherited Permissions on Maintenance Branches

Once a branch is in maintenance—for example, after you have shipped a version of your software—you can turn off inheriting permissions to lock down the tree. After you have done this, you can grant individual users the PendChange and Checkin permissions as needed for hot fixes.

Additional Resources

- For more information about removing permissions, see "How to: Remove Access to Source Control Files" at *http://msdn2.microsoft.com/en-us/library/ms400718(VS.80).aspx*

Deny Check-in Permissions to Developers You Do Not Yet Trust to Make Changes to Your Source

You can deny check-in permissions on the source tree for developers you do not trust, such as new hires or interns. Make sure that you set your desired permissions (including permissions for your own account) before turning off inheritance. Rather than check in directly, they can make pending changes and then shelve these changes. A more experienced developer can then unshelve the changes, review them, and check them in.

Additional Resources

- For more information about removing permissions, see "How to: Remove Access to Source Control Files" at *http://msdn2.microsoft.com/en-us/library/ms400718(VS.80).aspx*

Branch / Label / Merge

- **Use labels to mark builds you might need to return to.**
- **Use branches to isolate supported releases.**
- **Plan your branching structure along merge paths.**
- **Branch at a high level, including configuration and source files.**
- **Do not branch too deeply.**
- **Do not branch unless you need to.**
- **Avoid baseless merges where possible.**
- **Prefer full merges to "cherry-pick" merges.**
- **Merge frequently.**
- **Always create a top-level folder for a new team project to serve as a main branch.**
- **Consider using the candidate or preview switch to double-check before merging.**
- **When renames are part of the merge, pay close attention to the path that the tool recommends.**
- **Be careful when resolving merge conflicts.**
- **Check in the results of one merge at a time.**
- **Build and run tests after the merge and prior to check-in.**

Use Labels to Mark Builds You Might Need to Return To

Use labels to mark daily builds so that you can easily view and retrieve the set of files used for a particular build. Team Build automatically assigns a label to the set of files associated with each build that it creates. Team Build labels follow the format "ReleaseType_Build#"; for example, "Releasex86_20070226.1".

Although every team build is labeled, you might want to create your own labels for builds that you are likely to want to return to, such as:

- An internal milestone; e.g., alpha release
- A build created after branch or external dependency integration

You should use a label-naming convention that makes it easy to locate the build later and know what it represents. Use labels that are clear about what they represent. For example, use a convention such as "AlphaBuild_20070112" composed of "LabelName_Date".

When you release a build to a customer for whom you will need to provide maintenance, use a branch instead of a label to isolate future maintenance work on the release. You can subsequently merge the branch, with any fixes it might contain, back into to your main source tree.

To locate an existing label, on the **File** menu, point to **Source Control**, **Label** and then click **Find Label**. Once you have found the label, you can modify it or delete it from within the **Find Label** dialog box.

Additional Resources

- For more information, see "Working with labels" at *http://msdn2.microsoft.com/en-us/library/ms181439(VS.80).aspx*
- For more information about labels, see "How to: Apply Labels" at *http://msdn2.microsoft.com/en-us/library/ms181440(VS.80).aspx*

Use Branches to Isolate Supported Releases

Create a branch containing the source code used to generate a supported release build. This allows you to apply fixes and updates to the supported release version of your software without impacting the continued development of your source code base, which continues along the main branch.

You continue to develop the next version of your application along your main branch in parallel with the supported release branch. You can merge any stabilization changes you made to the supported release branch into the main branch prior to releasing the next version of your product.

The following is an example of what your branch structure might look like after you have created a Maintenance branch used to support released versions of your software:

Main—Integration Branch

  Source

  Other Asset Folders

Releases—Container for maintenance branches

  Release 1—Maintenance Branch

    Source

Additional Resources

- For an introduction to branching and merging, see "Branching and Merging Primer" at *http://msdn2.microsoft.com/en-us/library/aa730834(VS.80).aspx*
- For more information about branching, see "How to: Branch Files and Folders" at *http://msdn2.microsoft.com/en-us/library/ms181425(VS.80).aspx*
- For more information about merging, see "How to: Merge Files and Folders" at *http://msdn2.microsoft.com/en-us/library/ms181428(VS.80).aspx*
- For additional descriptions of how to branch and merge in Visual Studio 2005, see "Branching and Merging Team Foundation Source Control" at *http://msdn2.microsoft.com/en-us/library/ms181423(VS.80).aspx*

Plan Your Branching Structure Along Merge Paths

You can only merge along existing branch paths by using Source Control Explorer. You can do baseless merges along other paths from the command line, but this type of merge is less intelligent, resulting in more merge conflicts and additional conflicts in future merges.

Keep the following in mind when you perform merges:

- Merging along the hierarchy, from parent to child or from child to parent, results in fewer conflicts than merging across the hierarchy.
- The branch hierarchy is based on the branch parent and branch child, which may be different than the physical structure of the source code on disk. For example:

  Physical Structure:

  Development—Development branch

  Main—Integration branch

  Releases—Container for release branches

  Release 1—Release Branch

  Logical Structure:

  Main

  Development

  Release 1

Additional Resources

- For an introduction to branching and merging, see "Branching and Merging Primer" at *http://msdn2.microsoft.com/en-us/library/aa730834(VS.80).aspx*
- For more information about branching, see "How to: Branch Files and Folders" at *http://msdn2.microsoft.com/en-us/library/ms181425(VS.80).aspx*
- For more information about merging, see "How to: Merge Files and Folders" at *http://msdn2.microsoft.com/en-us/library/ms181428(VS.80).aspx*
- For additional descriptions of how to branch and merge in Visual Studio 2005, see "Branching and Merging Team Foundation Source Control" at *http://msdn2.microsoft.com/en-us/library/ms181423(VS.80).aspx*

Branch at a High Level, Including Configuration and Source Files

Branch at a high-enough level that the branch you create is still compilable. For instance, in the following source tree:

Main—container for all assets you need to ship the product

Source—container for everything you need to build

Code—container for source code

Shared Code—container for source code that is shared from other projects

Unit Tests—container for unit tests

Lib—container for binary dependencies

Docs—container for documentation that will ship with the product

Installer—container for installer source code and binaries

Tests—container for test team test cases

Branch at the level of the Source folder to ensure that the new branch contains all source and configuration files.

Additional Resources

- For an introduction to branching and merging, see "Branching and Merging Primer" at *http://msdn2.microsoft.com/en-us/library/aa730834(VS.80).aspx*
- For more information about branching, see "How to: Branch Files and Folders" at *http://msdn2.microsoft.com/en-us/library/ms181425(VS.80).aspx*
- For more information about merging, see "How to: Merge Files and Folders" at *http://msdn2.microsoft.com/en-us/library/ms181428(VS.80).aspx*
- For additional descriptions of how to branch and merge in Visual Studio 2005, see "Branching and Merging Team Foundation Source Control" at *http://msdn2.microsoft.com/en-us/library/ms181423(VS.80).aspx*

Do Not Branch Too Deeply

Do not branch too deeply because this will add to the time required to merge a change from a child branch up to the topmost parent. For example, in the following branching structure:

Development—Container for development branches

Development Branch

Sub-Branch

Sub-Sub-Branch

Main—Integration Branch

Source

Other Asset Folders

Merges result in fewer conflicts when performed along the branch hierarchy. Therefore, if there is a change in the **Sub-Sub-Branch** that you would like to merge into **Main**, you would first need to merge with the **Sub-Branch** and the **Development Branch** before you can merge into **Main.** Each merge takes time to complete, resolve conflicts, build, and test, which multiplies merge time by the level of branches you have created in your branch structure.

Additional Resources

- For an introduction to branching and merging, see "Branching and Merging Primer" at *http://msdn2.microsoft.com/en-us/library/aa730834(VS.80).aspx*
- For more information about branching, see "How to: Branch Files and Folders" at *http://msdn2.microsoft.com/en-us/library/ms181425(VS.80).aspx*
- For more information about merging, see "How to: Merge Files and Folders" at *http://msdn2.microsoft.com/en-us/library/ms181428(VS.80).aspx*
- For additional descriptions of how to branch and merge in Visual Studio 2005, see "Branching and Merging Team Foundation Source Control" at *http://msdn2.microsoft.com/en-us/library/ms181423(VS.80).aspx*

Do Not Branch Unless You Need To

Do not branch unless your development team needs to work on the same set of files concurrently. If you are unsure, you can label a build and create a branch from that build at a later point. Merging branches can be costly, especially if there are significant changes between them.

Merging requires one or more developers to execute the merge and sort out conflicts. The merged source must be thoroughly tested because it is not uncommon to make bad merge decisions that can destabilize the build.

Merging across the branch hierarchy is especially difficult and requires you to manually handle many conflicts that could otherwise be handled automatically.

Additional Resources

- For an introduction to branching and merging, see "Branching and Merging Primer" at *http://msdn2.microsoft.com/en-us/library/aa730834(VS.80).aspx*
- For more information about branching, see "How to: Branch Files and Folders" at *http://msdn2.microsoft.com/en-us/library/ms181425(VS.80).aspx*
- For more information about merging, see "How to: Merge Files and Folders" at *http://msdn2.microsoft.com/en-us/library/ms181428(VS.80).aspx*
- For additional descriptions of how to branch and merge in Visual Studio 2005, see "Branching and Merging Team Foundation Source Control" at *http://msdn2.microsoft.com/en-us/library/ms181423(VS.80).aspx*

Avoid Baseless Merges Where Possible

Avoid baseless merges where possible. When performing a baseless merge, TFS has no information describing the relationship of files and folders in the branches being merged. This generally results in more merge conflicts, and can lead to more conflicts in future merges.

Structure your branch trees so that you only need to merge along the hierarchy (up and down the branch tree) rather than across the hierarchy. Branching across the hierarchy forces you to use a baseless merge.

Keep the following in mind when performing merges:

Merging along the hierarchy, from parent to child or from child to parent, results in fewer conflicts than merging across the hierarchy.

The branch hierarchy is based on the branch parent and branch child, which may be different than the physical structure of the source code on disk. For example:

Physical Structure:

- **Development**—Development branch
- **Main**—Integration branch
- **Releases**—Container for release branches
  - **Release 1**—Release Branch

Logical Structure:

- **Main**
  - **Development**
  - **Release 1**

Additional Resources

- For an introduction to branching and merging, see "Branching and Merging Primer" at *http://msdn2.microsoft.com/en-us/library/aa730834(VS.80).aspx*
- For more information about branching, see "How to: Branch Files and Folders" at *http://msdn2.microsoft.com/en-us/library/ms181425(VS.80).aspx*
- For more information about merging, see "How to: Merge Files and Folders" at *http://msdn2.microsoft.com/en-us/library/ms181428(VS.80).aspx*
- For additional descriptions of how to branch and merge in Visual Studio 2005, see "Branching and Merging Team Foundation Source Control" at *http://msdn2.microsoft.com/en-us/library/ms181423(VS.80).aspx*

Prefer Full Merges to "Cherry-Pick" Merges

Rather than picking individual changes to merge between branches (a "cherry-pick" merge), choose to merge the entire branch at once. It can be convenient to select individual changes in a branch to merge with another branch. However, if a cherry-picked changeset falls in the middle of a future merge range, that changeset will be re-merged, potentially resulting in additional merge conflicts.

This is especially true for **/discard** merges run from the command line. The discarded changeset can be picked up if it falls in the middle of a future merge range.

Additional Resources

- For an introduction to branching and merging, see "Branching and Merging Primer" at *http://msdn2.microsoft.com/en-us/library/aa730834(VS.80).aspx*
- For more information about branching, see "How to: Branch Files and Folders" at *http://msdn2.microsoft.com/en-us/library/ms181425(VS.80).aspx*
- For more information about merging, see "How to: Merge Files and Folders" at *http://msdn2.microsoft.com/en-us/library/ms181428(VS.80).aspx*
- For additional descriptions of how to branch and merge in Visual Studio 2005, see "Branching and Merging Team Foundation Source Control" at *http://msdn2.microsoft.com/en-us/library/ms181423(VS.80).aspx*

Merge Frequently

Eliminate the latency between branches, especially when teams are working on the same release but in their own isolated branch. This ensures compatibility between changes.

The merge schedule depends on the complexity of your branch structure as well as the individual needs of your development team. As an example, in a moderately complex branch structure such as the one below, the development branches may merge up to the main branch daily and merge changes back from the integration branch every couple of days.

Development—Folder for isolated development branches

- **External**—External dependency branch
- **Team 1**—Team branch
- **Team 2**—Team branch
  - **Feature A**—Feature branch
  - **Feature B**—Feature branch
  - **Feature C**—Feature branch

Main—Integration branch

Releases—Folder for release branches

    Release 2—Release Branch

Safe Keeping—Folder for safekeeping branches

    Release 1—Safekeeping branch

Additional Resources

- For an introduction to branching and merging, see "Branching and Merging Primer" at *http://msdn2.microsoft.com/en-us/library/aa730834(VS.80).aspx*
- For more information about branching, see "How to: Branch Files and Folders" at *http://msdn2.microsoft.com/en-us/library/ms181425(VS.80).aspx*
- For more information about merging, see "How to: Merge Files and Folders" at *http://msdn2.microsoft.com/en-us/library/ms181428(VS.80).aspx*
- For additional descriptions of how to branch and merge in Visual Studio 2005, see "Branching and Merging Team Foundation Source Control" at *http://msdn2.microsoft.com/en-us/library/ms181423(VS.80).aspx*

Always Create a Top-Level Folder for a New Team Project to Serve as a Main Branch

Start any new team project by creating a folder, frequently named **Main**, underneath your team project. Put all source for the **Main** branch in this folder. When you need to create a new branch, branch directly from the Main folder.

The following example shows a typical branch structure:

Development—Folder for isolated development branches, branched from Main

    Feature A

        Source

    Feature B

        Source

Main—Integration Branch

    Source

    Other Asset Folders

Releases—Folder for release branches, branched from Main

    Release 1—Maintenance Branch

        Source

Additional Resources

- For an introduction to branching and merging, see "Branching and Merging Primer" at *http://msdn2.microsoft.com/en-us/library/aa730834(VS.80).aspx*
- For more information about branching, see "How to: Branch Files and Folders" at *http://msdn2.microsoft.com/en-us/library/ms181425(VS.80).aspx*
- For more information about merging, see "How to: Merge Files and Folders" at *http://msdn2.microsoft.com/en-us/library/ms181428(VS.80).aspx*
- For additional descriptions of how to branch and merge in Visual Studio 2005, see "Branching and Merging Team Foundation Source Control" at *http://msdn2.microsoft.com/en-us/library/ms181423(VS.80).aspx*

Consider Using the Candidate or Preview Switch to Double-Check Before Merging

Prior to performing a merge, use the candidate or preview switch to double-check your merge results. Although this option is only available from the command line, it is extremely beneficial to know which files and which versions will be merged when you perform the merge command. For example, this can help to ensure that the scope of your merge is not significantly greater than you were expecting and to make sure that you understand the impact of your merge command. For large merges, the merge report also helps you to divide the work between individuals or teams.

To preview the results of a merge, use the Tf.exe command-line tool with the **merge** command, together with the **preview** or **candidate** switches. For example:

```
Tf merge main/source development/feature/source /preview
```

The **preview** switch shows a preview of the merge, while the **candidate** switch prints a list of all changesets in the source that have not yet been merged into the destination. The list includes the changeset ID that has not been merged and other basic information about that changeset.

Additional Resources

- For an introduction to branching and merging, see "Branching and Merging Primer" at *http://msdn2.microsoft.com/en-us/library/aa730834(VS.80).aspx*
- For more information about branching, see "How to: Branch Files and Folders" at *http://msdn2.microsoft.com/en-us/library/ms181425(VS.80).aspx*
- For more information about merging, see "How to: Merge Files and Folders" at *http://msdn2.microsoft.com/en-us/library/ms181428(VS.80).aspx*
- For additional descriptions of how to branch and merge in Visual Studio 2005, see "Branching and Merging Team Foundation Source Control" at *http://msdn2.microsoft.com/en-us/library/ms181423(VS.80).aspx*

When Renames Are Part of the Merge, Pay Close Attention to the Path That the Tool Recommends

When renames are part of the merge, pay close attention to the path that the tool recommends and make changes as appropriate. All renames are marked as conflicts. The merge algorithm used by TFS tries to calculate the best target path when a rename is being merged over. In some cases the default target path is not the desired path, so you should always double-check prior to committing the merged file.

Additional Resources

- For an introduction to branching and merging, see "Branching and Merging Primer" at *http://msdn2.microsoft.com/en-us/library/aa730834(VS.80).aspx*
- For more information about branching, see "How to: Branch Files and Folders" at *http://msdn2.microsoft.com/en-us/library/ms181425(VS.80).aspx*
- For more information about merging, see "How to: Merge Files and Folders" at *http://msdn2.microsoft.com/en-us/library/ms181428(VS.80).aspx*
- For additional descriptions of how to branch and merge in Visual Studio 2005, see "Branching and Merging Team Foundation Source Control" at *http://msdn2.microsoft.com/en-us/library/ms181423(VS.80).aspx*

Be Careful When Resolving Merge Conflicts

Be careful when merging because it is easy to make mistakes that may result in build instability. When merging files:

- Double-check the code you are merging before committing the merges.
- Test that you can compile the resulting merged file before checking it back into source control.
- Verify that the associated unit tests run and succeed before checking the merged file back into source control.
- Make sure that you understand the nature of the changes made by another developer. If you are in doubt about merging some lines, talk to the developer who made the other changes so that you are sure of their purpose and to get a second view on the impact of your merge.

After you have finished merging, compile the resulting source and run unit tests to test for major breaks.

Additional Resources

- For more information about resolving merge conflicts, see "Resolving Conflicts" on the MSDN Web site at *http://msdn2.microsoft.com/en-us/library/ms181432(VS.80).aspx*

Check In the Results of One Merge At a Time

Check in the results of one merge before performing a second merge that involves the same files. After performing the first merge, compile the code and ensure that the unit tests succeed, and then check in your pending changes. Then begin the second merge and repeat the process.

This helps to reduce complexity and, by keeping the merges separate, enables you to undo changes if the need arises.

Additional Resources

- For an introduction to branching and merging, see "Branching and Merging Primer" at *http://msdn2.microsoft.com/en-us/library/aa730834(VS.80).aspx*
- For more information about branching, see "How to: Branch Files and Folders" at *http://msdn2.microsoft.com/en-us/library/ms181425(VS.80).aspx*
- For more information about merging, see "How to: Merge Files and Folders" at *http://msdn2.microsoft.com/en-us/library/ms181428(VS.80).aspx*
- For additional descriptions of how to branch and merge in Visual Studio 2005, see "Branching and Merging Team Foundation Source Control" at *http://msdn2.microsoft.com/en-us/library/ms181423(VS.80).aspx*

Build and Run Tests After the Merge and Prior to Check-in

Having performed a merge, make sure that you compile the code and run the associated tests before checking in the merged file. Do this to avoid introducing build instability as a result of your merges.

The results of a merge are initially isolated within your workspace and are not uploaded to the server until you check in the pending changes.

Additional Resources

- For an introduction to branching and merging, see "Branching and Merging Primer" at *http://msdn2.microsoft.com/en-us/library/aa730834(VS.80).aspx*
- For more information on branching, see "How to: Branch Files and Folders" at *http://msdn2.microsoft.com/en-us/library/ms181425(VS.80).aspx*
- For more information on merging, see "How to: Merge Files and Folders" at *http://msdn2.microsoft.com/en-us/library/ms181428(VS.80).aspx*
- For additional descriptions of how to branch and merge in Visual Studio 2005, see "Branching and Merging Team Foundation Source Control" at *http://msdn2.microsoft.com/en-us/library/ms181423(VS.80).aspx*

Check-in and Check-in Policies

- **Only check in your code when you are ready to share it.**
- **Use shelvesets to back up or share pending changes.**
- **Resolve one work item per check-in.**
- **Use check-in policies to enforce coding standards.**
- **Use check-in policies to enforce a code quality gate.**
- **Detect when a policy has been overridden.**
- **Plan to avoid conflicts.**

Only Check In Your Code When You Are Ready to Share It

Only check your updated code into source control when it is fully unit-tested and ready to share with the rest of the team. Use shelvesets for intermediate work that is not yet complete.

When you check in your code, it will be used as part of your next scheduled build. Any incomplete code is likely to cause build instability. Also when you check in your code, any other developer who does a **get latest** operation will pick up your changes. If they are incomplete or inadequately tested, they will cause problems for your colleague.

Additional Resources

- For more information about check-ins, see "How to: Check In Pending Changes" at *http://msdn2.microsoft.com/en-us/library/ms181411(VS.80).aspx*

Use Shelvesets to Back Up or Share Pending Changes

Use shelvesets to back up files that contain pending changes you are not yet ready to check in. You can also use shelvesets to share code for code review, or if you are passing off a development task to another developer. By using shelvesets, you can upload your pending changes to the server without checking in partially completed work that could potentially lead to build instability.

To shelve a set of pending changes, first view the changes by right-clicking your solution in Solution Explorer and then clicking **View Pending Changes**. Select the files you want to shelve and then click **Shelve**. Type a shelveset name and a comment that identifies the purpose of the shelveset, and then click **Shelve**.

► **To retrieve a shelveset**

1. On the **File** menu, point to **Source Control** and then click **Unshelve**.
2. In the **Owner name** text box, type the shelveset creator's name (for example, Contoso\JimB or simply JimB) and then click **Find**.

3. In the Results pane, select the shelveset you want to unshelve into your workspace, and then click **Details**.
4. If you want to delete the shelveset as you retrieve it from the TFS source control server, clear the **Preserve shelveset on server** option. Team Foundation Server restores each shelved revision into the destination workspace as a pending change as long as the revision does not conflict with a change that is already pending in your workspace.
5. Optionally, you can clear the **Restore work items and check-in notes** option if you do not want to have the work items and check-in notes associated with the shelveset restored. When the **Details** dialog box appears, select the shelveset or shelveset items you want to unshelve into your workspace, and then click **Unshelve**.

Additional Resources

- For more information, see "How to: Shelve and Unshelve Pending Changes" at *http://msdn2.microsoft.com/en-us/library/ms181404(VS.80).aspx*

Resolve One Work Item per Check-in

After resolving a work item, check in your pending changes and update the work item status. This practice serves the following purposes:

- It provides a consistent record in the source control database that can be used to review changes per work item, or to back a work item out if necessary in the future.
- It ensures that you do not wait too long between check-ins. The longer you wait between check-ins, the more likely that you will have a conflict that requires a manual merge and additional testing.

Additional Resources

- For more information about check-ins, see "How to: Check In Pending Changes" at *http://msdn2.microsoft.com/en-us/library/ms181411(VS.80).aspx*
- For more information about work items and changesets, see "How to: Associate Work Items with Changesets" at *http://msdn2.microsoft.com/en-us/library/ms181410(VS.80).aspx*
- For more information about reviewing work item details, see "How to: View Work Item Details from Pending Changes Window" at *http://msdn2.microsoft.com/en-us/library/ms245467(VS.80).aspx*

Use Check-in Policies to Enforce Coding Standards

Use check-in policies to enforce coding standards across your development team. Check-in policies help to ensure that all source code checked into TFS source control meets your defined coding standards.

The code analysis check-in policies that ship with TFS enables you to ensure that static code analysis has been run on code before it is checked in. You can fine-tune the code analysis policy to check many different rules. For example, you can check rules governing design, interoperability, maintainability, mobility, naming conventions, reliability, and more.

► **To enforce a code analysis check-in policy for a team project**

1. In Team Explorer, right-click your team project, point to **Team Project Settings**, and then click **Source Control**.
2. Click the **Check-in Policy** tab and then click **Add**.
3. In the **Add Check-in Policy** dialog box, select **Code Analysis** and then click **OK**.
4. In the **Code Analysis Policy Editor**, select either **Enforce C/C++ Code Analysis (/analyze)** or **Enforce Code Analysis For Managed Code**. Select both if your project contains a combination of managed and unmanaged code.
5. If you select **Enforce Code Analysis For Managed Code**, configure your required rule settings for managed code analysis based on your required coding standards. This determines precisely which rules are enforced.

You can also create a custom check-in policy to perform checks that are not available by default. For example, you can disallow code patterns such as banned application programming interface (API) calls, or you can write a policy to enforce your team's specific coding style guidelines, such as where braces should be positioned within your source code.

Additional Resources

- For more information about creating and using a custom check-in policy, see "How To: Step Through Creating Custom Check-in Policies for TFS" in this guide.
- To learn how to customize a check-in policy, see "Walkthrough: Customizing Check-in Policies and Notes" at *http://msdn2.microsoft.com/en-us/library/ms181281(VS.80).aspx*
- To view sample code that will disallow selected patterns on check-in, see "Check-in Policy to Disallow Certain Patterns" at *http://blogs.msdn.com/jmanning/archive/2006/02/02/523125.aspx*
- To view sample code that will enforce comments on check-in, see "Sample Check-in Policy: Make Sure the Comment Isn't Empty" at *http://blogs.msdn.com/jmanning/archive/2006/01/21/515858.aspx*
- To learn how to register a new check-in policy, see "I've Made a New Check-In Policy! How Do I Add It?" at *http://blogs.msdn.com/jmanning/archive/2006/02/07/526778.aspx*

Use Check-in Policies to Enforce a Code Quality Gate

Use a combination of code analysis and testing policies to enforce a code quality gate. For example, use the supplied testing policy to ensure that specific tests are executed and passed prior to allowing source to be checked into TFS source control. You can also configure a code analysis policy to help ensure that your code meets certain quality standards by ensuring that security, performance, portability, maintainability, and reliability rules are passed.

By enforcing this type of check-in policy in addition to policies that enforce coding standards and guidelines, you ensure your code meets a specific code quality gate.

► **To enforce a code analysis check-in policy for a team project**

1. In Team Explorer, right-click your team project, point to **Team Project Settings,** and then click **Source Control**.
2. Click the **Check-in Policy** tab, click **Add**, and then select and configure the appropriate policy.

Additional Resources

- For more information about creating and using a custom check-in policy, see "How To – Step Through Creating Custom Check-in Policies for TFS" in this guide.
- To learn how to customize a check-in policy, see "Walkthrough: Customizing Check-in Policies and Notes" at *http://msdn2.microsoft.com/en-us/library/ms181281(VS.80).aspx*
- To see sample code that will disallow selected patterns on check-in, see "Checkin Policy to Disallow Certain Patterns" at *http://blogs.msdn.com/jmanning/archive/2006/02/02/523125.aspx*
- To see sample code that will enforce comments on check-in, see "Sample Checkin Policy: Make Sure the Comment Isn't Empty" at *http://blogs.msdn.com/jmanning/archive/2006/01/21/515858.aspx*
- To learn how to register a new check-in policy, see "I've Made a New Check-In Policy! How Do I Add It?" at *http://blogs.msdn.com/jmanning/archive/2006/02/07/526778.aspx*

Detect When a Policy Has Been Overridden

Team Foundation Version Control does not prevent you from overriding a policy. However, you can use the following steps to detect if a policy has been overridden:

- Use the Team Foundation Eventing Service (from the Team Foundation Core Services API) for hooking into check-in events.
- Write a **Notify** method that parses the details of the changeset and then react to it if an override has occurred.

Alternatively, you can manually scan changeset history to discover policy overrides.

Additional Resources

- To learn more about overriding a check-in policy, see "How to: Override a Check-in Policy" at *http://msdn2.microsoft.com/en-us/library/ms245460(VS.80).aspx*
- To learn more about the Team Foundation Eventing Service, see "Eventing Service" at *http://msdn2.microsoft.com/en-us/library/bb130154(vs.80).aspx*
- To learn how to receive an e-mail message when a policy has been violated, see *http://blogs.infosupport.com/marcelv/archive/2005/10/18/1635.aspx*

Plan to Avoid Conflicts

Plan to avoid having multiple developers working in the same region of the same source file at the same time. Do this to avoid conflicts that are potentially difficult to correctly resolve. While automatic conflict resolution can resolve many conflicts, you should avoid situations where two or more developers are working on the same method, or on the same lines of code. Conflicts on the same lines of code require manual conflict resolution, which complicates the merge operation. Effective team communication is the key.

Before starting work on a file, make sure that you have the latest version from source control and check to see if anyone else has the file checked out before you begin work. If a colleague has the file checked out, ask your colleague what he or she is working on and then decide if you can wait until they complete their changes or if it is safe to continue to work in parallel on the same file because you are working on separate functionality in separate source code regions within the file.

► **To check if someone else has a file checked out**

1. In the Team Explorer window in Visual Studio, double-click **Source Control**.
2. Browse to the folder containing the file you want to check in the source control folder hierarchy.

   Any pending changes are listed together with the username of the user who owns those changes.

To check which files people currently have pending changes for, run the following command from a Visual Studio 2005 command prompt window.

```
Tf status /format:detailed /user:*
```

When you do begin working on a source file that you know others will work on in parallel, let other team members know that you are working on the file and which aspects you will be updating.

Additional Resources

- For more information on viewing pending changes in your workspace, see "How to: View and Manage All Pending Changes in Your Workspace" at *http://msdn2.microsoft.com/en-us/library/ms181400(VS.80).aspx*
- For more information on viewing pending changes in other workspaces, see "How to: View Pending Changes in Other Workspaces" at *http://msdn2.microsoft.com/en-us/library/ms181401(VS.80).aspx*

Checkout, Get, and Lock

- **Get the latest source before making changes.**
- **Use the lock command with discretion.**
- **Communicate with your teammates when locking files.**

Get the Latest Source Before Making Changes

To make sure that you have the latest versions of all the source files for the project you are working on, run a **get latest** command before you check out a file for editing. The danger of not doing so is that locally building your code against non-current source files increases the likelihood of your code causing build problems when you subsequently check it into the server.

To get the latest copies of the file set associated with a specific team project, right-click the team project in Source Control Explorer and then click **Get Latest Version**. If you currently have writable files with pending edits in your workspace, this command does not overwrite those files. You can run the same command from the command line by running the **Tf get /all** command from a directory mapped to the current workspace.

Additional Resources

- For more information about the Get command, see "Get Command" on the MSDN Web site at *http://msdn2.microsoft.com/en-us/library/fx7sdeyf(VS.80).aspx*

Use the lock Command with Discretion

Use the **lock** command sparingly because locking a file while you work on it can lead to bottlenecks in the development process by preventing other people from working on the same file at the same time. You should only lock a file while editing it if you are concerned that there will be a conflict resulting in a complicated manual merge operation. Where possible, prefer shared checkouts by selecting the lock type **None** when you check out the file.

The following are common scenarios where using a lock is appropriate to avoid conflicts:

- You are modifying a binary file format, such as an image or a document that cannot be easily merged.
- You are making such widespread changes to a file that any other developer working on the same file would be very likely to make changes to the same lines as you.

If you want to avoid any possibility of conflicts, use a checkout lock, which prevents other people from checking out and checking in the same file. If you do lock a file, notify your teammates when you lock a file and tell them why you are doing so and how long your work on the file is likely to take. Also let them know when you remove the lock and check your changes back in.

You specify your lock type when you check out a file for editing, or you can explicitly lock a file.

► To lock a file while checking it out

1. In Source Control Explorer, right-click the file and then click **Check Out for Edit**.
2. Specify your lock type: **None**, **Check Out**, or **Check In**.
3. To explicitly lock a file, right-click the file, click **Lock**, and then select the **Check Out** or **Check In** lock type.

Note that unlike Microsoft Visual Source Safe® (VSS) behavior, checking out a file does not implicitly get the latest version. Prior to locking a file, make sure that you have the latest version in your workspace by clicking **Get Latest Version**.

Additional Resources

- For more information about locks, see "How to: Lock and Unlock Folders or Files" at *http://msdn2.microsoft.com/en-us/library/ms181420(VS.80).aspx*
- For more informational about lock types, see *http://msdn2.microsoft.com/en-us/library/ms181419(VS.80).aspx*

Communicate with Your Teammates When Locking Files

If you do lock a source file, let your teammates know so that they can plan their work around the unavailability of the file. Explain why you need an exclusive lock on the file and how long you are likely to retain the lock. By locking a file, you potentially introduce a bottleneck into your development cycle, if other developers need to work on the same source file.

Only lock a file while editing it if you are concerned that there will be a conflict resulting in a complicated manual merge operation. Where possible, prefer shared checkouts by selecting the lock type **None** when you check out the file.

To lock a file from Source Control Explorer, right-click the file, click **Lock**, and then select the **Check Out** or **Check In** lock type.

Additional Resources

- For more information on lock types, see *http://msdn2.microsoft.com/en-us/library/ms181419(VS.80).aspx*

Dependencies

- **Use project references whenever possible.**
- **Use file references only where necessary.**
- **Use copy local = true for project and file references.**
- **Use dynamic URLs when referencing Web services.**

Use Project References Whenever Possible

You should use a project reference whenever possible because they provide the following advantages:

- They work on all development workstations where the solution and project set are loaded. This is because a project Globally Unique Identifier (GUID) is placed in the project file, which uniquely identifies the referenced project in the context of the current solution.
- They enable the Visual Studio build system to track project dependencies and determine the correct project build orders.
- They help you avoid the possibility of referenced assemblies being missing on a particular computer.
- They automatically track project configuration changes. For example, when you build using a debug configuration, any project references refer to debug assemblies generated by the referenced projects, while they refer to release assemblies in a release configuration. This means that you can automatically switch from debug to release builds across projects without having to reset references.
- They enable Visual Studio to detect and prevent circular dependencies.

You can use a project reference if the assembly is already within your solution's project set. If the assembly is outside of your solution's project set and you still want to use a project reference, you can branch the dependency from the originating project into your project. When you want to pick up a new version of the dependency, perform a merge from the originating project into your branch.

Additional Resources

- For more information about project and file references, see "Project References" at *http://msdn2.microsoft.com/en-us/library/ez524kew(VS.80).aspx*

- For more information about adding references, see "How to: Add or Remove References in Visual Studio" at *http://msdn2.microsoft.com/en-us/library/wkze6zky(VS.80).aspx*

Use File References Only Where Necessary

If you cannot use a project reference because you need to reference an assembly outside of your current solution's project set, and you do not want to create a branch from the originating project into your project, you must set a file reference.

Additional Resources

- For more information about project and file references, see "Project References" at *http://msdn2.microsoft.com/en-us/library/ez524kew(VS.80).aspx*

Use copy local = true for Project and File References

Every reference has an associated **copy local** attribute. Visual Studio determines the initial setting of this attribute (true or false) when the reference is initially added. It is set to false if the referenced assembly is found to be in the Global Assembly Cache (GAC); otherwise, it is set to true.

You should not change this default setting.

With **copy local** set to **true**, the Visual Studio build system copies any referenced assembly (and any dependent downstream assemblies) to the client project's output folder when the reference is set. For example, if your client project references an assembly named Lib1, and Lib1 depends on Lib2 and Lib3, then Lib1, Lib2, and Lib3 are copied to your project's local output folder automatically by Visual Studio at build time.

Additional Resources

- For more information about project and file references, see "Project References" at *http://msdn2.microsoft.com/en-us/library/ez524kew(VS.80).aspx*

Use Dynamic URLs When Referencing Web Services

If you want to call a Web service, you must first add a Web reference to your project. This generates a proxy class through which you interact with the Web service. The proxy code initially contains a static Uniform Resource Locator (URL) for the Web service; for example, http://localhost or http://SomeWebServer.

Important: For Web services in your current solution that execute on your computer, always use http://localhost rather than http://MyComputerName to ensure that the reference remains valid on all computers.

The static URL that is embedded within the proxy is usually not the URL that you require in either the production or test environment. Typically, the required URL varies as your application moves from development to test to production. You have three options to address this issue:

- You can programmatically set the Web service URL when you create an instance of the proxy class.
- A more flexible approach that avoids a hard-coded URL in the proxy is to set the **URL Behavior** property of the Web service reference to **Dynamic**. This is the preferred approach. When you set the property to **Dynamic**, code is added to the proxy class to retrieve the Web service URL from a custom configuration section of the application configuration file—Web.config for a Web application or SomeApp.exe.config for a Windows application.
- You can also generate the proxy by using the WSDL.exe command-line tool and specifying the **/urlkey** switch. This works in a similar way to setting the **URL Behavior** property in that it adds code to the proxy to retrieve the Web service URL, but in this case the URL is stored in the <applicationSettings> section of the application configuration file.

The dynamic URL approach also lets you provide a user configuration file, which can override the main application configuration file. This allows separate developers (and members of the test team) to temporarily redirect a Web service reference to an alternate location.

Additional Resources

- For more information, see Chapter 6, "Managing Source Control Dependencies in Visual Studio Team System" in this guide.

Distributed / Remote Development

- **Make sure that you get an appropriately sized disk drive for your proxy.**
- **Create a scheduled task to pull the latest files on a periodic basis.**
- **Periodically monitor proxy performance counters and the event log.**
- **Configure executionTimeout based on file sizes and bandwidth.**
- **Disable the proxy if it is going to be down for an extended time period.**
- **Consider workspace cloaking to reduce unnecessary file transfers.**

Make Sure That You Get an Appropriately Sized Disk Drive for Your Proxy

Be sure to follow the hardware recommendations in the TFS installation guide; specifically, make sure that you get a disk drive with sufficient capacity. A maximum limit is set on the amount of storage space the proxy can use for caching files. When this limit is reached, old files in the cache are deleted to free up some storage space so that the space can be used for caching newly requested files. Cleanup removes the files based on when they were last accessed. Those files that have not been served for the longest time are deleted first.

Additional Resources

- To learn more about the Team Foundation Server Proxy, see "Team Foundation Server Proxy and Source Control" on the MSDN Web site at *http://msdn2.microsoft.com/en-us/library/ms252490(VS.80).aspx*

Create a Scheduled Task to Pull the Latest Files on a Periodic Basis

Run a scheduled task to retrieve the latest files on a periodic basis to the proxy server. This helps to ensure that the latest version of the files are available in the proxy cache and to ensure that subsequent client requests for these files result in a cache hit.

Additional Resources

- To learn more about the Team Foundation Server Proxy, see "Team Foundation Server Proxy and Source Control" on the MSDN Web site at *http://msdn2.microsoft.com/en-us/library/ms252490(VS.80).aspx*

Periodically Monitor Proxy Performance Counters and the Event Log

Monitor Proxy Performance counters and the Windows event log for errors and warnings on a periodic basis, to get a good picture of how your proxy is functioning. Make sure that proxy caching is enabled and monitor the performance of your cache.

You should observe the following performance counters:

- Current Cache Size
- Total Cache Hits - count and percentage
- Total Download Requests
- Total Files in Cache
- Total Cache Miss - count and percentage

These performance counters are registered when you install the proxy. The proxy performance counters are multi-instanced, which means there is a set of counters for each application tier that you have configured in the Proxy.config file. By collecting this data, you get an understanding of the performance when the proxy server is running.

Note that the TFS proxy saves cache performance statistics to an Extensible Markup Language (XML) file named ProxyStatistics.xml, and you can change the interval for saving these statistics. The ProxyStatistics.xml file is located in the App_Data folder in the proxy installation directory.

Additional Resources

- To learn more about the Team Foundation Server Proxy, see "Team Foundation Server Proxy and Source Control" on the MSDN Web site at *http://msdn2.microsoft.com/en-us/library/ms252490(VS.80).aspx*

Configure executionTimeout Based on File Sizes and Bandwidth

If you know that large files are going to be downloaded over a low-bandwidth (< 3 megabits per second [Mbps]) network, set the **executionTimeout** configuration to an appropriate value in Web.config. Do this to reduce the likelihood of timeouts. The default value is one hour as shown here:
`<httpRuntime executionTimeout="3600"/>`.

Additional Resources

- To learn more about the Team Foundation Server Proxy, see "Team Foundation Server Proxy and Source Control" on the MSDN Web site at *http://msdn2.microsoft.com/en-us/library/ms252490(VS.80).aspx*

Disable the Proxy if It Is Going to Be Down for an Extended Time Period

Disable the proxy on the clients if the proxy is going to be down for an extended time period. Do this to prevent fruitless reconnections. By default, these are attempted every five minutes.

Additional Resources

- To learn more about the Team Foundation Server Proxy, see "Team Foundation Server Proxy and Source Control" on the MSDN Web site at *http://msdn2.microsoft.com/en-us/library/ms252490(VS.80).aspx*

Consider Workspace Cloaking to Reduce Unnecessary File Transfers

Consider using workspace cloaking to hide specific workspaces from being viewed and to prevent unnecessary file transfers. Cloaking not only hides specified workspace folders from view, but also increases performance bandwidth and conserves local disk space by preventing folders and files that you do not currently require from being copied to your local workspace. Although you can cloak an existing folder mapping in your workspace, a better approach is to create a new folder mapping specifically intended to be cloaked.

► **To cloak folders in a workspace**

1. In Visual Studio, on the **File** menu, point to **Source Control**, and then click **Workspaces**.
2. In the **Manage Workspaces** dialog box, select the workspace to which you want to apply cloaking, and then click **Edit**.

3. In the **Edit Workspace** dialog box, in the **Working folders** list, either highlight the folder mapping located under **Source Control Folder** and **Local Folder** that you want to cloak, or create a new one.
4. Click in the **Status** column and change the setting from **Active** to **Cloaked**.
5. Note that you can only cloak folders in an actively mapped TFS source control folder.
6. Click **OK** to close Edit Workspaces and click **Close** to close Manage Workspaces.

Note that your files do not disappear locally until you perform another **get** operation for the entire workspace.

Additional Resources

- To learn more about the Team Foundation Server Proxy, see "Team Foundation Server Proxy and Source Control" on the MSDN Web site at *http://msdn2.microsoft.com/en-us/library/ms252490(VS.80).aspx*

Migration

- **Use the VSS converter to migrate to Team Foundation Server Source Control.**
- **Migrate from other source-control systems to Team Foundation Server Source Control.**

Use the VSS Converter to Migrate to Team Foundation Server Source Control

Team Foundation Server ships with a VSS converter tool that allows you to migrate files, folders, version history, labels, and user information from a Visual SourceSafe database to Team Foundation Server Version Control.

The converter does have some limitations that are important to understand, for example:

- Historical information about file sharing is not preserved. Team Foundation Server does not support sharing. The migration of a shared file results in copying the file to the destination folder.
- Historical information about branching is not preserved.
- Team Foundation Server does not support pinning. Pinned files are migrated by creating two labels.
- Timestamps associated with actions are not preserved during migration.

Additional Resources

- For more information about migrating files, see "How To: Migrate Source Code to Team Foundation Server from Visual Source Safe" in this guide.

Migrate from Other Source-Control Systems to Team Foundation Server Source Control

You can manually export files from the version-control system you are migrating from and then import them into Team Foundation Server Version Control. If you need to preserve file history or other attributes from the version-control system you are migrating from, you can use the TFS Migration and Synchronization Toolkit, available at *http://www.codeplex.com/MigrationSyncToolkit*, to write your own migration tool.

Microsoft is currently working on a ClearCase converter. When this converter is ready, it will be announced on the TFS Migration blog at *http://blogs.msdn.com/tfs_migration*

Component Software has created a converter that is compatible with GNU RCS, CS-RCS, GNU CVS, Subversion (SVN), and Visual SourceSafe (VSS).

Additional Resources

- For more information about TFS migration, see the "TFS Migration blog" on the MSDN Web site at *http://blogs.msdn.com/tfs_migration*
- To download the TFS Migration and Synchronization Toolkit from CodePlex, go to *http://www.codeplex.com/MigrationSyncToolkit*
- For more information about the Component Software converter, see *http://www.componentsoftware.com/Products/Converter/*

Project / Workspace Management

- **Isolate a single developer using workspaces rather than branches.**
- **Delete and rename files by using source control, not Windows Explorer.**
- **Only delete and rename with your solution open.**
- **Create one team project per application if you want to move your assets between application versions.**
- **Create one team project per version if you want to start fresh with each application version.**
- **Use branching to share code and binaries that require integration testing.**
- **Avoid workspace mapping to support cross-project dependencies.**
- **Create workspace mappings at the team project root level.**
- **Use a unique local folder path on shared computers.**
- **Consider mapping only part of the source tree.**
- **Structure your source tree to support branching.**

Isolate a Single Developer Using Workspaces Rather Than Branches

To isolate your work from the rest of your team, use an additional workspace and do not create a new branch. Use your primary workspace to contain references to the files and folders being worked on by the rest of the team (that is, containing the shared source) and create a second workspace to maintain the files and folders that you want to isolate. You might want to isolate these files in order to evolve specific files in parallel with work that is happening elsewhere. For instance, this can be used to work on risky pending changes, or experimental changes. By using a second workspace, you reduce additional branch and merge complexity.

► **To create a secondary workspace**

1. In Source Control Explorer, click the **Workspace** drop-down list and then click **Workspaces**.
2. In the **Manage Workspaces** dialog box, click **Add**.
3. In the **Add Workspace** dialog box, enter a new workspace name such as **MyIsolatedWork** and provide a comment to serve as a future reminder about the purpose of the workspace.
4. In the **Working folders** list, set the workplace status to **Active**, identify the source control folder to be included in the workspace (this can be the team project root folder or any subfolder), and specify a local folder path on your own computer to contain the files from the workspace.
5. Click **OK** and then click **Close** to create the isolated workspace.

► **To retrieve the latest set of source to begin work in your isolated workspace**

1. In Source Control Explorer, make sure that your isolated workspace name is selected in the **Workspace** drop-down list.
2. Select your team project root folder (or a subfolder if you only need part of the source tree), right-click, and then click **Get Latest Version**.
3. This copies the folder structure and latest file set from the source control server to the local directory on your computer that you mapped to the new workspace.

Additional Resources

- For more information about creating a workspace, see "How to: Create a Workspace" at *http://msdn2.microsoft.com/en-us/library/ms181384(VS.80).aspx*
- For more information about editing a workspace, see "How to: Edit a Workspace" at *http://msdn2.microsoft.com/en-us/library/ms245466(VS.80).aspx*

Delete and Rename Files by Using Source Control, Not Windows Explorer

If you need to delete or rename files that have been added to source control, you should delete or rename them by using Source Control Explorer or by using Tf.exe from the command line. Do not delete or rename files by using Windows Explorer because doing so forces your local workspace files to become out of synchronization with the source control files maintained on the server.

► To delete a file or folder by using Source Control Explorer

1. In Source Control Explorer, select the file or folder.
2. Right-click the selected file or folder and then click **Delete**.

   An icon that indicates the item is deleted appears to the left and the status "delete" appears under the **Pending Change** column. The item is deleted the next time you check the file in.

Note: You cannot delete an item for which another pending change exists. For example, a checked out file cannot be deleted.

The **Tf move**, **delete**, and **rename** commands are particularly useful if you need to perform the operation on multiple files or folders. With Source Control Explorer, you can only move, rename, or delete a single file or folder at a time.

Additional Resources

- For more information about the Tf delete command, see "Delete Command" on the MSDN Web site at *http://msdn2.microsoft.com/en-us/library/k45zb450(VS.80).aspx*
- For more information about the Tf rename command, see "Rename Command" on the MSDN Web site at *http://msdn2.microsoft.com/en-us/library/a79bz90w(VS.80).aspx*

Only Delete and Rename with Your Solution Open

Delete and rename files inside Solution Explorer only with your solution open. Do not do this directly on disk. This approach ensures that when you next check in your pending changes, TFS source control is kept in synchronization.

Additional Resources

- For more information about the Tf delete command, see "Delete Command" on the MSDN Web site at *http://msdn2.microsoft.com/en-us/library/k45zb450(VS.80).aspx*
- For more information about the Tf rename command, see "Rename Command" on the MSDN Web site at *http://msdn2.microsoft.com/en-us/library/a79bz90w(VS.80).aspx*

Create One Team Project per Application if You Want to Move Your Assets Between Application Versions

If you want to carry forward not only source code but also work items and other TFS assets between releases, consider using one team project per application. When you use a single team project for multiple versions of the application, all of the TFS assets are carried forward automatically for you for the next release. When you are ready to release a new version of your application, you can create a branch within the project to represent the release and isolate that code.

If you choose to use one project per application, keep the following vulnerabilities in mind:

- Releases in parallel are forced to share work item schemas, check in policies, and process guidance.
- Reporting is more difficult. Because reports default to the entire project, you must add filtering by release.
- If you have hundreds of applications, each in its own project, you will run up against TFS performance and scale limits.
- You will accumulate 'baggage' over multiple releases. The easiest way to address this issue is to create a new project and then branch code you want to carry forward into that project.

Additional Resources

- For more information on using team projects, see "When to use Team Projects" at *http://blogs.msdn.com/ericlee/archive/2006/08/09/when-to-use-team-projects.aspx*

Create One Team Project Per Version If You Want to Start Fresh With Each Application Version

If you want each release to start fresh without carrying forward work items and other TFS assets, consider using one project per release. When you use a new project for each release, you can modify work item schemas, workflow, check-in policies, and other assets without impacting the old release. This can be especially useful if the old release will be maintained by a separate team such as a sustained engineering team who may have a different process and workflow than your main development team.

When using one project per release, keep the following in mind:

- Although it is very easy to move the source code from one project to another, it is difficult to move work items and other TFS assets from one project to another. Work items can only be copied one at a time to another project; if you want to copy sets of work items, you will need to write your own utility.
- If you have hundreds of applications and releases, each in its own project, you will run up against TFS performance and scale limits.

- Choose a structure you can live with in the long term because restructuring existing team projects is difficult.
- Source can be easily shared among team projects:
  - Branch source from one project to another.
  - Map source from another project into your workspace.
- Team Foundation Server can scale to ~500 projects by using the Microsoft Solution Framework (MSF) for Agile Software Development (MSF Agile) process template or to 250 projects by using the MSF CMMI process template. If you create your own process, or customize an existing process, keep in mind that the work item schema has the greatest impact on server scalability. A complex schema will result in a server capable of supporting fewer projects.

Additional Resources

- For more information on using team projects, see "When to use Team Projects" at *http://blogs.msdn.com/ericlee/archive/2006/08/09/when-to-use-team-projects.aspx*

Use Branching to Share Code and Binaries that Require Integration Testing

Managing shared code or binaries involves two steps:

1. Determine a location in which to store the dependency.
2. Branch the dependency into your project.

1. **Determine a location in which to store the dependency.**

   Options for storing:

   - If the shared dependency is clearly owned by a particular team, store it in that team's team project.
   - If the shared dependency has no clear ownership, create a team project specifically for the shared code.

2. **Branch the dependency into your project.**

   Once you have stored the dependency, branch the shared source or binaries into your project. Every time you perform a merge from shared to consuming project, you will pick up the latest source. This allows you to pick up changes on a regular schedule and to perform integration testing before impacting your main source tree.

Additional Resources

- For an introduction to branching and merging, see "Branching and Merging Primer" at *http://msdn2.microsoft.com/en-us/library/aa730834(VS.80).aspx*
- For more information about branching, see "How to: Branch Files and Folders" at *http://msdn2.microsoft.com/en-us/library/ms181425(VS.80).aspx*

- For more information about merging, see "How to: Merge Files and Folders" at *http://msdn2.microsoft.com/en-us/library/ms181428(VS.80).aspx*
- For additional descriptions of how to branch and merge in Visual Studio 2005, see "Branching and Merging Team Foundation Source Control" at *http://msdn2.microsoft.com/en-us/library/ms181423(VS.80).aspx*

Avoid Workspace Mapping to Support Cross-Project Dependencies

In general, you should avoid dependencies that cross team projects and try to have all the related/dependent solutions/projects under the same team project. This reduces the need for build script customization. If you have a dependency, use project references to define it, or branch the dependency from a shared project into your project. You should avoid file references because they are more difficult to manage. The exception is when the dependent project is developed in parallel and you need real-time changes. In this case, you can consider using workspace mapping. However, you can still use branching in this case to create a buffer of isolation, if the dependent code is causing too many breaking changes.

Additional Resources

- For more information about creating a workspace, see "How to: Create a Workspace" at *http://msdn2.microsoft.com/en-us/library/ms181384(VS.80).aspx*
- For more information about editing a workspace, see "How to: Edit a Workspace" at *http://msdn2.microsoft.com/en-us/library/ms245466(VS.80).aspx*

Create Workspace Mappings at the Team Project Root Level

For new team projects, map your team project root ($/MyTeamProject) to a folder with the same name on your local drive; for example, C:\TeamProjects. Because mappings are recursive, your entire local folder structure is created automatically and will be exactly the same as the structure in source control.

Additional Resources

- For more information about creating a workspace, see "How to: Create a Workspace" at *http://msdn2.microsoft.com/en-us/library/ms181384(VS.80).aspx*
- For more information about editing a workspace, see "How to: Edit a Workspace" at *http://msdn2.microsoft.com/en-us/library/ms245466(VS.80).aspx*

Use a Unique Local Folder Path on Shared Computers

Two users of a single computer cannot share the same workspace mapping. For example, you and a colleague cannot map the same team project ($/MyTeamProject) to the same folder on the local computer. Instead, create mappings beneath My Documents (although this leads to long location paths) or establish a team folder naming convention on the local computer (for example, C:\TeamProjects\User1, C:\TeampProjects\User2 etc).

Additional Resources

- For more information about creating a workspace, see "How to: Create a Workspace" at *http://msdn2.microsoft.com/en-us/library/ms181384(VS.80).aspx*
- For more information about editing a workspace, see "How to: Edit a Workspace" at *http://msdn2.microsoft.com/en-us/library/ms245466(VS.80).aspx*

Consider Mapping Only Part of the Source Tree

To improve performance and reduce disk-size requirements, only map the files you need for your development project. In general, you will only need the files and projects associated with the solution on which you will be working.

Additional Resources

- For more information about creating a workspace, see "How to: Create a Workspace" at *http://msdn2.microsoft.com/en-us/library/ms181384(VS.80).aspx*
- For more information about editing a workspace, see "How to: Edit a Workspace" at *http://msdn2.microsoft.com/en-us/library/ms245466(VS.80).aspx*

Structure Your Source Tree to Support Branching

Your source tree structure consists of a combination of folder structure, file structure, and branch structure. Within your main branch, the following folder and file structure has been proven to work for teams of various sizes:

- **Main**—container for all assets you need in order to ship the product
    - **Source**—container for everything you need to build
        - **Code**—container for source code
        - **Shared Code**—container for source code that is shared from other projects
        - **Unit Tests**—container for unit tests
        - **Lib**—container for binary dependencies
    - **Docs**—container for documentation that will ship with the product
    - **Installer**—container for installer source code and binaries
    - **Tests**—container for test team test cases

Any branches that you create off of **Main** will copy this folder and file structure into the new branch; for example:

- **Development**—Development branch
    - **Source**—container for everything you need to build
        - **Code**—container for source code

Shared Code—container for source code that is shared from other projects

Unit Tests—container for unit tests

Lib—container for binary dependencies

Main—Integration branch

Source—container for everything you need to build

Code—container for source code

Shared Code—container for source code that is shared from other projects

Unit Tests—container for unit tests

Lib—container for binary dependencies

Docs—container for documentation that will ship with the product

Installer—container for installer source code and binaries

Tests—container for test team test cases

Additional Resources

- For more information about creating a workspace, see "How to: Create a Workspace" at *http://msdn2.microsoft.com/en-us/library/ms181384(VS.80).aspx*
- For more information about editing a workspace, see "How to: Edit a Workspace" at *http://msdn2.microsoft.com/en-us/library/ms245466(VS.80).aspx*

Shelving

- **Use shelving to share pending changes for review or handoff.**
- **Use shelving to back up pending changes to the server.**
- **Use shelving if interrupted by higher-priority work.**

Use Shelving to Share Pending Changes for Review or Handoff

Use shelving if you want to discuss or review your work-in-progress code with a remote team member. Rather than e-mailing the code to your teammate, you can shelve the code and then have your remote colleague retrieve the files from the shelf.

Similarly, if you want to pass partially finished work to another developer for completion, you can use shelving to hand the code off.

Additional Resources

- For more information on shelving pending changes, see "How to: Shelve and Unshelve Pending Changes" at *http://msdn2.microsoft.com/en-us/library/ms181404(VS.80).aspx*

Use Shelving to Back Up Pending Changes to the Server

Use shelving if you have not completed work at the end of the day but want to ensure that your current work is backed up on the server. By shelving your current changes, the changes are applied to the TFS server and can be retrieved by you (or others) the next day.

Additional Resources

- For more information on shelving pending changes, see "How to: Shelve and Unshelve Pending Changes" at *http://msdn2.microsoft.com/en-us/library/ms181404(VS.80).aspx*

Use Shelving if Interrupted by Higher-Priority Work

Use shelving if you are midway through making changes to a set of source code, when new higher-priority work is allocated (for example, an emergency bug fix is required). At this point, you need to go back to a stable version of the code but you do not want to lose your changes. Before doing so, you can shelve your code and easily retrieve it later.

Additional Resources

- For more information on shelving pending changes, see "How to: Shelve and Unshelve Pending Changes" at *http://msdn2.microsoft.com/en-us/library/ms181404(VS.80).aspx*

Source Control Resources

- For more information on Team Foundation Server Source Control, see "Team Foundation Source Control" at *http://msdn2.microsoft.com/en-us/library/ms181237(VS.80).aspx*

Guidelines: Reporting

Index

Administration

- *Ensure that users are in the correct security groups.*
- *Create a report dashboard to view project status and health metrics in one location.*

Creating / Customizing

- *Make sure that the server name is correct when deploying reports.*
- *Create scheduled report snapshots that you can view over time.*
- *Modify existing reports to gain access to additional data.*

Viewing

- *Ensure that the warehouse Web service has run if you want the latest data.*

Administration

- **Ensure that users are in the correct security groups.**
- **Create a report dashboard to view project status and health metrics in one location.**

Ensure That Users Are in the Correct Security Groups

If you want a user to be able to deploy reports, make sure that the user is assigned the report server's Content Manager Role. The Content Manager role is a predefined Report Services role for users who deploy and manage reports and data source connections on the Web server. For a Microsoft® Visual Studio® 2005 Team Foundation Server (TFS) user to be able to deploy reports to the report server, the user must be a member of this role.

► **To add a user to the Content Manager role**

1. Open the report site for the project. In Team Explorer, right-click the **Reports** entry for your team project and then select **Show Report Site**.
2. At the top of the window, click the **Properties** tab.

3. At the left side of the window, click **Security**.
4. Click **New Role Assignment**.
5. In the **Group or user name:** field, enter the name of the user or group you want to add to the Content Manager role
6. Select the **Content Manager** check box.
7. Click **OK**.

Additional Resources

- For more information about the Content Manager role, see "Content Manager Role" at *http://technet.microsoft.com/en-us/library/ms159693(SQL.90).aspx*
- For more information about security roles in the data tier, see "Securing Access Through Analysis Services" at *http://msdn2.microsoft.com/en-us/library/ms174839.aspx*
- For more information about security roles in the application tier, see "Securing Reporting Services" at *http://msdn2.microsoft.com/en-us/library/ms157198.aspx*

Create a Report Dashboard to View Project Status and Health Metrics in One Location

A reporting dashboard allows you and your team to quickly access important project information on a single page. The default Microsoft Office SharePoint® portal page for Microsoft Solution Framework (MSF) for Agile Software Development (MSF Agile) projects contains a single report as well as links to others. To create a single repository for project information, you can modify the portal page for MS Agile or MSF for CMMI® (MS CMMI) projects to include as many reports on the page as you want.

For example, a useful reporting dashboard could contain the following reports:

- Remaining Work
- Quality Indicators
- Bug Rates
- Project Velocity

You can add new reports to your SharePoint portal page by adding a Report Viewer Web Part for each report you want displayed on the page.

► **To modify the team project portal and create a reporting dashboard**

1. Install the Report Viewer Web Part on your report server using the stsadm.exe tool and RSWebParts.cab, both of which are included with SharePoint and the Report Services installation package.
   - STSADM.EXE can be found in the following path: C:\Program Files\Common Files\Microsoft Shared\web server extensions\60\BIN

   - RSWebParts.Cab can be found in the following path: C:\ Program Files\Microsoft SQL Server\90\Tools\Reporting Services\SharePoint
   - Example: STSADM.EXE -o addwppack -filename "C:\ Program Files\Microsoft SQL Server\90\Tools\Reporting Services\SharePoint\RSWebParts.cab" -globalinstall
2. In Team Explorer, right-click your project.
3. Click **Show Project Portal**.
4. Click **Modify Shared Page**.
5. Point to **Browse** and then click **Add Web Parts**.
6. Click **Virtual Server Gallery**.
7. In the **Web Part List**, select **Report Viewer**.
8. Click **Add**.
9. Enter the Report Manager name, such as http://*<report server>*/reports.
10. Enter the path for the report you want to display, such as *<my project>*/Quality Indicators.

Additional Resources

- For more information about adding a Report Viewer Web Part, see "Viewing Reports with SharePoint 2.0 Web Parts" at *http://msdn2.microsoft.com/en-us/library/ms159772(SQL.90).aspx*
- For more information about the team project portal, see "Using the Team Project Portal" at *http://msdn2.microsoft.com/en-us/library/ms242883(VS.80).aspx*

Creating / Customizing

- **Make sure that the server name is correct when deploying reports.**
- **Create scheduled report snapshots that you can view over time.**
- **Modify existing reports to gain access to additional data.**

Make Sure That the Server Name Is Correct When Deploying Reports

If either the report server's Uniform Resource Locator (URL) or Target Folder Name is specified incorrectly, your report cannot be deployed to the report server. When you deploy a report from Visual Studio 2005, specify the URL of the server to which the report should be deployed and the name of the team project of which the report is a part. The URL of the report server to which the report is to be deployed is http://TeamServerName/**ReportServer**, where **ReportServer** is the endpoint of the Report Server Web service.

Specify the team project name in the **TargetReportFolder** field of the deployment properties dialog box. This value is case-sensitive; if you get the case wrong, the report will be deployed but will not appear in the list of reports for your team project in Team Explorer.

Additional Resources

- For more information about setting the deployment properties, see "How to: Set Deployment Properties (Report Designer)" at *http://technet.microsoft.com/en-us/library/ms155802(SQL.90).aspx*

Create Scheduled Report Snapshots That You Can View over Time

Use report history to build snapshots of project data at regular intervals. You can view these snapshots over a specified time period to better understand trends, or to remember important data points throughout the duration of your project.

► **To create a scheduled report snapshot**

1. Open a report from the report portal.
2. Click the **Properties** tab.
3. Click the **History** link.
4. Set up a schedule for when you want the snapshot to run.

After the schedule has been set up, you can find the snapshots on the **History** tab for that report. You can also create manual snapshots on the **History** tab.

Modify Existing Reports to Gain Access to Additional Data

Modify reports by using the Microsoft SQL Server™ 2005 Reporting Services Designer inside Visual Studio (Business Intelligence Development Studio), which ships with the SQL Server 2005 client tools.

Customizing a report enables you to add functionality to an existing report without having to build a new report. If a report you need is similar to one that already exists, customize the existing report to save time. To customize an existing report, you must export it from the report server, add it to an existing report project in Visual Studio, and then redeploy it to the reporting portal after changes are made.

Note: Although you can use the Report Builder that is available from the team reporting site, this tool is not well supported for Visual Studio reporting scenarios and therefore is not recommended.

Additional Resources

- For a more detailed How To article, see "How To: Customize a Report in Visual Studio Team Foundation Server" in this guide.
- For more information about reporting, see Chapter 15, "Reporting Explained" in this guide.
- For more tutorials explaining how to work with reporting projects, see "Reporting Services Tutorials" at *http://msdn2.microsoft.com/en-us/library/ms170246.aspx*
- To read a Microsoft MSDN® article about editing reports, see "How to: Edit Reports in Report Designer" at *http://msdn2.microsoft.com/en-us/library/ms244655(VS.80).aspx*

Viewing

- **Ensure that the warehouse Web service has run if you want the latest data.**

Ensure That the Warehouse Web Service Has Run If You Want the Latest Data

Manually run the warehouse Web service if you want to ensure that your reports have the latest data. By default, the warehouse Web service runs once every hour to generate the data for your reports. If you are about run a report and want to ensure that your reports contain the latest data, you can run the service manually.

► To run the warehouse service manually

1. Open Internet Information Services (IIS) Manager.
2. Select the **Team Foundation Server** Web site.
3. Within the Web site, open the Warehouse\v1.0 directory.

   This displays a page with a list of the operations available on the warehouse.
4. Right-click warehousecontroller.asmx and then click Browse.
5. Click Run and then click Invoke.

   This opens a second browser window showing the status of the run request. It should show the value **true**.
6. Go back to the first browser window and navigate back to the operations page.
7. Select **GetwareHouseStatus** and then click **Invoke**.

This displays the current status of the warehouse Web service. A value of **idle** indicates that the warehouse has run. Other values display the status of service.

Additional Resources

- For more information about troubleshooting the warehouse, see "Troubleshooting the Data Warehouse" at *http://msdn2.microsoft.com/en-us/library/ms244674(vs.80).aspx*

Team Foundation Reporting Resources

- For more information about reporting, see "Team Foundation Server Reporting" at *http://msdn2.microsoft.com/en-us/library/ms194922(VS.80).aspx*

Guidelines: Project Management

Index

Areas and Iterations

- *Use areas for better traceability.*
- *Use iterations to represent milestones in your project.*
- *Determine appropriate iteration cycle duration.*

Check-in Policies

- *Use check-in policies to enforce code quality.*
- *Use check-in policies to ensure that developers associate work items with check-ins.*
- *Create check-in policies to enforce coding standards.*
- *Set up notifications to inform you when developers bypass check-in policies.*

Process Templates

- *Use the MSF Agile process template when working on projects that only require a light-weight or informal process.*
- *Use the MSF CMMI process template when working on projects requiring a more formal process or conformance with CMMI standards.*
- *Consider using a minimal process template.*
- *Modify an existing process template to match your team's process.*

Security Groups and Permissions

- *Create security groups to grant a specific set of permissions.*
- *Assign team members to the appropriate security group.*

Team Projects

- *Create one team project per application if you want to migrate work items and other assets between application versions.*
- *Create one team project per version if you want to start with new work items and other assets with each application version.*
- *Grant only required permissions on project assets.*
- *Structure your source tree to support branching.*

Work Items

- *Capture your scenarios at the start of your project.*
- *Define your Quality of Service requirements appropriately.*
- *Break scenarios into manageable, modular development tasks.*
- *Set acceptance criteria for each task.*
- *Link requirements and tasks to scenarios.*
- *Use Microsoft Excel for bulk editing of work items.*

Areas and Iterations

- **Use areas for better traceability.**
- **Use iterations to represent milestones in your project.**
- **Determine appropriate iteration cycle duration.**

Use Areas for Better Traceability

Use areas in your team project to keep project tasks, bugs, requirements, and other work items organized. You can also set permissions on areas to restrict access to various parts of your team project.

Use areas to represent logical or physical components, and then create sub-areas to represent specific features. This structure helps you keep your work items organized and can be used to improve traceability by component or feature.

► **To create areas for your project**

1. In Team Explorer, click your team project.
2. On the **Team** menu, point to **Team Project Settings**, and then click **Areas and Iterations**.
3. In the **Areas and Iterations** dialog box, click the **Area** tab.
4. Click the **Add a child node** toolbar button.
5. Right-click the new node, click **Rename**, and then type the area name you want.
6. Click the **Area** node.
7. Repeat steps 2, 3, and 4 to create additional areas and to create a hierarchy for your project structure.

Beware of creating too complex area structure, while areas allow you to partition work items permissions, there is overhead associated with managing those permissions for complex trees. It may also be problematic to copy over the structure/ permissions to other Team projects.

Additional Resources

- For more information about using areas, see "How To: Manage Projects in Visual Studio Team Foundation Server" in this guide.

Use Iterations to Represent Milestones in Your Project

Use iterations to define how many times your team will repeat a particular set of major activities (such as planning, implementation, or testing) during the course of application development. This set of major activities should represent a milestone for the project with a quantifiable outcome such as feature complete or component complete.

► To create an iteration

1. In Team Explorer, click your team project.
2. On the **Team** menu, point to **Team Project Settings**, and then click **Areas and Iterations**.
3. In the **Areas and Iterations** dialog box, click the **Iteration** tab.
4. Click the **Add a child node** toolbar button.
5. Right-click the new node, click **Rename**, and then type the iteration name.
6. Click the **Iteration** node.
7. Repeat steps 2, 3, and 4 to create additional iterations identified for your project.
8. Click **Close**.

Note: The Microsoft® Solutions Framework (MSF) for Agile Software Development (MSF Agile) process template includes three predefined iterations. Depending on your specific requirements, you can delete these iterations, rename them instead of creating new ones, or leave them unchanged.

Additional Resources

- For more information about using iterations, see "How To: Manage Projects in Visual Studio Team Foundation Server" in this guide.

Determine Appropriate Iteration Cycle Duration

When setting up your team project, determine the appropriate iteration cycle duration based on the size and complexity of your project.

Keep the following key points in mind when determining iteration cycle duration:

- The iteration cycle should be long enough to allow team members to get substantial work done, and should cover at least a few different scenarios.
- The iteration cycle should be short enough to flexibly accommodate changes and priorities.

In practice, a two-week iteration cycle works for most projects.

Additional Resources

- For more information about iteration cycle duration, see "How To: Manage Projects in Visual Studio Team Foundation Server" in this guide.
- For further information about iteration cycle duration, see Chapter 11, "Project Management Explained" in this guide.

Check-in Policies

- **Use check-in policies to enforce code quality.**
- **Use check-in policies to ensure that developers associate work items with check-ins.**
- **Create check-in policies to enforce coding standards.**
- **Set up notifications to inform you when developers bypass check-in policies.**

Use Check-in Policies to Enforce Code Quality

Use a combination of code analysis and testing policies to improve check-in quality for your project. For example, use the supplied testing policy to ensure that specific tests are executed and passed prior to allowing source to be checked into Microsoft Visual Studio® 2005 Team Foundation Server (TFS) source control. You can also configure a code analysis policy to help ensure that your code meets certain quality standards by ensuring that security, performance, portability, maintainability, and reliability rules are passed.

By enforcing this type of check-in policy in addition to policies that enforce coding standards and guidelines, you ensure that your code meets a specific quality standard.

► **To enforce a code analysis check-in policy for a team project**

1. In Team Explorer, right-click your team project, point to **Team Project Settings**, and then click **Source Control**.
2. Click the **Check-in Policy** tab, click **Add**, and then select and configure the appropriate policy.

Additional Resources

- For more information about creating and using a custom check-in policy, see "How To: Step Through Creating Custom Check-in Policies for TFS" in this guide.

Use Check-in Policies to Ensure That Developers Associate Work Items with Check-ins

Set the Work Items check-in policy to force developers to associate their check-in with a work item.

If a build breaks, it is important that you know what changesets are associated with the build, and what work items those changesets are associated with, so that you can identify the developer responsible for checking in this code and the area of the project on which the developer is working.

► **To set the Work Items check-in policy to force developers to associate their check-in with a work item**

1. In Team Explorer, right-click your team project, select **Team Project Settings**, and then click **Source Control**.
2. Click the **Check-in Policy** tab.
3. Click **Add** and then select and configure the **Work Item** check-in policy.

Additional Resources

- For more information about check-ins, see "How to: Check In Pending Changes" at *http://msdn2.microsoft.com/en-us/library/ms181411(VS.80).aspx*
- For more information about work items and changesets, see "How to: Associate Work Items with Changesets" at *http://msdn2.microsoft.com/en-us/library/ms181410(VS.80).aspx*

Create Check-in Policies to Enforce Coding Standards

The project you are working on may require coding standards that are not covered by static code analysis or by existing check-in policies. For example, your project may require that your code never uses the tab character, or that all check ins require comments. You can create new check-in policies to cover these scenarios.

► **To enforce a code analysis check-in policy for a team project**

1. In Team Explorer, right-click your team project, point to **Team Project Settings**, and then click **Source Control**.
2. Click the **Check-in Policy** tab and then click **Add**.
3. In the **Add Check-in Policy** dialog box, select **Code Analysis** and then click **OK**.
4. In the **Code Analysis Policy Editor**, select either **Enforce C/C++ Code Analysis (/analyze)** or **Enforce Code Analysis For Managed Code**. Select both if your project contains a combination of managed and unmanaged code.
5. If you select managed code analysis, configure your required rule settings for managed code analysis based on your required coding standards.

   This determines precisely which rules are enforced.

You can also create a custom check-in policy to perform checks that are not available by default. For example, you can disallow code patterns such as banned application programming interface (API) calls, or you can write a policy to enforce your team's specific coding style guidelines, such as where braces should be positioned within your source code.

Additional Resources

- For more information about creating check-in policies, see "How To: Create Custom Check-in Policies in Visual Studio Team Foundation Server" in this guide.

Set Up Notifications to Inform You When Developers Bypass Check-in Policies

Team Foundation Server Version Control does not prevent you from overriding a check-in policy. However, you can use the following steps to detect if a check-in policy has been overridden:

1. Use the Team Foundation Server Eventing Service (from the Team Foundation Core Services API) for hooking check-in events.
2. Write a **Notify** method that parses the details of the changeset and then reacts to it if an override has occurred.

Alternatively, you can manually scan changeset history to discover policy overrides.

Additional Resources

- To learn more about overriding a check-in policy, see "How to: Override a Check-in Policy" at *http://msdn2.microsoft.com/en-us/library/ms245460(VS.80).aspx*

Process Templates

- **Use the MSF Agile process template when working on projects that only require a lightweight or informal process.**
- **Use the MSF CMMI process template when working on projects requiring a more formal process or conformance with CMMI standards.**
- **Consider using a minimal process template.**
- **Modify an existing process template to match your team's process.**

Use the MSF Agile Process Template When Working on Projects That Only Require a Lightweight or Informal Process

When using Test-Driven Development (TDD) or other agile methodologies, you should use the MSF for Agile Software Development (MSF Agile) process template. This is a lightweight process for agile software projects. You should use this project template as your first choice, unless you specifically need the additional process improvement features provided by the MSF for CMMI Software Development (MSF CMMI) process template.

You can easily edit the MSF Agile process template and modify it to suit your process requirements.

Additional Resources

- For more information, see Chapter 11, "Project Management Explained" in this guide.
- For more information about the MSF Agile process template, see Chapter 13, "MSF for Agile Software Development Projects" in this guide.
- For more information about customizing the process template, see "How To: Customize a Process Template in Visual Studio Team Foundation Server" in this guide.

Use the MSF CMMI Process Template When Working on Projects Requiring a More Formal Process or Conformance with CMMI Standards

When using a formal software development process aimed at improving the existing process, you should use the MSF for CMMI Software Development (MS CMMI) process template.

You can easily edit and modify this process template to suit your process requirements.

Additional Resources

- For more information, see Chapter 11, "Project Management Explained" in this guide.
- For more information about customizing the template, see "How To: Customize a Process Template in Visual Studio Team Foundation Server" in this guide.

Consider Using a Minimal Process Template

Many teams do not require support for all parts of a standard team project. For example, many teams want to use the source control portion of a team project but not the Microsoft Office SharePoint® portal. Team project templates can be modified, and it is possible to remove some parts of the template that you do not need. When you modify the template, you will need to keep the Group Permissions and Classifications sections; however, you can keep or remove the other sections as you see fit.

In order to create a minimal process template, you use the Process Template Manager to download the template to your local computer, edit the template to remove the sections you are not going to use, and then upload the template back to the server.

Additional Resources

- For more information about process templates, see Chapter 13, "Process Templates Explained" in this guide.
- For more information about customizing process templates, see "How To: Customize a Process Template in Visual Studio Team Foundation Server" in this guide.
- For further information about customizing process templates, see "Customizing Process Templates" at *http://msdn2.microsoft.com/en-us/library/ms243782(VS.80).aspx*
- For more information on using a minimal process template see, "How to use TFS for source control only" at *http://blogs.msdn.com/richardb/archive/2007/05/10/how-to-use-tfs-for-source-control-only.aspx*

Modify an Existing Process Template to Match Your Team's Process

The project you are working on might not fit the out-of-box process templates provided with Microsoft Visual Studio Team System (VSTS). You might need a different work item type, or you might be using an entirely different process methodology. In this case, you should modify the existing process template. Choose the process template that most closely meets your process requirements and then modify the template as necessary.

The following areas of the process templates commonly need to be customized:

- Groups and Permissions
- Work Item Types
- Source Control Check-in Notes and Policies
- Areas and Iterations
- Reports
- Team Portal
- Process Guidance

Additional Resources

- For more information about process templates, see Chapter 13, "Process Template Explained" in this guide.
- For more information about customizing the template, see "How To: Customize a Process Template in Visual Studio Team Foundation Server" in this guide.

Security Groups and Permissions

- **Create security groups to grant a specific set of permissions.**
- **Assign team members to the appropriate security group.**

Create Security Groups to Grant a Specific Set of Permissions

When you create a project in Team Foundation Server, four default groups are created for that project regardless of your choice of process template. By default, each of these groups has a set of permissions defined for it that governs what members of those groups are authorized to do. The four groups are:

- Project Administrator
- Contributor
- Reader
- Build Services.

You can create security groups for your team project to better meet your organization's security requirements. Creating a security group is an efficient way to grant a specific set of permissions to a group of users on your team project. Make sure that you allow only the minimum permissions necessary for the group, and add only those users or groups who must belong to this new team project group.

Additionally use the following guidelines:

- Do not change the permissions on default groups (or if you do, do it in every project the same way)
- Use Active Directory (AD) groups for membership on server level only
- Use TFS groups for permissions settings (rather than AD groups)
- Never deny anything (usually deny means that the partitioning you use is less than ideal); make sure you reason is sound when you do

Additional Resources

- For more information on creating security groups, see "How To: Manage Projects in Visual Studio Team Foundation Server" in this guide.
- For more information on TFS permissions, see "Team Foundation Server Permissions" at *http://msdn2.microsoft.com/en-us/library/ms252587(VS.80).aspx*

Assign Team Members to the Appropriate Security Group

Identify the team members who will be working on the project and their roles, and assign these team members to TFS by using existing team project groups, server-level groups, or custom security groups that you create.

When assigning members to a security group, assign only those members who need the permissions available to that security group. If necessary, you can create custom security groups with appropriate security permissions and then assign users to those security groups.

Additional Resources

- For more information about security groups, see "How To: Manage Projects in Visual Studio Team Foundation Server" in this guide.

Team Projects

- **Create one team project per application if you want to migrate work items and other assets between application versions.**
- **Create one team project per version if you want to start with new work items and other assets with each application version.**
- **Create one team project per team when working with large projects that span multiple projects.**
- **Grant only required permissions on project assets.**
- **Structure your source tree to support branching.**

Create One Team Project per Application if You Want to Migrate Work Items and Other Assets Between Application Versions

If you want to carry forward not only source code but also work items and other TFS assets between releases, consider using one team project per application. When you use a single team project for multiple versions of the application, all of the TFS assets are carried forward automatically for the next release. When you are ready to release a new version of your application, you can create a branch within the project to represent the release and isolate that code.

Keep the following key points in mind when using one project per application:

- Parallel releases are forced to share work items schema, check in policies, and process guidance.
- Reporting is more difficult; because reports default to the entire project, you must add filtering by release.
- If you have hundreds of applications, each in its own project, you will run up against TFS performance and scale limits.
- You will accumulate 'baggage' over multiple releases. The easiest way to address this issue is to create a new project and branch the code you want to carry forward into that project.

Additional Resources

- For more information about using team projects, see "When to use Team Projects" at *http://blogs.msdn.com/ericlee/archive/2006/08/09/when-to-use-team-projects.aspx*

Create One Team Project per Version if You Want to Start with New Work Items and Other Assets with Each Application Version

If you want each release to start fresh without carrying forward work items and other TFS assets, consider using one project per release. When you use a new project for each release, you can modify work item schema, workflow, check-in policies, and other assets without impacting the old release. This can be especially useful if the old release will be maintained by a separate team such as a sustained engineering team who may have a different process and workflow than your main development team.

Keep the following key points in mind when using one project per release:

- Although it is very easy to move the source code from one project to another, it is difficult to move work items and other TFS assets from one project to another. Because work items can only be copied one at a time to another project, if you want to copy sets of work items, you will need to write your own utility.
- If you have hundreds of applications and releases, each in its own project, you will run up against TFS performance and scale limits.
- Choose a structure you can live with in the long term because restructuring existing team projects is difficult.
- Source can be easily shared among team projects as follows:
  - Branch source from one project to another.
  - Map source from another project into your workspace.
- Team Foundation Server can scale to ~500 projects by using the MSF Agile process template or 250 projects using the MSF CMMI process template. If you create your own process template or customize an existing process template, keep in mind that the work item schema has the largest impact on server scalability. A complex schema will result in a server capable of supporting fewer projects.
- You will have to carry over all the areas from the original project; and perhaps also change the permissions in source control.

Additional Resources

- For more information about using team projects, see "When to use Team Projects" at *http://blogs.msdn.com/ericlee/archive/2006/08/09/when-to-use-team-projects.aspx*

Grant Only Required Permissions on Project Assets

When creating team projects, review the default security groups created by the process and, if necessary, create security groups with appropriate permissions. You then assign the project members to appropriate groups to ensure that each member gets only the permissions he or she requires on project assets.

Additional Resources

- For more information about granting permissions, see "How To: Manage Projects in Visual Studio Team Foundation Server" in this guide.

Structure Your Source Tree to Support Branching

When creating your source tree structure, make sure that it supports branching. Keep separate folders for source and for other project assets, so that if isolation development is required in the future, you can simply branch the source folder. Also make sure that you maintain separate folders for each component within the source folder, so that partial branching can be performed if required.

Segregate other entities such as shared code, unit tests, library dependencies, and so on by using folders so that they can be excluded or included during branching as required.

The following is an example of a source tree structure that supports branching:

Main—Container for all assets you need to ship the product

- **Source**—Container for everything you need in order to build
  - **Code**—Container for source code
  - **Shared Code**—Container for source code that is shared from other projects
  - **Unit Tests**—Container for unit tests
  - **Lib**—Container for binary dependencies
- **Docs**—Container for documentation that will ship with the product
- **Installer**—Container for installer source code and binaries
- **Builds**—Container for Team Build scripts
- **Tests**—Container for test team test cases

Additional Resources

- For more information about source tree structure, see Chapter 5, "Defining Your Branching and Merging Strategy" in this guide.

Work Items

- **Capture your scenarios at the start of your project.**
- **Define your Quality of Service requirements appropriately.**
- **Break scenarios into manageable, modular development tasks.**
- **Set acceptance criteria for each task.**
- **Link requirements and tasks to scenarios.**
- **Use Microsoft Excel for bulk editing of work items.**

Capture Your Scenarios at the Start of Your Project

Create and capture a set of project scenarios at the start of your project. This helps you to gain a complete picture of your project and can later be used track progress. During the course of development, you can modify existing scenarios or add new scenarios to represent what you learn over time.

► To capture scenarios at the start of the project

1. Use the project back log (PBL) document, which is a requirement document based on input from various stakeholders (including customers, business analysts, end users, and product managers), and scope out the scenarios for your project.
2. In Team Explorer, expand the project node, right-click the Work Items folder, point to **Add Work Item**, and then click **Scenario**.
3. On the New Scenario page, enter the details for the scenario. Make sure to set the Iteration to **Iteration 999**.
4. Save your new scenario.
5. Repeat the above steps for all scenarios that you have identified for the project.

Additional Resources

- For more information about capturing scenarios, see "How To: Manage Projects in Visual Studio Team Foundation Server" in this guide.

Define Your Quality of Service Requirements Appropriately

Define your Quality of Service (QoS) requirements for each of the scenarios to be worked on during the iteration cycle. This helps to define the acceptance criteria for the scenario. The inputs for the QoS requirements come from project goals and requirements and specification documentation, if available.

► To define your QoS requirements

1. Right-click your project's Work Items folder, point to **Add Work Item**, and then click **Quality of Service Requirements**.

2. On the New Quality of Service Requirements page, add the following details:
   a. Set the **Type** to an appropriate value such as performance, scalability, stress, or security.
   b. Set the **Iteration** to the current iteration cycle.
   c. From the **Links** tab, link the QoS to a specific scenario for easier traceability.
3. Save the new QoS requirement.
4. Create one QoS requirement for each discipline or type of quality requirement, bearing in mind that each scenario can have multiple QoS requirements.
5. Make sure that you create QoS requirements for all of the scenarios being worked on during a specific iteration cycle.

Important: You can break down the QoS requirements into test tasks later.

Additional Resources

- For more information about defining QoS requirements, see "How To: Manage Projects in Visual Studio Team Foundation Server" in this guide.
- For more information about work items, see "Managing Team Foundation Work Items" at *http://msdn2.microsoft.com/en-us/library/ms181314(VS.80).aspx*

Break Scenarios into Manageable, Modular Development Tasks

During iteration planning, break your scenarios into user stories and then further break the user stories into development tasks. Make sure that the development tasks you create are manageable and modular. The tasks should not last for more than one or two days. If they are larger than this, you need to break the tasks down into smaller tasks or sub-tasks. Doing this contributes to schedule flexibility and improved manageability of the project.

► **To break scenarios into manageable, modular development tasks**

1. Break down the chosen scenarios into developer stories.
2. Subdivide the developer stories into developer tasks.
3. Capture developer tasks in TFS as task work items as follows:
   a. In Team Explorer, under your project node, right-click the Work Items folder, point to **Add Work Item**, and then click **Task**.
   b. On the New Task page, add the following details:
      i. Set the Discipline to Development.
      ii. Set the Iteration to the current iteration cycle.
      iii. On the Links tab, link the task to the specific scenario for easier traceability.
      iv. On this tab, along with the description, you can capture the acceptance

criteria for the task, which can determine if the task has been successfully completed.

v. Set the Assigned to field to the developer who will work on the task.

c. Save the new task.

d. Repeat the above steps for all the identified tasks.

4. Repeat the above steps for all the identified scenarios for the iteration.

Additional Resources

- For more information about scenarios, see "How To: Manage Projects in Visual Studio Team Foundation Server" in this guide.
- For more information about work items, see "Managing Team Foundation Work Items" at *http://msdn2.microsoft.com/en-us/library/ms181314(VS.80).aspx*

Set Acceptance Criteria for Each Task

Development tasks, when defined, should include acceptance criteria that allow a developer to decide when the task is complete. Depending on the process template you are using, this could be done in two different ways:

- **MSF Agile**—If you are using MSF Agile without a formal work item type requirement, it is best to include acceptance criteria as text in the work item itself. Start with a bulleted list and add more detail as necessary.
- **MSF CMMI**—If you are using MSF CMMI, you can use formal requirements to define acceptance criteria for a task. The first step is to define your requirements. You then create the development task that will be used to implement these requirements and link the task to the requirements so that the developer can check against them, and so that there is traceability from requirements to task.

The acceptance criteria are most often defined as a user experience requirement in the form of a mini-scenario or a QoS requirement. After the acceptance criteria have been met, the developer can mark the task as complete and move to the next task.

Additional Resources

- For more information about work items, see "Managing Team Foundation Work Items" at *http://msdn2.microsoft.com/en-us/library/ms181314(VS.80).aspx*

Link Requirements and Tasks to Scenarios

When creating new work items such as tasks, bugs, issues, or QoS requirements, make sure that you link these work items to the scenarios that drove their creation. This helps ensure that each work item is driven by a real user scenario and can be used to better track scenario completion progress during the course of your development iterations.

To links new tasks, bugs, issues, or QoS work items to scenarios

1. In the **New work item** page, click the **Links** tab, on the Links tab click the **Add** button.
2. In the **Add Link** dialog box, under **Link Type**, select **Scenario**.
3. Click **Browse** to find the scenarios in your team project.
4. In the list, select the scenario to which you want to link and then click **OK**.
5. In the **Comment** box, type a comment that explains how the work item is related. The **Description** box is filled in automatically.
6. Click **OK**.

Additional Resources

- For more information, see "How To: Manage Projects in Visual Studio Team Foundation Server" in this guide.
- For more information about work items, see "Managing Team Foundation Work Items" at *http://msdn2.microsoft.com/en-us/library/ms181314(VS.80).aspx*

Use Microsoft Excel for Bulk Editing of Work Items

Team Foundation Server does not support bulk editing of work items. Instead, you must edit each work item individually. If you need to modify a large number of work items in a short period of time—for example, during a triage meeting—consider using Microsoft Office Excel® to ease the task. Work items can be exported from TFS to Excel, modified, and then imported back into TFS to retain any edits that you made.

To create a work item list in Excel and edit it

1. In Microsoft Office Excel, on the **Team** menu, click **New List**.
2. Under **Connect to a Team Foundation Server**, select the server to connect to, or click **Servers** to enter the server information.
3. Under **Team Projects**, select the team project on the Team Foundation Server with which you want to work.

   The document will be bound to this team project.
4. Click **OK**.
5. Select the type of list you want. To create a query list, select the **Query List** option and then select a team query from the **Select a Query** drop-down list.
6. Select the columns you want to appear in the new work item list.
7. Import the desired work items. For more information, see How to: Import Work Items in Microsoft Excel or Microsoft Project at *http://msdn2.microsoft.com/en-us/library/ms181676(VS.80).aspx*
8. You can now edit the work items and then publish the updated work items to the work item database by clicking **Publish Changes** on the **Team** menu.

Additional Resources

- For more information about using Microsoft Office Excel for project-management tasks, see "Working with Work Item Lists in Microsoft Excel" at *http://msdn2.microsoft.com/en-us/library/ms181694(VS.80).aspx*

Team Foundation Project Management Resources

- For more information about MSF process templates, see "Process Templates" at *http://msdn2.microsoft.com/en-us/teamsystem/aa718801.aspx*

Practices at a Glance: Team Build

Index

Administration

- *How to secure your build server.*
- *How to delete a build.*
- *How to delete a build type.*
- *How to associate a work item with a build.*

Check-in Policies

- *How to use check-in policies to improve check-in quality.*
- *How to use check-in policies to associate work items with the build.*

Continuous Integration Builds

- *How to automatically run Continuous Integration (CI) builds.*
- *How to determine if you need a rolling build.*
- *How to determine your rolling build time interval.*

Customization

- *How to modify the build number*
- *How to set up workspace mapping to get and build a subset of the tree*
- *How to build a project with dependencies on another team project.*
- *How to change the build configuration (release/debug).*

Deployment

- *How to set up a build server.*
- *How to determine if you need multiple build servers.*

General

- *How to build and deploy an ASP.NET application with Team Build.*
- *How to build a Microsoft® .NET 1.1 application with Team Build.*
- *How to build setup and deployment projects with Team Build.*

- *How to create a team build.*
- *How to create multiple build types.*
- *How to create a team build for a project that references assemblies from another project.*
- *How to subscribe to build e-mail events.*
- *How to receive notification when a build has failed.*
- *How to start a build.*
- *How to verify that the build succeeded.*
- *How to view the build output.*
- *How to change the build server location.*
- *How to change the build output location.*
- *How to determine what changesets are part of the build.*
- *How to change the reported build quality.*

Projects

- *How to use a single-solution strategy.*
- *How to use a partitioned-solution strategy.*
- *How to use a multiple-solution strategy.*

Reporting

- *How to view build quality.*
- *How to view all the check-ins for a build.*
- *How to view work items or bugs closed for a build.*
- *How to view open work items or bugs for a build.*
- *How to track velocity from build to build.*
- *How to track test case pass/fail results for a build.*
- *How to review build status (BVT results).*

Scheduled Builds

- *How to automatically run nightly builds.*
- *How to decide on a build frequency and type for your project.*

Test-Driven Development

- *How to create a "hello world" acceptance test.*
- *How to run automated tests as part of the build.*
- *How to run code analysis as part of the build.*
- *How to get failed tests to fail a build.*

Administration

- **How to secure your build server.**
- **How to delete a build.**
- **How to delete a build type.**
- **How to associate a work item with a build.**

How to Secure Your Build Server

► **To secure your build server**

1. Deploy build services on a separate server, rather than sharing a server with the Microsoft Visual Studio® 2005 Team Foundation Server (TFS) application-tier or data-tier.
2. Grant the build process read/write access to the builds directory. Ensure that the account running the build is able to access this directory.
3. Grant the build process read/write access to the build drop network share. Ensure that the account running the build is able to access this share.
4. Ensure that the account used to run the team build is a member of the Team Project's **Build Services** group.

To improve Team Foundation Server security, you should install the build server on its own computer rather than on the application tier or data tier. Certain deployment or build steps may require elevated privileges; for example, creating a virtual directory to deploy a Web application requires administrative rights on the build server. This means that the Microsoft Windows® account running the build requires these rights. If the build computer is on the application tier, then this could present a security risk. Similarly, if the build computer is on the data tier, the build account could access and change the databases on that tier.

Note: For security reasons, do not add the account running the team build to the SERVER\ Service Accounts group. Members of this group have full administration rights in TFS.

Additional Resources

- For more information about TFS groups and permissions, see "Team Foundation Server Default Groups, Permissions, and Roles" at *http://msdn2.microsoft.com/en-us/library/ms253077(VS.80).aspx*

How to Delete a Build

To delete a build, you use the TFSBuild command-line tool. Specify the address of the TFS server, the name of the team project, and the build name; for example:

```
TfsBuild delete http://mytfsserver:8080 myproject build20070606.4
```

Additional Resources

- For more information about deleting a completed build, see "How to: Delete a Completed Build" at *http://msdn2.microsoft.com/en-us/library/aa337656(VS.80).aspx*
- For more information about the delete command, see "Delete Command (Team Foundation Build)" at *http://msdn2.microsoft.com/en-us/library/ms244360(VS.80).aspx*

How to Delete a Build Type

You cannot delete Team Build types by using Team Explorer. Instead, you should remove the build type from source control.

► **To delete an existing build type**

1. Open Source Control Explorer.
2. In Source Control Explorer, expand your team project folder.
3. Expand the TeamBuildTypes folder.
4. Right-click the Team Build folder that represents the Team Build type you want to delete and then click **Delete**.
5. Right-click the Team Build folder again and then click **Check In Pending Changes…**
6. Open Team Explorer.
7. Right-click the Team Builds folder and then click **Refresh**.
8. Expand the Team Builds folder and confirm that the Team Build has been deleted.

Additional Resources

- For more information about Team Build, see "Overview of Team Foundation Build" at *http://msdn2.microsoft.com/en-us/library/ms181710(vs.80).aspx*

How to Associate a Work Item with a Build

Use the **Check In** dialog box to associate work items with a check-in. This automatically associates these work items with the next build.

► **To associate a work item with a build**

1. Make code changes that you want to have included in the build and that will be associated with a work item.
2. Check in the pending changes.
3. In the **Check In** dialog box, click **Work Items**.
4. Select the work item(s) you want to associate with this check-in.

All changesets that have occurred since the last successful build will be associated with the next build. After the next build, Team Build will list this changeset in the associated changesets for the build and will include the selected work item as being associated with the changeset.

Additional Resources

- For more information about checking in pending changes, see "How to: Check In Pending Changes" at *http://msdn2.microsoft.com/en-us/library/ms181411(VS.80).aspx*

Check-in Policies

- **How to use check-in policies to improve check-in quality.**
- **How to use check-in policies to associate work items with the build.**

How to Use Check-in Policies to Improve Check-in Quality

Use a combination of code analysis and testing policies to improve check-in quality. For example, use the default testing check-in policy to ensure that specific tests are executed and passed prior to allowing source to be checked into TFS source control. You can also configure a code analysis policy to help ensure that your code meets certain quality standards by ensuring that security, performance, portability, maintainability, and reliability rules are passed.

► **To enforce a code analysis check-in policy for a team project**

1. In Team Explorer, right-click your team project, select **Team Project Settings**, and then click **Source Control**
2. Click the **Check-in Policy** tab.
3. Click **Add** and then select and configure the code analysis and testing policies.

Additional Resources

- For more information about creating and using a custom check-in policy, see "How To: Step Through Creating Custom Check-in Policies for TFS" in this guide.
- To learn how to customize a check-in policy, see "Walkthrough: Customizing Check-in Policies and Notes" at *http://msdn2.microsoft.com/en-us/library/ms181281(VS.80).aspx*
- To see sample code that will disallow selected patterns on check-in, see "Checkin Policy to Disallow Certain Patterns" at *http://blogs.msdn.com/jmanning/archive/2006/02/02/523125.aspx*
- To see sample code that will enforce comments on check-in, see "Sample Checkin Policy: Make Sure the Comment Isn't Empty" at *http://blogs.msdn.com/jmanning/archive/2006/01/21/515858.aspx*

- To learn how to register a new check-in policy, see "I've Made a New Check-In Policy! How Do I Add It?" at *http://blogs.msdn.com/jmanning/archive/2006/02/07/526778.aspx*

How to Use Check-in Policies to Associate Work Items with the Build

Use a check-in policy to enforce that each check-in has associated work items. Developers use the **Check In** dialog box to associate work items with a check-in. This automatically associates these work items with the next build.

► **To set the work item check-in policy to force developers to associate their check-in with a work item**

1. In Team Explorer, right-click your team project, select **Team Project Settings**, and then click **Source Control**.
2. Click the **Check-in Policy** tab.
3. Click **Add** and then select and configure the **Work Item** check-in policy.

Additional Resources

- For more information about creating and using a custom check-in policy, see "How To: Step Through Creating Custom Check-in Policies for TFS" in this guide.
- To learn how to customize a check-in policy, see "Walkthrough: Customizing Check-in Policies and Notes" at *http://msdn2.microsoft.com/en-us/library/ms181281(VS.80).aspx*

Continuous Integration Builds

- **How to automatically run Continuous Integration (CI) builds.**
- **How to determine if you need a rolling build.**
- **How to determine your rolling build time interval.**

How to Automatically Run Continuous Integration Builds

Although Visual Studio 2005 Team Foundation Server does not provide a Continuous Integration (CI) solution out of the box, it does provide the framework for you to implement your own CI solution.

► **To set up a CI build solution**

1. **Create and test your build.** Make sure that you have a Team Build type in place and that you can run it without errors.
2. **Install the Continuous Integration add-on.** Install the CI add-on from *http://msdn2.microsoft.com/en-us/library/ms364045(VS.80).aspx.*
3. **Configure the Continuous Integration add-on.** Ensure that the CI Web application virtual root runs in the **TFSAppPool** application pool. Update the CI Web

application Web.config file so that it works with your team server and team build by adding the following key:

```
<add key="1" value="TeamServer=http://TFSRTM:8080;TeamProjectName=AdventureWork
s;BuildType=Test Build"/>
```

4. **Register for the CheckinEvent event.** Use the **BisSubscribe.exe** tool to register for the check-in event, by using the following command line:

```
Bissubscribe /eventType CheckinEvent /address http://TFSRTM:8080/ci/notify.asmx
/deliveryType Soap /domain http://TFSRTM:8080
```

5. **Test the CI build.** Test the build by completing a check-in. Wait a few minutes for the build to complete, and then view the builds page to see if the build completed successfully.
6. **Set up e-mail alerts.** Set up alerts so that concerned parties can be notified when the build completes. Open the **Project Alerts** dialog box from the team project context menu, and then select the **A build completes** alert check box.

For more information and expanded steps, see "How To: Set Up a Continuous Integration Build with Visual Studio Team Foundation Server" in this guide.

Additional Resources

- For more information, see Chapter 8, "Setting up a Continuous Integration Build with Team Build" in this guide.
- For more information about setting up a CI build, see "How To: Set Up a Scheduled Build with Visual Studio Team Foundation Server" in this guide.
- For more information about how to use the Visual Studio Team System CI solution, see "Continuous Integration Using Team Foundation Build" at *http://msdn2.microsoft.com/en-us/library/ms364045(VS.80).aspx*
- To download the Visual Studio Team System CI solution MSI, go to *http://download.microsoft.com/download/6/5/e/65e300ce-22fc-4988-97de-0e81d3de2482/ci.msi*
- For more information about agile development and CI in TFS, see "Extend Team Foundation Server To Enable Continuous Integration" at *http://msdn.microsoft.com/msdnmag/issues/06/03/TeamSystem/default.aspx*

How to Determine if You Need a Rolling Build

Building immediately after every check-in is the simplest CI strategy and generally gives you the most rapid feedback. However, if check-ins occur rapidly enough to overwhelm the build server, you should use a rolling build approach where you build after a specified number of check-ins or after a specified time period. To find out if you need to use a rolling build, determine the following:

- Length of your team build in minutes
- Average frequency of check-ins in minutes
- Time window during which frequent check-ins occur

If the length of the build is longer than the average frequency of check-ins, your builds run continuously because the first build will not complete before the next check-in occurs, which starts another build. If check-ins continue to occur before each build is complete, this impacts the performance of the build server and will block other builds from being started, such as scheduled builds. Review the time window during which frequent check-ins occur and determine if CI builds are likely to impact the delivery of scheduled builds or other important team builds.

Additional Resources

- For more information, see Chapter 8, "Setting Up a Continuous Integration Build with Team Build" in this guide.

How to Determine Your Rolling Build Time Interval

It is important to determine the rolling build time interval to ensure an efficient build process. You will want a timely build while at the same time not overloading the build process.

To determine the ideal rolling build interval, divide the average frequency of check-ins by the length of your build. For example, if you have a build that takes 10 minutes and you average a check-in every 5 minutes, you could set a check-in interval of two check-ins and a timeout period of 10 minutes. This helps to ensure that the build is complete before the next build is started. If you notice excessive load on your build server, you can increase these values.

Additional Resources

- For more information, see Chapter 8, "Setting Up a Continuous Integration Build with Team Build" in this guide.

Customization

- **How to modify the build number.**
- **How to set up workspace mapping to get and build a subset of the tree.**
- **How to build a project with dependencies on another team project.**
- **How to change the build configuration (release/debug).**

How to Modify the Build Number

In order to customize the build number in your compiled assemblies, you need to generate the replacement build number and then write it to the assemblyinfo source file.

In order to customize the build number property displayed in the Team Build interface, you need to override the $(**BuildNumber**) property in the **BuildNumberOverride** target.

► To customize the build number in both the assembly and in the Team Build interface

1. Override the $(BuildNumber) in the BuildNumberOverride target.
2. Override the BeforeCompile target to write the AssemblyInfo.cs or .vb file.

   Example

```
<Target Name="BuildNumberOverrideTarget">
  <Message Importance="High" Text="$(BuildNumber)" />

  <ConvertTFSBuildNumberToSolutionBuildNumber
    MajorAndMinorVersion="1.0"
    TFSBuildNumber="$(BuildNumber)"
    TFSLastBuildNumber="$(LastBuildNumber)">
    <Output TaskParameter="SolutionBuildNumber" PropertyName="SolutionBuildN
umber" />
    <Output TaskParameter="TFSBuildNumber" PropertyName="BuildNumber" />
  </ConvertTFSBuildNumberToSolutionBuildNumber>
  <Message Importance="High" Text="$(SolutionBuildNumber)" />
  <Message Importance="High" Text="$(BuildNumber)" />
</Target>

<Target Name="BeforeCompile">
  <Message Importance="High" Text="$(SolutionBuildNumber)" />
  <CreateItem Include="$(SolutionRoot)\**\AssemblyInfo.cs">
    <Output TaskParameter="Include" ItemName="AssemblyInfoFiles"/>
  </CreateItem>
  <CreateItem Include="$(SolutionRoot)\**\AssemblyInfo.vb">
    <Output TaskParameter="Include" ItemName="AssemblyInfoFiles"/>
  </CreateItem>
  <RewriteFileVersions
    AssemblyInfoFiles="@(AssemblyInfoFiles)"
    AssemblyVersionNumber="$(SolutionBuildNumber)"
    AssemblyFileVersionNumber="$(SolutionBuildNumber)"
    AssemblyInformationalVersionNumber="$(SolutionBuildNumber)" />
</Target>
```

Additional Resources

- For another method to modify assembly versioning, see Aaron Halberg's blog post "Team Build and the AssemblyInfo Task" at *http://blogs.msdn.com/aaronhallberg/archive/2007/06/08/team-build-and-the-assembly-info-task.aspx*

- The AssemblyInfo task, referenced in the blog post above, has a new home on GotDotNet. You can find it here *http://www.gotdotnet.com/Community/UserSamples/Details.aspx?SampleGuid=5C455590-332C-433B-A648-E368B9515580*
- For more information about customizing Team Foundation Build, see "Customizing Team Foundation Build" at *http://msdn2.microsoft.com/en-us/library/ms400688(VS.80).aspx*

How to Set Up Workspace Mapping to Get and Build a Subset of the Tree

The workspace mapping file defines the source control folders that are retrieved by the build server. It is not always necessary to check out all of the files in order to perform the build. You can change your workspace definition to reduce the number of folders included, or you can cloak unnecessary files so that they are not retrieved as part of the build.

For example, the default mapping for a new project is $/TeamProject. If all your source files are under $/TeamProject/foo/bar/foobar/sources, you should map only that directory

► To cloak files and folders

1. Check out WorkspaceMapping.xml from source control.
2. Add the appropriate cloak entries to this file.
3. Check in WorkspaceMapping.xml.

   The WorkspaceMapping.xml file looks like the following:

```
<Mappings>
  <InternalMapping ServerItem="$/MyTeamProject" LocalItem="c:\projects\teampro-
ject" Type="Map" />
  <InternalMapping ServerItem="$/MyTeamProject/documentation" Type="Cloak" />
</Mappings>
```

Additional Resources

- For more information about cloaking folders in a workspace, see "How to: Cloak and Decloak Folders in a Workspace" at *http://msdn2.microsoft.com/en-us/library/ms181378(VS.80).aspx*
- For more information about making Team Build ignore folders, see "How to make 'Team Build' skip getting certain folders?" at *http://blogs.msdn.com/manishagarwal/archive/2005/10/13/480584.aspx*
- For more information about the WorkspaceMapping schema, see "Schema for the WorkspaceMapping.xml file" at *http://blogs.msdn.com/buckh/archive/2007/02/28/schema-for-the-workspacemapping-xml-file.aspx*

How to Build a Project with Dependencies on Another Team Project

Team Build does not support building solutions that cross team projects. To enable this, you must customize the TFSBuild.proj file to check out the code you need from the other projects on which your build depends.

To build a project with dependencies on another team project, you need to get the source or assemblies from that project into the workspace on your build server. To do this, you need to edit your TFSBuild.proj file to add the assembly or the solution reference and override the **BeforeGet** event to get assemblies or sources from each of the team projects on which you have a dependency.

► **To build a project that has dependencies on another team project**

1. Check out the TFSBuild.proj script from Source Control Explorer.
2. Add the following configuration setting under the **PropertyGroup** section:

```
<!-- to be added under PropertyGroup -->
<TfCommand>$(TeamBuildRefPath)\..\tf.exe</TfCommand>
<SkipInitializeWorkspace>true</SkipInitializeWorkspace>
```

   SkipInitializeWorkSpace allows you to skip invoking the default tasks to delete and re-create the workspace on the build machine. The new property is used in the custom target **BeforeGet** (see below).

3. Add the following configuration setting to the **ItemGroup** entries that map both the Team Projects and the solutions. Make sure that you provide the correct local paths for the build machine. Multiple mappings cannot share the same local folder and will result in a **MappingConflictException** exception in the CreateWorkspace task.

```
<ItemGroup>
  <!-- add one entry for every solution you reference -->
  <SolutionToBuild Include="$(SolutionRoot)\DependentApp\DependentApp.sln" />
  <SolutionToBuild Include="$(SolutionRoot)\YourApp\YourApp.sln" />
</ItemGroup>

<ItemGroup>
  <!-- add one entry for every Team Project you reference -->
  <Map Include="$/YourApp/YourApp">
    <LocalPath>$(SolutionRoot)\YourApp</LocalPath>
  </Map>
  <Map Include="$/DependentApp/DependentApp">
    <LocalPath>$(SolutionRoot)\DependentApp</LocalPath>
  </Map>
</ItemGroup>
```

4. Override the **BeforeGet** event to retrieve the workspaces for each Team Project:

```
<Target Name="BeforeGet">
  <DeleteWorkspaceTask
      TeamFoundationServerUrl="$(TeamFoundationServerUrl)"
      Name="$(WorkspaceName)" />
  <Exec
    WorkingDirectory="$(SolutionRoot)"
    Command="&quot;$(TfCommand)&quot; workspace /new $(WorkSpaceName) /server:$
(TeamFoundationServerUrl)"/>
  <Exec
   WorkingDirectory="$(SolutionRoot)"
   Command="&quot;$(TfCommand)&quot; workfold /unmap /workspace:$(WorkSpaceName
) &quot;$(SolutionRoot)&quot;"/>
  <Exec
    WorkingDirectory="$(SolutionRoot)"
    Command="&quot;$(TfCommand)&quot; workfold /map /workspace:$(WorkSpaceName)
/server:$(TeamFoundationServerUrl) &quot;%(Map.Identity)&quot; &quot;%(Map.
LocalPath)&quot;"/>
</Target>
```

5. Check in the build script and run the build.

Additional Resources

- For more information, see Manish Agarwal's blog entry, "Working with multiple team projects in Team Build," at *http://blogs.msdn.com/manishagarwal/archive/2005/12/22/506635.aspx*

How to Change the Build Configuration (Release/Debug)

In order to change build configuration in an existing build, you need to modify the **<ConfigurationToBuild>** tag in TFSBuild.proj.

► To change the build configuration

1. Open Source Control Explorer.
2. In Source Control Explorer, expand your team project folder.
3. Expand the TeamBuildTypes folder.
4. Select the team build folder for which you want to turn on code analysis.
5. Check out the TFSBuild.proj file from source control. You might need to perform a **Get Latest Version** operation on the folder first.
6. In Source Control Explorer, double-click TFSBuild.Proj to open it.
7. Modify the **<ConfigurationToBuild>** tag to the new build configuration.
8. Save TFSBuild.proj and check it back into source control.

Additional Resources

- For more information about customizing Team Foundation Build, see "Customizing Team Foundation Build" at *http://msdn2.microsoft.com/en-us/library/ms400688(VS.80).aspx*

Deployment

- **How to set up a build server.**
- **How to determine if you need multiple build servers.**

How to Set Up a Build Server

You install the build server separately from your installation of TFS. Because the build server needs to be able to compile your code, run tests, and perform code analysis, all tools that are needed by the build process must be installed.

► **To set up a build server**

1. Install Visual Studio.
   - If you want to ensure you have all the tools necessary for any build scenario, install the entire Team Suite.
   - If you want to run Team Build but do not need to run test cases, install Visual Studio Team Developer Edition.
   - If you want to run automated tests cases as part of your build process, install Visual Studio Team Test Edition.
2. On the Team Foundation Server DVD, open the \build folder.
3. Run the Setup wizard.

The account used to run the build server:

- Must have **Log On Locally** permission on the TFS computers.
- Should not be a local administrator account on TFS computers.
- Should be marked **Account is sensitive and cannot be delegated** for Microsoft Active Directory® on the domain.

Additional Resources

- You can download the Team Foundation Server Installation Guide from *http://www.microsoft.com/downloads/details.aspx?familyid=e54bf6ff-026b-43a4-ade4-a690388f310e&displaylang=en*

How to Determine if You Need Multiple Build Servers

If you have multiple build types all executing on a single build server, you can overload the build server. If this becomes an issue, consider executing different build types on different build servers.

A build can take a long time to execute, especially if the build is for a large project. If you are using Continuous Integration or frequent scheduled builds, it is possible that the build server will not be able to keep up with the volume of builds being generated. You can install multiple build servers to distribute the load. Assign different build types to each server to even out the build load.

General

- **How to build and deploy an ASP.NET application with Team Build.**
- **How to build a .NET 1.1 application with Team Build..**
- **How to build setup and deployment projects with Team Build.**
- **How to create a team build.**
- **How to create multiple build types.**
- **How to create a team build for a project that references assemblies from another project.**
- **How to subscribe to build e-mail events.**
- **How to receive notification when a build has failed.**
- **How to start a build.**
- **How to verify that the build succeeded.**
- **How to view the build output.**
- **How to change the build server location.**
- **How to change the build output location.**
- **How to determine what changesets are part of the build.**
- **How to change the reported build quality.**

How to Build and Deploy an ASP.NET Application with Team Build

If you want to build a solution that contains only ASP.NET Web applications, you must ensure that you choose the appropriate configuration. When creating the build type, when you select the configuration and the platform, make sure that the platform is set to **.NET** and that the **Configuration** is set to **Debug**:

► **To build a solution that contains only ASP.NET Web applications projects**

1. Run the New Team Build Type Creation Wizard.
2. Give the build a name.

3. Select the solution that contains only the ASP.NET Web application.
4. Select the appropriate configuration.
5. Click the Platform drop-down list and select .NET as the platform.
6. Specify the location information for the build type.
7. Choose the tests and code analysis rules to run.
8. Save the build type by selecting Finish.

If you are building a solution that contains both ASP.NET Web applications and other .NET projects, you must set the platform type to **Mixed Platforms**.

► **To build a solution that contains ASP.NET Web applications and other .NET projects**

1. Run the New Team Build Type Creation Wizard.
2. Give the build a name.
3. Select the solution that contains only ASP.NET Web applications and other projects.
4. Select the appropriate configuration.
5. Click the Platform drop-down list and select Mixed as the platform.
6. Specify the location information for the build type.
7. Choose the tests and code analysis rules to run.
8. Save the build type by selecting Finish.

You will find the compiled binaries in the drop location under {BuildType}\{Configuration Name}\{Platform}_PublishedWebsites

Deploying a Web application to Internet Information Services (IIS) is not supported natively by Team Build. If you want to deploy the application to IIS as part of the team build, you have two choices: you can: add a custom step to the build type, or you can use a Web Deployment Project.

If you are at the start of a Team Project, examine the Web Deployment Project option to see if you can use this option in your development. If you already have existing Web sites, using Web Deployment Projects may disrupt application development. Consider using an MSBuild post-build step instead. In both cases, you must ensure that the service account used to run the build is a member of the local administrators group to allow it to create a virtual directory in IIS.

► **To use a post build step to deploy your Web application**

1. Download the SDC Tasks Library from Codeplex at *http://www.codeplex.com/sdctasks*
2. Check out the Team Build type that you are going to use to deploy the Web application.
3. Extract the file Microsoft.Sdc.Tasks.dll from the downloaded zip file into the folder where you checked out the build type.

4. Add the DLL to source control and check it in.
5. Amend the TFSBuild.proj file so that the build copies the files to the correct directory, and then create that directory as a virtual directory as follows:
   a. Add a **<PropertyGroup>** element specifying the location of the compiled Web application:

   ```
   <PropertyGroup>
    <WebBinariesLocation>$(SolutionRoot)\..\Binaries\.NET\Release\_
   PublishedWebSites\MyWebSite</WebBinariesLocation>
   </PropertyGroup>
   ```

   b. Add two **UsingTask** elements that add a references to the CreateVirtualDirectory and DeleteVirtualDirectory tasks:

   ```
   <UsingTask TaskName="Microsoft.Sdc.Tasks.Web.WebSite.CreateVirtualDirectory"
   AssemblyFile="Microsoft.Sdc.Tasks.dll" />

   <UsingTask TaskName="Microsoft.Sdc.Tasks.Web.WebSite.CreateVirtualDirectory"
   AssemblyFile="Microsoft.Sdc.Tasks.dll" />
   ```

   c. Add an **AfterCompile** target to create the virtual directory and copy the files into that directory:

   ```
   <Target Name="AfterCompile">
    <MakeDir Directories="C:\Deploy\MyWebsite" />
    <CreateVirtualDirectory VirtualDirectoryName="MyWebSite" Path="C:\Deploy\
   Website" />
    <DeleteVirtualDirectory VirtualDirectoryName="MyWebSite" />
    <Exec Command="xcopy /y /e $(WebBinariesLocation) C:\Deploy\MyWebsite"/>
   </Target>
   ```

6. Save the file and commit it to the source control repository.

If you run the team build, it will now build the Web application, create a virtual directory, and copy the Web application to that directory.

► **To use a Web deployment project**

1. Download and install the Visual Studio 2005 Web Deployment Projects onto your client computer.
2. Download and install the Visual Studio 2005 Web Deployment Projects onto your build server.
3. Open the solution containing the Web application.
4. Click the **Build** menu and then select **Add Web Deployment Project...**
5. Specify the name and location of the deployment project.

6. In Solution Explorer, right-click the Web Deployment Project and then select **Property Pages**.
7. In the dialog box, choose the **Configuration** that Team Build should build (Debug or Release).
8. In the **Deployment** section, select the **Create an IIS virtual directory for the output folder** check box and then specify the virtual directory name.
9. Click **OK**.
10. Check the solution changes into source control.

If you run the team build containing this solution, it will build the Web application and create a virtual directory in the directory where the Web application is built. This will be Build Directory}\{Team Project Name}\{Build Type}\Binaries\{Configuration Name}\{Platform}_PublishedWebSite\{Web Deployment Project Name.

Additional Resources

- To download the SDC Tasks, go to *http://www.codeplex.com/sdctasks*
- For more information about building ASP.NET applications with Team Build, see "TN_1600: Building ASP.NET projects with Team Build" at *http://msdn2.microsoft.com/en-us/teamsystem/aa718894.aspx*
- For more information about using Web Deployment Projects, see "TN_1601: Team Build and Web Deployment Projects" at *http://msdn2.microsoft.com/en-us/teamsystem/aa718895.aspx*
- For more information about building Web Deployment Projects, see "Visual Studio 2005 Web Deployment Projects" at *http://msdn2.microsoft.com/en-us/asp.net/aa336619.aspx*

How to Build a .NET 1.1 Application with Team Build

Because .NET 1.1 is not directly supported by MSBuild, it is not supported by Team Build. Microsoft has released a project on CodePlex named MSBuild Extras (MSBee) that supports building .NET 1.1 applications.

In order to build your .NET 1.1 applications, you need to upgrade your project file to a .NET 2.0 project file. You will also need to edit the Team Build project file so that it builds using the .NET 1.1 tools rather than the .NET 2.0 tools.

► To build a .NET 1.1 applications with Team Build

1. Upgrade your .NET 1.1 solutions to .NET 2.0. You can do this by opening the solution in Visual Studio 2005 and running the Conversion Wizard, or by running devenv [projectname] /upgrade.

2. Ensure that the .NET 1.1 Software Development Kit (SDK) is installed on your build server.
3. Download and install MSBuild Extras from *http://www.codeplex.com/MSBee*
4. Download BuildingFx11inTB.targets from *http://blogs.msdn.com/gautamg/attachment/578915.ashx*
5. Check out the build type from source control that will build your .NET 1.1 project.
6. Copy BuildingFx11inTB.targets to the directory containing the build type and check the file into source control.
7. Edit TFSBuild.proj file:
    a. Import the BuildingFx11inTB.targets file:
    ```
    <Import Project="$(MSBuildProjectDirectory)\BuildingFx11inTB.targets" />
    ```
    b. Add a property defining the CSharp targets:
    ```
    <PropertyGroup>

         <AdditionalPropertiesForBuildTarget>CustomAfterMicrosoftCommonTar
    gets=$(ProgramFiles)\MSBuild\MSBee\MSBuildExtras.Fx1_1.CSharp.targets</
    AdditionalPropertiesForBuildTarget>

     </PropertyGroup>
    ```
8. Check TFSBuild.proj into source control.

Additional Resources

- For more information about MSBuild Extras, see "MSBuild Extras - Toolkit for .NET 1.1 "MSBee" at *http://www.codeplex.com/MSBee*
- For more information about using MSBuild Extras to build .NET 1.1 applications, see "Building .NET 1.1 application using Team Build" at *http://blogs.msdn.com/gautamg/archive/2006/04/19/578915.aspx*

How to Build Setup and Deployment Projects with Team Build

Team Build does not support setup projects by default. Use a custom post-build step to compile the setup project and copy the binaries to the build drop location as follows.

1. Test the build.

    Make sure that the Team Build that you want to use for the setup project works. If it does not, fix it before moving on.

Tip: Most builds include the main project build as well as the setup build. If you are creating a new team build for the setup project only, do this before moving to step 2.

2. Ensure that the setup project is built by default.
   a. In Solution Explorer, right-click the installer project for which you need to create a team build.
   b. Click **Properties**.
   c. Click **Configuration Manager...**
   d. Select the build configuration(s) you want to build; for example, Debug, Release.
   e. Select the **Build** check box for the installer project.
3. Ensure that all build paths in the project file are relative.
   a. Open the solution folder for the installer project.
   b. Open the .vdproj file in an editor other than Visual Studio.
   c. Check out the .vdproj file for editing.
   d. Search for each of the following entries: **SccLocalPath**, **SccAuxPath**, **OutputFileName**, and **SourcePath**.
   e. Ensure that the path for each entry is relative and not absolute. (This is the default when a setup project is created.) Absolute paths start with a drive letter. Relative paths start with a double forward slash ('\\') or nothing.
   f. If you find an absolute path, replace it with a relative path. Do not modify any constant expressions. These are expanded by the installer later; for example:

```
"OutputFileName" = "8:c:\\temp\\SetupProject.msi" would be replaced with
"OutputFileName" = "8:debug\\SetupProject.msi"
```

> **Tip:** Relative paths will be directly off of the project folder.

> **Tip:** Always use double forward slash ('\\') when creating paths because it will be passed through code that decodes to a single forward slash ('\').

   g. If you had to make any changes, check the .vdproj file back in.
4. Add a post-compile task to your team build.
   a. Open the team build you want to use for the setup project.
   b. Check out the build type from source control:
      i. You can find the build type beneath your team project in source control, in a subfolder of the TeamBuildTypes folder named TFSBuild.proj.
      ii. You might need to perform a **Get Latest Version** operation on the folder first.

c. In Source Control Explorer, double-click TFSBuild.Proj to open it.

Note: Viewing the build type from the Team Explorer will not work; because this opens a read-only copy of the build file.

d. Add the following code to the end of the file between the last **</ItemGroup>** tag and the last **</Project>** tag:

```
<Target Name="AfterCompile">

        <Exec Command="&quot;C:\Program Files\Microsoft Visual
Studio 8\Common7\IDE\devenv&quot; &quot;C:\Documents and Settings\
darren\My Documents\Visual Studio 2005\Projects\HelloWorldTest\
HelloWorldTestInstaller\HelloWorldTestInstaller.vdproj&quot; /Build
&quot;Debug&quot;"/>

        <Copy SourceFiles="C:\Documents and Settings\
darren\My Documents\Visual Studio 2005\Projects\HelloWorldTest\
HelloWorldTestInstaller\Debug\HelloWorldTestInstaller.msi" DestinationFo
lder="$(OutDir)" />

        <Copy SourceFiles="C:\Documents and Settings\
darren\My Documents\Visual Studio 2005\Projects\HelloWorldTest\
HelloWorldTestInstaller\Debug\setup.exe" DestinationFolder="$(OutDir)"
/>

</Target>
```

e. Check the paths in the pasted code to make sure that they are accurate for your build server.

Tip: Use the command line to test the path in the exec command tag. Replace each " with a quote when testing on the command line, for example: "C:\Program Files\Microsoft Visual Studio 8\Common7\IDE\devenv" "C:\Documents and Settings\darren\My Documents\Visual Studio 2005\Projects\HelloWorldTest\HelloWorldTestInstaller\HelloWorldTestInstaller.vdproj" /Build "Debug"

Tip: Use the command line to test the SourceFiles paths as well.

5. Test the build changes.
   a. In Team Explorer, right-click the build type and then click **Build Team Project**.
   b. Review the build summary to determine if the build passed or failed.

c. If the build failed, click the link to the build log. Common reasons for failure include:

   i. **Exec command path is incorrect.**

   ii. **Permissions are not set to allow the output files to be copied to the build directory.** Make sure that the tfsservice user account has permissions to copy from the binaries folder and to the build folder. The binaries folder is the location where the msi file will be placed after the solution builds. The build folder is specified in tfs.proj in the <BuildDirectoryPath> tag.

   iii. **Permissions are not set to allow the installer to build.** Make sure that the tfsserver user account has permissions to read the .vdproj file and source files for your installer project as well as the application with which the installer is associated. Also make sure that the tfsserver user account has permissions to write binary files to the output directory; for example, Debug or Release.

   iv. **Build configuration is incorrect.** Make sure that the build configuration you specify in the exec command exists for your project. For instance, your project might have "Debug | Any CPU" but not "Debug". You can check this by looking at the solution properties in Solution Explorer.

d. If the build log does not give you enough information, create an output file for the exec command and review this log for more information. For example:

```
<Exec Command="&quot;C:\Program Files\Microsoft Visual Studio 8\Common7\
IDE\devenv&quot; &quot;C:\Documents and Settings\darren\My Documents\
Visual Studio 2005\Projects\HelloWorldTest\HelloWorldTestInstaller\
HelloWorldTestInstaller.vdproj&quot; /Build &quot;Debug&quot; > c:\temp\
output.txt"/>
```

Additional Resources

- For more information, see "Walkthrough: Configuring Team Foundation Build to Build a Visual Studio Setup Project" at *http://msdn2.microsoft.com/en-us/library/ms404859(VS.80).aspx*

How to Create a Team Build

You can create a new team build from the Team Builds folder in Team Explorer.

To create a team build

1. Open Team Explorer.
2. Expand the team project for which you want to create a build.

3. Right-click the Team Builds folder in the tree.
4. Select **New Team Build Type...**
5. Specify the name of the new team build type and click **Next**.
6. Select the projects you wish to build, this should include the project that contains your unit tests.
7. Select a build configuration (e.g. release or debug) and click **Next**.
8. Specify the name of your build server, e.g. **TFSRTM**
9. Specify a local build directory on your build server, e.g. **c:\builds**
10. Specify a drop location for your build output, e.g. **\\TFSRTM\NightlyBuilds** and then click **Next**.
11. Click the **Run tests** checkbox, select the test list you want to associate with the build, and then click **Next**.
12. Click **Finish** to create the team build type.

How to Create Multiple Build Types

To create multiple build types—for example, Release for Customers or Debug for Test Team—use separate team builds for each build type that interests you.

► **To create a team build**

1. Open Team Explorer.
2. Expand the team project for which you want to create a build.
3. Right-click the Team Builds folder in the tree.
4. Select **New Team Build Type...**
5. Specify the name of the new team build type and click **Next**.
6. Select the projects you wish to build, this should include the project that contains your unit tests.
7. Select a build configuration (e.g. release or debug) and click **Next**.
8. Specify the name of your build server, e.g. **TFSRTM**
9. Specify a local build directory on your build server, e.g. **c:\builds**
10. Specify a drop location for your build output, e.g. **TFSRTM\NightlyBuilds** and then click **Next**.
11. Click the **Run tests** checkbox, select the test list you want to associate with the build, and then click **Next**.
12. Click **Finish** to create the team build type.

How to Create a Team Build for a Project That References Assemblies from Another Project

To build a project that has dependencies on another team project, you need to get the source or assemblies from that project into the workspace on your build server. To do this, you need to edit your TFSBuild.proj file in order to add the assembly or the solution reference and override the **BeforeGet** event to get assemblies or sources from each of the required team projects.

To build a project that references assemblies in another team project

1. Check out the TFSBuild.proj script from Source Control Explorer.
2. Add the following configuration setting under the **PropertyGroup** section:

```
<!-- to be added under PropertyGroup -->
<TfCommand>$(TeamBuildRefPath)\..\tf.exe</TfCommand>
<SkipInitializeWorkspace>true</SkipInitializeWorkspace>
```

   SkipInitializeWorkSpace allows you to skip invoking the default tasks to delete and re-create the workspace on the build machine. The new property is used in the custom target **BeforeGet** (see below).

3. Add the following configuration setting to the **ItemGroup** entries that map both the Team Projects and the solutions. Make sure that you provide the correct local paths for the build machine. Multiple mappings cannot share the same local folder and will result in a **MappingConflictException** exception in the CreateWorkspace task.

```
<ItemGroup>
  <!-- add one entry for every solution you reference -->
  <SolutionToBuild Include="$(SolutionRoot)\DependentApp\DependentApp.sln" />
  <SolutionToBuild Include="$(SolutionRoot)\YourApp\YourApp.sln" />
</ItemGroup>

<ItemGroup>
  <!-- add one entry for every Team Project you reference -->
  <Map Include="$/YourApp/YourApp">
    <LocalPath>$(SolutionRoot)\YourApp</LocalPath>
  </Map>
  <Map Include="$/DependentApp/DependentApp">
    <LocalPath>$(SolutionRoot)\DependentApp</LocalPath>
  </Map>
</ItemGroup>
```

4. Override the **BeforeGet** event to retrieve the workspaces for each Team Project:

```
<Target Name="BeforeGet">
  <DeleteWorkspaceTask
      TeamFoundationServerUrl="$(TeamFoundationServerUrl)"
      Name="$(WorkspaceName)" />
  <Exec
    WorkingDirectory="$(SolutionRoot)"
```

```
    Command="&quot;$(TfCommand)&quot; workspace /new $(WorkSpaceName) /server:$
(TeamFoundationServerUrl)"/>
  <Exec
   WorkingDirectory="$(SolutionRoot)"
   Command="&quot;$(TfCommand)&quot; workfold /unmap /workspace:$(WorkSpaceName
) &quot;$(SolutionRoot)&quot;"/>
  <Exec
    WorkingDirectory="$(SolutionRoot)"
    Command="&quot;$(TfCommand)&quot; workfold /map /workspace:$(WorkSpaceName)
/server:$(TeamFoundationServerUrl) &quot;%(Map.Identity)&quot; &quot;%(Map.
LocalPath)&quot;"/>
</Target>
```

5. Check in the build script and run the build.

Additional Resources

- For more information, see "Working with multiple team projects in Team Build" at *http://blogs.msdn.com/manishagarwal/archive/2005/12/22/506635.aspx*

How to Subscribe to Build E-mail Events

You can create a new project alert in order to subscribe to build e-mail events.

► **To set up build e-mail alerts**

1. Right-click the relevant team project in Team Explorer.
2. Select **Project Alerts**.
3. Select each alert option you would like to receive and enter an e-mail address for notification.

Additional Resources

- For more information about project alerts, see "Setting Alerts" at *http://msdn2.microsoft.com/en-us/library/ms181334(VS.80).aspx*

How to Receive Notification When a Build Has Failed

You can create a new project alert with a filter to receive e-mails only when the build fails.

► **To create a project alert to notify you when a build fails**

1. **Create and Test your Build.** Make sure that you have a Team Build type in place and that it runs without errors.

2. **Register for BuildCompletionEvent event.** Use the **BisSubscribe.exe** tool to register for the **BuildCompletionEvent** event with a filter specifying that you only want the e-mail notification when the build fails, by using the following command-line syntax:

```
bissubscribe /eventType BuildCompletionEvent /address myemail@domain.com /de-
liveryType EmailPlaintext /server tfsserver1 /filter "TeamProject = 'MyTeamPro-
ject' AND CompletionStatus='Failed'"
```

3. **Test the build.** Test the build by checking in code that fails to compile, execute the build, and ensure that an e-mail notification is received.

Additional Resources

- For more information about filtering the build completion event, see "How to Filter the Build Completion Event" at *http://blogs.msdn.com/jpricket/archive/2006/09/05/how-to-filter-the-build-completion-event.aspx*
- For more information about BuildCompletionEvent filters, see "Useful BuildCompletionEvent Filters" at *http://blogs.msdn.com/jpricket/archive/2006/09/05/useful-buildcompletionevent-filters.aspx*

How to Start a Build

You can start a build type from the Team Builds folder in Team Explorer.

► To manually start a build

1. Open Team Explorer.
2. Expand the team project for which you want to start a build.
3. Expand the Team Builds folder in the tree.
4. Right-click the Team Build type you want to start.
5. Select **Build Team Project**.

How to Verify That the Build Succeeded

You can check build status from the Builds window, accessible from Team Explorer.

► To verify that a build succeeded

1. Open Team Explorer.
2. Expand the team project for which you want to see results.
3. Expand the Team Builds folder in the tree.
4. Double-click the Team Build type for which you want to see results

How to View the Build Output

You can view build output from the Builds window, accessible from Team Explorer.

► **To view build output**

1. Open Team Explorer.
2. Expand the team project for which you want to see build output.
3. Expand the Team Builds folder in the tree.
4. Double-click the Team Build type for which you want to see build output.
5. Double-click the Team Build result entry for the build number for which you want to see output.
6. If you want to see the build output folder, click the **Build name** link.
7. If you want to see the build log, click the **Log** link.

How to Change the Build Server Location

In order to change the build server location for an existing Team Build, you modify the <**BuildMachine**> tag in TFSBuild.proj.

► **To change the build server location for an existing Team Build type**

1. Open Source Control Explorer.
2. In Source Control Explorer, expand your team project folder.
3. Expand the TeamBuildTypes folder.
4. Select the Team Build folder for which you want to turn on code analysis.
5. Check out the TFSBuild.proj file from source control. You might need to perform a **Get Latest Version** operation on the folder first.
6. In Source Control Explorer, double-click TFSBuild.Proj to open it.
7. Modify the **<BuildMachine>** tag to point to the new server.
8. Save TFSBuild.proj and check it back into source control.

Additional Resources

- For more information about customizing Team Foundation Build, see "Customizing Team Foundation Build" at *http://msdn2.microsoft.com/en-us/library/ms400688(VS.80).aspx*

How to Change the Build Output Location

In order to change the build output location for an existing Team Build, modify the <**DropLocation**> tag in TFSBuild.proj.

► **To change the build server location for an existing Team Build type**

1. Open Source Control Explorer.
2. In Source Control Explorer, expand your team project folder.

3. Expand the TeamBuildTypes folder.
4. Select the team build folder for which you want to turn on code analysis.
5. Check out the TFSBuild.proj file from source control. You might need to perform a **Get Latest Version** operation on the folder first.
6. In Source Control Explorer, double-click TFSBuild.Proj to open it.
7. Modify the **<DropLocation>** tag to point to the new location.
8. Save TFSBuild.proj and check it back into source control.

Additional Resources

- For more information about customizing Team Foundation Build, see "Customizing Team Foundation Build" at *http://msdn2.microsoft.com/en-us/library/ms400688(VS.80).aspx*

How to Determine What Changesets Are Part of the Build

You can view changesets associated with each build from the Builds window, accessible from Team Explorer.

► To view changesets associated with a build

1. Open Team Explorer.
2. Expand the team project for which you want to view changesets.
3. Expand the Team Builds folder in the tree.
4. Double-click the Team Build type for which you want to view changesets.
5. Double-click the Team Build result entry for the build number for which you want to view changesets.
6. Expand the **Associated changesets** item.
7. If you want to see more information about a particular changeset, click the **ID** link.

How to Change the Reported Build Quality

You can change build quality from the Builds window, accessible from Team Explorer.

► To change the build quality

1. Open Team Explorer.
2. Expand the team project for which you want to change the build quality.
3. Expand the Team Builds folder in the tree.
4. Double-click the Team Build type for which you want to change the build quality.
5. In the **Build Quality** drop down list, select the build for which you want to set build quality, and then set a build quality value.

Projects

- **How to use a single-solution strategy.**
- **How to use a partitioned-solution strategy.**
- **How to use a multiple-solution strategy.**

How to Use a Single-Solution Strategy

If you work on a small system, consider using a single Visual Studio solution to contain all of your projects. This strategy simplifies development because all of the code is available when you open the solution. This strategy also makes it easy to set up references, because all references are between projects in your solution. You might still need to use file references to reference third-party assemblies (such as purchased components) that are outside your solution.

Additional Resources

- For more information, see Chapter 3, "Structuring Projects and Solutions in Source Control" in this guide.

How to Use a Partitioned-Solution Strategy

If you work on a large system, consider using multiple Visual Studio solutions, each representing a subsystem of your application. These solutions can be used by developers to work on smaller parts of your system without having to load all code across all projects. Design your solution structure so that any projects that have dependencies are grouped together. This enables you to use project references rather than file references. Consider creating a master solution file that contains all of the projects, if you want to use this to build the entire application.

When working with multiple solutions, use a flat file structure for all of your projects. A typical example is an application that has a Microsoft Windows Forms project, an ASP.NET project, a Windows service, and a set of class library projects shared by some or all of those projects.

You can use the following flat structure for all projects:

- /Source
  - /WinFormsProject
  - /WebProject
  - /WindowsServiceProject
  - /ClassLibrary1
  - /ClassLibrary2
  - /ClassLibrary3
  - Web.sln
  - Service.sln
  - All.sln

By keeping the structure flat, you gain a lot of flexibility and the ability to use solutions for presenting different views of the projects. Designing the physical folder structure around solution files is very hard to change, especially if you realize that you need to reuse a class library from another solution.

Note: If you are building with Team Build (which relies on MSBuild), it is possible to create solution structures that do not include all referenced projects. As long as the entire solution has been built first, generating the binary output from each solution, MSBuild is able to follow project references outside the boundaries of your solution and build successfully. You cannot build solutions created in this way from the Visual Studio build command, and this approach only works with Team Build and MSBuild.

Additional Resources

- For more information, see Chapter 3, "Structuring Projects and Solutions in Source Control" in this guide.

How to Use a Multiple-Solution Strategy

If you work on a very large solution requiring many dozens of projects, you might run up against solution scalability limits. In this scenario, you should break your application into multiple solutions, but do not create a master solution for the entire application because all references inside each solution are project references. References to projects outside of each solution (for example, to third-party libraries or projects in another sub-solution) are file references. This means that there can be no "master" solution. Instead, a script must be used that understands the order in which the solutions must be built. One of the maintenance tasks associated with a multiple-solution structure is ensuring that developers do not inadvertently create circular references between solutions. This structure requires complex build scripts and explicit mapping of dependency relationships. In this structure, it is not possible to build the application in its entirety within Visual Studio. Instead, you use TFS Team Build

Additional Resources

- For more information, see Chapter 3, "Structuring Projects and Solutions in Source Control" in this guide.

Reporting

- **How to view build quality.**
- **How to view all the check-ins for a build.**
- **How to view work items or bugs closed for a build.**
- **How to view open work items or bugs for a build.**
- **How to track velocity from build to build.**

- **How to track test case pass/fail results for a build.**
- **How to review build status (BVT results).**

How to View Build Quality

You can view build quality from the Builds window, accessible from Team Explorer.

► **To view build quality**

1. Open Team Explorer.
2. Expand the team project for which you want to view build quality.
3. Expand the Team Builds folder in the tree.
4. Double-click the Team Build type to view build quality.

If you are using the Microsoft Solutions Framework (MSF) for CMMI® Process Improvement (MSF CMMI) process template, you can view the Builds report in order to see build quality as well as additional information on test results, code coverage and code churn.

► **To view build quality in MSF CMMI**

1. In Team Explorer, expand your team project node.
2. Right-click **Reports** and then click **Show Report Site**.
3. In the report site, select the **Builds** report.

How to View All the Check-ins for a Build

You can view check-ins associated with each build from the Builds window, accessible from Team Explorer.

► **To view check-ins associated with a build**

1. Open Team Explorer.
2. Expand the team project for which you want to view check-ins for a build.
3. Expand the Team Builds folder in the tree.
4. Double-click the Team Build type for which you want to view check-ins for a build.
5. Double-click the Team Build result entry for which you want to view check-ins for a build.
6. Expand the **Associated changesets** item to see all check-ins associated with the build.
7. If you want to see more information on a particular changeset (which represents a check-in), click the **ID** link.

How to View Work Items or Bugs Closed for a Build

You can view work items and bugs that have been closed for each build from the Builds window, accessible from Team Explorer.

To view work items associated with a build

1. Open Team Explorer.
2. Expand the team project for which you want to view work items.
3. Expand the Team Builds folder in the tree.
4. Double-click the Team Build type for which you want to view work items.
5. Double-click the Team Build result entry for the build number for which you want to view work items.
6. Expand the **Associated work items** item.

How to View Open Work Items or Bugs for a Build

If you are using the MSF CMMI process template, you can view the Open Issues and Blocked Work Items Trend report to view open, resolved, and closed work items over a given time period. However, because the report presents the information by date instead of by build, you need to translate the results into builds according to the date on which the build was produced.

To view open work items or bugs for a build

1. In Team Explorer, expand your team project node.
2. Right-click **Reports** and then click **Show Report Site**.
3. In the report site, select the **Open Issues and Blocked Work Items Trend** report.

How to Track Velocity from Build to Build

You can use the Velocity report to track the progress and the rate at which work items are getting completed from build to build. This report is available in both MSF CMMI and MSF for Agile Software Development (MSF Agile).

To track velocity from build to build

1. In Team Explorer, expand your team project node.
2. Right-click **Reports** and then click **Show Report Site**.
3. In the report site, select the **Velocity** report.

How to Track Test Case Pass/Fail results for a Build

You can use the Quality Indicators report to track the number of test cases that pass and fail over a given time period. The report presents the information by date instead of by build. As a result, you need to translate the results into builds according to the date at which the build was produced. This report is available in both MSF CMMI and MSF Agile.

To track test case pass/fail for a build

1. In Team Explorer, expand your team project node.
2. Right-click **Reports** and then click **Show Report Site**.
3. In the report site, select the **Quality Indicators** report.

How to Review Build Status (BVT Results)

If you are using the MSF CMMI process template, you can view the Builds report in order to see BVT results.

To review build status

1. In Team Explorer, expand your team project node.
2. Right-click **Reports** and then click **Show Report Site**.
3. In the report site, select the **Builds** report.

Scheduled Builds

- **How to automatically run nightly builds.**
- **How to decide on a build frequency and type for your project.**

How to Automatically Run Nightly Builds

The Team Build feature in TFS does not support scheduled builds from the user interface. Instead, you can use the Microsoft Windows Task Scheduler to run the TFSBuild command utility to start builds at predetermined time.

To create a scheduled build

1. Create a TFSBuild command line as follows:

```
TfsBuild start <<TeamFoundationServer>> <<TeamProject>> <<BuildTypeName>>
```

2. Place the command line in a batch file.
3. Create a Windows Scheduled Task that runs the batch file at your desired interval.

For more information and expanded steps, see "How To: Set Up a Scheduled Build with Visual Studio Team Foundation Server" in this guide.

Additional Resources

- For more information, see Chapter 9, "Setting Up a Scheduled Build with Team Build" in this guide.

How to Decide on a Build Frequency and Type for Your Project

The frequency of your builds is one of the most important decisions to make when creating a scheduled build.

If you are working on a project that has enough check-ins to cause significant changes within an hour, and you do not use Continuous Integration (CI) builds, you can choose an hourly build frequency. Hourly builds provide rapid feedback to developers and can also be made available to testers and other team members to solicit their feedback.

If you are working on a project that has enough check-ins to cause significant changes within a day, you can use daily scheduled build frequency because it gives your test and development teams a new build every morning that incorporates the changes from the previous day, ready to be tested.

If you are working on a large, complex project where the build time can last for days, you should opt for weekly builds. This ensures that your test team will have a build at the start of each week incorporating the changes from the previous week, ready to be tested.

Additional Resources

- For more information about setting up scheduled builds, see "How To: Set Up a Scheduled Build with Visual Studio Team Foundation Server" in this guide.
- For more information, see Chapter 9, "Setting Up Scheduled Build with Team Build" in this guide.

Test-Driven Development

- **How to create a "hello world" acceptance test.**
- **How to run automated tests as part of the build.**
- **How to run code analysis as part of the build.**
- **How to get failed tests to fail a build.**

How to Create a "Hello World" Acceptance Test

A "hello world" acceptance test is a simple test that you can use to prove that you can create unit tests and hook them up to your build process.

In order to create a test list to associate with the build you must have either Visual Studio Test Edition or Visual Studio Team Suite installed. In order to run automated tests on the build server you must have either Visual Studio Developer Edition, Visual Studio Test Edition, or Visual Studio Team Suite installed on the build server.

To create a hello world test

1. On the **Test** menu, click **New Test**…
2. Click **Unit Test** and then click **OK**.
3. Enter a name for your test project and then click **Create**.
4. Compile your new project.
5. Check the project into source control.
6. With your unit test solution still open in Visual Studio, on the **Test** menu, click **Create New Test List...**
7. Specify a test list name in the **Create New Test List** dialog and then click **OK**.
8. In the Test Manager, click on the **All Loaded Tests** node.
9. Drag and drop tests from the available tests into your test list node in the tree.
10. Check the modified unit test project VSMDI file into source control.

The test list you have created is available when you create a new Team Build and can be run automatically as part of the build process.

Additional Resources

- For more information about automatically running Build Verification Tests, see "How to: Configure and Run Build Verification Tests (BVTs)" at *http://msdn2.microsoft.com/en-us/library/ms182465(VS.80).aspx*
- For more information about how to run automated build tests without Visual Studio Test Edition or a VSMDI file, see "How to run tests in a build without test metadata files and test lists (.vsmdi files)" at *http://blogs.msdn.com/buckh/archive/2006/11/04/how-to-run-tests-without-test-metadata-files-and-test-lists-vsmdi-files.aspx*

How to Run Automated Tests as Part of the Build

You can run automated tests to automatically gain feedback on build quality after every build. In order to run automated tests, you must have Visual Studio Developer Edition as well as Visual Studio Test Edition on the build server, or you can install the entire Team Suite. Developer Edition is necessary in order to run the build, while Test Edition is necessary in order to set up tests and test lists that can be run.

To run automated tests as part of the Team Build process

1. Create one or more automated tests that you want to run with the build.
2. On the **Test** menu, click **Create New Test List...**
3. Use the Test Manager to group tests into the new Test List by dragging and dropping the tests from the Test View to the Test List in the Test Manager.
4. Create a new Team Build type.
5. Select the check box to run automated tests.

6. Select the test project within which your tests and test list were created.
7. Select the test list you want to run.

Additional Resources

- For more information about automatically running Build Verification Tests, see "How to: Configure and Run Build Verification Tests (BVTs)" at *http://msdn2.microsoft.com/en-us/library/ms182465(VS.80).aspx*
- For more information about how to run automated build tests without Visual Studio Test Edition or a VSMDI file, see "How to run tests in a build without test metadata files and test lists (.vsmdi files)" at *http://blogs.msdn.com/buckh/archive/2006/11/04/how-to-run-tests-without-test-metadata-files-and-test-lists-vsmdi-files.aspx*

How to Run Code Analysis as Part of the Build

To turn on code analysis for a build type, you can either select the code analysis check box in the New Team Build Type Creation Wizard when you create the new Team Build type, or you can modify the TFSBuild.proj file after the build type has been created.

► To enable code analysis in the TFSBuild.proj file

- If you want all projects to run code analysis, regardless of project settings, change the **<RunCodeAnalysis>** tag to **Always**.
- If you want to run code analysis on each project based on project settings, change the **<RunCodeAnalysis>** tag to **Default**.

Additional Resources

- For more information about automatic code analysis as part of the build, see "How To: Automatically Run Code Analysis with Team Build in Visual Studio Team Foundation Server" in this guide.
- For more information about code analysis tools, see "Guidelines for Using Code Analysis Tools" at *http://msdn2.microsoft.com/en-us/library/ms182023(VS.80).aspx*

How to Get Failed Tests to Fail a Build

When a build fails because of compilation errors, a work item is created to track the failure and the build is marked as failed. When an automated test fails, however, the build does not fail. The test failure is converted into a warning and the build continues.

You might want to fail the build if an associated automated test fails. You might also want to generate a work item automatically to track the failure.

To fail the build upon test failure

1. Open the Microsoft.TeamFoundation.Build.targets file from Program Files\MSBuild\Microsoft\VisualStudio\v8.0\TeamBuild.
2. Check out for edit and open the TFSBuild.proj file for the Team Build type you want to have failed upon test failure.
3. Copy the **RunTestWithConfiguration** target from Microsoft.TeamFoundation.Build.targets to the end of the TFSBuild.proj file, just before the closing </Project> tag.
4. Modify the **ContinueOnError** attribute from **true** to **false**.

Note: There will be two test tool tasks. Modify the end-to-end task in order to only modify the behavior of builds on the build server. Use the desktop build task when building on a developer's desktop.

Alternatively, if you want all Team Build types to fail upon test failure, you can modify Microsoft.TeamFoundation.Build.targets directly. This change will modify behavior for all Team Build types.

The solution recommended above is straightforward to implement but is not guaranteed to continue working for future versions of Visual Studio. If you want to implement a solution that is guaranteed to continue working after upgrade, see Aaron Hallberg's blog entry "Determining Whether Tests Passed in Team Build" at *http://blogs.msdn.com/aaronhallberg/archive/2006/09/21/determining-whether-tests-passed-in-team-build.aspx*

Additional Resources

- For more information about setting up the build to create a work item upon test failure, see "Create Workitems for Test Failures in TeamBuild" at *http://blogs.msdn.com/nagarajp/archive/2005/10/14/481290.aspx*
- For more information about a solution that is guaranteed to continue working after a Visual Studio upgrade, see "Determining Whether Tests Passed in Team Build" at *http://blogs.msdn.com/aaronhallberg/archive/2006/09/21/determining-whether-tests-passed-in-team-build.aspx*

Team Build Resources

- For an overview of Team Foundation Build, see "Overview of Team Foundation Build" at *http://msdn2.microsoft.com/en-us/library/ms181710(vs.80).aspx*

Practices at a Glance: Source Control

Index

Accessing Version Control

- *How to use version control from non-Visual Studio clients.*
- *How to automate common version-control tasks.*
- *How to work offline.*

Administration

- *How to add a new developer to your project.*
- *How to remove a developer who has left your project.*
- *How to grant permissions within your source tree.*
- *How to move Team Foundation Server Version Control to another server.*

Branch/Label/Merge

- *How to use labels.*
- *How to branch.*
- *How to plan your branching structure.*
- *How to use branching to support a release.*
- *How to use branching to maintain a previous release.*
- *How to use branching to stabilize your development and build process.*
- *How to use branching to stabilize feature development.*
- *How to use branching to stabilize development across teams.*
- *How to use branching to isolate external dependencies.*
- *How to retire an old release.*
- *How to perform a merge.*
- *How to perform a baseless merge.*
- *How to resolve merge conflicts.*

Builds

- *How to use TFS to perform Continuous Integration builds.*

Check-ins and Check-in Policies

- *How to work with source control change sets.*
- *How to enforce coding standards prior to check-in.*
- *How to override a check-in policy.*
- *How to undo a check-in.*
- *How to resolve a conflict.*
- *How to avoid conflicts.*
- *How to create a custom check-in policy.*

Checkout, Get, and Lock

- *How to synchronize your computer with TFS.*
- *How to prepare a file for editing.*

Code Sharing

- *How to share code.*
- *How to manage shared binaries.*

Dependencies

- *How to manage Web service dependencies.*
- *How to manage database dependencies.*

Distributed/Remote Development

- *How to access TFS over the Internet.*
- *How to optimize TFS Version Control proxy performance.*

Migration

- *How to migrate your source from Visual SourceSafe.*
- *How to migrate your source from other version-control systems.*

Project/Workspace Management

- *How to choose one team project versus multiple team projects.*
- *How to organize your source tree.*
- *How to define workspace mappings.*
- *How to use workspaces to isolate code changes on your computer.*

Security

- *How to secure the channel between a developer workstation and TFS.*

Shelving

- *How to use shelving to back up pending work.*
- *How to use shelving to share code with a team member.*

Accessing Version Control

- **How to use version control from non–Visual Studio clients.**
- **How to automate common version-control tasks.**
- **How to work offline.**

How to Use Version Control from Non–Visual Studio Clients

You can access Microsoft® Visual Studio® 2005 Team System (VSTS) Team Foundation Server (TFS) Version Control from other clients by using one of the following approaches:

- Microsoft Source Code Control Interface (MSSCCI) integration
- Third-party integration
- Custom integration

MSSCCI Integration

The following clients can work directly with TFS Version Control by using the MSSCCI provider:

- Microsoft Visual Studio .NET 2003
- Microsoft Visual C++® 6 SP6
- Microsoft Visual Basic® 6 SP6
- Microsoft Visual FoxPro® 9 SP1
- Microsoft Access™ 2003 SP2
- Microsoft SQL Server™ Management Studio
- Sparx Systems Enterprise Architect 61
- Sybase PowerBuilder 105
- Toad for SQL Server 2.0

The MSSCCI provider behaves differently than TFS Version Control in Visual Studio 2005 in the following ways:

- Checkout also performs a **GetLatest** operation.
- An exclusive check-in lock is applied at checkout.
- **Open-from source control** and **save-to source control** behave as they do in Microsoft Visual SourceSafe® (VSS).

You can download the MSSCCI provider from Microsoft MSDN® at *http://www.microsoft.com/downloads/details.aspx?FamilyId=87E1FFBD-A484-4C3A-8776-D560AB1E6198&displaylang=en*

The MSSCCI provider is not supported by Microsoft. If you have questions, consult the MSDN forums at *http://forums.microsoft.com/MSDN/ShowForum.aspx?ForumID=22&SiteID=1*

Third-Party Integration

The following clients have integration solutions provided by other vendors:

- Eclipse
- Linux client
- Apple Macintosh client
- HTML Web client

If you want to access TFS Version Control from Eclipse IDE, Linux, or Macintosh clients, consider installing Teamprise from *http://www.teamprise.com/*

If you would like read-only access to TFS Version Control from the Internet, consider using Team System Web Access from *http://msdn2.microsoft.com/en-us/teamsystem/bb676728.aspx*

Custom Integration

Other clients have no integration solution currently available. You can either access TFS Version Control from the command line or build your own integration solution.

To learn more about working with TFS Version Control, see "Walkthrough: Working with Team Foundation Source Control from Command Line" on the MSDN Web site at *http://msdn2.microsoft.com/en-us/library/zthc5x3f(VS.80).aspx*

You can use control scripts and command files to automate the use of the command line. To learn more about working with control scripts and command files, see "Team Foundation Source Control Scripts and Command Files" on the MSDN Web site at *http://msdn2.microsoft.com/en-us/library/1az5ay5c(VS80).aspx*

Additional Resources

- To download the MSSCCI provider from MSDN, go to *http://www.microsoft.com/downloads/details.aspx?FamilyId=87E1FFBD-A484-4C3A-8776-D560AB1E6198&displaylang=en*
- If you want to access TFS Version Control from Eclipse IDE, Linux, or Macintosh clients, consider installing Teamprise at *http://www.teamprise.com/*
- If you would like to access TFS Version Control from the Internet, consider installing Team System Web Access at *http://msdn2.microsoft.com/en-us/teamsystem/bb676728.aspx*

- To learn more about working with TFS Version Control, see "Walkthrough: Working with Team Foundation Source Control from Command Line" at *http://msdn2.microsoft.com/en-us/library/zthc5x3f(VS.80).aspx*
- To learn more about working with control scripts and command files, see "Team Foundation Source Control Scripts and Command Files" at *http://msdn2.microsoft.com/en-us/library/1az5ay5c(VS80).aspx*
- To learn more about TFS Version Control extensibility, see "Walkthru: The Version Control Object Model" at *http://msdn2.microsoft.com/en-us/library/bb187335(VS.80).aspx*

How to Automate Common Version-Control Tasks

To automate common version-control tasks, use the Team Foundation command-line tool (tf.exe). With this tool, you can do everything that you can do with Source Control Explorer, including source control operations (**add**, **check-in**, **checkout**, **get**, **lock**, **label**, and more), branching, shelving, workspace manipulation, and general administration tasks.

The main reasons for using the command-line tool include automating repetitive operations and scheduling operations to run at specific times or on specific events by using the Microsoft Windows® Task Scheduler. The following commands are also only available from the command line:

- Deleting another user's workspace
- Undoing another user's checkout
- Unlocking another user's lock
- Defining label scope
- Performing a baseless merge

To ensure that the appropriate path and other environment variables are set up, run the command-line tool from the Visual Studio 2005 Command Prompt window, or run the Vsvars32 batch file, which is normally located in *DriveLetter*:\Program Files\Microsoft Visual Studio 8\Common7\Tools.

Tf.exe is installed as part of the TFS client and is located by default in the following folder:

```
C:\Program Files\Microsoft Visual Studio 8\Common 7\IDE.
```

To run the command-line tool, you must specify a server name with the **/s** switch. The following command shows how to view the files in source control on the server named YourTFSServer:

```
tf.exe dir /s:YourTFSServer
```

Additional Resources

- For more information, see "Walkthrough: Working with Team Foundation Source Control from Command Line" on the MSDN Web site at *http://msdn2.microsoft.com/en-us/library/zthc5x3f(VS.80).aspx*
- For more information, see "MSDN Team Foundation Source Control Command-Line Reference" at *http://msdn2.microsoft.com/en-us/library/cc31bk2e(VS.80).aspx*

How to Work Offline

Offline working is not supported natively by TFS Version Control.

To work offline, you need to use the following strict workflow:

1. **Manually remove read-only flags.** By default, all files in the workspace that have not been checked out are marked as read-only. When you work without a server connection, you must manually remove the read-only flag from files before editing or deleting them. To do this, right-click the file in Windows Explorer, click **Properties**, clear the **Read-only** check box, and then click **OK**. Alternatively, you can use the DOS command **attrib -r**
2. **Edit files.** You can now edit any files for which you have removed the read-only flag.
3. **Add or delete files.** You can add or delete files for which you have removed the read-only flag. Do not rename files, because the **TFPT online** tool cannot distinguish a **rename** from a **deletion** paired with an **add** operation.

   Note: You must specify an option to the TFPT online command to get it to look for deletions because this is a more time-consuming operation.

4. **Run the TFPT online command.** When you are back online, run the **TFPT online** command by typing **TFPT online** at the command line. This command scans your workspace for writable files and determines what changes should be pended on the server. If you have deleted any files, use the **/delete** switch. This tells the tool to scan for deleted files in your local workspace as well. The tool then displays the online window from which you can choose which changes to pend into the workspace.

Important: You must not rename any files while you are offline.

Additional Resources

- To download the TFPT tool from MSDN, go to *http://www.microsoft.com/downloads/details.aspx?FamilyID=7324C3DB-658D-441B-8522-689C557D0A79&displaylang=en*
- To learn about the Visual Studio Team Foundation Power Tool, see "Power Toy: tfptexe" at *http://blogs.msdn.com/buckh/archive/2005/11/16/493401.aspx*

Administration

- How to add a new developer to your project.
- How to remove a developer who has left your project.
- How to grant permissions within your source tree.
- How to move Team Foundation Version Control to another server.

How to Add a New Developer to Your Project

To add a new developer to your project, grant the developer appropriate access to the team project and associated Microsoft Office SharePoint® project site. To enable the developer to view reports, grant the developer's account access to SQL Server Reporting Services.

► To grant access to the team project

1. Log on to Visual Studio with an account that is a member of the Team Foundation Administrators application group.
2. Add the required project to Team Explorer (if it is not already listed).
3. Right-click the team project, point to **Team Project Settings**, and then click **Group Membership**.
4. Select **Project\Contributors**, click **Properties**, and then add the new developer's account to this group.

Note: Membership in the Contributors group provides the typical set of permissions that a developer requires, including the ability to add, modify, and delete items within the team project and perform builds.

► To grant access to the SharePoint project site

1. Access the team project site with an account that is a member of the SharePoint Administrator site group. The project site for a project named YourProject is located by default at *http://server/sites/YourProject/default.aspx*
2. Click **Site Settings**.
3. Under the **Administration** title, click **Manage Users**.
4. Click **Add Users**.
5. Enter the account name of the new developer's account in the form domain\useraccount, select **Contributor**, and then click **Next**.
6. Enter the developer's e-mail address, and optionally type a message to welcome the developer to the site.
7. Click **Finish**.

Note: Membership in the Contributors group provides the typical set of permissions that a developer requires, including the ability to add, modify, and delete items within the team project and perform builds. If you need to restrict access to specific Visual Studio solutions or to specific folders in your team project, you can also assign permissions at the folder or file level.

► **To grant access to SQL Server Reporting Services**

1. Log on to the SQL Server Reporting Services administration Web site using an administrator account. The site is located at *http://server/reports*.
2. Click your team project name.
3. Click the **Properties** tab.
4. Click the **Security** tab.
5. Click **New Role Assignment**.
6. Enter your developer's Windows account name, select **Browser**, and then click **OK**.

Note: Membership in the Browser group enables the developer to view and subscribe to reports.

Additional Resources

- For more information, see "Team Foundation Server Default Groups, Permissions, and Roles" on the MSDN Web site at *http://msdn2.microsoft.com/en-us/library/ms253077.aspx*
- For more information, see "Source Control Security Rights and Permissions" on the MSDN Web site at *http://msdn2.microsoft.com/en-us/library/ms181761.aspx*

How to Remove a Developer Who Has Left Your Project

If a developer has left your project, make sure that you delete that developer's workspace. This operation not only helps to ensure the security of your project, but also removes any of the developer's pending changes and undoes any locks held by the developer.

Note: You cannot undo the locks without undoing the changes if an exclusive lock has been turned on for the team project.

To find out which files the developer has locked out, run the following command:

```
tf workspaces /owner:domain\devuser /computer:* /server:servername
```

To delete the workspace and remove locks, run the following command:

```
tf workspace /delete workspacename;domain\devuser /s:servername
```

Next, remove the developer's account from the security groups. To do so, make changes in the following three places:

- **TFS team project**—Log on to Visual Studio with an account that is a member of the Team Foundation Administrators application group. Using Team Explorer, right-click the project, point to **Team Project Settings**, click **Group Membership**, and then remove the developer's account from the relevant groups (normally Contributors).
- **SharePoint team project site**—Log on to the team site, located at http://server/sites/*yourprojectname*/default.aspx with an administrator account. Click **Site Settings**, **Manage Users** and then remove the developer account.
- **SQL Server Reporting Services**—Log on to the SQL Server Reporting Services administration Web site using an administrator account. The site is located at *http://server/reports*. Click your team project name, click the **Properties** tab, click the **Security** tab, and then delete the developer's account.

Additional Resources

- For more information about cleaning up after a developer who has left a project, see "How to: Clean Up Files When Users Leave" at *http://msdn2.microsoft.com/en-us/library/ms194958(VS.80).aspx*
- For more information about the Workspace command, see "Workspace Command" at *http://msdn2.microsoft.com/en-us/library/y901w7se(VS.80).aspx*
- For more information about finding pending changes, see "How do I tell who has files checked out or locked?" at *http://blogs.vertigosoftware.com/teamsystem/archive/2006/07/24/3125.aspx*

How to Grant Permissions Within Your Source Tree

You can set permissions on a file or folder within your source tree by right-clicking the file or folder in Source Control Explorer, clicking **Properties**, clicking the **Security** tab, selecting the user or group for which you want to change permissions, and then editing the permissions. You can also set permissions by using the **Permission** switch with the tf.exe command-line utility for source control.

Although you can apply source control permissions to specific folders and files, by default, permissions within your source tree are inherited from the permissions applied to the project folder. If your developers are members of the Project\Contributors application group, they will be able to read, check out, check in, label, and lock source files. If you need to provide restricted access to a subset of folders or source files within your team project—for example to enable a developer only to work on certain source files within your team project—you can set permissions at the folder or file level.

Additional Resources

- For more information about granting permissions, see "Team Foundation Server Default Groups, Permissions, and Roles" on the MSDN Web site at *http://msdn2.microsoft.com/en-us/library/ms253077.aspx*
- For further information about granting permissions, see "Source Control Security Rights and Permissions" at *http://msdn2.microsoft.com/en-us/library/ms181761.aspx*
- For more information about the tf permission command, see "Permission Command" at *http://msdn2.microsoft.com/en-us/library/0dsd05ft(VS.80).aspx*

How to Move Team Foundation Version Control to Another Server

Team Foundation Server does not support copying a server from one location to another, nor does it support mirroring. You can back up and restore a complete server, move your existing server hardware to a new domain, or upgrade to a dual-server deployment. You cannot perform partial moves; for example, moving some projects from your server but keeping others.

Team Foundation Server supports the following three move types:

- **Backup Restore**—Use this move type when you need to move your Team Foundation Server to a new machine. For specific steps, see "How to: Move Your Team Foundation Server from One Hardware Configuration to Another" at *http://msdn2.microsoft.com/en-us/library/ms404869(VS.80).aspx*
- **Environment**—Use this move type when you need to move your Team Foundation Server to a new domain or workgroup. For specific steps, see "How to: Move Your Team Foundation Server from One Environment to Another" at *http://msdn2.microsoft.com/en-us/library/ms404883(VS.80).aspx*
- **Single Server to Dual Server**—Use this move type when you need to move from a single-server deployment to a dual-server deployment. For specific steps, see "How to: Move from a Single-Server to a Dual-Server Deployment" at *http://msdn2.microsoft.com/en-us/library/ms404854(VS.80).aspx*

Keep the following considerations in mind when moving a Team Foundation Server:

- Changing the TFS application-tier server name requires that all TFS clients must connect to a new server name.
- All query-bound Microsoft Office documents will no longer work if the server name is changed. The documents are bound to the server for which they were created. This includes all of the query-bound Microsoft Office documents that are created automatically at project creation time in the project **Documents** node.
- Any embedded links to documents will point to an unknown server name if the server name is changed.

- Local accounts existed on the original TFS. You must decide whether these accounts will be re-created as local accounts on the moved TFS, or as domain accounts in the moved Team Foundation Server's new domain.
- Domain accounts existed on the original TFS, but you are moving TFS to a domain that does not trust the original domain. You must decide whether these accounts will be re-created as local accounts on the moved TFS, or as domain accounts in the moved Team Foundation Server's new domain.

Test your server after the move to ensure that nothing serious was broken in the transition. Testing should check the following areas:

- Were all the assets moved correctly? Look at your source tree, work items, and team pages to be sure that they are all in place.
- Are the user accounts still operative? Try logging in with a few different account types to make sure that they still work.

Additional Resources

- For more information about moving TFS, see *http://msdn2.microsoft.com/en-us/library/ms404879(VS.80).aspx*

Branch/Label/Merge

- **How to use labels.**
- **How to branch.**
- **How to plan your branching structure.**
- **How to use branching to support a release.**
- **How to use branching to maintain a previous release.**
- **How to use branching to stabilize your development and build process.**
- **How to use branching to stabilize feature development.**
- **How to use branching to stabilize development across teams.**
- **How to use branching to isolate external dependencies.**
- **How to retire an old release.**
- **How to perform a merge.**
- **How to perform a baseless merge.**
- **How to resolve merge conflicts.**

How to Use Labels

Use labels to group a set of files and folders together for future operations. You can use labels for branching, merging, diffing, or getting files. A label provides a marker to which you can return when performing one of the above operations at a later date.

► To apply a label to a file or folder

1. Right-click the file or folder in Source Control Explorer and then click **Apply Label**.
2. In the **Choose Item Version** dialog box, modify your choice of file or folder, choose the version of the file or folder that you would like to label, and then click **OK** to apply the label.

When applying labels, consider the following:

- Labels are markers that you can apply to only one version of a file or folder at a time.
- You can apply multiple labels to a version of a file or folder.
- Labels that you apply by using Source Control Explorer are automatically scoped to the root folder of the team project within which they are created. You cannot create two labels with the same name within the same scope.
- Labels are un-versioned objects and there is no history associated with them.
- Labels are applied instantly, and they do not require a check-in
- Team Build automatically assigns a label to the set of files associated with each build that it creates.
- Labels are not applied to deleted items; this means that merge-by-label will not pick up deleted files.

► To locate an existing label

1. On the **File** menu, point to **Source Control**, point to **Label**, click **Find Label**, and then navigate to the label.
2. After finding the label, you can modify it or delete it from within the **Find Label** dialog box.

Additional Resources

- For more information about using labels, see "Working with Labels" at *http://msdn2.microsoft.com/en-us/library/ms181439(VS.80).aspx*
- For more information about applying labels, see "How to: Apply Labels" at *http://msdn2.microsoft.com/en-us/library/ms181440(VS.80).aspx*

How to Branch

To create a branch, either use Source Control Explorer or use the **tf branch** command from the command line.

To branch from Source Control Explorer, right-click the top-level folder containing your project source, click **Branch**, and then specify a target folder location with a folder name to indicate the purpose of the branch; for example, **MyProject_Release1.0_Branch**.

To branch from the command line, use the **tf branch** command from a Visual Studio 2005 Command Prompt; for example:

```
tf branch C:\MyProject $/MyProject_Release1.0_Branch
```

Use branches only when you need to provide isolation while you do parallel development. When using branches you will have to eventually merge the changes to the main branch and as merging incurs overhead and requires you to manage conflicts, do not branch unless you need the file isolation that branching provides. You can label a build and branch later if needed.

Additional Resources

- For an introduction to branching and merging, see "Branching and Merging Primer" at *http://msdn2.microsoft.com/en-us/library/aa730834(VS.80).aspx*
- For more information about branching, see "How to: Branch Files and Folders" at *http://msdn2.microsoft.com/en-us/library/ms181425(VS.80).aspx*
- For more information about merging, see "How to: Merge Files and Folders" at *http://msdn2.microsoft.com/en-us/library/ms181428(VS.80).aspx*
- For additional descriptions of how to branch and merge in Visual Studio 2005, see "Branching and Merging Team Foundation Source Control" at *http://msdn2.microsoft.com/en-us/library/ms181423(VS.80).aspx*

How to Plan Your Branching Structure

Branches are a mechanism to enable isolation; they are used to allow multiple developers to work on the same files in isolation. To plan your branching approach, evaluate common branching scenarios and choose a strategy based on team size, composition, release schedule, and build stability requirements.

Common branch scenarios include:

- **Release**—Branch to stabilize code you want to release. You can branch before release, avoiding the need to lock down the main branch.
- **Maintenance**—Branch to maintain a previously released build.

- **Feature**—Branch to isolate feature development that might make the rest of the project unstable.
- **Team**—Branch to isolate sub-teams so that they can work without being subject to breaking changes, or that they can work towards unique milestones. These are very similar to feature branches.

Do not branch unless it becomes necessary for your development team. Branching introduces additional source tree maintenance and merging tasks. Most development teams working on short release cycles (e.g., Line-of-Business [LOB] applications) will never need a branch. Development teams working on longer release cycles (e.g., packaged Independent Software Vendor [ISV] applications) are more likely to employ branching as part of the development process.

Additional Resources

- For an introduction to branching and merging, see "Branching and Merging Primer" at *http://msdn2.microsoft.com/en-us/library/aa730834(VS.80).aspx*
- For more information about branching, see "How to: Branch Files and Folders" at *http://msdn2.microsoft.com/en-us/library/ms181425(VS.80).aspx*
- For more information about merging, see "How to: Merge Files and Folders" at *http://msdn2.microsoft.com/en-us/library/ms181428(VS.80).aspx*
- For additional descriptions of how to branch and merge in Visual Studio 2005, see "Branching and Merging Team Foundation Source Control" at *http://msdn2.microsoft.com/en-us/library/ms181423(VS.80).aspx*

How to Use Branching to Support a Release

Use a Release branch when you are ready to stabilize your build prior to release.

The following is an example of what your branch structure might look like after you have created a Release branch:

Main—Integration Branch

  Source

  Other Asset Folders

Releases—Container for release branches

  Release 1—Release branch

    Source

Keep the following recommendations in mind when working with Release branch:

- **When to branch**—When you are ready to release, integrate everything into the Main branch and then create Release branch that can be used to stabilize the application prior to release.

- **When not to branch**—If you are using one TFS project per release, you can use the new project to continue development, instead of a branch in the current project.
- **Permissions on branch**:
  - **Prior to release**—assign read/write permissions to all developers.
  - **After release**—Assign read/write permissions to developers working on hotfixes, read-only for everyone else.
- **Build frequency in branch**—The builds are performed on-demand.
- **Testing focus in branch**—Sign off on release.

You should use the Release branch for the targeted fixes and changes necessary in order to stabilize a build prior to release. Development of the next version of your application can occur in parallel in your Development or Main (integration) branches so that they can get the benefit of the stabilization changes you made prior to release. After a final release build has been created, you can merge the changes from the Release branch back into your Development and Main (integration) branches.

Additional Resources

- For an introduction to branching and merging, see "Branching and Merging Primer" at *http://msdn2.microsoft.com/en-us/library/aa730834(VS.80).aspx*
- For more information about branching, see "How to: Branch Files and Folders" at *http://msdn2.microsoft.com/en-us/library/ms181425(VS.80).aspx*
- For more information about merging, see "How to: Merge Files and Folders" at *http://msdn2.microsoft.com/en-us/library/ms181428(VS.80).aspx*
- For additional descriptions of how to branch and merge in Visual Studio 2005, see "Branching and Merging Team Foundation Source Control" at *http://msdn2.microsoft.com/en-us/library/ms181423(VS.80).aspx*

How to Use Branching to Maintain a Previous Release

Use maintenance branches to support previously released builds. This is very similar to branching for release, but at this point the branch is maintained over time in order to support the release.

The following is an example of what your branch structure might look like after you have released your application and maintain a branch to support the release:

Main—Integration Branch

Source

Other Asset Folders

Releases—Container for release branches

Release 1—Maintenance Branch

Source

Other Asset Folders

Keep the following recommendations in mind when working with a maintenance branch:

- **When to branch**—After you have released, support the release with a branch in the Releases folder.
- **When not to branch**—If you will never need to maintain the release, you can use a label to mark the old released build and continue work in the main branch.
- **Permissions on branch**—Assign read/write permissions to developers working on hot fixes, and read-only permissions to everyone else.
- **Build frequency in branch**—The builds are performed on-demand.
- **Testing focus in branch**—Sign off on release.

You should use maintenance branches to support an older version of your application. You might choose to merge these changes into your Main (integration) branch, or leave them specific to the maintenance branch.

Additional Resources

- For an introduction to branching and merging, see "Branching and Merging Primer" at *http://msdn2.microsoft.com/en-us/library/aa730834(VS.80).aspx*
- For more information about branching, see "How to: Branch Files and Folders" at *http://msdn2.microsoft.com/en-us/library/ms181425(VS.80).aspx*
- For more information about merging, see "How to: Merge Files and Folders" at *http://msdn2.microsoft.com/en-us/library/ms181428(VS.80).aspx*
- For additional descriptions of how to branch and merge in Visual Studio 2005, see "Branching and Merging Team Foundation Source Control" at *http://msdn2.microsoft.com/en-us/library/ms181423(VS.80).aspx*

How to Use Branching to Stabilize Your Development and Build Process

Use a Development branch for active development and a Main branch for your integration build, thus avoiding build breaks.

The following is an example of what your branch structure might look like after you have created a Development branch:

Development—Development Branch

  Source

Main—Integration Branch

  Source

  Other Assets folders

Keep the following recommendations in mind when working with a Development branch:

- **When to branch**—If you are creating daily builds and are having problems with build stabilization and integration, create both a Main and a Development branch to provide more predictability to your daily build. You might also want to consider more stringent check-in policies to improve check-in quality.
- **When not to branch**—If you are only creating Continuous Integration (CI) builds, or your daily builds are already predictably stable, you might not need the extra overhead of an integration branch.
- **Permissions on branch:**
  - The Main branch should be read/write for developers responsible for merging and integration, but read-only for everyone else.
  - The Development branch should be read/write for everyone.
- **Build frequency in branch:**
  - Daily builds on the Main branch.
  - Continuous Integration builds on the Development branch.
- **Testing focus on branch:**
  - Perform integration, performance, and security testing on the Main branch.
  - Perform feature and quick feedback testing on the Development branch.

Use the Main branch as a staging ground for integrating changes that have been checked into the development branch. Perform all active development in the Development branch, and integrate non-breaking changes into the Main branch.

Additional Resources

- For an introduction to branching and merging, see "Branching and Merging Primer" at *http://msdn2.microsoft.com/en-us/library/aa730834(VS.80).aspx*
- For more information about branching, see "How to: Branch Files and Folders" at *http://msdn2.microsoft.com/en-us/library/ms181425(VS.80).aspx*

- For more information about merging, see "How to: Merge Files and Folders" at *http://msdn2.microsoft.com/en-us/library/ms181428(VS.80).aspx*
- For additional descriptions of how to branch and merge in Visual Studio 2005, see "Branching and Merging Team Foundation Source Control" at *http://msdn2.microsoft.com/en-us/library/ms181423(VS.80).aspx*

How to Use Branching to Stabilize Feature Development

Use Feature branches to improve the integration and stabilization of breaking changes across features.

The following is an example of what your branch structure might look like after you have created Feature branches:

Development—Container for feature branches

  Feature A—Feature branch

    Source

  Feature B—Feature branch

    Source

  Feature C—Feature branch

    Source

Main—Integration branch

  Source

  Other Asset Folders

Keep the following recommendations in mind when working with Feature branch:

- **When to branch**—Feature teams often have source file overlap, increasing the potential for build breaks and check-in conflicts. If you are experiencing these problems, consider feature branches for each feature to provide feature isolation. You can create these off Main branch for small teams, or off a Team branches for larger teams.
- **When not to branch**—If you are only creating CI builds, or your daily builds are already predictably stable, you might not need the extra overhead of Feature branches.
- **Permissions in branch**—Assign read/write permissions to developers on the feature branch, and read-only permissions to everyone else.
- **Build frequency on branch**—Continuous integration builds are performed on the branch.
- **Testing focus in branch**—Perform feature and quick feedback testing.

Use the Feature branch to allow each feature to be developed in parallel. Perform all active development in the Feature branches and then integrate your code into the Main branch.

Additional Resources

- For an introduction to branching and merging, see "Branching and Merging Primer" at *http://msdn2.microsoft.com/en-us/library/aa730834(VS.80).aspx*
- For more information about branching, see "How to: Branch Files and Folders" at *http://msdn2.microsoft.com/en-us/library/ms181425(VS.80).aspx*
- For more information about merging, see "How to: Merge Files and Folders" at *http://msdn2.microsoft.com/en-us/library/ms181428(VS.80).aspx*
- For additional descriptions of how to branch and merge in Visual Studio 2005, see "Branching and Merging Team Foundation Source Control" at *http://msdn2.microsoft.com/en-us/library/ms181423(VS.80).aspx*

How to Use Branching to Stabilize Development Across Teams

Use Team branches to improve the integration and stabilization of breaking changes across teams.

The following is an example of what your branch structure might look like after you have created Team branches:

Development—Container for team branches

  Team 1—Team branch

    Source

  Team 2—Team branch

    Source

Main—Integration branch

  Source

  Other Asset Folders

Keep the following recommendations in mind when you work with Team branch:

- **When to branch**—If your development teams overlap on files and components, use Team branches to isolate each team's work. You might also choose to create Feature branches beneath the Team branches.
- **When not to branch**—If your source tree is organized by component, and you are confident that there will not be breaking interface changes or a large number of check-in conflicts across your teams, you probably do not need Team branches.
- **Permissions in branch**—Assign read/write permissions to developers on the team, and read-only permissions to everyone else
- **Build frequency on branch**—Continuous integration builds are performed on the branch.
- **Testing focus in branch**—Perform feature and quick feedback testing.

The Team branches should be used to allow teams to complete development tasks in parallel. This can be useful to isolate teams from breaking changes originating on other teams, or to allow teams to work toward unique milestones. All active development should occur in the Team branches and then be integrated into the Main branch. You might also want to create Feature branches beneath each Team branch.

Additional Resources

- For an introduction to branching and merging, see "Branching and Merging Primer" at *http://msdn2.microsoft.com/en-us/library/aa730834(VS.80).aspx*
- For more information about branching, see "How to: Branch Files and Folders" at *http://msdn2.microsoft.com/en-us/library/ms181425(VS.80).aspx*
- For more information about merging, see "How to: Merge Files and Folders" at *http://msdn2.microsoft.com/en-us/library/ms181428(VS.80).aspx*
- For additional descriptions of how to branch and merge in Visual Studio 2005, see "Branching and Merging Team Foundation Source Control" at *http://msdn2.microsoft.com/en-us/library/ms181423(VS.80).aspx*

How to Use Branching to Isolate External Dependencies

Use an External branch to improve the integration and stabilization of breaking changes caused by external dependencies.

The following is an example of what your branch structure might look like after you have created an External branch:

External—External branch

  Source

Main—Integration branch

  Source

  Other Asset Folders

Keep the following recommendations in mind when working with an External branch:

- **When to branch**—When you have external dependencies that might cause breaking changes in your project. If your dependencies are making interface changes or substantial logic changes that will impact your code, create an External branch to isolate these changes.
- **When not to branch**—When your external dependencies are stable or you are confident they will not introduce breaking changes.
- **Permissions in branch**—Read/write for developers responsible for external dependency integration, read-only for everyone else.
- **Build frequency on branch**—Builds are performed on-demand.
- **Testing focus in branch**—Integration testing.

You should use the External branch as an isolated location to test changes in external dependencies before you integrate them into the Main branch. This can be useful to isolate the development team from breaking changes caused by external dependencies such as headers and libraries.

Additional Resources

- For an introduction to branching and merging, see "Branching and Merging Primer" at *http://msdn2.microsoft.com/en-us/library/aa730834(VS.80).aspx*
- For more information about branching, see "How to: Branch Files and Folders" at *http://msdn2.microsoft.com/en-us/library/ms181425(VS.80).aspx*
- For more information about merging, see "How to: Merge Files and Folders" at *http://msdn2.microsoft.com/en-us/library/ms181428(VS.80).aspx*
- For additional descriptions of how to branch and merge in Visual Studio 2005, see "Branching and Merging Team Foundation Source Control" at *http://msdn2.microsoft.com/en-us/library/ms181423(VS.80).aspx*

How to Retire an Old Release

When a Release branch in your Releases folder is old enough that you no longer have to support it, create a Safe Keeping folder in which to store the old release. The following is an example of what your branch structure might look like after you have created a Safe Keeping folder:

Main—Integration Branch

- **Source**
- **Other Asset Folders**

Releases—Container for release branches

- **Release 2**—Maintenance Branch
  - **Source**
  - **Other Asset Folders**

Safe Keeping—Container for safe keeping branches

- **Release 1**—Safe keeping branch
  - **Source**
  - **Other Asset Folders**

The goal of moving the branch from the Releases folder to the Safe Keeping folder is to reduce clutter in the Releases folder without having to delete old releases. This is not a new branch, but rather the moving of an old branch to a new folder.

Additional Resources

- For an introduction to branching and merging, see "Branching and Merging Primer" at *http://msdn2.microsoft.com/en-us/library/aa730834(VS.80).aspx*
- For more information about branching, see "How to: Branch Files and Folders" at *http://msdn2.microsoft.com/en-us/library/ms181425(VS.80).aspx*
- For more information about merging, see "How to: Merge Files and Folders" at *http://msdn2.microsoft.com/en-us/library/ms181428(VS.80).aspx*
- For additional descriptions of how to branch and merge in Visual Studio 2005, see "Branching and Merging Team Foundation Source Control" at *http://msdn2.microsoft.com/en-us/library/ms181423(VS.80).aspx*

How to Perform a Merge

Use the **merge** command to integrate changes from one branch into another. To perform a merge, you can use the merge functionality in Source Control Explorer, or you can use the **tf merge** command line. You can merge by changeset, label, date, or version. To start a merge, right-click the branch in Source Control Explorer and then click **Merge**. The Source Control Merge Wizard allows you to choose the target branch with which to merge.

Depending on your branch structure, you might need to merge changes up the branch hierarchy, down the hierarchy, or across the hierarchy. If you are merging across the hierarchy, you are performing a baseless merge and you must use the **tf merge** command line, because you cannot do this with Visual Studio. A baseless merge allows you to merge files and folders that do not have a branch/merge relationship. After a baseless merge, a merge relationship exists and future merges are not baseless. You still need to execute the merges from the command line, but the number of merge conflicts will be reduced.

Keep the following in mind when performing merges:

- Merging along the hierarchy—from parent to child or from child to parent—results in fewer conflicts than merging across the hierarchy.
- The branch hierarchy is based on the branch parent and branch child, which might be different from the physical structure of what you see in Source Control Explorer; for example:
  - **Physical structure:**

    Development—Development branch

    Main—Integration branch

    Releases—Container for release branches

    Release 1 – Release Branch
  - **Logical structure:**

    Main

Development

Release 1

Additional Resources

- For more information about merging, see "Understanding Merging" at *http://msdn2.microsoft.com/en-us/library/ms181427(VS.80).aspx*
- For a walkthrough describing how to perform a merge, see "How to: Merge Files and Folders" at *http://msdn2.microsoft.com/en-us/library/ms181428(VS.80).aspx*

How to Perform a Baseless Merge

To perform a baseless merge, you use the **tf merge /baseless** command from the Visual Studio 2005 Command Prompt.

For example, the following command line will perform a baseless merge from the source branch to the target branch. The **/recursive** switch is used to perform a recursive merge of all the files and folders within the specified branch path:

```
tf merge /baseless <<source path>> <<target path>> /recursive
```

Example

```
tf merge /baseless c:\data\proj1 c:\data proj2 /recursive
```

The process of merging items that are not directly branched from each other is known as a *baseless merge*. For example, you might want to merge a change between two release branches that are siblings of each other without merging up to the parent branch. Baseless merging only works from the command line; you cannot perform a baseless merge from Visual Studio.

When you perform a baseless merge, TFS does not have any information about the relationship between the files in the branches. For instance, a file rename will be viewed as a deleted file and a new file in the branch. For this reason you will have to perform more manual conflict resolution than you would when performing a normal merge. However, you only have to perform this conflict resolution one time. After you have performed the baseless merge, TFS records history and establishes a relationship between the folders/files.

Baseless merges can only be created from the command line. Even after the first baseless merge, when a relationship has been created between the branches, future merges still need to be created from the command line.

Additional Resources

- For an explanation of merge command syntax, see "Merge Command" at *http://msdn2.microsoft.com/en-us/library/bd6dxhfy(VS.80).aspx*
- For more information about merging, see "Understanding Merging" at *http://msdn2.microsoft.com/en-us/library/ms181427(VS.80).aspx*
- For a walkthrough describing how to perform a merge, see "How to: Merge Files and Folders" at *http://msdn2.microsoft.com/en-us/library/ms181428(VS.80).aspx*

How to Resolve Merge Conflicts

To resolve merge conflicts, you use the Visual Studio merge tool. If a conflict is detected during a merge, you can resolve conflicts either automatically or manually. If you choose to resolve the conflict manually, you can keep the source changes, keep the target changes, or resolve the conflict in the merge tool.

You might need to resolve conflicts when merging changes between branches, getting files into your workspace, or checking in new versions of files. There are three conflict types:

- **Version**—The file has evolved along divergent paths. This could be the result of a file edit, rename, delete, or undelete operation.
- **File Name Collision**—Two or more items are trying to occupy the same path.
- **Local Overwrite**—Only occurs during a **get** operation, if you are trying to overwrite a local, editable file.

Most conflicts can be resolved automatically; version conflicts are the only conflict type that might result in a manual merge operation. Manual merge is most common in the following scenarios:

- A file has been edited in both branches, with changes to the same lines of code.
- A baseless merge is being conducted in which the branch file relationships are not known to TFS.

The merge tool shows you the details for each conflict and allows you to choose which change you want to keep in the final merged file. You can choose to keep the source change or the destination change, integrate both changes, or manually modify the final version by typing directly into the file.

After resolving every conflict in the file, save the final version as a pending change to be checked into the target branch.

Be careful when merging because it is easy to make mistakes that may result in build instability. After you have finished merging, compile the resulting source and run unit tests to test for major breaks.

Additional Resources

- For more information about resolving conflicts, see "How to: Resolve Conflicts" at *http://msdn2.microsoft.com/en-us/library/ms181433(VS.80).aspx*

Builds

- **How to use TFS to perform Continuous Integration builds.**

How to Use TFS to Perform Continuous Integration Builds

To perform continuous integration and rebuild your project every time a file is checked in, you need to use a Web service to trigger the build process. You subscribe the Web service to check-in events so that the build is triggered each time someone checks in a file. To trigger the build, you also need to use an appropriate build type that determines what configuration is built, what post-build steps and tests are executed, what drop location is used, and so on.

Additional Resources

- To download a Web service to trigger the build process available from Microsoft, go to *http://download.microsoft.com/download/6/5/e/65e300ce-22fc-4988-97de-0e81d3de2482/ci.msi*

Check-ins and Check-in Policies

- **How to work with source control change sets.**
- **How to enforce coding standards prior to check-in.**
- **How to override a check-in policy.**
- **How to undo a check-in.**
- **How to resolve a conflict.**
- **How to avoid conflicts.**
- **How to create a custom check-in policy.**

How to Work with Source Control Change Sets

A *changeset* groups together a set of changes associated with a given check-in. The common operations you need to perform on changesets are:

- Checking in a changeset associated with a work item
- Labeling a changeset
- Viewing details about a changeset.
- Changing details about a changset.
- Rolling back a changeset

► **To check in a changeset associated with a work item**

1. On the Visual Studio **View** menu, point to **Other Windows** and then click **Pending Changes**.
2. Enter a suitable comment to reflect the nature of the changes.
3. Click the **Work Items** icon to display the list of associated work items.
4. Update the associated work items by selecting them and then specifying the check-in action **Associate** or **Resolve** (if the check-in means that the work item is resolved).
5. Click **Check In** to check the changeset into the source control server.

► **To label a change set**

1. In Visual Studio, in Source Control Explorer, right-click your Team Project folder and then click **Apply Label**.
2. In the **Version** drop-down list, select **Changeset**, enter a **Changeset number**, and then click **OK**.
3. In the **Apply Label** dialog box, enter a label name and comment, and then click **OK**.

► **To view changeset details**

- Use the **tf changeset** command.

  The following command displays details about changeset number 1234 by displaying the **Details for Changeset** dialog box:

  ```
  tf changeset 1234
  ```

  By using the dialog box, you can view the source files contained in the changeset, view the check-in comments and notes, view associated work items, and view any policy warnings that were generated when the changeset was checked into the server.

► **To change details about a changeset**

Use the **tf changeset** command to alter the comments and/or notes associated with the changeset.

- The following command displays the **Details for Changeset** dialog box for changeset 1234 and updates the displayed comment field, allowing you to change the comment:

  ```
  tf changeset /comment:"This is a much better comment than the last one." 1234
  ```

  The following command updates the code reviewer and security reviewer notes associated with changeset 1234:

  ```
  tf changeset /notes:"Code Reviewer"="C Davis";"Security Reviewer"="F Smith"
  1234
  ```

To roll back a changeset and remove the changes from the source control server, you use the Team Foundation Power Tool.

► **To roll back a changeset using the Team Foundation Power Tool**

- Use the **Tfpt rollback** command.

  The following command rolls back change set number 1234.

  ```
  TFPT rollback /changeset:1234
  ```

  This command causes the Roll Back Changeset window to display. You can select the files contained within the changeset to roll back.

Additional Resources

- For more information about the tf changeset command, see "Changeset Command" at *http://msdn2.microsoft.com/en-us/library/w51xa47k(VS.80).aspx*
- For more information about retrieving changesets, see "How to: Retrieve Old Versions of Files from Changesets" at *http://msdn2.microsoft.com/en-us/library/ms181416(VS.80).aspx*
- To download the Team Foundation Power Tool (TFPT) from MSDN, go to *http://www.microsoft.com/downloads/details.aspx?FamilyID=7324C3DB-658D-441B-8522-689C557D0A79&displaylang=en*
- To learn more about the Team Foundation Power Tool, see "Power Toy: tfptexe" at *http://blogs.msdn.com/buckh/archive/2005/11/16/493401.aspx*

How to Enforce Coding Standards Prior to Check-in

Use TFS check-in policies to ensure that all code checked into the server meets your required coding standards.

The following check-in policies are available by default:

- **Code Analysis**—Requires that code analysis be run before check-in.
- **Test Policy**—Requires that check-in tests be completed before check-in.
- **Work Items**—Requires that one or more work items be associated with the check-in.

The default code analysis check-in policy provides code analysis checks for both managed and unmanaged code. Managed code statically analyzes your code to ensure that it conforms to standard .NET design rules, globalization rules, interoperability rules, naming rules, performance rules, security rules, and more. If you need to extend the code analysis, you can develop your own code analysis rules.

To configure the code analysis check-in policy

1. In Team Explorer, right-click your team project, point to **Team Project Settings**, and then click **Source Control**.
2. Click **Check-in Policy** and then click **Add**.
3. In the **Check-in policy** list, select **Code Analysis** and then click **OK**.
4. Specify the type of code analysis that you want performed by selecting the appropriate check boxes. If you select **Enforce Code Analysis For Managed Code**, select the required rules in the **Rule settings for Managed Code Analysis** list.
5. Click **OK** twice.

Important: Although the above procedure ensures that the configured policy is executed whenever a developer checks in a source file, developers can always override policy at check-in time. If you want to monitor this in order to manage this scenario, you can hook the policy override event.

You can create your own custom check-in policies that will enforce your project-specific quality gates; for example, if you want to enforce the following:

- Users should add comments at the time of check-in.
- Users should run additional acceptance tests before checking in the code.
- Users do not use certain pragma directives in C# to suppress XML documentation warnings
- Ensure that the projects are configured to generate XML documentation during compilation.

To create custom policy plug-ins that will appear in the **Add Checkin Policy** dialog box, use the extensibility features provided in the Visual Studio Team Foundation Server Software Development Kit (SDK).

Additional Resources

- For more information about creating and using a custom check-in policy, see "How To: Create Custom Check-In Policies in Visual Studio Team Foundation Server" in this guide.
- To learn how to customize a check-in policy, see "Walkthrough: Customizing Check-in Policies and Notes" at *http://msdn2.microsoft.com/en-us/library/ms181281(VS.80).aspx*
- To view sample code that will disallow selected patterns upon check-in, see "Checkin Policy to Disallow Certain Patterns" at *http://blogs.msdn.com/jmanning/archive/2006/02/02/523125.aspx*
- To view sample code that will enforce comments upon check-in, see "Sample Checkin Policy: Make Sure the Comment Isn't Empty" at *http://blogs.msdn.com/jmanning/archive/2006/01/21/515858.aspx*

- To learn how to register a new check-in policy, see "I've Made a New Check-In Policy! How Do I Add It?" at *http://blogs.msdn.com/jmanning/archive/2006/02/07/526778.aspx*
- For more information about how to use code analysis tools, see "Guidelines for Using Code Analysis Tools" at *http://msdn2.microsoft.com/en-us/library/ms182023(VS.80).aspx*

How to Override a Check-in Policy

To override a check-in policy, select the **Override policy failure and continue check-in** check box in the **Policy Failure** dialog box. Any user who has permission to check in files can override a check-in policy.

If you would like to detect when a member of your team overrides a check-in policy, you can use the Team Foundation Eventing Service to hook check-in events.

Additional Resources

- To learn more about overriding a check-in policy, see "How to: Override a Check-in Policy" at *http://msdn2.microsoft.com/en-us/library/ms245460(VS.80).aspx*
- To learn more about the Team Foundation Eventing Service, see "Eventing Service" at *http://msdn2.microsoft.com/en-us/library/bb130154(vs.80).aspx*
- To learn how to use the TFS Object Model to detect a policy override, instead of eventing, see James Manning's blog post on MSDN at *http://blogs.msdn.com/jmanning/archive/2005/11/04/489193.aspx*

How to Undo a Check-in

To undo the check-in of a file, use the Team Foundation Power Tools (TFPT) **rollback** command to revert the file to the previous version. The **rollback** command enables you to roll back an entire changeset at a time, but you can also select individual files from within the changeset to roll back. This is useful if you need to undo a change to a file that was mistakenly checked in, or where you want to undo the check-in because the changes are causing serious integration build issues.

► **To undo a file check-in and revert to the previous version**

1. Run the following command from a command window that includes the \program files\microsoft team foundation server power tools folder in the path:

```
TFPT rollback filename.cs
```

Note: If you know the changeset number of the changeset containing the check-in you want to undo, you can supply the changeset number on the command line as follows.

```
TFPT rollback filename.cs /changeset:54
```

2. The **rollback** command needs to ensure that your local workspace is up to date. Click **Yes** in response to the **Roll Back Changeset** message. At this point your workspace is updated with files from the server.
3. If you did not specify a changeset number on the command line, the **Find Changeset** dialog box is displayed. Enter search criteria, or simply click **Find** and then locate and select the changeset that contains the check-in you want to undo, and then click **Roll Back**.
4. The **Roll Back Changeset** dialog box is displayed .Because the changeset might contain multiple check-ins, you should select the file for which you want to undo the check-in and then click **Roll Back**.

Note: If you specified the filename on the command line, only this file in the changeset will be selected.

When undoing check-ins by using the **TFPT rollback** command, you should be aware of the following:

- **Workspace location**—TFPT locates workspaces as follows: If you specify a file path as an argument to filter the rollback, the file paths are used to find the workspace. If you do not specify file paths, the local directory is used to identify the workspace, if the local directory is mapped. The simplest approach to ensure that the tool locates the right workspace is to run the command from a locally mapped directory.
- **Pending changes**—You cannot roll back a changeset that contains pending changes. If you attempt to do so, the tool reports an error. In this instance, you must move pending changes to a shelveset and then undo or check in all pending changes before running the **rollback** command.
- **Merge scenarios**—If you are undoing the check-in of a file that has very recently been checked in, you probably will not need to merge changes because it is unlikely that anyone else will have updated the item in the intervening period. However, if you want to undo a check-in, and the check-in to be undone is not the latest change to a file, a three-way merge is required. The current version on the server, the version you have in your workspace, and the version you want to roll back to must be merged together. If there are no conflicts, the changes from the version to be rolled back are extracted from the file, and any changes that came after that version are preserved.
- **Resolving conflicts**—If you do need to perform a merge, the merge window is displayed. To resolve the merge, select the item and then click **Merge**. An automatic merge is initially attempted; if it fails, the merge tool is invoked to resolve the merge. The **Auto-Merge All** button attempts to automatically merge each of the items in the merge list, but does not attempt to invoke the merge tool.

Additional Resources

- To download the TFPT tool from MSDN, go to *http://www.microsoft.com/downloads/details.aspx?FamilyID=7324C3DB-658D-441B-8522-689C557D0A79&displaylang=en*
- To learn more about the TFPT, see "Power Toy: tfptexe" at *http://blogs.msdn.com/buckh/archive/2005/11/16/493401.aspx*

How to Resolve a Conflict

To resolve merge conflicts, use the Visual Studio merge tool. If a conflict is detected during a merge, you can resolve conflicts either automatically or manually. If you choose to resolve the conflict manually, you can keep the source changes, keep the target changes, or resolve the conflict in the merge tool.

You might need to resolve conflicts when merging changes between branches, getting files into your workspace, or checking in new versions of files. There are three conflict types:

- **Version**—The file has evolved along divergent paths. This could be the result of a file edit, rename, delete, or undelete operation.
- **File Name Collision**—Two or more items are trying to occupy the same path.
- **Local Overwrite**—Only occurs during a **get** operation, if you are trying to overwrite a local, editable file.

Most conflicts can be resolved automatically; version conflicts are the only conflict type that might result in a manual merge operation. Manual merge is most common in the following scenarios:

- A file has been edited in both branches, with changes to the same lines of code.
- A baseless merge is being conducted in which the branch file relationships are not known to TFS.

The merge tool shows you the details for each conflict and allows you to choose which change you want to keep in the final merged file. You can choose to keep the source change or the destination change, integrate both changes, or manually modify the final version by typing directly into the file.

After resolving every conflict in the file, save the final version as a pending change to be checked into the target branch.

Be careful when merging because it is easy to make mistakes that might result in build instability. After you have finished merging, compile the resulting source and run unit tests to test for major breaks.

Additional Resources

- For more information about resolving conflicts, see "How to: Resolve Conflicts" at *http://msdn2.microsoft.com/en-us/library/ms181433(VS.80).aspx*

How to Avoid Conflicts

To help avoid conflicts:

- **Ensure effective team communication.** When you work on a source file, let other team members know that you are working on the file and which aspects you will be updating. Although automatic conflict resolution can resolve many conflicts, you should avoid situations where two or more developers are working on the same functional areas in the same source file where there is a strong likelihood of you both making changes to the same lines of code. Conflicts on the same lines of code require manual conflict resolution, which complicates the merge operation.
- **Determine who else has a file checked out.** Before updating a file, check to see if another team member has already checked out the file. If so, ask your colleague what he or she is working on and then decide if you can wait until they complete their changes or if it is safe to continue to work in parallel on the same file because you are working on separate functionality in separate source code regions within the file.

► **To view pending changes**

1. In Source Control Explorer, right-click the solution, project, folder, or file for which you want to see pending changes.
2. Select **View Pending Changes**.

This method shows you all of the pending changes within the scope you have selected. You can also use the command-line checkout tool as follows to learn about pending changes:

```
tf status /format:detailed /user:*
```

This command displays detailed status information about any pending changes made by all users. In the resulting list, you can see who has which files checked out, along with pending changes. To view the pending changes for a specific file, specify the filename as the first argument to tf.exe.

Additional Resources

- For more information about viewing pending changes in your workspace, see "How to: View and Manage All Pending Changes in Your Workspace" at *http://msdn2.microsoft.com/en-us/library/ms181400(VS.80).aspx*
- For more information about viewing pending changes in other workspaces, see "How to: View Pending Changes in Other Workspaces" at *http://msdn2.microsoft.com/en-us/library/ms181401(VS.80).aspx*

- For more information about the tf status command see "Status Command" at *http://msdn2.microsoft.com/en-us/library/9s5ae285(VS.80).aspx*

How to Create a Custom Check-in Policy

To create a custom check-in policy, use the plug-in model exposed by the policy framework.

You can create a custom check-in policy to implement your own policy logic; for example, if you want to check if users have been adding comments or using regular expressions correctly at the time of check-in.

Plug-ins are used both within the policy definition process and during the policy evaluation process. Policy plug-ins are installed either as stand-alone utilities or as part of a separate application, and are registered with the policy framework so that they can be loaded as needed.

A policy plug-in must expose the following interfaces:

- **IPolicyDefinition**—The **IPolicyDefinition** interface exposes methods that are used in the process of defining policy requirements for a team project. This interface includes methods for invoking a user interface specific to the policy plug-in in order to allow users to easily define a check-in policy.
- **IPolicyEvaluation**—The **IPolicyEvaluation** interface exposes methods that are used in the process of evaluating policy compliance during the check-in process. This interface includes methods that accept the contents of a check-in operation and analyze them to establish whether the defined policy is satisfied.

You can package multiple policy plug-ins n the same assembly. The only requirement is that you implement the plug-ins as separate classes.

Note: These interfaces are exposed in PolicyBase class. As an alternative to implementing IPolicyDefinition and IPolicyEvaluation interfaces, you can derive a class from PolicyBase.

Additional Resources

- For more information about creating and using a custom check-in policy, see "How To: Create Custom Check-In Policies in Visual Studio Team Foundation Server" in this guide.
- To learn how to customize a check-in policy, see "Walkthrough: Customizing Check in Policies and Notes" at *http://msdn2.microsoft.com/en-us/library/ms181281(VS.80).aspx*
- To view sample code that will disallow selected patterns upon check-in, see "Checkin Policy to Disallow Certain Patterns" at *http://blogs.msdn.com/jmanning/archive/2006/02/02/523125.aspx*

- To see sample code that will enforce comments upon check-in, see "Sample Checkin Policy: Make Sure the Comment Isn't Empty" at *http://blogs.msdn.com/jmanning/archive/2006/01/21/515858.aspx*
- To learn how to register a new check-in policy, see "I've Made a New Check-In Policy! How Do I Add It?" at *http://blogs.msdn.com/jmanning/archive/2006/02/07/526778.aspx*
- For more information about using code analysis tools, see "Guidelines for Using Code Analysis Tools" at *http://msdn2.microsoft.com/en-us/library/ms182023(VS.80).aspx*
- For more information about creating a new policy, see "Policy Plug-ins" at *http://msdn2.microsoft.com/en-us/library/bb130343(VS.80).aspx*

Checkout, Get, and Lock

- **How to synchronize your computer with TFS.**
- **How to prepare a file for editing.**

How to Synchronize Your Computer with TFS

To synchronize your computer with the version control server, use the **tf get** command. This is a quick way of ensuring that your computer is synchronized with the rest of your team to ensure that you have the latest copy of shared work. To download all files and not just those that are out of date, run the following command from a Visual Studio 2005 command prompt window:

```
tf get /all
```

When you use this command, any local writable files that you might have on your computer are not overwritten. If you want to overwrite local writable files to completely synchronize your computer with the server, use the **/force** switch as follows:

```
tf get /force
```

Although this command overwrites local writable files, it does not overwrite writable files for which you also have pending edits. If you have pending edits on a file that you need to keep, check in or shelve your edits prior to re-synchronizing with the server.

► To perform the same operation from Visual Studio

1. In Team Explorer, double-click the Source Control folder, right-click your server or team project, and then click **Get Specific Version**.
2. Select **Overwrite writable files that are not checked out** and **Force get of file versions already in workspace**.

3. In the **Type** drop-down list, ensure that **Latest Version** is selected, and then click **Get**.

If you want to completely synchronize your computer with the version control server, do not use the **Get Latest Version** option available in Visual Studio. Because this command only downloads those files that are not already in your workspace and does not overwrite writable files that you have checked out in your local directory, your computer remains out of synchronization with the server.

Additional Resources

- For more information about the get command, see "Get Command" at *http://msdn2.microsoft.com/pt-br/library/fx7sdeyf(VS.80).aspx*

How to Prepare a File for Editing

In order to prepare a file for editing you must first get the latest version from Team Foundation Server source control and then check it out for editing.

► To prepare a file for editing

1. In Source Control Explorer, select the file, right-click and then click **Get Latest Version**.
2. This downloads a read-only copy of the latest version of the file into the workspace on your computer.
3. Right-click the file and then click **Check Out for Edit**.
4. Choose your required lock type. Select **None** to allow other users to check the file in and out during the time period when you are working on the file.
5. This type of shared checkout is generally recommended because most conflicts that might arise can be resolved automatically.

Note: The get latest version operation does not check out the file, and the check out for edit operation does not perform a get. You need to perform both steps individually. This behavior is different from Microsoft Visual SourceSafe behavior.

When selecting your lock type, consider the following:

- A shared checkout (**None**) avoids introducing potential bottlenecks into your development process by preventing someone else from working in the same file.
- You should only lock a file while editing it if you are concerned that there will be a conflict resulting in a complicated manual merge operation.
- Select the **Check Out** lock type to prevent other users from checking out and checking in the file. This option prevents other people from editing the file, which could represent a potential bottleneck in your development process. This option ensures that you can apply your changes back to the source control database without the possibility of other changes having been made to the file by other users.

- Select the **Check In** lock type to allow other users to check out the file while preventing them from checking it in. Again, this option ensures that you will be able to check in your edits without conflicts.

Additional Resources

- For more information about the checkout command, see "Checkout and Edit Commands" at *http://msdn2.microsoft.com/pt-br/library/1yft8zkw(VS.80).aspx*

Code Sharing

- **How to share code.**
- **How to manage shared binaries.**

How to Share Code

If you have source code that is used by multiple team projects, you can either manage the source code within the team project of the owning team or create a team project specifically for the shared source code.

Teams consuming shared source code have the following two options:

1. Reference the code from a shared location.
2. Branch the shared code.

1. **Reference the code from a shared location.**

   In this case, the projects consuming the shared code can simply map the source from the shared location into their workspaces on the client machine. This creates a configuration that unifies the source from the shared location with the projects on the client-side.

   The advantage of this approach is that changes to shared source are picked up every time the latest source is retrieved into the workspace. For example, consider that you have two team projects named Client and Shared Code, where Shared Code is the location of the shared source. To reference the code from a shared location, these projects will share a common path on the client's hard drive as shown below:

   - c:\TestProject\Client
   - c:\TestProject\Shared Code

   Both projects will have workspace mappings to those local hard drive paths.

Source control folder	Local folder
$/Client	c:\TestProject\Client
$/Shared Code	c:\TestProject\Shared Code

For more information, see "Working with multiple team projects in Team Build" at *http://blogs.msdn.com/manishagarwal/archive/2005/12/22/506635.aspx*

2. **Branch the shared code.**

   In this case, the projects consuming the shared code can branch the source from the shared location into their respective team projects. This creates a configuration that unifies the source from the shared location with the projects on the server-side.

   The difference is that changes to the shared source are picked up as part of a merge process between the branches. This makes the decision to pick up changes in the shared source much more explicit.

   For example, consider that you have two team projects named Client and Shared Code, where Shared Code is the location of the shared source. Use the following steps to branch the code from the shared location:

   a. In Source Control Explorer, right-click the root folder of Shared Code.
   b. Select the **Branch** option.
   c. In the **Branch** dialog box, set the **Target** to the root folder of the Client team project, and then click **OK**.
   d. After the branch operation completes, do not forget to check in the branched source code.

Additional Resources

- For more information, see "Working with multiple team projects in Team Build" at *http://blogs.msdn.com/manishagarwal/archive/2005/12/22/506635.aspx*
- For an introduction to branching and merging, see "Branching and Merging Primer" at *http://msdn2.microsoft.com/en-us/library/aa730834(VS.80).aspx*
- For more information about project references, see "Project References" at *http://msdn2.microsoft.com/en-us/library/ez524kew(VS.80).aspx*

How to Manage Shared Binaries

Managing shared binaries is similar to managing shared source: you must decide where you want to store the binaries and how you want your team to access the binaries.

The following options are available for storing the binaries:

- If the shared binaries are clearly owned by a particular team, store the binaries in their team project.
- If the shared binaries have no clear ownership, create a team project specifically for the shared binaries.

The following options are available for using the binaries in another project:

- Shared binaries are usually updated only periodically. If this is the case, branch from the shared location into the consuming team project. When the binaries change, you can execute a merge to get the latest version.
- If you need to stay synchronized with the shared binaries at all times, map the source from the shared location into a local workspace on the client machines.

► To branch shared binaries into your project

1. In Source Control Explorer, right-click the root folder of Shared Binaries.
2. Select the **Branch** option.
3. In the **Branch** dialog box, set the **Target** to the root folder of the Client team project, and then click **OK**.
4. After the branch operation has completed, do not forget to check in the branched source code.

Whether you use workspace mapping or branching, you should use naming conventions that make it clear where the shared binary location is in your project; for example:

Main

Source—Contains code for this project

Lib—Contains shared binaries

Additional Resources

- For more information, see "Working with multiple team projects in Team Build" at *http://blogs.msdn.com/manishagarwal/archive/2005/12/22/506635.aspx*
- For an introduction to branching and merging, see "Branching and Merging Primer" at *http://msdn2.microsoft.com/en-us/library/aa730834(VS.80).aspx*
- For more information about project references, see "Project References" at *http://msdn2.microsoft.com/en-us/library/ez524kew(VS.80).aspx*

Dependencies

- **How to manage Web service dependencies.**
- **How to manage database dependencies.**

How to Manage Web Service Dependencies

Generally, the Web service Uniform Resource Locator (URL) reference in production is different from that for the development and test environments. To facilitate management of each of these Web service URL references, the URL value should be specified in a user configuration file that can be changed by individual developers and testers without impacting the main App.config file. To do this, you set the **URL Behavior** property of your Web service reference to **Dynamic**. Store and reference the Web service URL from a user configuration file.

By default, Visual Studio sets the value of this property to **Dynamic** when you add a Web reference.

► **To verify that this value is still set to Dynamic**

1. In Solution Explorer, expand the list of Web references.
2. Select each Web reference in the list.
3. For each Web reference, check that the value of the **URL Behavior** property is set to **Dynamic**.

Specify a Web Service URL in a user configuration file

When you first add a Web reference, the App.config file looks like the following:

```
<configuration>
    <configSections>
        <sectionGroup name="applicationSettings" type="System.Configuration.Appli-
cationSettingsGroup, System, Version=2.0.0.0, Culture=neutral, PublicKeyToken=b77
a5c561934e089" >
            <section name=" SomeService.Properties.Settings" type="System.Configu-
ration.ClientSettingsSection, System, Version=2.0.0.0, Culture=neutral, PublicKeyT
oken=b77a5c561934e089" requirePermission="false" />
        </sectionGroup>
    </configSections>
    <applicationSettings>
        <YourProject.Properties.Settings>
            <setting name="SomeService_ localhost _Service" serializeAs="String">
                <value>http://localhost/someservice/Service.asmx</value>
            </setting>
        </ YourProject.Properties.Settings>
    </applicationSettings>
</configuration>
```

This file has a new configuration section that contains the address of the Web service that Visual Studio found when generating this proxy.

► **To create a User.config file**

1. In Solution Explorer, right-click the project that contains the Web service reference, point to **Add**, and then click **New Item**.
2. Select **Application Configuration File**, change the name to **User.config**, and then click **Add**.

3. Copy the *<YourProject.Properties.Settings>* element setting from your application configuration file (App.config) to the User.config file. This file should contain only the element for which the runtime is redirected. Delete the <?xml> directive and the <configuration> element if present, as shown in the following example:

```
<YourProject.Properties.Settings>
    <setting name="SomeService_localhost_Service" serializeAs="String">
       <value>http://localhost/someservice/Service.asmx</value>
    </setting>
</YourProject.Properties.Settings>
```

4. In Solution Explorer, right-click the User.config file, click **Properties**, and then set the **Copy To Output Directory** property to **Copy if newer**.

Individual developers should set their User.config file to reference the appropriate Web service URL reference.

► **To update the App.config file to reference User.config file when accessing the Web service URL**

1. Add a **configSource="user.config"** attribute to the *<YourProject.Properties.Settings>* element of your main application configuration file.

   This silently redirects the runtime to the named user configuration file when it accesses information from this section.

2. Delete the content from the *<YourProject.Properties.Settings>* element.

Your App.config should now look like the following:

```
<?xml version="1.0" encoding="utf-8" ?>
<configuration>
    <configSections>
        <sectionGroup name="applicationSettings" type="System.Configuration.Appli-
cationSettingsGroup, System, Version=2.0.0.0, Culture=neutral, PublicKeyToken=b77
a5c561934e089" >
            <section name="SomeService.Properties.Settings" type="System.Configura-
tion.ClientSettingsSection, System, Version=2.0.0.0, Culture=neutral, PublicKeyTok
en=b77a5c561934e089" requirePermission="false" />
        </sectionGroup>
    </configSections>
  <applicationSettings>
    <YourProject.Properties.Settings  configSource="user.config">
    </YourProject.Properties.Settings>
  </applicationSettings>
</configuration>
```

In the preceding example, *YourProject* is the name of the project that contains the Web service reference. Make sure that the *<SomeService.Properties.Service>* element is empty in the App.config file.

Important:

- Do not add your User.config file to source control. By not doing so, each developer (and the test team) can explicitly bind to specific URLs by using his or her own User.config files. To prevent this, clear the User.config file check box when you first check in the file. You can then right-click the file in Solution Explorer and select the **Undo Pending Changes** option to ensure that the file is not subject to source control.
- Source control may contain other User.config files; for example, for testing and production. These files should be managed by the users responsible for managing the testing and production environments. These test and production User.config files should not be stored as part of the Web service projects but should be in different areas of the source control system.
- Store a global User.config file in source control. This could either contain only the root element (no <setting> element), or it could specify the default location of the Web service. The User.config file must be present for the configuration system to work.

It is important to understand that the User.config file must be present if you are using this mechanism. Some team member must be responsible for ensuring that the environment is correct when creating builds for production releases and for any test environments. As part of this build step, the appropriate User.confg file must be retrieved from the source control system and copied into the correct location in order for MSBuild to be able to find it.

Additional Resources

- For more information, see "Web Projects and Source Control Integration in Visual Studio .NET" at *http://msdn2.microsoft.com/en-US/library/aa290068(VS.71).aspx*
- For more information about the ApplicationSettingsGroup class, see "ApplicationSettingsGroup Class" at *http://msdn2.microsoft.com/en-us/library/system.configuration.applicationsettingsgroup.aspx*

How to Manage Database Dependencies

The following procedure explains how to store and then reference a database connection string within a user configuration file.

► **To use a user configuration file to store database connection strings**

1. Add a **configSource="user.config"** attribute to the <connectionStrings> element of your main application configuration file as follows:

```
<configuration>
   <connectionStrings configSource="user.config"/>
</configuration>
```

2. To override the main application configuration file, create a User.config file (located in the same folder as the application configuration file), and then add a similar <connectionStrings> entry to the file.

   Notice that the following connection string references a local database:

```
<connectionStrings>
      <add name="DBConnStr"
     connectionString="server=localhost;Integrated Security=SSPI;database=Acco
unts"/>
   </connectionStrings>
</configuration>
```

3. Within your project, use the following code to obtain the connection string from the user configuration file.

   This code uses the static **ConnectionStrings** property of the **System.Configuration.ConfigurationManager** class. In the Win Form application, you must add a reference to **System.Configuration.dll** explicitly.

```
using System.Configuration;
private string GetDBaseConnectionString()
{
  return ConfigurationManager.ConnectionStrings["DBConnStr"].ConnectionString;
}
```

4. Ensure that the User.config file is deployed along with the application code. To do so, in Solution Explorer, right-click the User.config file, click **Properties**, and then in the Properties pane, set the **Copy To Output Directory** property to **Copy if newer**.

Do not add the User.config file to source control. By not doing so, each developer (and the test team) can explicitly specify the connection string through his or her own User.config file. Source control might contain other User.config files; for example, for testing and production. These files should be managed by the users responsible for managing the testing and production environments. These test and production User.config files should not be stored as part of the database projects but should be stored in different areas of the source control system.

In source control you should have a User.config file for each of the environments that you use, such as production and test. These configuration files should specify the connection string for the database. The User.config file must be present for the configuration system to work.

Tip: By default, the user configuration file is automatically added to source control when you add the solution. To prevent this, when you first check in the files, clear the User.config file check box. You can then right-click the file in Solution Explorer and select Undo Pending Changes to ensure that the file never comes under source control.

It is important to understand that the User.config file must be present if you are using this mechanism. Some team member will need to be responsible for ensuring that the environment is correct when creating builds for production releases and for any test environments. As part of this build step, the appropriate User.confg file will need to be retrieved from the source control system and copied into the correct location in order for MSBuild to be able to find it.

Additional Resources

- For more information about using a configuration file to define a data source, see "Walkthrough: Using a Configuration File to Define a Data Source" at *http://msdn2.microsoft.com/en-us/library/ms243192(VS.80).aspx*
- For more information about the configSource attribute, see "SectionInformation. ConfigSource Property" at *http://msdn2.microsoft.com/en-us/library/system.configuration.sectioninformation.config-source.aspx*

Distributed/Remote Development

- **How to access TFS over the Internet.**
- **How to optimize TFS Version Control proxy performance.**

How to Access TFS over the Internet

You can choose from one of the following three solutions to provide access to TFS over the Internet:

- **Use a VPN connection.** You can provide access to TFS over a virtual private network (VPN).
- **Publish your TFS through a reverse proxy.** You can provide access to TFS through a reverse proxy such as Microsoft Internet Security and Acceleration (ISA) Server.
- **Locate your TFS in the extranet ("hosted scenario").** You can host your TFS server on an extranet.

If you are supporting remote users with VPN access, use the VPN solution. This is the easiest solution to enable, provides well-understood security, allows remote access to all TFS features, and allows you to use the TFS Proxy to improve performance. In this solution Your TFS sits inside the internal network, and external users access it over a VPN. Internal users access a TFS directly

If you are supporting remote users without VPN access or without access to the domain, use the reverse proxy scenario. This solution is more difficult to set up, but it enables remote users to access an internally located TFS without the need for VPN. In this solution your TFS sits inside the internal network, and one or more reverse proxy machines, such as ISA Server, bring in client requests from the Internet to your TFS.

If you are supporting a set of remote users who will be using a TFS installation dedicated to their use, such as a community development site, use the extranet scenario. This solution gives you the most separation between the remote users and your internal network resources. In this solution only external clients access your TFS, and it is located outside of the firewall on an extranet

If you are supporting an office with multiple clients connecting to a remote Team Foundation Server, you should install and configure Team Foundation Server Proxy in the remote office. This improves performance by caching source control files on the remote office's proxy server.

If you are supporting a single client connecting to a remote TFS, configure the client to connect directly to the TFS.

Additional Resources

- To learn more about TFS remote access scenarios, see Chapter 17, "Providing Internet Access to Team Foundation Server" in this guide.
- To learn more about the Team Foundation Server Proxy, see "Team Foundation Server Proxy and Source Control" at *http://msdn2.microsoft.com/en-us/library/ms252490(VS.80).aspx*
- For more information about examining TFS proxy performance, see "How to: Examine Cache Performance for Team Foundation Server Proxy" at *http://msdn2.microsoft.com/en-us/library/ms252455(VS.80).aspx*

How to optimize TFS Version Control proxy performance

At your remote location, install and configure Team Foundation Server Proxy. This improves performance by caching source control files in the remote office's proxy.

► To configure and optimizing proxy performance

1. Make sure that caching is enabled, and monitor the performance of your cache. Monitor the performance counters (installed by default) and event logs (for errors/warnings) on your proxy server on a periodic basis, to see how your proxy is performing.

   Note: The TFS proxy saves cache performance statistics to an XML file named ProxyStatistics.xml; you can change the interval for saving these statistics. The ProxyStatistics.xml file is located in the App_Data folder in the proxy installation directory.

2. Run a scheduled task to retrieve the latest files to the proxy server on a periodic basis. This helps to ensure that the latest versions of the files are available in the proxy cache, and to ensure that subsequent client requests for these files result in a cache hit.
3. If you know that large files are going to be downloaded over a low-bandwidth (< 3 megabits per second [Mbps]) network, set the **executionTimeout** configuration

to an appropriate value in Web.config. The default value is one hour <httpRuntime executionTimeout="3600" />.

Additional Resources

- To learn more about TFS remote access scenarios, see Chapter 17, "Providing Internet Access to Team Foundation Server" in this guide
- To learn more about the Team Foundation Server Proxy, see "Team Foundation Server Proxy and Source Control" at *http://msdn2.microsoft.com/en-us/library/ms252490(VS.80).aspx*
- For more information about examining TFS proxy performance, see *http://msdn2.microsoft.com/en-us/library/ms252455(VS.80).aspx*
- To learn more about the TFS Proxy File Cache Server, see the MSDN Webcast at *http://msevents.microsoft.com/CUI/WebCastEventDetails.aspx?culture=en-US&EventID=1032291120&CountryCode=US*

Migration

- **How to migrate your source from Visual SourceSafe.**
- **How to migrate your source from other version-control systems.**

How to Migrate Your Source from Visual SourceSafe

To migrate your source from VSS, perform the following steps.

Note: To perform these steps, you must be a member of the Team Foundation Administrators group.

---

1. **Prepare VSS.** Prepare to migrate by backing up your VSS database, ensuring that files are checked in and running the Visual SourceSafe Analyze tool to identify and resolve data integrity issues in your existing database.
2. **Analyze your projects.** Use the converter command-line tool (VSSConverter.exe), passing the analyze command switch together with the name of a settings XML file as follows

   VSSConverter analyze conversionsettings.xml

   The following is a sample XML settings file:

```
<?xml version="1.0" encoding="utf-8"?>
<SourceControlConverter>
   <ConverterSpecificSetting>
         <Source name="VSS">
               <VSSDatabase name="c:\VSSDatabase"></VSSDatabase>
         </Source>
         <ProjectMap>
```

```
            <Project Source="$/MyFirstProject"></Project>
            <Project Source="$/MySecondProject"></Project>
            </ProjectMap>
      </ConverterSpecificSetting>
   </SourceControlConverter>
```

The settings file contains the name of the VSSDatabase. You set the **name** attribute to point to the folder that contains your source safe .ini file. The Project elements define the path to the projects you want to convert within your VSS database. To migrate an entire VSS database, use <Project Source="$/"></Project>.

The VssConverter.exe **analyze** command also generates a usermap.xml file. By adding mappings to this file, you can change the names associated with version history and so on from VSS login names to your TSF Windows login names.

3. **Migrate your projects.** Choose the folders you want to migrate and then use VSSConverter.exe with the **migrate** argument as follows:

   VSSConverter migrate conversionsettings.xml

   You again pass the configuration settings XML file, but with two important additions as follows:

```
<?xml version="1.0" encoding="utf-8"?>
<SourceControlConverter>
   <ConverterSpecificSetting>
         <Source name="VSS">
               <VSSDatabase name="c:\VSSDatabase"></VSSDatabase>
         </Source>
         <ProjectMap>
           <Project Source="$/MyFirstProject" Destination="$/MyTeam_
                ProjectOne"></Project>
           <Project Source="$/MySecondProject" Destination="$/MyTeam_
                ProjectTwo"></Project>
         </ProjectMap>
   </ConverterSpecificSetting>
   <Settings>
     <TeamFoundationServer name="YourTFSServerName" port="PortNumber"
                protocol="http"></TeamFoundationServer>
   </Settings>
</SourceControlConverter>
```

Notice the addition of the **Destination** attribute on the <Project> elements. This attribute points to your team project in TFS (which you must have previously created). Also notice the addition of the <Settings> element that contains connection details for your TFS application tier.

Additional Resources

- For more information about how to prepare for migration, see "Walkthrough: Preparing to Migrate from Visual SourceSafe to Team Foundation" at *http://msdn2.microsoft.com/en-us/library/ms181246(en-us,vs.80).aspx*

- For more information about how to perform the migration, see "Walkthrough: Migrating from Visual SourceSafe to Team Foundation" at *http://msdn2.microsoft.com/en-us/library/ms181247(VS.80).aspx*
- For more information about the limitations of the Visual SourceSafe converter, see "Visual SourceSafe Converter Limitations" at *http://msdn2.microsoft.com/en-us/library/ms252491(VS.80).aspx*

How to Migrate Your Source from other Version-Control Systems

You can manually export files from the version-control system you are migrating from and then import them into Team Foundation Server Version Control. If you want to preserve file history or other attributes from the version-control system you are migrating from, you can use the Team Foundation Server Version Control object model to write your own migration tool.

Microsoft is currently working on a ClearCase converter. When this converter is ready, it will be announced on the TFS Migration blog at *http://blogs.msdn.com/tfs_migration*

ComponentSoftware has created a converter that is compatible with GNU RCS, CS-RCS, GNU CVS, Subversion (SVN), and Visual SourceSafe (VSS).

Additional Resources

- To download the Visual Studio Team Foundation Server SDK, go to *http://go.microsoft.com/fwlink/?linkid=68586*
- To learn more about Team Foundation Version Control extensibility, see "Walk-thru: The Version Control Object Model" at *http://msdn2.microsoft.com/en-us/library/bb187335(VS.80).aspx*
- For more information about the ComponentSoftware converter, see the ComponentSoftware Web site at *http://www.componentsoftware.com/Products/Converter/*

Project/Workspace Management

- **How to choose one team project versus multiple team projects.**
- **How to organize your source tree.**
- **How to define workspace mappings.**
- **How to use workspaces to isolate code changes on your computer.**

How to Choose One Team Project vs. Multiple Team Projects

To plan your project structure, evaluate common project organization strategies and choose the one that best fits your organization's size, server constraints, and process workflow. Projects are intended to represent the largest unit of work possible in your organization. You should preferably choose a single project versus creating multiple projects. Use multiple projects when there is strong reason for doing so; for example, the team changes, or there is significant change from one release to another and you do not want to carry the unwanted work items (bugs, etc.) forward, or there is change in the process template, and so on.

The main advantages of creating a single project versus multiple projects are that it simplifies the moving of requirements, features, scenarios, and bugs between releases.

The most important decision points are:

- Do you want to maintain work items and other assets from release to release? If so, choose to keep all releases in the same project.
- Do you want to create a new process and work item structure from scratch when you move to a new release? If so, choose to create a new project for each release.

Common project structures include:

- **One project per application.** Use a single project to contain all versions of your application. Create one branch per release within that project.
  - **Reasons to use this structure:** Makes it easy to carry forward code, work items and other assets.
  - **Reasons not to use this structure:**
    - Releases in parallel are forced to share work items' schema, check-in policies, and process guidance.
    - Reporting is more difficult; because reports default to the entire project, you must add filtering by release.
    - If you have hundreds of applications, each in its own project, you may run up against TFS scalability limits.
    - You will accumulate 'baggage' over multiple releases. The easiest way to clean this up is to create a new project and branch the code you want to carry forward into that project.
- **One project per release.** Create a new project for each version of your application.
  - **Reasons to use this structure:**
    - It works well if you want to start with a clean project after every release.
    - The old project can be used for maintenance and handed off to a separate sustained engineering team.
    - It is easy to move source from one project to another.
  - **Reasons not to use this structure:**
    - It is difficult to move work items and TFS assets from one project to another. Work items can only be copied one at a time to another project. If you want to move sets of items, you will need to do so manually or write your own utility.
    - If you are managing hundreds of projects, you may run up against TFS scalability limits.

Keep the following considerations in mind when choosing your strategy:

- Choose a structure you can live with in the long term because restructuring existing team projects can be difficult.
- Source can be easily shared among team projects:
  - Branch source from one project to another.
  - Map source from another project into your workspace.
- Team Foundation Server can scale to ~500 projects using the Microsoft Solution Framework (MSF) for Agile Software Development Process (MS Agile) or 250 projects using the MSF CMMI process. If you create your own process or customize an existing process, keep in mind that the work item schema has the greatest impact on server scalability. A complex schema will result in a server capable of supporting fewer projects.

Additional Resources

- For more information about project strategy, see Eric Lee's blog post "When to use Team Projects" at *http://blogs.msdn.com/ericlee/archive/2006/08/09/when-to-use-team-projects.aspx*

How to Organize Your Source Tree

Your source tree structure consists of a combination of folder structure, file structure, and branch structure. Within your main branch, the following folder and file structure has been proven to work for teams of various sizes:

Main—Container for all assets you need in order o ship the product

- **Source**—Container for everything you need to build
  - **Code**—Container for source code
  - **Shared Code**—Container for source code that is shared from other projects
  - **Unit Tests**—Container for unit tests
  - **Lib**—Container for binary dependencies
- **Docs**—Container for documentation that ships with your product
- **Installer**—Container for installer source code and binaries
- **Tests**—Container for test team tests

Any branches that you create off of the Main branch will copy this folder and file structure into the new branch; for example:

Development—Development branch

- **Source**—Container for everything you need in order to build
  - **Code**—Container for source code

Shared Code—Container for source code that is shared from other projects

Unit Tests—Container for unit tests

Lib—Container for binary dependencies

Main—Integration branch

Source—Container for everything you need in order to build

Code—Container for source code

Shared Code—Container for source code that is shared from other projects

Unit Tests—Container for unit tests

Lib—Container for binary dependencies

Docs—Container for documentation that ships with your product

Installer—Container for installer source code and binaries

Tests—Container for test team tests

Additional Resources

- For more information about creating a workspace, see "How to: Create a Workspace" at *http://msdn2.microsoft.com/en-us/library/ms181384(VS.80).aspx*

How to Define Workspace Mappings

Define a workspace mapping to map source control files and folder on the server to your local drive.

► **To create a workspace mapping for a project that is not yet on your hard drive**

1. In Source Control Explorer, select the root source folder.
2. Right-click and select **Get Latest Version.**
3. Choose the local folder to which you want to map the workspace.

► **To modify a workspace mapping for a project that is already on your hard drive**

1. Select File->Source Control->Workspaces.
2. Use the Manage Workspaces dialog box to add, remove, or edit existing workspaces.

► **To view an existing workspace mapping**

1. In Source Control Explorer, select a source folder.
2. Right-click and then click **Properties**.

   The workspace mapping to your local drive appears in the **Local Name** field.

Consider the following best practices for creating workspace mappings:

- **Create mappings at the team project root level.** For new team projects, map your team project root ($/MyTeamProject) to a folder with the same name on your local drive; for example, C:\TeamProjects. Because mappings are recursive, your entire local folder structure is created automatically and will be exactly the same as the structure in source control.
- **On shared computers, use a unique local folder path.** Two users of a single computer cannot share the same workspace mapping. For example, you and a colleague cannot map the same team project ($/MyTeamProject) to the same folder on the local computer. Instead, create mappings beneath My Documents (although this leads to long location paths) or establish a team folder-naming convention on the local computer (e.g., C:\TeamProjects\User1, C:\TeampProjects\User2 etc).
- **You might not need the entire tree.** To improve performance and reduce disk size requirements, only map the files you need for your development project. In general, you will only need the files and projects associated with the solution on which you will work.
- **Avoid using workspace mapping to support cross-project dependencies.** In general, you should avoid dependencies that cross team projects and try to have all the related/dependent solutions/projects under same team project. This reduces the need for build script customization. If you have a dependency, use project references to define the dependency, or branch the dependency from a shared project into your project. You should avoid file references because they are more difficult to manage. The exception is when the dependent project is developed in parallel and you need real-time changes. In this case, you can consider the **using workspace** mapping. You can still consider branching to create a buffer of isolation, if the dependent code is causing too many breaking changes.

Additional Resources

- For more information about creating a workspace, see "How to: Create a Workspace" at *http://msdn2.microsoft.com/en-us/library/ms181384(VS.80).aspx*
- For more information about editing a workspace, see "How to: Edit a Workspace" at *http://msdn2.microsoft.com/en-us/library/ms245466(VS.80).aspx*

How to use Workspaces to Isolate Code Changes on Your Computer

As a developer, you can create two workspaces, one containing references to files and folders being worked on by the rest of the team, and another containing files and folders that you want to isolate. You might want to isolate these files in order to evolve specific files in parallel with work that is happening elsewhere. For instance, this can be used to work on risky pending changes, or to conduct a code review.

► **To create a secondary workspace**

1. In Source Control Explorer, click the **Workspace** drop-down list and then click **Workspaces**.
2. In the **Manage Workspaces** dialog box, click **Add**.
3. In the **Add Workspace** dialog box, enter a new workspace name such as **MyIsolatedWork** and provide a comment to serve as a future reminder about the purpose of the workspace.
4. In the **Working folders** list, set the workplace status to **Active**, identify the source control folder to be included in the workspace (this can be the team project root folder or any subfolder), and then specify a local folder path on your own computer to contain the files from the workspace.
5. Click **OK** and then click **Close** to create the isolated workspace.

► **To retrieve the latest set of source to begin work in your isolated workspace**

1. In Source Control Explorer, make sure that your isolated workspace name is selected in the **Workspace** drop-down list.
2. Select your team project root folder (or a subfolder if you only need part of the source tree), right-click, and then click **Get Latest Version**.

   This copies the folder structure and latest file set from the source control server to the local directory on your computer that you mapped to the new workspace.

Additional Resources

- For more information about creating a workspace, see "How to: Create a Workspace" at *http://msdn2.microsoft.com/en-us/library/ms181384(VS.80).aspx*
- For more information about editing a workspace, see "How to: Edit a Workspace" at *http://msdn2.microsoft.com/en-us/library/ms245466(VS.80).aspx*

Security

- **How to secure the channel between a developer workstation and TFS.**

How to Secure the Channel Between a Developer Workstation and TFS

To secure the channel between a developer workstation and TFS, you can configure your TFS to use HTTPS and Secure Sockets Layer (SSL) encryption. You can configure your TFS to use only HTTPS and SSL while disallowing HTTP connections. In order to do this, you must first configure TFS to allow HTTPS and SSL, and then perform the additional steps to require HTTPS and SSL.

Using HTTPS and SSL encrypts the network traffic between TFS and the Team Foundation clients that request access to Team Foundation Server's Web resources, including team project portals, reports, and work items.

Additional Resources

- For more information, see "Securing Team Foundation Server with HTTPS and Secure Sockets Layer (SSL)"at *http://msdn2.microsoft.com/en-us/library/aa395265(VS.80).aspx*
- For more information on how to set up TFS with Secure Socket Layer (SSL), see "Walkthrough: Setting up Team Foundation Server with Secure Sockets Layer (SSL)" at *http://msdn2.microsoft.com/en-us/library/ms242875(VS.80).aspx*
- For more information on how to configure TFS for HTTPS and SSL only, see "How to: Configure Team Foundation Server for HTTPS and SSL Only" at *http://msdn2.microsoft.com/en-us/library/aa395285(VS.80).aspx*

Shelving

- **How to use shelving to back up pending work.**
- **How to use shelving to share code with a team member.**

How to Use Shelving to Back Up Pending Work

To back up pending changes to the server, shelve the files that you are not yet ready to check in. This ensures that the source is uploaded to the server without checking in partially completed work that could potentially lead to build instability.

► **To shelve a set of pending changes**

1. View the pending changes by right-clicking your solution in Solution Explorer and then clicking **View Pending Changes**.
2. Select the files you want to shelve and then click **Shelve**.
3. Type a shelveset name and a comment that identifies the purpose of the shelveset, and then click **Shelve**.

► **To restore your work the following day**

1. On the **File** menu, point to **Source Control** and then click **Unshelve**.
2. Select the required shelveset and click **Unshelve**.

   Team Foundation Server restores each shelved revision into the destination workspace as a pending change, as long as the revision does not conflict with a change that is already pending in your workspace.

Additional Resources

- For more information about shelving pending changes, see "How to: Shelve and Unshelve Pending Changes" at *http://msdn2.microsoft.com/en-us/library/ms181404(VS.80).aspx*

How to Use Shelving to Share Code with a Team Member

To shelve source code for sharing with a team member, perform a **Get Latest** operation to synchronize your workspace with the latest server version and then build your application to ensure that it compiles. Shelve the source using Source Control Explorer. The team member to whom you have handed off the code then needs to unshelve the code.

Shelving is useful when you have work in progress that is to be completed by another team member; in this case, you can shelve your changes to make a handoff easier. By synchronizing the latest code, you get an opportunity to incorporate changes to source files that have been made outside of your workspace.

► **To shelve folders and files from Source Control Explorer**

1. In Source Control Explorer, right-click and then select **Shelve Pending Changes**.
2. In the **Shelve - Source Files** dialog box, in the **Shelveset name** box, type the shelveset name; for example, **shelvetest**.
3. In the **Comment** box, type **Testing my shelveset** and then click **Shelve**.

   The files and folders are copied to the source control server and are available for other team members to unshelve.

When the other team member unshelve a shelveset, TFS restores each shelved revision into the destination workspace as a pending change, as long as the revision does not conflict with a change that is already pending in the workspace.

► **To unshelve a set of pending changes**

1. In Visual Studio 2005 Team System, click **File**, point to **Source Control**, and then click **Unshelve**.
2. In the **Owner name** box, type the shelveset creator's name (for example, ADVENTUREWORKS\JuanGo or simply juango) and then click **Find**.
3. In the Results pane, select the shelveset you want to unshelve into your workspace, and then click **Details**.
4. If you want to delete the shelveset from the TFS source control server, clear the **Preserve shelveset on server** option.
5. (Optional) Clear the **Restore work items and check-in notes** option if you do not want to have the work items and check-in notes associated with the shelveset restored.
6. When the **Details** dialog box appears, select the shelveset or shelveset items you want to unshelve into your workspace, and then click **Unshelve**.

Additional Resources

- For more information, see "How to: Shelve and Unshelve Pending Changes" at *http://msdn2.microsoft.com/en-us/library/ms181404(VS.80).aspx*

Source Control Resources

- For more information about Team Foundation Server Source Control, see "Team Foundation Source Control" at *http://msdn2.microsoft.com/en-us/library/ms181237(VS.80).aspx*

Practices at a Glance: Reporting

Index

Administration

- *How to set up a report dashboard.*
- *How to set permissions on reports.*

Creation / Customization

- *How to customize an existing report.*
- *How to create a new report in Visual Studio.*
- *How to create a new report in Excel.*
- *How to create a scheduled report snapshot.*
- *How to create a report subscription.*
- *How to add a new report to an existing process template.*

Viewing

- *How to analyze the status of a project.*
- *How to analyze application quality.*
- *How to review remaining work.*
- *How to review build status.*
- *How to review bugs and test results.*
- *How to review scheduled work versus actual work on an iteration.*
- *How to determine the owner of the last edit on a file.*
- *How to discover all the code changes made by a developer.*
- *How to discover all the code changes made to a file.*
- *How to discover all the code changes associated with a specific work item .*
- *How to generate code churn metrics.*
- *How to generate workspace metrics such as number of files, lines of code, and number of projects.*

Administration

- **How to set up a report dashboard.**
- **How to set permissions on reports.**

How to Set Up a Report Dashboard

Modify the team project Microsoft® Office SharePoint® portal site in order to create a report dashboard that enables you to display a variety of project information in one location.

For example, a useful reporting dashboard could contain the following reports:

- Remaining Work
- Quality Indicators
- Bug Rates
- Project Velocity

You can add new reports to your SharePoint portal page by adding a Report Viewer Web Part for each report you want displayed on the page.

► **To modify the team project portal and create a reporting dashboard**

1. Install the Report Viewer Web Part on your report server by using the stsadm.exe tool and RSWebParts.cab, both of which are included with SharePoint and the Report Services installation package.
   - STSADM.EXE can be found in the following path: C:\Program Files\Common Files\Microsoft Shared\web server extensions\60\BIN
   - RSWebParts.Cab can be found in the following path: C:\ Program Files\Microsoft SQL Server\90\Tools\Reporting Services\SharePoint
   - Example: STSADM.EXE -o addwppack -filename "C:\ Program Files\Microsoft SQL Server\90\Tools\Reporting Services\SharePoint\RSWebParts.cab" -globalinstall
2. In Team Explorer, right-click your project.
3. Click **Show Project Portal**.
4. Click **Modify Shared Page**.
5. Point to **Browse** and click **Add Web Parts**.
6. Click **Virtual Server Gallery**.
7. In the **Web Part List**, select **Report Viewer**.
8. Click **Add**.
9. Enter the Report Manager name, such as http://*<report server>*/reports.
10. Enter the path for the report you want to display, such as *<my project>*/Quality Indicators.

Additional Resources

- For more information about adding a Report Viewer Web Part, see "Viewing Reports with SharePoint 2.0 Web Parts" at *http://msdn2.microsoft.com/en-us/library/ms159772(SQL.90).aspx*
- For more information about the team project portal, see "Using the Team Project Portal" at *http://msdn2.microsoft.com/en-us/library/ms242883(VS.80).aspx*

How to Set Permissions on Reports

You can modify report permissions to define who can edit or view reports. You must be a member of the Microsoft SQL Server™ Reporting Services Content Manager role in order to be able to set report permissions.

► **To set permissions for all reports in your team project**

1. In Team Explorer, expand you team project node.
2. Right-click **Reports** and then click **Show Report Site**.
3. Click the **Properties** tab.
4. Click **Security**.
5. Click **Edit Item Security**.
6. If you want to edit security on a role that is already defined for the report, click **Edit**.
7. If you want to define security for a role that is not listed, click **New Role Assignment**.

► **To set permissions on a single report**

1. In Team Explorer, expand you team project node.
2. Right-click **Reports** and then click **Show Report Site**.
3. On the report site, select the report for which you want to set permissions.
4. Click the **Properties** tab.
5. Click **Security**.
6. Click **Edit Item Security**.
7. If you want to edit security on a role that is already defined for the report, click **Edit**.
8. If you want to define security for a role that is not listed, click **New Role Assignment**.

Additional Resources

- For more information about setting report permissions, see "How to: Set Permissions for a Report" at *http://msdn2.microsoft.com/en-us/library/ms181645(VS.80).aspx*

Creation / Customization

- How to customize an existing report.
- How to create a new report in Visual Studio.
- How to create a new report in Excel.
- How to create a scheduled report snapshot.
- How to create a report subscription.
- How to add a new report to an existing process template.

How to Customize an Existing Report

You can modify reports by using the SQL Server 2005 Reporting Services Designer inside Visual Studio (Business Intelligence Development Studio), which ships with the SQL Server 2005 client tools. Modifying an existing report is often easier than creating a new report.

► **To customize an existing report in TFS**

1. Create a reporting project as follows:
   a. In Visual Studio, click **File**, click **New**, and then click **Project**.
   b. Select the **Business Intelligence Project** type.
   c. Select the **Report Server Project** template.
   d. Set your project's **Name** and **Location** and then click **OK**.
2. Export the report you want to customize as follows:
   a. Right-click your team project and then click **Show Project Portal**.
   b. In the Quick Launch bar on the left side of the portal Web site, click **Reports**.
   c. Click the report you want to customize.
   d. Click **Properties**.
   e. Select **Edit**.
   f. Save the report .rdl file into the reporting project folder you created in step 1.
3. Add data sources as follows:
   a. To create the warehouse data source:
      i. In the Visual Studio Solution Explorer, right-click Shared Data Sources and then click Add New Data Source.
      ii. On the **General** tab, in the **Name** text box, type **TfsReportDS**
      iii. In the **Type** combo box, select **Microsoft SQL Server**.
      iv. Click **Edit**.
      v. Fill in your data tier server name.
      vi. Select the **TFSWarehouse** database.
      vii. Click the **OK** button twice to add the data source.

   b. To create the OLAP data source:
      i. In Solution Explorer, right-click **Shared Data Sources** and then click **Add New Data Source**.
      ii. On the **General** tab, in the **Name** text box, type **TfsOlapReportDS**
      iii. In the **Type** combo box, select **Microsoft SQL Server Analysis Services**.
      iv. Click **Edit**.
      v. Fill in your data tier server name.
      vi. Select the **TFSWarehouse** database.
      vii. Click the **OK** button twice to add the data source.
4. Add the report to your project as follows:
   a. In Solution Explorer, right-click **Reports** and then click **Add->Existing Item**.
   b. Browse to the rdl file you exported in step 2.
5. Modify the report as follows:
   a. Modify query statements in the Data Pane.
   b. Drag new measures or members into the Data Pane.
   c. Modify the report layout in the Layout Pane.

Note: Although you can use the Report Builder that is available from the team reporting site, this tool is not well supported for Visual Studio reporting scenarios and therefore is not recommended.

Additional Resources

- For more information, see "How To: Customize a Report in Visual Studio Team Foundation Server" in this guide.

How to Create a New Report in Visual Studio

You can create reports by using the SQL Server 2005 Reporting Services Designer inside Visual Studio (Business Intelligence Development Studio), which ships with the SQL Server 2005 client tools.

Create a new report if there are no existing reports that can be modified to meet your needs. Modifying an existing report is often easier than creating a new report.

► **To create a new report in TFS**

1. Create a reporting project as follows:
   a. In Visual Studio, click **File**, click **New**, and then click **Project**.
   b. Select the **Business Intelligence Project** type.
   c. Select the **Report Server Project** template.
   d. Set your project's **Name** and **Location** and then click **OK**.

2. Add data sources as follows:
   a. To create the warehouse data source:
      i. In Visual Studio Solution Explorer, right-click **Shared Data Sources** and then click **Add New Data Source**.
      ii. On the **General** tab, in the **Name** text box, type **TfsReportDS**
      iii. In the **Type** combo box, select **Microsoft SQL Server**.
      iv. Click **Edit**.
      v. Fill in your data tier server name.
      vi. Select the **TFSWarehouse** database.
      vii. Click the **OK** button twice to add the data source.
   b. To create the Online Analytical Processing (OLAP) data source:
      i. In Solution Explorer, right-click **Shared Data Sources** and then click **Add New Data Source**.
      ii. On the **General** tab, in the **Name** text box, type **TfsOlapReportDS**
      iii. In the **Type** combo box, select **Microsoft SQL Server Analysis Services**.
      iv. Click **Edit**.
      v. Fill in your data tier server name.
      vi. Select the **TFSWarehouse** database.
      vii. Click the **OK** button twice to add the data source.
3. Create a new report as follows:
   a. In Solution Explorer, right-click **Reports**, point to **Add**, and then click **New Item**.
   b. Select the **Report** template.
   c. Name the report and then click **OK**.
4. Modify the report as follows:
   a. If the Report Designer does not open automatically, open the report for modification by double-clicking it in Solution Explorer.
   b. In the **Dataset** drop-down list, select **<New Dataset...>**.
   c. Name the dataset; for example TestDataSet.
   d. Select **TFSOlapReportDS (shared)**.
   e. Click **OK**.
   f. Click the ellipsis (**...**) button next to **Build** (just below the **Dataset** drop-down list), and then select **Team System**.

You can now modify your report by dragging measures and dimensions from the **Dataset** tree into the Query Pane and Filter Pane. You can modify the report's layout by clicking the **Layout** tab. You can preview your report by clicking the **Preview** tab.

Note: Although you can use the Report Builder that is available from the team reporting site, this tool is not well supported for Visual Studio reporting scenarios and therefore is not recommended.

Additional Resources

- For more information, see "How To: Create a Custom Report for Visual Studio Team Foundation Server" in this guide.

How to Create a New Report in Excel

You can create ad-hoc reports by connecting Microsoft Office Excel® directly to the TFS Reporting OLAP cube. By using Excel, you can display report data in the form of pivot tables or pivot charts.

► **To create an Excel pivot table report**

1. Ensure that you have the Microsoft SQL Server 2005 Analysis Services 9.0 OLE DB Provider installed. You can install it from *http://www.microsoft.com/downloads/details.aspx?FamilyID=d09c1d60-a13c-4479-9b91-9e8b9d835cdc*
2. Start Excel.
3. Select the worksheet to which you want to add the pivot table report.
4. On the **Data** menu, select **PivotTable and PivotChart Report**.
5. Select **External Data Source**.
6. Click **Next**.
7. Click **Get Data**.
8. Click the **OLAP Cubes** tab.
9. Select **<New Data Source>** and then click **OK**.
10. Enter a name for the data source.
11. Select the Microsoft SQL Server 2005 Analysis Services 9.0 OLE DB provider.
12. Click **Connect**.
13. Select **Analysis Server**.
14. Enter the name of your reporting server; for example, TFSRTM.
15. Click **Next**.
16. Select **TFSWarehouse** and then click **Finish**.
17. Select the cube from which you want to build a report (e.g., Code Churn, Work Items, and Test Result) and then click **OK**.
18. Click **OK** again to return to the Pivot Table and Pivot Chart Wizard.
19. Click **Finish** to add the pivot table to the worksheet.

Use the **PivotTable Field List** to drag and drop columns and measures into the pivot table. For example, to see a line count for each Team Project on your server:

1. Choose the **Code Churn** cube in step 17 above.
2. Drag **TeamProject.TeamProject** into the **Column Fields** section of the pivot table.
3. Drag **Total Lines** into the **Data Items** section of the pivot table.

Additional Resources

- For more information about using Excel to create ad-hoc reports, see "Using Microsoft Excel for Team Foundation Server Reporting" at *http://msdn2.microsoft.com/en-us/library/ms244713(VS.80).aspx*
- Install the Microsoft SQL Server 2005 Analysis Services 9.0 OLE DB Provider from *http://www.microsoft.com/downloads/details.aspx?FamilyID=d09c1d60-a13c-4479-9b91-9e8b9d835cdc*

How to Create a Scheduled Report Snapshot

You can use scheduled report snapshots to better understand trends over time, or to remember important data points throughout the duration of your project.

► To create a scheduled report snapshot

1. In Team Explorer, right-click **Reports** for your team project, and then click **Show Report Site**.
2. Open a report from the report site.
3. Click the **Properties** tab.
4. Click the **History** link.
5. Set up a schedule for when you want the snapshot to run.

After the schedule has been set up, you can find the snapshots on the **History** tab for that report. You can also create manual snapshots on the **History** tab.

How to Create a Report Subscription

You can use report subscriptions to generate reports and export them to a file share for further use. You can set the subscription to overwrite old reports, or you can build a set of reports over time to view snapshots of project data.

► To create a report subscription

1. In Team Explorer, right-click **Reports** for your team project, and then click **Show Report Site**.
2. Open a report from the report site.
3. Click the **Subscriptions** tab.
4. Click **New Subscription** to create the report subscription.

How to Add a New Report to an Existing Process Template

You can use the Process Editor tool, available with the latest version of the Team Foundation Server Power Tool, to add new reports to an existing process template. You can download the Team Foundation Server Power Tool from *http://msdn2.microsoft.com/en-us/vstudio/aa718351.aspx.*

► **To add new reports**

1. Download the process template that most closely meets your requirements as follows:
   a. In Visual Studio, click **Team** and then select **Team Foundation Server Settings**.
   b. Click **Process Template Manager**.
   c. In the **Process Template Manager** dialog box, select the process template you want to modify, and then click **Download**.
   d. In the **Download Process Template** dialog box, select the folder location on your local drive, and then click **Save**.
2. Open the Process Template in the Process Editor as follows:
   a. In Visual Studio, click the **Team** menu.
   b. Click **Process Editor**, and then click **Open Process Template**.
   c. In the **Open Process Template fileset** dialog box, navigate to the downloaded process template and then click **Open**.

      This opens the ProcessTemplate.xml file in Visual Studio.
   d. Set the **Name** of the methodology to which you are applying customizations.
3. In the Process Template Explorer, click **Reports**.
4. On the toolbar, click **Add**.
5. In the **Report** dialog box, on the **Report Detail** tab, enter a name for the report.
6. Browse to the .rdl file you want to add in the **File Name** field.

   Leave the other fields unchanged and do not make any changes to the data on the **Properties** and **Parameters** tabs.
7. On the **DataSources** tab, enter the appropriate data sources.

   The default data sources for process templates shipped with TFS are /TfsOlapReportDS and /TfsReportDS.
8.. Click **OK**.

Additional Resources

- You can download the Team Foundation Server Power Tool from *http://msdn2.microsoft.com/en-us/vstudio/aa718351.aspx*
- For more information about using the Process Editor tool for customizing work item types, see "How To: Customize a Process Template in Visual Studio Team Foundation Server" in this guide.

Viewing

- **How to analyze the status of a project.**
- **How to analyze application quality.**
- **How to review remaining work.**
- **How to review build status.**
- **How to review bugs and test results.**
- **How to review scheduled work versus actual work on an iteration.**
- **How to determine the owner of the last edit on a file.**
- **How to discover all the code changes made by a developer.**
- **How to discover all the code changes made to a file.**
- **How to discover all the code changes associated with a specific work item.**
- **How to generate code churn metrics.**
- **How to generate workspace metrics such as number of files, lines of code, and number of projects.**

How to Analyze the Status of a Project

You can use the Velocity report to analyze the status of a project.

► To review application status

1. In Team Explorer, expand your team project node, right-click **Reports**, and then click **Show Report Site**.
2. On the report site, select the **Velocity** report.

This report shows how quickly the team is completing work and indicates rates of change from day to day.

How to Analyze Application Quality

You can use the Quality Indicators report to analyze application quality.

► To analyze application quality

1. In Team Explorer, expand your team project node, right-click **Reports**, and then select **Show Report Site**.
2. On the report site, select the **Quality Indicators** report.

This report collects test results, bugs, code coverage, and code churn into a single report that you can use to track project health.

How to Review Remaining Work

You can use the Remaining Work report to review remaining work.

▶ **To review the remaining work**

1. In Team Explorer, expand your team project node, right-click **Reports**, and then select **Show Report Site**.
2. On the report site, select the **Remaining Work** report.

This report shows work that is remaining, resolved, and closed over time. By projecting remaining work trends forward, you can predict the point at which you will be code complete.

How to Review Build Status

If you are using the Microsoft Solution Framework (MSF) for CMMI® (MS CMMI) process template, you can view the Builds report in order to see BVT results.

▶ **To review build status**

1. In Team Explorer, expand your team project node.
2. Right-click **Reports** and then click **Show Report Site**.
3. In the report site, select the **Builds** report.

This report provides a list of available builds and includes build quality and other detailed information.

How to Review Bugs and Test Results

You can use the Bugs by Priority report to review bugs. This report shows you the rate of high-priority bugs found versus low-priority bugs.

You can use the Quality Indicators report to view test results, bugs, code coverage, and code churn in a single report.

▶ **To view either the Bugs by Priority or Quality Indicators report**

1. In Team Explorer, expand your team project node.
2. Right-click **Reports** and then click **Show Report Site**.
3. Select the **Bugs by Priority** report to review bugs, or select the **Quality Indicators** report to view test results.

How to Review Scheduled Work versus Actual Work on an Iteration

You can use the Unplanned Work report to review scheduled work versus actual work. This report charts total work versus remaining work and distinguishes planned from unplanned tasks.

▶ **To view the Unplanned Work report**

1. In Team Explorer, expand your team project node.
2. Right-click **Reports** and then click **Show Report Site**.
3. In the report site, select the **Unplanned Work** report.

How to Determine the Owner of the Last Edit on a File

You can use source file history from Source Control Explorer to determine the owner of the last edit on a file.

To determine who made the last edit on a file

1. In Source Control Explorer, select the file of interest.
2. Right-click the file and then click **View History**.
3. In the History pane, review change history, including the owner.

Additional Resources

- For more information about Source Control Explorer, see "Using Source Control Explorer" at *http://msdn2.microsoft.com/en-us/library/ms181370(VS.80).aspx*

How to Discover All the Code Changes Made by a Developer

You can use the **TF History** command to find all the code changes in your project that have been made by a specific developer.

For example, the following command shows you all changes made by the user Mario:

```
tf history $/ /r  /user:Mario
```

In the preceding example, $/ is used to search the entire repository. You can replace this with $/TeamProjectName to restrict your search to a specific team project.

Additional Resources

- For more information about the TF History command, see "History Command" at *http://msdn2.microsoft.com/en-us/library/yxtbh4yh(VS.80).aspx*

How to Discover All the Code Changes Made to a File

You can use source file history from Source Control Explorer to determine the changes made to a file.

To determine all changes made to a file

1. In Source Control Explorer, select the file of interest.
2. Right-click the file and then click **View History**.
3. In the History pane, review change history to see all changes that have been applied to this file.

Additional Resources

- For more information about Source Control Explorer, see "Using Source Control Explorer" at *http://msdn2.microsoft.com/en-us/library/ms181370(VS.80).aspx*

How to Discover All the Code Changes Associated with a Specific Work Item

If a work item has been associated with a set of code changes at the time of check-in, you can view these changes from the work item **Links** tab.

To view code changes associated with a work item

1. Open the work item in question.
2. Click the **Links** tab.

   If a changeset is associated with this work item, it will be listed in the Links pane in the work item.
3. Double-click the linked changeset to view the files and comments that were checked in.

Additional Resources

- For more information about changesets, see "Working with Source Control Changesets" at *http://msdn2.microsoft.com/en-us/library/ms181408(VS.80).aspx*

How to Generate Code Churn Metrics

You can use the Quality Indicators report to view code churn details.

To view the Quality Indicators report

1. In Team Explorer, expand your team project node.
2. Right-click **Reports** and then click **Show Report Site**.
3. Select the **Quality Indicators** report.

This report collects test results, bugs, code coverage, and code churn into a single report that you can use to track project health.

Alternatively, you use Excel to generate a report on code churn. To learn more, see "How to Create a New Report in Excel" in this document.

How to Generate Workspace Metrics Such as Number of Files, Lines of Code, and Number of Projects

Create reports on various workspace metrics by connecting Excel directly to the TFS Reporting OLAP cube. By using Excel, you can display report data in the form of pivot tables or pivot charts.

To create an Excel pivot table report

1. Ensure that you have the Microsoft SQL Server 2005 Analysis Services 9.0 OLE DB Provider installed. You can install it from *http://www.microsoft.com/downloads/details.aspx?FamilyID=d09c1d60-a13c-4479-9b91-9e8b9d835cdc*

2. Start Excel.
3. Select the worksheet to which you want to add the pivot table report.
4. On the **Data** menu, select **PivotTable and PivotChart Report**.
5. Select **External Data Source**.
6. Click **Next**.
7. Click **Get Data**.
8. Click the **OLAP Cubes** tab.
9. Select **<New Data Source>** and then click **OK**.
10. Enter a name for the data source.
11. Select the Microsoft SQL Server 2005 Analysis Services 9.0 OLE DB provider.
12. Click **Connect**.
13. Select **Analysis Server**.
14. Enter the name of your reporting server; for example, TFSRTM.
15. Click **Next**.
16. Select **TFSWarehouse** and then click **Finish**.
17. Select the **Code Churn** cube from which to build a report, and then click **OK**.
18. Click **OK** again to return to the Pivot Table and Pivot Chart Wizard.
19. Click **Finish** to add the pivot table to the worksheet.

You can use the **PivotTable Field List** to drag and drop columns and measures into the pivot table.

► **To view a file count for each team project on your server**

1. Drag **TeamProject.TeamProject** into the **Page Fields** section of the pivot table.
2. Drag **File Name.FilePath** into the **Row Fields** section of the pivot table.
3. Use the **Team Project** drop-down list in the **Page Fields** section of the pivot table to filter each team project.

   Note the number of rows displayed. This will give you your file count.

► **To view a line count for each team project on your server**

1. Drag **TeamProject.TeamProject** into the **Column Fields** section of the pivot table.
2. Drag **Total Lines** into the **Data Items** section of the pivot table.

► **To view a team project count for your server**

- Drag **TeamProject.TeamProject** into the **Row Fields** section of the pivot table.

  Note the number of rows displayed. This will give you your project count.

Additional Resources

- For more information about using Excel to create ad-hoc reports, see "Using Microsoft Excel for Team Foundation Server Reporting" at *http://msdn2.microsoft.com/en-us/library/ms244713(VS.80).aspx*
- Install the Microsoft SQL Server 2005 Analysis Services 9.0 OLE DB Provider from *http://www.microsoft.com/downloads/details.aspx?FamilyID=d09c1d60-a13c-4479-9b91-9e8b9d835cdc*

Team Foundation Reporting Resources

- For more information on reporting, see "Team Foundation Server Reporting" at *http://msdn2.microsoft.com/en-us/library/ms194922(VS.80).aspx*

Practices at a Glance: Project Management

Index

Check-in Policies

- **How to set up check-in policies to enforce code quality.**
- **How to set up check-in policies to ensure that developers associate work items with check-ins.**
- **How to set up check-in policies to enforce coding standards.**

How to Set Up Check-in Policies to Enforce Code Quality

Use a combination of code analysis and testing policies to enforce a standard of code quality. For example, use the testing policy available out-of-box with VSTS, to ensure that specific tests are executed and passed prior to allowing source to be checked into Microsoft® Visual Studio® 2005 Team Foundation Server (TFS) source control. You can also configure a code analysis policy to help ensure that your code meets certain quality standards by ensuring that security, performance, portability, maintainability, and reliability rules are passed.

By enforcing this type of check-in policy in addition to policies that enforce coding standards and guidelines, you ensure that your code meets a specific code quality gate.

► **To enforce a code analysis check-in policy for a team project**

1. In Team Explorer, right-click your team project, point to **Team Project Settings**, and then click **Source Control**.
2. Click the **Check-in Policy** tab.
3. Click **Add** and then select and configure the appropriate policy.

Additional Resources

- For more information about creating and using a custom check-in policy, see "How To: Step Through Creating Custom Check-in Policies for TFS" In this guide.
- To learn how to customize a check-in policy, see "Walkthrough: Customizing Check-in Policies and Notes" at *http://msdn2.microsoft.com/en-us/library/ms181281(VS.80).aspx*
- To view sample code that will disallow selected patterns on check-in, see "Check-in Policy to Disallow Certain Patterns" at *http://blogs.msdn.com/jmanning/archive/2006/02/02/523125.aspx*
- To see sample code that will enforce comments on check-in, see "Sample Checkin Policy: Make Sure the Comment Isn't Empty" at *http://blogs.msdn.com/jmanning/archive/2006/01/21/515858.aspx*
- To learn how to register a new check-in policy, see "I've Made a New Check-In Policy! How Do I Add It?" at *http://blogs.msdn.com/jmanning/archive/2006/02/07/526778.aspx*

How to Set Up Check-in Policies to Ensure That Developers Associate Work Items with Check-ins

Configure the out-of-box **Work Item** check-in policy, so that developers are forced to associate work items with a check-in. This association helps maintain traceability between the changes made to the source code and the work items tracking bugs and tasks.

► To configure the work item check-in policy to force developers to associate check-ins with a work item

1. In Team Explorer, right-click your team project, select **Team Project Settings**, and then click **Source Control**.
2. Click the **Check-in Policy** tab.
3. Click **Add** and then select and configure the **Work Item** check-in policy.

Additional Resources

- For more information about creating and using a custom check-in policy, see "How To: Step Through Creating Custom Check-in Policies for TFS" in this guide.
- To learn how to customize a check-in policy, see "Walkthrough: Customizing Check-in Policies and Notes" at *http://msdn2.microsoft.com/en-us/library/ms181281(VS.80).aspx*

How to Set Up Check-in Policies to Enforce Coding Standards

The code analysis check-in policies that ship with Team Foundation Server enable you to automatically run static code analysis on code as it is checked in, to ensure that the relevant rules are satisfied. You can fine-tune the code analysis policy to check many different rules. For example, you can check rules governing design, interoperability, maintainability, mobility, naming conventions, reliability, and more.

► To enforce a code analysis check-in policy for a team project

1. In Team Explorer, right-click your team project, point to **Team Project Settings**, and then click **Source Control**.
2. Click the **Check-in Policy** tab and then click **Add**.
3. In the **Add Check-in Policy** dialog box, select **Code Analysis** and then click **OK**.
4. In the **Code Analysis Policy Editor**, select either **Enforce C/C++ Code Analysis (/analyze)** or **Enforce Code Analysis For Managed Code**. Select both if your project contains a combination of managed and unmanaged code.
5. If you select manage code analysis, configure your required rule settings for managed code analysis based on your required coding standards. This determines precisely which rules are enforced.

You can also create a custom check-in policy to perform checks that are not available by default. For example, you can disallow code patterns such as banned API calls, or you can write a policy to enforce your team's specific coding style guidelines, such as where braces should be positioned within your source code.

Additional Resources

- For more information about creating and using a custom check-in policy, see "How To: Step Through Creating Custom Check-in Policies for TFS" in this guide.
- To learn how to customize a check-in policy, see "Walkthrough: Customizing Check-in Policies and Notes" at *http://msdn2.microsoft.com/en-us/library/ms181281(VS.80).aspx*
- To see sample code that will disallow selected patterns on check-in, see "Checkin Policy to Disallow Certain Patterns" at *http://blogs.msdn.com/jmanning/archive/2006/02/02/523125.aspx*
- To see sample code that will enforce comments on check-in, see "Sample Checkin Policy: Make Sure the Comment Isn't Empty" at *http://blogs.msdn.com/jmanning/archive/2006/01/21/515858.aspx*
- To learn how to register a new check-in policy, see "I've Made a New Check-In Policy! How Do I Add It?" at *http://blogs.msdn.com/jmanning/archive/2006/02/07/526778.aspx*

Project Management

- **How to use Microsoft Project to manage your project.**
- **How to use Microsoft Excel to manage your project.**
- **How to create a minimal process template.**
- **How to customize a process template.**
- **How to customize a work item type within a process template.**
- **How to customize a work item type within an existing team project.**
- **How to create an iteration.**
- **How to create an area.**
- **How to add a check-in event notification.**
- **How to set up a report dashboard.**
- **How to create folders in your source control repository.**
- **How to delete a project from Team Foundation Server.**

How to Use Microsoft Project to Manage Your Project

Use Microsoft Office Project to create and schedule tasks, lay out task dependencies, load-balance resources, and estimate end dates. You can use these features to track your projects.

► **To track a project, you need to perform the following high-level steps**

- Create a project plan.
- Create a set of tasks, schedule them, and publish them to Team Foundation Server.

- The tasks show up in the appropriate developer's work item queue.
- The team members work on their tasks and report their progress in Team Explorer by setting the work item status.

- Refresh the project plan to retrieve the latest information. This enables you to track the progress of the project in Microsoft Project.

► **To publish a project plan to TFS**

1. If you are creating a new project plan, set up your tasks, durations, resource assignments, dependencies, and other details as you would normally do with Microsoft Office Project.
2. In Microsoft Office Project, on the **Team** menu, click **Choose Team Project**.
3. Select the Team Foundation Server for your team project.
4. Select your team project.
5. Click **OK**.
6. In the **Work Item Type** column, set the work item type for each work item that you want published to TFS.
7. In the **Sync** column, for summary tasks that you do not want to publish to TFS, select **Do Not Publish**.
8. If you have any tasks that are assigned to more than one resource, divide them into separate tasks that can be assigned to one resource. (Team Foundation Server does not currently support assigning a work item to multiple resources.) Optionally, you can group the separate tasks into a summary task to receive the automatic calculation benefits.

   To group sets of tasks, create a set of areas in TFS, and then group tasks by setting the Area column. TFS, see "How to: Modify the Team Project Areas" at *http://msdn2.microsoft.com/en-us/library/ms181479(VS.80).aspx*
9. On the **Work Item** toolbar, select **Publish** to publish the project plan to TFS.

Additional Resources

- For more information, see "Working with Work Items in Microsoft Project" at *http://msdn2.microsoft.com/en-us/library/ms244368(VS.80).aspx*
- For more information, see "How to: Import Work Items in Microsoft Excel or Microsoft Project" at *http://msdn2.microsoft.com/en-us/library/ms181676(VS.80).aspx*
- For more information, see "Tracking Team Projects in Microsoft Excel and Microsoft Project" at *http://msdn2.microsoft.com/en-us/library/ms244373(VS.80).aspx*

How to Use Microsoft Excel to Manage Your Project

Use Microsoft Office Excel® to store, sort, filter, and manage requirements, scenarios, issues, bugs, risks, and work items.

There are two ways to create a work item list. With the first approach, from Team Explorer you can select a work item query and create a new data-bound spreadsheet. The new spreadsheet contains a work item list that is populated with the data from the query. You can also create a work item list from within Excel by using the add-in to select a project and import work items.

► **To create a work item list with Excel**

1. In Microsoft Office Excel, on the **Team** menu, click **New List**.
2. Under **Connect to a Team Foundation Server**, select the server to connect to, or click **Servers** to enter the server information.
3. Under **Team Projects**, select the team project on the TFS server with which you want to work. The document is bound to this team project.
4. Click **OK**.
5. Select the type of list you want. To create a query list, select the **Query List** option and then click a team query from the **Select a Query** drop-down list.
6. Select the columns you want to appear in the new work item list.
7. Import the desired work items.

   For more information, see "How to: Import Work Items in Microsoft Excel or Microsoft Project" at *http://msdn2.microsoft.com/en-us/library/ms181676(VS.80).aspx*
8. You should now either save the spreadsheet, or publish the new work items to the work item database by clicking **Publish Changes** on the **Team** menu.

Additional Resources

- For more information, see "Working with Work Item Lists in Microsoft Excel" at *http://msdn2.microsoft.com/en-us/library/ms181694(VS.80).aspx*
- For more information, see "How to: Create a Work Item List" at *http://msdn2.microsoft.com/en-us/library/ms181695(VS.80).aspx*
- For more information, see "How to: Import Work Items in Microsoft Excel or Microsoft Project" at *http://msdn2.microsoft.com/en-us/library/ms181676(VS.80).aspx*

How to Create a Minimal Process Template

If you do not require support for any project management–related features of TFS beyond source control, a minimal process template may be sufficient for your needs. In order to create a minimal process template, you use the Process Template Manager to download the template to your local computer, edit the template to remove the sections you are not going to use, and then upload the template back to the server.

► **To create a custom project template that supports only source control**

1. In Team Explorer, right-click the server name, click **Team Foundation Server Settings**, and then click **Process Template Manager**.

2. Choose the template you want to edit and then select **Download**.
3. From the folder where you saved the template, open Process Template.xml for editing.
4. Change the name of the process to a name of your choice by editing the **<name>** element.
5. In the <plugins> section, remove the plug-ins for **Reporting**, **Portal**, and **WorkItemTracking**.
6. In the <groups> section, remove the groups for **Reporting**, **Portal**, and **WorkItem-Tracking**.
7. In the **VersionControl** group, find the <dependencies> section and then remove the **WorkItemTracking** dependency.
8. In the folder where the template was saved, remove the Reports, Windows Share-point Services, and WorkItem Tracking folders.
9. Save all of your changes.
10. In Team Explorer, right-click the server name, click **Team Foundation Server Settings**, and then click **Process Template Manager**.
11. Select **Upload** and choose the template you want to upload.

After you have uploaded the modified process template, you can create new team projects by using this template.

Additional Resources

- For more information, see Chapter 13, "Process Templates Explained" in this guide.
- For more information, see "How To: Customize a Process Template in Visual Studio Team Foundation Serve" in this guide.
- For more information, see "Customizing Process Templates" at *http://msdn2.microsoft.com/en-us/library/ms243782(VS.80).aspx*

How to Customize a Process Template

Customize a process template to change the default work item types, security settings, source control settings, and reports that are set up when a new team project is created to match your organization's process requirements.

► To customize a process template

1. Review the out-of-box process templates and choose the one that most closely suits your organizational process.
2. Download the chosen process template.
3. Customize the process template and change the work item types, security settings, and source control settings as appropriate.

4. Upload the customized template to TFS.
5. Verify that the changes you made suit your process requirements.

To implement the proceeding process you have two options:

- **Manually customize the XML files.** Although this is manual process and hence is error-prone, it does enable you to customize the process template with a fine degree of control. For more information, see "Customizing Process Templates" at *http://msdn2.microsoft.com/en-us/library/ms243782(VS.80).aspx*
- **Use the Process Template Editor tool available with the Microsoft Visual Studio 2005 Team Foundation Server Power Tool.** The latest version of the TFS Power Tool provides a graphical tool for viewing and customizing process templates. When connected to TFS, you can use this tool to customize work item type definitions and global lists on an active project. For more information, see "How To: Customize a Process Template in Visual Studio Team Foundation Serve" in this guide.

Additional Resources

- For more information, see Chapter 13, "Process Templates Explained" in this guide.
- For more information, see "How To: Customize a Process Template in Visual Studio Team Foundation Serve" in this guide.
- For more information, see "Customizing Process Templates" at *http://msdn2.microsoft.com/en-us/library/ms243782(VS.80).aspx*

How to Customize a Work Item Type Within a Process Template

Use the Process Editor tool, available with the latest version of the TFS Power Tool, to customize work item types. You can download the TFS Power Tool from *http://msdn2.microsoft.com/en-us/vstudio/aa718351.aspx.*

► **To customize work item types**

1. Download the process template that most closely meets your requirements, as follows:
   a. In Visual Studio, on the **Team** menu, select **Team Foundation Server Settings**.
   b. Click **Process Template Manager**.
   c. In the **Process Template Manager** dialog box, select the process template you want to modify and then click **Download**.
   d. In the **Download Process Template** dialog box, select the folder location on your local drive where you want to save the template, and then click **Save**.
2. Open the process template in the Process Editor as follows:
   a. In Visual Studio, click the **Team** menu.
   b. Click **Process Editor**, and then click **Open Process Template**.

   c. In the **Open Process Template fileset** dialog box, navigate to the downloaded process template and then click **Open**.
   d. The ProcessTemplate.xml file is loaded by Visual Studio.
   e. Set the **Name** of the methodology you are customizing.
3. In the Process Template Explorer, click **Work Item Tracking**.
4. In the right pane, click the **Type Definitions** tab.
5. To create a new work item, click **Add** in the toolbar in the right pane.
6. In the **New Work Item Type** dialog box, enter a name for the work item type and select an existing work item type from the **Copy From** drop-down list.

   The new work item type is created and is available in the **Item List** on the **Type Definitions** tab in the right pane.
7. To save changes, on the **File** menu, click **Save**.
8. Optionally, add/remove attributes or fields to/from the new work item type or an existing work item type.
9. On the **Type Definitions** tab, right-click the work item type you want to edit, and then click **Open**.

   The selected work item type opens in a new Visual Studio window.
10. Add or remove attributes as necessary.

Additional Resources

- To download the TFS Power Tool, go to *http://msdn2.microsoft.com/en-us/vstudio/aa718351.aspx*
- For more information about work items, see Chapter 12, "Work Items Explained" in this guide.
- For more information on using the Process Editor tool to customize work item types, see "How To: Customize a Process Template in Visual Studio Team Foundation Server" in this guide.

How to Customize a Work Item Type Within an Existing Team Project

You have two options for editing an existing work item type: you can use the command line or you can use the Process Template Editor tool, available as part of the TFS Power Tool.

To edit a work item type from the command line, use the witexport and witimport tools available at, "%programfiles%\Program Files\Microsoft Visual Studio 8\Common7\IDE" on a computer with Team Explorer installed.

► To export the work item type from the project, edit it, and re-import the type

1. Run **witexport** as follows to export the work item type:

```
witexport /f task.xml /t http://TFSServer:8080 /p MyTeamProject /n Task
```

2. Edit the work item type definition.
3. Run **witimport** as follows to import the changed type:

```
witimport /f task.xml /t http://TFSServer:8080 /p MyTeamProject
```

The preceding command line shows how to export the **Task** work item type from the MyTeamProject project to a server named TFSServer.

► **To edit a work item type by using the Process Template Editor tool**

1. Export the work item type you want to edit as follows:
   a. In Visual Studio, on the **Team** menu, select **Process Editor** and then click **Work Item Types** and then select **Export WIT**.
   b. In the **Connect to Team Foundation Server** dialog box, enter the URL of your server.
   c. In the **Select Work Item Type** dialog box, choose the work item type you want to export.
   d. Save the work item type.
   e. Save any global lists you also want to edit.
   f. Edit the work item type and then save your edits.
2. Import the edited work item type as follows:
   a. In Visual Studio, on the **Team** menu, select **Process Editor** and then click **Work Item Types** and then select **Import WIT**.
   b. In the **Connect to Team Foundation Server** dialog box, enter the URL of your server.
   c. In the **Import Work Item Type** dialog box, browse to the edited work item type and then choose the team project into which you want to import the changed work item type.
   d. Click **OK** to import the new work item type definition.

Additional Resources

- To download the TFS Power Tool, go to *http://msdn2.microsoft.com/en-us/vstudio/aa718351.aspx*
- For more information about using the Process Editor tool to customize work item types, see "How To: Customize a Process Template in Visual Studio Team Foundation Server" in this guide
- For more information about using witimport, see "witimport" at *http://msdn2.microsoft.com/en-us/library/ms253163(VS.80).aspx*
- For more information about using witexport, see "witexport" at *http://msdn2.microsoft.com/en-us/library/ms253051(VS.80).aspx*

How to Create an Iteration

Iterations are used to group work items and therefore impact work item creation, work item queries, and reporting.

► **To create an iteration**

1. In Team Explorer, click your team project.
2. On the **Team** menu, point to **Team Project Settings** and then click **Areas and Iterations**.
3. In the **Areas and Iterations** dialog box, click the **Iteration** tab.
4. Click the **Add a child node** toolbar button.
5. Right-click the new node, click **Rename**, and then type iteration name.
6. Click the **Iteration** node.
7. Repeat steps 2, 3, and 4 to create additional iterations identified for your project.
8. Click **Close**.

Note: The Microsoft Solution Framework (MSF) for Agile Software Development (MS Agile) process template includes three predefined iterations. You can delete these iterations, rename them instead of creating new ones, or simply leave them unchanged.

Additional Resources

- For more information, see "Walkthrough: Creating a New Team Project" at *http://msdn2.microsoft.com/en-us/library/dhedaeb2(VS.80).aspx*

How to Create an Area

Create areas to organize team project work into project sub-areas. For example, you could organize your project work into areas such as UI, Application, and Database. Once you have created areas, you can assign scenarios and work items to these areas.

You can start with a single root-level area and then later, as your project matures, you can create areas whenever you need them.

► **To create areas for your project**

1. In Team Explorer, click your team project.
2. On the **Team** menu, point to **Team Project Settings**, and then click **Areas and Iterations**.
3. In the **Areas and Iterations** dialog box, click the **Area** tab.
4. Click the **Add a child node** toolbar button.
5. Right-click the new node, click **Rename**, and then type the area name you want.
6. Click the **Area** node.
7. Repeat steps 2, 3, and 4 to create additional areas. In this way, you can create a hierarchy for your project structure.

Additional Resources

- For more information, see "Walkthrough: Creating a New Team Project" at *http://msdn2.microsoft.com/en-us/library/dhedaeb2(VS.80).aspx*

How to Add a Check-in Event Notification

Use the **bissubscribe** tool, available at %programfiles%\Microsoft Visual Studio 2005 Team Foundation Server\TF Setup\BisSubscribe.exe, on your TFS server to subscribe to check-in notifications.

► To set up a check-in event notification

1. Open a command prompt and change to the following location:

   C:\Program Files\Microsoft Visual Studio 2005 Team Foundation Server\TF Setup\
2. If you want to set up an e-mail notification, use the following command:

```
bissubscribe /eventType CheckinEvent /address someone@domain.com  /deliveryType
EmailHtml /domain http://TFSRTM:8080
```

3. If you want to set up a Web service notification, use the following command:

```
bissubscribe /eventType CheckinEvent /address http://TFSRTM:8080/ci/notify.asmx
/deliveryType Soap /domain http://TFSRTM:8080
```

4. If you get any errors or you want to confirm that you have registered correctly, do the following:
   a. Open SQL Server Management Studio.
   b. Open the **tfsIntegration** database.
   c. Review the **tbl_subscription** table.

The **tbl_subscription** table lists all the events that are already subscribed. By viewing this table, you should be able to find the entry for the event to which you subscribed. You can unsubscribe any registered event by deleting the entry from the table. You can also unsubscribe an event by running **bissubscribe**, passing it the **/unsubscribe** command line parameter and the **id** of the event as follows:

```
bissubscribe /delete/id [id] /server http://TFSRTM:8080
```

Additional Resources

- For more information, see "How To: Set Up a Continuous Integration Build in Visual Studio Team Foundation Server" in this guide.
- For more information, see "Adding a path filter to a CheckinEvent subscription using bissubscribe" at *http://blogs.msdn.com/buckh/archive/2006/09/29/checkinevent-path-filter.aspx*

- For more information, see "Continuous Integration using Team Build" at *http://blogs.msdn.com/khushboo/archive/2006/01/04/509122.aspx*

How to Set Up a Report Dashboard

Modify the team project portal Microsoft Office SharePoint® site in order to create a report dashboard that can provide a variety of project information in one location.

For example, a useful reporting dashboard might contain the following reports:

- Remaining Work
- Quality Indicators
- Bug Rates
- Project Velocity

You can add new reports to your SharePoint portal page by adding a Report Viewer Web Part for each report you want displayed on the page.

► **To modify the team project portal and create a reporting dashboard**

1. Install the Report Viewer Web part on your report server by using the stsadm. exe tool and RSWebParts.cab, included with the Microsoft Office SharePoint and Report Services installation package.
   - STSADM.EXE can be found in the following path: C:\Program Files\Common Files\Microsoft Shared\web server extensions\60\BIN
   - RSWebParts.Cab can be found in the following path: C:\ Program Files\Microsoft SQL Server\90\Tools\Reporting Services\SharePoint

     Example: STSADM.EXE -o addwppack -filename "C:\ Program Files\Microsoft SQL Server\90\Tools\Reporting Services\SharePoint\RSWebParts.cab" -globalinstall
2. In Team Explorer, right-click your project and then click **Show Project Portal**.
3. Click **Modify Shared Page**, point to **Browse**, and then click **Add Web Parts**.
4. Click **Virtual Server Gallery**.
5. From the **Web Part List**, select **Report Viewer**.
6. Click **Add**.
7. Enter the Report Manager name, such as http://*<report server>*/reports.
8. Enter the path for the report you want to display, such as *<my project>*/Quality Indicators.

Additional Resources

- For more information about adding a Report Viewer Web Part, see "Viewing Reports with SharePoint 2.0 Web Parts" at *http://msdn2.microsoft.com/en-us/library/ms159772(SQL.90).aspx*
- For more information about the team project portal, see "Using the Team Project Portal" at *http://msdn2.microsoft.com/en-us/library/ms242883(VS.80).aspx*

How to Create Folders in Your Source Control Repository

You can create folders in your source control repository by using Team Explorer, or you can create the folder structure in your workspace on the client and then check in pending changes.

► **To create a folder structure on the server**

1. In Team Explorer, expand your team project.
2. Double-click **Source Control** beneath your team project.
3. In Source Control Explorer, select the root node, right-click in the Local Path: pane, and then click **New Folder**.
4. Type the name of the root folder and then press ENTER.
5. Repeat steps 3 and 4 and create the required folders in the source control repository.

► **To create a folder structure on the client**

1. Create a workspace mapping on your local computer.
2. Create the folder structure as required by your project.

   When you check in pending changes for the first time, the folder structure is copied to the server.

Additional Resources

- For more information about creating a workspace, see "How to: Create a Workspace" at *http://msdn2.microsoft.com/en-us/library/ms181384(VS.80).aspx*
- For more information about creating a source tree, see "How To: Create Your Source Tree in Visual Studio Team Foundation Server" in this guide.

How to Delete a Project from Team Foundation Server

You cannot delete a project by using Team Explorer. Instead, you must use the **TfsDeleteProject** command-line tool. You can find this tool in Program Files\Microsoft Visual Studio 8\Common7\IDE on a computer with Team Explorer installed.

► **To delete a project from Team TFS**

1. Open a command prompt and switch to the following location:

   C:\Program Files\Microsoft Visual Studio 2005 Team Foundation Server\TF Setup\
2. Run **TfsDeleteProject** as follows to delete the project:

```
TfsDeleteProject /server:TfsServer TeamProjectName
```

Additional Resources

- For more information about deleting projects, see "TFSDeleteProject" at *http://msdn2.microsoft.com/en-us/library/ms181482(VS.80).aspx*

Team Foundation Project Management Resources

- For more information about MSF process templates, see "Process Templates" at *http://msdn2.microsoft.com/en-us/teamsystem/aa718801.aspx*

Questions and Answers: Source Control

Index

- *How do I merge two branches?*
- *Can I merge across team projects?*
- *What is a baseless merge?*
- *What is the code promotion model?*
- *What is the difference between the logical and physical view of branches?*
- *If I use the code promotion model, how often should I merge?*

Check-ins and Check-in Policies

- *What is a changeset?*
- *What is a check-in policy?*
- *When and how can I override a check-in policy?*
- *How do I enforce a policy?*
- *How do I use a check-in verification system?*
- *If I modify file names or delete files on the disk, does version control get out of sync?*
- *How does automatic conflict resolution work?*
- *How do I resolve conflicts manually?*
- *How do I avoid conflicts?*

Checkout, Get, and Lock

- *How do I find out who was the last developer to modify a file?*
- *How does the get command work?*
- *What is the difference between shared and exclusive checkout?*
- *When should I use the lock command?*
- *What lock types does TFS support?*

Distributed/Remote Development

- *How do I work offline?*
- *How do I optimize for distributed team development?*
- *What is the TFS Version Control proxy?*
- *How do I optimize TFS Version Control proxy performance?*

Migration

- *How is TFS version control different from VSS?*
- *How is the checkout model different from VSS?*
- *How should I migrate my source from VSS to TFS?*
- *How should I migrate my source from other version-control systems?*

Project/Workspace Management

- *How should I organize my team projects?*
- *How should I manage dependencies between projects?*
- *What is a workspace?*
- *How do I use workspaces to isolate a developer?*
- *What are the proven practices for workspace mapping?*
- *What are the proven practices for managing shared components and code?*
- *When should I create a new team project versus a new branch?*
- *How should I manage source code that is shared across multiple projects?*
- *How should I manage binaries that are shared across multiple projects?*
- *How should I organize my source tree?*

Shelving

- *What is shelving?*
- *What is a shelveset?*
- *When would I typically use shelving?*
- *How do I use shelving to back up my work?*
- *Why would I want to unshelve a shelveset?*

Accessing Version Control

- **What is the MSSCCI Provider and when is it used?**
- **What other IDEs support TFS?**
- **When should I use the Team Foundation Server Power Tool?**
- **What are the most common version control extensibility scenarios?**
- **How do I work with version control from the command line?**

What is the MSSCCI Provider and when is it used?

The Microsoft® Source Code Control Interface (MSSCCI) provider is used to provide an integrated version control user experience with products that do not support the Microsoft Visual Studio® Team Explorer. For example, if you use Visual Studio 6.0, you can use the MSSCCI client or command line to interact with Microsoft Visual Studio Team System (VSTS) Team Foundation Version Control.

The following clients can work directly with Team Foundation Version Control by using the MSSCCI provider:

- Microsoft Visual Studio .NET 2003
- Microsoft Visual C++® 6 Service Pack 6 (SP6)

- Microsoft Visual Basic® 6.0 SP6
- Microsoft Visual FoxPro® 9.0 SP1
- Microsoft Access 2003 SP2
- Microsoft SQL Server™ Management Studio
- Sparx Systems Enterprise Architect 6.1
- Sybase PowerBuilder 105
- Toad for SQL Server 2.0

The MSSCCI Provider behaves differently from Team Foundation Version Control in Visual Studio 2005 in the following ways:

- Checkout also performs a **GetLatest** operation.
- An exclusive check-in lock is applied at checkout.
- The **Open from Source Control** and **Save to Source Control** menu options behave similarly to Microsoft Visual SourceSafe®.

Additional Resources

- To read more about MSSCCI on Microsoft MSDN®, see "The Microsoft Source-Code Control Interface" at *http://msdn.microsoft.com/library/default.asp?url=/library/en-us/vcug98/html/_asug_the_microsoft_source_code_control_interface.asp*
- To learn more about the MSSCCI Provider, see "Update on the TFS MSSCCI Provider" at *http://blogs.msdn.com/bharry/archive/2006/03/24/559876.aspx*
- The MSSCCI add-in is a TFS Power Tool developed but not officially supported by Microsoft. To download the tool from MSDN, go to *http://www.microsoft.com/downloads/details.aspx?FamilyId=87E1FFBD-A484-4C3A-8776-D560AB1E6198&displaylang=en*

What other IDEs support TFS?

Team Foundation Server can be used from any edition of Visual Studio 2005 that has Team Explorer installed. You can also run Team Explorer side-by-side with any non–Visual Studio 2005 integrated development environment (IDE) in order to work with team projects and manage work items.

The following clients have integration solutions provided by other vendors:

- Eclipse
- Linux client
- Apple Macintosh client
- Hypertext Markup Language (HTML) Web client

If you want to access Team Foundation Version Control from Eclipse IDE, Linux, or Macintosh clients, consider installing the Teamprise suite of client applications, available at *http://www.teamprise.com/*

If you want read-only access to Team Foundation Version Control from the Web, consider installing Team System Web Access, available at *http://msdn2.microsoft.com/en-us/teamsystem/bb676728.aspx*

Additional Resources

- For more information about using Team Explorer, see "Working with Older Visual Studio Projects or Other Code Projects" at *http://msdn2.microsoft.com/en-us/library/ms242912(vs.80).aspx*
- For more information on Teamprise, see *http://www.teamprise.com*
- For more information on Team System Web Access, see *http://msdn2.microsoft.com/en-us/teamsystem/bb676728.aspx*

When should I use the Team Foundation Server Power Tool?

The Team Foundation Power Tool (TFPT) provides version-control functionality that is not available from the Visual Studio 2005 user interface (UI). For example, you can use TFPT to help support working offline, or to perform rollback operations to undo check-ins of a changeset. Consider using TFPT if you need to perform any of the following operations:

- **Unshelve**—The **unshelve** operation that is supported by TFS does not allow shelved changes and local changes to be merged together. When you use TFPT to unshelve a change from a changeset, if an item in your local workspace has a pending change that is an edit, and the shelved change is also an edit, then TFPT can merge the changes by performing a three-way merge.
- **Roll back**—The ability to undo a check-in of a changeset is not directly supported by TFS. By using the TFPT **rollback** command, you can attempt to undo any changes made in a specified changeset. Not all changes can be rolled back, but the rollback works for most scenarios.
- **Work offline**—The TFPT online tool allows you to work without a server connection for a period of time by providing functionality that informs the server about changes you make to your local workspace.
- **Get a changeset**—The TFPT **GetCS** command enables you to get all the items listed in a changeset based on the given changeset version. This is useful if a colleague has checked in a change that you need to have in your workspace, but you cannot update your entire workspace to the latest version.

- **Remove pending edits**—The TFPT **UU** (Undo Unchanged) command removes pending edits from files that have not actually been edited. This is useful in a scenario where you check out a large number of files for edit, but only actually make changes to a small number of the files. You can back out your edits on the unchanged files by running the TFPT **UU** command, which compares hashes of the files in the local workspace to hashes on the server in order to determine whether the file has actually been edited.

You run each of these commands from the command line by using Tfpt.exe.

Additional Resources

- To download TFPT, go to *http://www.microsoft.com/downloads/details.aspx?FamilyID=7324c3db-658d-441b-8522-689c557d0a79&DisplayLang=en*
- To view a forum discussing TFPT, go to *http://forums.microsoft.com/MSDN/ShowForum.aspx?ForumID=930&SiteID=1*

What are the most common version control extensibility scenarios?

The most common version control extensibility scenario is customizing a check-in policy in order to enforce standards at check-in time. To create custom policy plug-ins that appear in the **Add Checkin Policy** dialog box, use the extensibility features provided in the Visual Studio Team Foundation Server Software Development Kit (SDK). You can download the TFS SDK from *http://go.microsoft.com/fwlink/?linkid=68586*

Although not as common, it is also possible to write an integration layer to allow a non–Visual Studio 2005 client to work with Team Foundation Version Control.

Additional Resources

- To learn how to customize a check-in policy, see "Walkthrough: Customizing Check-in Policies and Notes" at *http://msdn2.microsoft.com/en-us/library/ms181281(VS.80).aspx*
- To see sample code that will disallow selected patterns on check-in, see "Checkin Policy to Disallow Certain Patterns" at *http://blogs.msdn.com/jmanning/archive/2006/02/02/523125.aspx*
- To see sample code that will enforce comments on check-in, see "Sample Checkin Policy: Make Sure the Comment Isn't Empty" at *http://blogs.msdn.com/jmanning/archive/2006/01/21/515858.aspx*
- To learn how to register a new check-in policy, see "I've Made a New Check-In Policy! How Do I Add It?" at *http://blogs.msdn.com/jmanning/archive/2006/02/07/526778.aspx*
- To download the TFS SDK, go to *http://go.microsoft.com/fwlink/?linkid=68586*

- To learn more about Team Foundation Version Control extensibility, see "Walk-thru: The Version Control Object Model" at *http://msdn2.microsoft.com/en-us/library/bb187335(VS.80).aspx*

How do I work with version control from the command line?

Team Foundation Server provides the TF command line tool (Tf.exe) to enable you to perform source control operations. For example, you can use the command line to schedule operations by using the Microsoft Windows® Task Scheduler.

To ensure that the appropriate path and other environment variables are set up, run the tool from the Visual Studio 2005 Command Prompt window, or run the Vsvars32 batch file, which is normally located in *DriveLetter*:\Program Files\Microsoft Visual Studio 8\Common7\Tools. The command line supports most source control commands, including **Checkin**, **Checkout**, **Get**, **History**, **Shelve**, **Branch**, **Merge**, **Label**, **Status**, **Undelete**, and **Undo**.

The following are common operations you might want to execute from the command line:

- Synchronize files from the server to your local machine—**tf get**
- Add a file to the server—**tf add**
- Check out a file for editing—**tf checkout**
- Check in pending changes—**tf checkin**
- Retrieve a particular changeset from the server—**tf get /version**

The following operations can only be performed from the command line:

- Delete another user's workspace—**tf workspace /delete**
- Undo another user's check-in—**tf undo**
- Unlock another user's lock—**tf lock**
- Define label scope—**tf label**
- Perform a baseless merge—**tf merge**

Additional Resources

- For more information about working with Tf.exe commands, see "MSDN: Walk-through: Working with Team Foundation Source Control from Command Line" at *http://msdn2.microsoft.com/en-us/library/zthc5x3f.aspx*
- For more information about commands that are only available from the command line, see "Operations Available Only From the Command-Line (Team Foundation Source Control)" at *http://msdn2.microsoft.com/en-us/library/ms194957(VS.80).aspx*

Administration

- **How do I grant permissions on a file within a folder that has inherited permissions?**
- **What should I do if a developer has left the project?**
- **How do I manage interns or other developers that I do not trust to perform check-ins?**
- **How should I modify permissions after my application has shipped?**

How do I grant permissions on a file within a folder that has inherited permissions?

You set permissions by right-clicking the folder or file in Source Control Explorer, clicking **Properties**, and then on the **Security** tab, selecting the user or group for which you want to change permissions, and editing the permissions listed under **Permissions**. You can also set these permissions on the command line by using the **Permission** command of the TF command-line utility.

Team Foundation Source Control allows you to grant access-control permissions to Windows Groups, Windows Users, and Team Foundation Groups. Permissions can be inherited from the containing folder, or you can declare permissions explicitly.

Permission settings are in the form of either Allow or Deny. Deny always overrides Grant, even if Deny is inherited and Grant is explicitly defined. The inherited permissions are combined with the explicit permissions to determine a user's or group's effective permissions on an item. Because Deny always overrides Allow, you can keep inherit turned on and deny check-in, for example.

Be careful when turning inheritance off; for example, you should first set the explicit permissions required and make sure to assign your own account-specific permissions before turning inheritance off. If you turn inheritance off without setting the desired permissions, you can lock yourself out of a file or folder and require a TFS administrator who is also an administrator on the application tier computer to fix the permissions. Application tier local administrators can never completely lock themselves out by design.

Additional Resources

- For more information about permissions, see "Team Foundation Server Default Groups, Permissions, and Roles" on MSDN at *http://msdn2.microsoft.com/en-us/library/ms253077.aspx*
- For further information about permissions, see "Source Control Security Rights and Permissions" on MSDN at *http://msdn2.microsoft.com/en-us/library/ms181761.aspx*

What should I do if a developer has left the project?

If a developer has left your project, make sure that you delete that developer's workspace. This operation also removes any of the developer's pending changes and undoes any locks held by the developer.

Note: You cannot undo the locks without undoing the changes if an exclusive lock has been turned on for the team project.

To find out which files the developer has locked out, run the following command:

```
tf workspaces /owner:domain\devuser /computer:* /server:servername
```

To delete the workspace and remove locks, run the following command:

```
Tf workspace /delete workspacename;domain\devuser /s:servername
```

Additional Resources

- For more information about cleaning up after a developer who has left a project, see "How to: Clean Up Files When Users Leave" at *http://msdn2.microsoft.com/en-us/library/ms194958(VS.80).aspx*
- For more information about the Workspace command, see "Workspace Command" at *http://msdn2.microsoft.com/en-us/library/y901w7se(VS.80).aspx*

How do I manage interns or other developers that I do not trust to perform check-ins?

If your team includes developers that you do not yet trust, such as new hires or interns, you can deny these developers check-in permission on the source tree. Make sure that you set your desired permissions (including permissions for your own account) before turning off inheritance. Rather than check in directly, untrusted developers can make pending changes and then shelve these changes. A more experienced developer can then unshelve the changes, review them, and check them in later.

Additional Resources

- For more information about removing permissions, see "How to: Remove Access to Source Control Files" at *http://msdn2.microsoft.com/en-us/library/ms400718(VS.80).aspx*

How should I modify permissions after my application has shipped?

When a branch is in maintenance mode — for example, after it has been shipped — you can turn off permissions inheritance to lock down the tree. After you have turned off the permissions, you can allow individual users the **pend-change** and **check-in** permissions as needed for hotfixes.

Additional Resources

- For more information about removing permissions, see "How to: Remove Access to Source Control Files" at *http://msdn2.microsoft.com/en-us/library/ms400718(VS.80).aspx*

Branch/Label/Merge

- **When should I use labels?**
- **How do TFS labels differ from VSS labels?**
- **What is branching?**
- **When should I consider branching?**
- **What are the reasons not to branch?**
- **How do I use branching to release my application?**
- **How do I use branching to maintain my application?**
- **How do I use branching to reduce conflicts between teams?**
- **How do I use branching to reduce conflicts between features?**
- **What are the proven practices for branching and merging?**
- **What is the difference between branching and labeling?**
- **What is the "path space" branching model?**
- **How does the TFS promotion model work?**
- **How do I merge two branches?**
- **Can I merge across team projects?**
- **What is a baseless merge?**
- **What is the code promotion model?**
- **What is the difference between the logical and physical view of branches?**
- **If I use the code promotion model, how often should I merge?**

When should I use labels?

Use labels to group a set of files and folders together for future operations. You can use labels for branching, merging, diffing, or getting files. A label provides a marker to which you can return when performing one of the above operations at a later date.

Team Foundation Build automatically labels the file versions associated with each build that it creates.

Note: If you are unsure whether or not you need a branch, you can label a set of files and later create a branch based on this label.

Additional Resources

- For more information about labels, see "Working with labels" at *http://msdn2.microsoft.com/en-us/library/ms181439(VS.80).aspx*
- For further information about labels, see "How to: Apply Labels" at *http://msdn2.microsoft.com/en-us/library/ms181440(VS.80).aspx*

How do TFS labels differ from VSS labels?

Team Foundation Server labels differ significantly from VSS labels. Because VSS labels are "point in time" labels that you normally assign to all or part of a tree in VSS, VSS displays labels according to time sequence along with the file history. Everything that appears on the list before the labeled file is included in the label, while everything later in the list is not.

In TFS, instead of being a single point in time, labels tie together specific versions of a set of source files. A common scenario for labels is to use them to mark daily builds. This allows you to easily retrieve the source file set corresponding to a particular build; for example, if you need to apply a fix.

Additional Resources

- For more information about comparing TFS and VSS labels, see "Comparing SourceSafe Labels to Team Foundation Server Labels" at *http://blogs.vertigosoftware.com/teamsystem/archive/2006/05/03/Comparing_SourceSafe_Labels_to_Team_Foundation_Server_Labels.aspx*

What is branching?

Branching (also known as forking) is the act of splitting a collection of files into separate development paths. Team Foundation Server supports branching and sophisticated merging that allows you to join together files from separate branches. For example, you can use branching to isolate major releases of your application. After you have branched the released version of your application, you can more easily maintain it in the future. Merging allows you to selectively make fixes to both branches.

The purpose of branching and merging is to allow you to isolate concurrent streams of development. For instance, you create a branch when your team has produced a build that you want to maintain going forward. You could also choose to branch in order to isolate feature teams in a very large development organization, or to support development on multiple versions of your application at once.

Because TFS Version Control does not make separate copies of the file content when you branch, it does not consume a lot of additional space in the source control database. A branch consists of a pointer in the database to the source content in the list of deltas that modify it from the base version.

Additional Resources

- For an introduction to branching and merging, see "Branching and Merging Primer" at *http://msdn2.microsoft.com/en-us/library/aa730834(VS.80).aspx*
- For more information about branching, see "How to: Branch Files and Folders" at *http://msdn2.microsoft.com/en-us/library/ms181425(VS.80).aspx*
- For more information about merging, see "How to: Merge Files and Folders" at *http://msdn2.microsoft.com/en-us/library/ms181428(VS.80).aspx*
- For additional descriptions of how to branch and merge in Visual Studio 2005, see "Branching and Merging Team Foundation Source Control" at *http://msdn2.microsoft.com/en-us/library/ms181423(VS.80).aspx*

When should I consider branching?

Branches enable multiple developers to work on the same files in isolation. Because merging incurs overhead and requires you to manage conflicts, you should not branch unless you need the file isolation that branching provides. You can label a build and branch later if needed.

The decision whether to create a branch can be summarized as follows: will the cost of merging conflicts in real time be higher, or will the overhead cost of merging conflicts between branches be higher?

Common reasons to branch include:

- **Release**—Branch for builds you want to maintain, or branch for multiple releases in parallel.
- **Maintenance**—Branch to maintain a previously released build.
- **Feature**—Isolate work on experimental or risky features that might make the rest of the project unstable. Isolate work on interface changes that will cause instability for the rest of the project.
- **Team**—Isolate sub-teams so that they can work without being subject to breaking changes from other teams. Isolate sub-teams so they can work toward unique milestones. These are very similar to feature branches.

Additional Resources

- For an introduction to branching and merging, see "Branching and Merging Primer" at *http://msdn2.microsoft.com/en-us/library/aa730834(VS.80).aspx*

- For more information about branching, see "How to: Branch Files and Folders" at *http://msdn2.microsoft.com/en-us/library/ms181425(VS.80).aspx*
- For more information about merging, see "How to: Merge Files and Folders" at *http://msdn2.microsoft.com/en-us/library/ms181428(VS.80).aspx*
- For additional descriptions of how to branch and merge in Visual Studio 2005, see "Branching and Merging Team Foundation Source Control" at *http://msdn2.microsoft.com/en-us/library/ms181423(VS.80).aspx*

What are the reasons not to branch?

Do not branch unless development team members need to work on the same set of files concurrently. If you are unsure, you can label a build and then create a branch from that labeled build at a later point. Merging branches can be costly, especially if there are significant changes between the branches being merged.

Merging requires one or more developers to execute the merge and sort out conflicts. The merged source must be thoroughly tested because it is not uncommon to make bad merge decisions that can destabilize the build.

Merging across the branch hierarchy is especially difficult and requires you to manually handle many conflicts that could otherwise be handled automatically.

Additional Resources

- For an introduction to branching and merging, see "Branching and Merging Primer" at *http://msdn2.microsoft.com/en-us/library/aa730834(VS.80).aspx*
- For more information about branching, see "How to: Branch Files and Folders" at *http://msdn2.microsoft.com/en-us/library/ms181425(VS.80).aspx*
- For more information about merging, see "How to: Merge Files and Folders" at *http://msdn2.microsoft.com/en-us/library/ms181428(VS.80).aspx*
- For additional descriptions of how to branch and merge in Visual Studio 2005, see "Branching and Merging Team Foundation Source Control" at *http://msdn2.microsoft.com/en-us/library/ms181423(VS.80).aspx*

How do I use branching to release my application?

Use a Release branch when you are ready to stabilize your build prior to release.

The following is an example of what your branch structure might look like after you have created a Release branch:

Main—Integration branch

  Source

  Other asset folders

Release 1—Release branch

  Source

Keep the following recommendations in mind when working with a Release branch:

- **When to branch:** When you are ready to release, integrate everything into the Main branch and then create a Release branch that can be used to stabilize the application prior to release.
- **When not to branch:** If you are using one TFS project per release, you can use the new project to continue development instead of a branch in the current project.
- **Permissions on branch:**
  - Prior to release – Read/write for all developers.
  - After release – Read/write for developers working on hotfixes, read-only for everyone else.
- **Build frequency on branch:** On-demand builds.
- **Testing focus on branch:** Sign off on release.

You should use the Release branch for the targeted fixes and changes necessary in order to stabilize a build prior to release. Development of the next version of your application can occur in parallel in your main Development or Integration branch so that the new version can get the benefit of the stabilization changes you made prior to release. After a final release build has been created, you can merge the changes from the Release branch back into your main Development and Integration branches.

Additional Resources

- For an introduction to branching and merging, see "Branching and Merging Primer" at *http://msdn2.microsoft.com/en-us/library/aa730834(VS.80).aspx*
- For more information about branching, see "How to: Branch Files and Folders" at *http://msdn2.microsoft.com/en-us/library/ms181425(VS.80).aspx*
- For more information about merging, see "How to: Merge Files and Folders" at *http://msdn2.microsoft.com/en-us/library/ms181428(VS.80).aspx*
- For additional descriptions of how to branch and merge in Visual Studio 2005, see "Branching and Merging Team Foundation Source Control" at *http://msdn2.microsoft.com/en-us/library/ms181423(VS.80).aspx*

How do I use branching to maintain my application?

Use Maintenance branches to support previously released builds.

The following is an example of what your branch structure might look like after you have moved a release to the Maintenance folder:

Main—Integration branch

  Source

  Other asset folders

Releases—Container for Release branches

    Release 1—Maintenance branch

        Source

Keep the following recommendations in mind when working with a Maintenance branch:

- **When to branch:** After you have released, support the release with a branch in the Maintenance folder.
- **When not to branch:** If you will never need to maintain the release, you can use a label to mark the old released build and continue work in the Main branch.
- **Permissions on branch:**
  - Read/write for developers working on hotfixes.
  - Read-only for everyone else.
- **Build frequency on branch:** On-demand builds.
- **Testing focus on branch:** Sign off on release.

You should use Maintenance branches to support an older version of your application. You might choose to merge these changes into your main Integration branch, or leave the changes specific to the Maintenance branch.

Additional Resources

- For an introduction to branching and merging, see "Branching and Merging Primer" at *http://msdn2.microsoft.com/en-us/library/aa730834(VS.80).aspx*
- For more information about branching, see "How to: Branch Files and Folders" at *http://msdn2.microsoft.com/en-us/library/ms181425(VS.80).aspx*
- For more information about merging, see "How to: Merge Files and Folders" at *http://msdn2.microsoft.com/en-us/library/ms181428(VS.80).aspx*
- For additional descriptions of how to branch and merge in Visual Studio 2005, see "Branching and Merging Team Foundation Source Control" at *http://msdn2.microsoft.com/en-us/library/ms181423(VS.80).aspx*

How do I use branching to reduce conflicts between teams?

Use Team branches to improve the integration and stabilization of breaking changes across teams.

The following is an example of what your branch structure might look like after you have created Team branches:

Development—Container for Team branches

    Team 1—Team branch

        Source

        Team 2—Team branch

            Source

    Main—Integration branch

        Source

            Other asset folders

Keep the following recommendations in mind when working with a Release branch:

- **When to branch:** If your development teams' work overlaps on files and components, use Team branches to isolate each team's work. You might also choose to create Feature branches beneath the Team branches.
- **When not to branch:** If your source tree is organized by component, and you are confident that there will not be breaking interface changes or a large number of check-in conflicts across your teams, you probably do not need team branches.
- **Permissions on branch:**
    - Read/write for developers on the team.
    - Read-only for everyone else.
- **Build frequency on branch:** Continuous Integration (CI) builds.
- **Testing focus on branch:** Feature and quick feedback testing.

Use the Team branches to allow teams to complete development tasks in parallel. This can be useful to isolate teams from breaking changes originated by other teams, or to allow teams to work toward unique milestones. All active development should occur in the Team branches and then be integrated into the Main branch. You might also want to create Feature branches beneath each team branch.

Additional Resources

- For an introduction to branching and merging, see "Branching and Merging Primer" at *http://msdn2.microsoft.com/en-us/library/aa730834(VS.80).aspx*
- For more information about branching, see "How to: Branch Files and Folders" at *http://msdn2.microsoft.com/en-us/library/ms181425(VS.80).aspx*
- For more information about merging, see "How to: Merge Files and Folders" at *http://msdn2.microsoft.com/en-us/library/ms181428(VS.80).aspx*
- For additional descriptions of how to branch and merge in Visual Studio 2005, see "Branching and Merging Team Foundation Source Control" at *http://msdn2.microsoft.com/en-us/library/ms181423(VS.80).aspx*

How do I use branching to reduce conflicts between features?

Use Feature branches to improve the integration and stabilization of breaking changes across features.

The following is an example of what your branch structure might look like after you have created Feature branches:

Development—Container for Feature branches

  Feature A—Feature branch

    Source

  Feature B—Feature branch

    Source

  Feature C—Feature branch

    Source

Main—Integration branch

  Source

  Other asset folders

Keep the following recommendations in mind when working with Release branches:

- **When to branch:** Feature teams often have source file overlap, thereby increasing the potential for build breaks and check-in conflicts. If you are experiencing these types of problems, consider feature branches for each feature to provide feature isolation. You can create these off a Main branch for small teams, or off Team branches for larger teams.
- **When not to branch:** If you are only creating CI builds, or your daily builds are already predictably stable, you might not need the extra overhead of feature branches.
- **Permissions on branch:**
  - Read/write permissions for developers on the Feature branch.
  - Read-only for everyone else.
- **Build frequency on branch:** CI builds.
- **Testing focus on branch:** Feature and quick feedback testing.

Use Feature branches to allow each feature to be developed in parallel. Perform all active development on the Feature branches and then integrate your code into the Main branch.

Additional Resources

- For an introduction to branching and merging, see "Branching and Merging Primer" at *http://msdn2.microsoft.com/en-us/library/aa730834(VS.80).aspx*
- For more information about branching, see "How to: Branch Files and Folders" at *http://msdn2.microsoft.com/en-us/library/ms181425(VS.80).aspx*

- For more information about merging, see "How to: Merge Files and Folders" at *http://msdn2.microsoft.com/en-us/library/ms181428(VS.80).aspx*
- For additional descriptions of how to branch and merge in Visual Studio 2005, see "Branching and Merging Team Foundation Source Control" at *http://msdn2.microsoft.com/en-us/library/ms181423(VS.80).aspx*

What are the proven practices for branching and merging?

When branching, consider the following guidelines:

- Structure your branch trees so that you only need to merge along the hierarchy (up and down the branch tree) rather than across the hierarchy. Branching across the hierarchy requires that you use a baseless merge, which requires more manual conflict resolution.
- The branch hierarchy is based on the branch parent and branch child, which may be different than the physical structure of the source code on disk. When planning your merges, keep the logical branch structure in mind rather than the physical structure on disk.
- Do not branch too deeply. Because there is latency involved in merging branches, a deep branching structure can mean that changes in a child branch might take a very long time to propagate to the main branch. This can negatively impact project schedules and increase the time required to fix bugs.
- Branch at a high level, and include configuration and source files.
- Allow your branching structure to evolve over time to suit changing needs.
- Do not branch unless your development team needs to work on the same set of files concurrently. If you are unsure, you can label a build and then create a branch from the labeled build at a later point. Merging branches can be costly, especially if there are significant changes between them.
- Merging requires one or more developers to execute the merge and sort out conflicts. The merged source must be thoroughly tested because it is not uncommon to make bad merge decisions that can destabilize the build.
- Merging across the branch hierarchy is especially difficult and requires you to manually handle many conflicts that could otherwise be handled automatically.

Additional Resources

- For an introduction to branching and merging, see "Branching and Merging Primer" at *http://msdn2.microsoft.com/en-us/library/aa730834(VS.80).aspx*
- For more information about branching, see "How to: Branch Files and Folders" at *http://msdn2.microsoft.com/en-us/library/ms181425(VS.80).aspx*
- For more information about merging, see "How to: Merge Files and Folders" at *http://msdn2.microsoft.com/en-us/library/ms181428(VS.80).aspx*

- For additional descriptions of how to branch and merge in Visual Studio 2005, see "Branching and Merging Team Foundation Source Control" at *http://msdn2.microsoft.com/en-us/library/ms181423(VS.80).aspx*

What is the difference between branching and labeling?

Branches are designed to split a collection of files into separate development paths. You use branching to isolate two sets of file versions so that you can evolve the two paths separately. For example, you can use branches to manage and maintain older released versions of your application. You can also use branches to isolate risky code changes that span multiple developers, so that team impact is minimized. However, if you need to isolate only a single developer, use workspaces to reduce branch and merge complexity.

Labels are used to tag a file or collection of files with distinct notation so that the file or collection can be easily retrieved later. For instance, you can use labels to mark daily builds in order to ease future retrieval; for example, if you want to address an issue related to that release.

Additional Resources

- For more information about the branch command, see "Branch Command" at *http://msdn2.microsoft.com/en-us/library/d73s8b27(VS.80).aspx*
- For more information about the label command, see "Label Command" at *http://msdn2.microsoft.com/en-us/library/9ew32kd1(VS.80).aspx*

What is the "path space" branching model?

Branches are created within the path structure of the repository, similar to file copy operations. This is different than the pin-and-share mechanism used by Visual SourceSafe. This approach makes it easier to maintain old versions of your software, because it is simpler to merge changes from one branch to another or make changes in two branches at once.

Team Foundation Server Version Control does not make separate copies of the file content when you branch it, so it does not consume a lot of additional space in the source control database. A branch consists of a pointer in the database to the source content in the list of deltas that modify it from the base version.

Additional Resources

- For an introduction to branching and merging, see "Branching and Merging Primer" at *http://msdn2.microsoft.com/en-us/library/aa730834(VS.80).aspx*

How does the TFS promotion model work?

A *promotion model* is the means by which a change is propagated from one branch to another. Visual SourceSafe also allowed branching and merging, but in practice customers used pinning and sharing as a crude promotion model. Team Foundation Server Version Control uses branching and merging to support promotion modeling. You can use multiple branches to isolate specific versions of the application on which you are working. You can propagate a change by merging from files in one branch to the files in another branch.

Additional Resources

- For more information about branching, see "How to: Branch Files and Folders" at *http://msdn2.microsoft.com/en-us/library/ms181425(VS.80).aspx*
- For more information about merging, see "How to: Merge Files and Folders" at *http://msdn2.microsoft.com/en-us/library/ms181428(VS.80).aspx*
- To learn more about the differences between Visual SourceSafe and Team Foundation Server Version Control, see "Visual Source Safe vs. Team Foundation Server" at *http://msmvps.com/blogs/vstsblog/archive/2005/07/02/56401.aspx*

How do I merge two branches?

To perform a merge, you can use the merge functionality in Source Control Explorer, or you can use the **merge** command-line tool. You can merge based on changeset, label, date, or version.

You might find that your branching structure becomes deeper than one level. If this happens, keep in mind that it is only possible to merge one level at a time. For example, consider the following source tree structure:

Development—Container for isolation development branches.

  Feature A

    Source

  Feature B

    Source

Main—Main integration build branch

  Source

  Other asset folders

Releases—Container for Release branches

  Release 1

    Source

  Release 2—Current release being locked down

    Source

When the source code contained in the **Release 2** branch changes, you might want to eventually merge that change into a Feature branch; for example, to incorporate a bug fix into the latest feature code. It is not easy to merge directly from **Release 2** into **Feature B**; instead, you merge from **Release 2** into its logical parent, **Main**, and then from **Main** into its logical child **Feature B**. If you need to merge between branches that do not have a direct parent-child relationship, you need to perform a baseless merge.

Additional Resources

- To learn how to merge files and folders, see "How to: Merge Files and Folders" at *http://msdn2.microsoft.com/en-us/library/ms181428(VS.80).aspx*
- To learn more about baseless merge, see the /baseless option in "Merge Command" at *http://msdn2.microsoft.com/en-us/library/bd6dxhfy(VS.80).aspx*

Can I merge across team projects?

Yes, there is nothing special about merging across team projects. Regular merges work in this scenario. The Team Project Creation Wizard enables you to create a team project as a branch of a different project.

Additional Resources

- For more information about merging, see "How to: Merge Files and Folders" at *http://msdn2.microsoft.com/en-us/library/ms181428(VS.80).aspx*

What is a baseless merge?

The **branch** command will create a relationship between two folders. You can leverage this connection to perform merges of code between the branches. Branches that are not a direct child or a direct parent of the merge target do not have this relationship. As defined in MSDN, a *baseless merge* "performs a merge without a basis version. That is, allows the user to merge files and folders that do not have a branch/merge relationship. After a baseless merge, a merge relationship exists and future merges do not have to be baseless".

A baseless merge will result in many more conflicts than a normal merge. However, after the first baseless merge, future merges between these branches will no longer be baseless, thus minimizing conflicts.

Baseless merges can only be created from the command line. Even after the first baseless merge, when a relationship has been created between the branches, future merges still need to be created from the command line.

Additional Resources

- To learn how to merge files and folders, see "How to: Merge Files and Folders" at *http://msdn2.microsoft.com/en-us/library/ms181428(VS.80).aspx*
- To learn more about baseless merges and other merging options, see the /baseless option in "Merge Command" at *http://msdn2.microsoft.com/en-us/library/bd6dxhfy(VS.80).aspx*

What is the code promotion model?

Code promotion is a strategy that uses branches to promote code through some stabilization phases. For example, you might have a Development branch in which your team does active development, a Main branch in which your team is integrating and testing, and a Production branch that your team uses for final release stabilization.

Additional Resources

- For more information on branching, see "How to: Branch Files and Folders" at *http://msdn2.microsoft.com/en-us/library/ms181425(VS.80).aspx*

What is the difference between the logical and physical view of branches?

The *physical view* is the hierarchy that appears within your source tree, as shown in the following example:

$/MyTeamProject

Development

Source

Main

Source

Releases

Release1

Source

Release2

Source

Development, Main, Release1, and Release2 are branches that directly contain source code. Releases is a folder that contains multiple branches.

The *logical view* is the hierarchy of parent and child branches as they were created. This hierarchy is not shown in the source tree but can be visualized based on how each branch was created; for example:

Main

Development

Release1

Release2

The logical view is important because merging is easiest when you do it up and down, rather than across, the logical hierarchy. If you execute a merge across the hierarchy, you must perform a baseless merge, which requires use of the command line and significantly more conflict resolution.

Additional Resources

- For more information about branching, see "How to: Branch Files and Folders" at *http://msdn2.microsoft.com/en-us/library/ms181425(VS.80).aspx*
- To learn how to merge files and folders, see "How to: Merge Files and Folders" at *http://msdn2.microsoft.com/en-us/library/ms181428(VS.80).aspx*
- To learn more about baseless merges, see the /baseless option in "Merge Command" at *http://msdn2.microsoft.com/en-us/library/bd6dxhfy(VS.80).aspx*

If I use the code promotion model, how often should I merge?

Merge frequency depends on your branch structure. For example, a common branch structure is as follows:

Development—Container for isolation development branches

Feature A

Source

Feature B

Source

Main—Main integration build branch

Source

Other asset folders

Releases—Container for Release branches

Release 1

Source

Release 2—Release currently locked down

Source

In this case, active development is occurring in the Feature branches and you have two merge frequency decisions to make:

1. How often should feature teams merge changes from the Main branch into their Feature branch?
2. How often should feature teams merge their changes into the Main branch?

The following merge frequency is a proven strategy to reduce breaking changes and reduce migration times:

1. Feature teams should merge their changes into the Main branch as soon as the feature is complete.
2. Feature teams should merge changes from the Main on a regular basis to ensure integration compatibility of their features when they are complete. Ideally, you should merge once per day, and not go more than two days between merges.

Additional Resources

- To learn how to merge files and folders, see "How to: Merge Files and Folders" at *http://msdn2.microsoft.com/en-us/library/ms181428(VS.80).aspx*

Check-in and Check-in Policies

- **What is a changeset?**
- **What is a check-in policy?**
- **When and how can I override a check-in policy?**
- **How do I enforce a policy?**
- **How do I use a check-in verification system?**
- **If I modify file names or delete files on the disk, does version control get out of sync?**
- **How does automatic conflict resolution work?**
- **How do I resolve conflicts manually?**
- **How do I avoid conflicts?**

What is a changeset?

A *changeset* represents the set of changes associated with a check-in. All changes in the changeset are applied to TFS in an atomic fashion when you check-in the changeset. Changesets are identified by unique, sequentially increasing numbers.

You can retrieve a changeset at a later time to view details of what files changed, check-in comments, and associated work items. You can also retrieve the file versions associated with the changeset if you need to review, test, or build with the old change.

Additional Resources

- For more information about retrieving changesets, see "How to: Retrieve Old Versions of Files from Changesets" at *http://msdn2.microsoft.com/en-us/library/ms181416(VS.80).aspx*

What is a check-in policy?

You can use check-in policies to enforce coding standards upon check-in. For example, you can require that each developer runs static code analysis on the code before it is checked in,.

The following check-in policies are available by default with VSTS:

- **Code Analysis**—Requires that code analysis be run before check-in.
- **Test Policy**—Requires that check-in tests be completed before check-in.
- **Work Items**—Requires that one or more work items be associated with the check-in.

You can create a custom check-in policy to perform checks that are not available by default. For example, you can disallow code patterns such as banned API calls, force the use of check-in comments, or check against your team's style guidelines.

Additional Resources

- To learn how to customize a check-in policy, see "Walkthrough: Customizing Check-in Policies and Notes" at *http://msdn2.microsoft.com/en-us/library/ms181281(VS.80).aspx*
- To see sample code that will disallow selected patterns on check-in, see "Checkin Policy to Disallow Certain Patterns" at *http://blogs.msdn.com/jmanning/archive/2006/02/02/523125.aspx*
- To see sample code that will enforce comments on check-in, see "Sample Checkin Policy: Make Sure the Comment Isn't Empty" at *http://blogs.msdn.com/jmanning/archive/2006/01/21/515858.aspx*
- To learn how to register a new check-in policy, see "I've Made a New Check-In Policy! How Do I Add It?" at *http://blogs.msdn.com/jmanning/archive/2006/02/07/526778.aspx*

When and how can I override a check-in policy?

You can override a check-in policy by selecting the **Override policy failure and continue check-in** checkbox. Any team member who has permission to check in files can override a check-in policy.

If you want to detect when a member of your team overrides check-in policy, you can use the Team Foundation Eventing Service to hook check-in events.

Additional Resources

- To learn more about overriding a check-in policy, see "How to: Override a Check-in Policy" at *http://msdn2.microsoft.com/en-us/library/ms245460(VS.80).aspx*
- To learn more about the Team Foundation Eventing Service, see "Eventing Service" at *http://msdn2.microsoft.com/en-us/library/bb130154(vs.80).aspx*

How do I enforce a policy?

Team Foundation Version Control will not prevent someone from overriding a policy. However, you can use the following steps to detect if a policy has been overridden:

- Use the Team Foundation Eventing Service (from the Team Foundation Core Services API) for hooking into check-in events.
- Write a **Notify** method that parses the details of the changeset, and then react to it if an override has occurred.

Alternatively, you can manually scan changeset history to discover policy overrides.

Additional Resources

- To learn how to receive an e-mail notification when a policy has been violated, see *http://blogs.infosupport.com/marcelv/archive/2005/10/18/1635.aspx*

How do I use a check-in verification system?

You can use Team Foundation Version Control check-in policies as a check-in verification system. Team Foundation Server ships with check-in policies to ensure that the following is true before a check-in can be committed:

- A work item is associated with the change.
- Unit tests have all passed.
- Static analysis has run cleanly.

You can create your own check-in requirements by creating new policy plug-ins. Your plug-in can ensure that code matches your team's coding standards, has run build verification tests, or any other requirement that is critical to your team's needs.

Additional Resources

- To learn more about creating and customizing check-in policies, see "Walkthrough: Customizing Check-in Policies and Notes" at *http://msdn2.microsoft.com/en-us/library/ms181281(VS.80).aspx*

If I modify file names or delete files on the disk, does version control get out of sync?

Yes. If you accidentally delete files or folders, the TFS server still thinks you have the latest versions on your local machine. This means that the **get latest version** command will not add the deleted files back onto your disk. In this case, use the **force get** command to restore the files or folders.

If you need to rename files or delete files or folders, do so by using Source Explorer so that the server stays synchronized with your local changes.

How does automatic conflict resolution work?

A conflict can occur as a result of a pending **change**, **merge**, or **get** operation. When you opt to resolve the conflict, you can choose to have Visual Studio resolve the conflict automatically. Automatic conflict resolution only works on non-binary files that have no overlapping changes (for example, changes applied to the same line of code). In this case, changes for both file versions are merged into a new file version.

If automatic conflict resolution does not work, you can choose to only accept changes from one of the files, or you can perform a manual merge by using the graphical compare and differencing tools provided by VSTS.

Additional Resources

- For more information about resolving conflicts, see "How to: Resolve Conflicts" at *http://msdn2.microsoft.com/en-us/library/ms181433(VS.80).aspx*

How do I resolve conflicts manually?

To resolve merge conflicts, use the Visual Studio merge tool. If a conflict is detected during a merge, you can resolve the conflict either automatically or manually. If you choose to resolve the conflict manually, you can keep the source changes, keep the target changes, or resolve the conflict in the merge tool.

You might need to resolve conflicts when merging changes between branches, getting files into your workspace, or checking in new versions of files. There are three conflict types:

- **Version**—The file has evolved along divergent paths. This could be the result of a file edit, rename, delete, or undelete.
- **File name collision**—Two or more items are trying to occupy the same path.
- **Local overwrite**—Only occurs during a **get** operation, if you are trying to overwrite a local, editable file.

Most conflicts can be resolved automatically; version conflicts are the only conflict type that might result in a manual merge operation. Manual merge is most common in the following scenarios:

- A file has been edited in both branches, with changes to the same lines of code.
- A baseless merge is being conducted in which the branch file relationships are not known to TFS.

The merge tool shows you the details for each conflict and allows you to choose which change you want to keep in the final merged file. You can choose to keep the source change, keep the destination change, integrate both changes, or manually modify the final version by typing directly into the file.

After resolving every conflict in the file, save the final version as a pending change to be checked into the target branch.

Be careful when merging because it is easy to make mistakes that might result in build instability. After you have finished merging, compile the resulting source and run unit tests to test for major breaks.

Additional Resources

- For more information about resolving conflicts, see "How to: Resolve Conflicts" at *http://msdn2.microsoft.com/en-us/library/ms181433(VS.80).aspx*

How do I avoid conflicts?

Most conflicts can be automatically resolved by Team Foundation Version Control. The scenarios in which you are most likely to need a manual merge and therefore are worth avoiding are scenarios in which there are overlapping changes to the same lines of code, or where more than two developers are working on a file at the same time.

► **To view pending changes**

1. In Source Control Explorer, right-click the solution, project, folder, or file for which you want to see pending changes.
2. Select **View Pending Changes**.

This method will show you all of the pending changes within the scope you have selected.

If you use the command line checkout tool, it will indicate which other users have checked out this file, including information about the nature of the users' pending changes. In the following example, a file named Math.cs is checked out, and TFS provides a notification that two other users (James and Sally) are working on the file. The notification indicates exactly what type of pending change each user has in his or her local workspace (Edit and Rename) and confirms that the local version of the file (the current workspace version) is not based on the latest repository version.

```
c:\dev\projects\calc\src>tf edit math.cs
ExplorerScc.cs

$/MathProject/dev/calc/src/math.cs:
   opened for edit in Workspace21;contoso\james
   opened for rename in WS24;contoso\sally
   newer version exists in the repository
```

Communicate regularly with other developers to indicate the nature of your changes to a particular file, to help avoid overlapping changes that would need to be manually merged. Coordination is a good way to make sure that two developers do not work on the same part of the code, but otherwise there is nothing wrong with having two or more people editing different parts of the same file.

Additional Resources

- For more information about viewing pending changes in your workspace, see "How to: View and Manage All Pending Changes in Your Workspace" at *http://msdn2.microsoft.com/en-us/library/ms181400(VS.80).aspx*
- For more information about viewing pending changes in other workspaces, see "How to: View Pending Changes in Other Workspaces" at *http://msdn2.microsoft.com/en-us/library/ms181401(VS.80).aspx*

Checkout, Get, and Lock

- **How do I find out who was the last developer to modify a file?**
- **How does the get command work?**
- **What is the difference between shared and exclusive checkout?**
- **When should I use the lock command?**
- **What lock types does TFS support?**

How do I find out who was the last developer to modify a file?

You can determine who last modified a file by examining the file's history. To do so, right-click the file in Solution Explorer and then click **View History**. This displays the History window, which shows a list of modifications and the users who made those modifications. The last developer to modify a given file is shown at the top of the list. You can also view version history for a file from the command line by using the **history** command from the tf.exe command line tool.

Additional Resources

- For more information about file history, see "How to: View Historical Data" at *http://msdn2.microsoft.com/en-us/library/ms181415(VS.80).aspx*

How does the get command work?

Use the **get** command to synchronize the files on your machine with the files on the Team Foundation Server. When you perform a **get** operation, Visual Studio performs the following steps. Note that the following sequence assumes that you have installed TFS proxy in order to boost performance:

1. The server determines which files are out of date based on the fact that it knows which versions are on your disk.
2. The server then tells the client what it needs to do to update its workspace.
3. The client downloads, moves, and deletes files as necessary and then notifies the server of which operations it accomplished.

A **get** operation does not mark any files for editing and by default will not overwrite any files you have checked out for editing.

Additional Resources

- For more information about the get command, see "Get Command" at *http://msdn2.microsoft.com/pt-br/library/fx7sdeyf(VS.80).aspx*

What is the difference between shared and exclusive checkout?

Team Foundation Server source control supports both shared and exclusive checkouts.

With an *exclusive checkout*, nobody else can check out a file until you check it back into source control. This can lead to bottlenecks in the development process.

By default, TFS also enables multiple users to check out the same source-controlled item concurrently. This is referred to as *shared checkout*. With this model, multiple developers can be working on copies of the same source file in their own workspaces. Team Foundation Server knows which version is in a given developer's workspace, and that developer must resolve conflicts prior to check-in.

In most collaborative development environments, it is unlikely that that you will make a change in your workspace that conflicts with a pending change in another user's workspace, or vice versa. A great majority of the workspace conflicts that do occur are resolved automatically by TFS. For conflicts that cannot be resolved automatically, you can use the **resolve** command to safely decide which change (yours or someone else's) you want to keep.

Additional Resources

- For more information about locks, see "How to: Lock and Unlock Folders or Files" at *http://msdn2.microsoft.com/en-us/library/ms181420(VS.80).aspx*

When should I use the lock command?

Use the **lock** command to prevent other developers from checking out or checking in their changes until you unlock the file on which they are working. You should only lock a file if you are concerned that there will be a conflict resulting in a complicated manual merge operation. Because most conflicts can be resolved automatically, you should use the **lock** command sparingly, if at all.

Additional Resources

- For more informational about lock types, see *http://msdn2.microsoft.com/en-us/library/ms181419(VS.80).aspx*

What lock types does TFS support?

Team Foundation Server provides two types of locks: check-in and checkout locks. A check-in lock is less restrictive than a checkout lock. When you apply a check-in lock, users can continue to make local changes to the item in other workspaces. The changes cannot be checked in until you explicitly remove the check-in lock from the workspace or you check in the file.

A checkout lock is more restrictive than a check-in lock. When you apply a checkout lock to a source-controlled file or folder, users can neither check out the file for editing nor check in pre-existing pending changes. You cannot acquire a checkout lock if an item currently has any pending changes.

Additional Resources

- For more informational about lock types, see *http://msdn2.microsoft.com/en-us/library/ms181419(VS.80).aspx*

Distributed/Remote Development

- **How do I work offline?**
- **How do I optimize for distributed team development?**
- **What is the TFS Version Control proxy?**
- **How do I optimize TFS Version Control proxy performance?**

How do I work offline?

Team Foundation Version Control does not natively support offline working. If you want to work offline you must strictly adhere to the following workflow:

1. Manually remove read-only flags.
2. Edit files.
3. Add or delete files.
4. Run the Team Foundation Power Tool (TFPT) online command.

Note: You must not rename any files while you are offline.

---

1. **Manually remove read-only flags.**

   By default, all files in the workspace that have not been checked out are marked as read-only. When you are working without a server connection, you must manually remove the read-only flag from files before editing or deleting them. To do this, right-click the file in Windows Explorer, click **Properties**, clear the **Read-only** check box, and then click **OK**. Alternatively, you can use the DOS command **attrib -r**

2. **Edit files.**

   You can now freely edit any files for which you have removed the read-only flag.

3. **Add or delete files.**

   You can add files or delete files for which you have removed the read-only flag. Do not rename files, as the TFPT online tool cannot distinguish a rename from a delete paired with an add.

   Note: You must specify an option to the TFPT online command to get it to look for delete instances, as this is a more time-consuming operation.

   ---

4. **Run the TFPT online command.**

   When you are back online, run the TFPT online command by typing **TFPT online** at the command line. This command scans your workspace for writable files and determines what changes should be pended on the server. If you have deleted any files, use the **/deletes** command-line option to scan for deleted files in your local workspace as well. The tool then displays the **Online** window from which you can choose which changes to pend into the workspace.

Additional Resources

- To download the TFPT online tool from MSDN, go to *http://www.microsoft.com/downloads/details.aspx?familyid=7324C3DB-658D-441B-8522-689C557D0A79&displaylang=en*
- To learn more about the Team Foundation Power Tool, see "Power Tools: tfpt.exe" at *http://blogs.msdn.com/buckh/archive/2005/11/16/493401.aspx*

How do I optimize for distributed team development?

You can choose from one of the following three solutions to provide access to TFS over the Internet:

- **Use a VPN connection.** You can provide access to TFS over a virtual private network (VPN).
- **Publish your TFS through a reverse proxy.** You can provide access to TFS through a reverse proxy such as Microsoft Internet Security and Acceleration (ISA) Server.
- **Locate your TFS in the extranet ("hosted scenario").** You can host your TFS server on an extranet.

If you are supporting remote users with VPN access, use the VPN solution. This is the easiest solution to enable, provides well-understood security, allows remote access to all TFS features, and allows you to use the TFS Proxy to improve performance. In this solution Your TFS sits inside the internal network, and external users access it over a VPN. Internal users access a TFS directly

If you are supporting remote users without VPN access or without access to the domain, use the reverse proxy scenario. This solution is more difficult to set up, but it enables remote users to access an internally located TFS without the need for VPN. In this solution your TFS sits inside the internal network, and one or more reverse proxy machines, such as ISA Server, bring in client requests from the Internet to your TFS.

If you are supporting a set of remote users who will be using a TFS installation dedicated to their use, such as a community development site, use the extranet scenario. This solution gives you the most separation between the remote users and your internal network resources. In this solution only external clients access your TFS, and it is located outside of the firewall on an extranet

If you are supporting an office with multiple clients connecting to a remote Team Foundation Server, you should install and configure Team Foundation Server Proxy in the remote office. This improves performance by caching source control files on the remote office's proxy server.

If you are supporting a single client connecting to a remote TFS, configure the client to connect directly to the TFS.

Additional Resources

- To learn more about the TFS Proxy, see "Team Foundation Server Proxy and Source Control" on MSDN at *http://msdn2.microsoft.com/en-us/library/ms252490(VS.80).aspx*
- To learn more about the TFS Proxy File Cache Server, see the MSDN Webcast at *http://msevents.microsoft.com/CUI/WebCastEventDetails.aspx?culture=en-US&EventID=1032291120&CountryCode=US*

What is the TFS Version Control proxy?

Client-server communication in TFS uses Hypertext Transfer Protocol (HTTP). The TFS Version Control proxy is installed on a server at remote locations team locations separated by a wide-area network (WAN) connection from the TFS database to boost performance and to avoid unnecessary roundtrips to the server. The proxy caches copies of source-controlled files in the remote location, away from the central TFS server. When a file is not in the local cache, the file is downloaded by the proxy to the local cache from TFS before returning the files to the client.

Although remote access is the most common scenario for using the proxy, you can also use it anytime you want to take load off of the main server. For instance, if your server is overloaded by many local simultaneous requests to get the latest source, you can offload this work to the proxy. Because every application tier install includes a proxy. there is generally nothing to be gained by putting a proxy in front of an AT.

Additional Resources

- For more information about the TFS Version Control proxy, see "Team Foundation Server Proxy and Source Control" at *http://msdn2.microsoft.com/en-us/library/ms252490(VS.80).aspx*

How do I optimize TFS Version Control proxy performance?

Consider the following approaches to optimizing proxy performance:

- Make sure that caching is enabled, and monitor the performance of your cache. Monitor the performance counters (installed by default) and event logs (for errors/warnings) on your proxy server on a periodic basis, to see how your proxy is performing. Note that TFS Proxy saves cache performance statistics to an Extensible Markup Language (XML) file named ProxyStatistics.xml, and that you can change the interval for saving these statistics. The ProxyStatistics.xml file is located in the App_Data folder in the proxy installation directory.
- Run a scheduled task to retrieve the latest files to the proxy server on a periodic basis. This helps to ensure that the latest versions of the files are available in the proxy cache, and to ensure that subsequent client requests for these files result in a cache hit.
- If you know that large files are going to be downloaded over a low bandwidth (< 3-Mbps) network, set the **executionTimeout** configuration to an appropriate value in Web.config. The default value is one hour <httpRuntime executionTimeout="3600"/>.

Additional Resources

- For more information about examining TFS proxy performance, see *http://msdn2.microsoft.com/en-us/library/ms252455(VS.80).aspx*

Migration

- **How is TFS version control different from VSS?**
- **How is the checkout model different from VSS?**
- **How should I migrate my source from VSS to TFS?**
- **How should I migrate my source from other version-control systems?**

How is TFS version control different from VSS?

Microsoft Visual SourceSafe is targeted at individual developers and small teams, while TFS version control is designed for professional developers and very large teams with up to 2,500 users per server. Other major improvements introduced with TFS version control include deep integration with Visual Studio 2005 as well as distributed team support enabling efficient file access over WANs. The major differences between the two systems include the following:

- **Code churn**—Visual SourceSafe has no features that support code churn metrics. TFS version control gives you code churn metrics for every file that you check into the data warehouse, and you can slice the data in any way that you want.
- **Checkout**—Visual SourceSafe always gets the latest file or the pinned file from the database and overwrites your local version. TFS version control makes your workspace version of the file writable, but does not overwrite your version with a version from the database.
- **File locking**—Visual SourceSafe automatically applies an exclusive lock to a file when you check it out. By default, TFS version control allows multiple developers to check out a file concurrently. When conflicts do occur, they usually can be automatically resolved.
- **Branching**—Visual SourceSafe uses a pin-and-share branching method. Pinning is not supported in TFS version control, which instead uses path-space branching. This makes it easier to maintain old versions of your software, because it facilitates merging changes from one branch to another or making changes in two branches at once.
- **Sharing**—TFS version control does not support sharing. The migration of a shared file results in copying the file to the destination folder.
- **Workflow integration**—Visual SourceSafe is a stand-alone version-control system. TFS version control is integrated with work item tracking and TFS reporting.

Additional Resources

- To learn more about the differences between Visual SourceSafe and TFS version control, see "Visual Source Safe vs. Team Foundation Server" at *http://msmvps.com/blogs/vstsblog/archive/2005/07/02/56401.aspx*

How is the checkout model different from VSS?

When you check out a file from TFS version control, the file is marked as writable in your workspace but is not synchronized with the database server. To get the latest version from the database server, you must first use the **get** command. In contrast, a VSS check-out operation gets the file from the database server and marks it as writable in your workspace.

Visual SourceSafe uses exclusive checkout by default, while TFS uses shared checkout by default. Shared checkout enables multiple developers to make changes to a file at the same time. Unlike in Visual SourceSafe, most conflicts in TFS can be resolved automatically.

Additional Resources

- For more information about the differences between VSS checkout and TFS version control checkout, see "Team Foundation vs. SourceSafe | Checking Out" at *http://blogs.msdn.com/korbyp/archive/2004/07/28/199720.aspx*

How should I migrate my source from VSS to TFS?

Team Foundation Server ships with a VSS converter that allows you to migrate files, folders, version history, labels, and user information from a VSS database to TFS version control.

The converter does have some limitations that are important to understand; for example:

- Historical information about file sharing is not preserved. Team Foundation Server does not support sharing. The migration of a shared file results in copying the file to the destination folder.
- Historical information about branching is not preserved.
- Team Foundation Server does not support pinning. Pinned files are migrated by creating two labels.
- Timestamps associated with actions are not preserved during migration.

Additional Resources

- For more information about how to prepare for migration, see *http://msdn2.microsoft.com/en-us/library/ms181246(en-us,vs.80).aspx*
- For more information about how to perform the migration, see *http://msdn2.microsoft.com/en-us/library/ms181247(VS.80).aspx*
- For more information about the limitations of the VSS converter, see *http://msdn2.microsoft.com/en-us/library/ms252491(VS.80).aspx*
- For more information about the VSS Analyze tool, see *http://msdn2.microsoft.com/en-us/library/ysxsfw4x.aspx.*
- For more information about the VSSConverter command-line utility's migrate command, see *http://msdn2.microsoft.com/en-us/library/ms400685(VS.80).aspx*

How should I migrate my source from other version-control systems?

You can manually export files from the version-control system from which you are migrating and then import the files into TFS version control. To preserve file history or other attributes from the version-control system from which you are migrating, you can use the TFS version control object model to write your own migration tool.

Microsoft is currently working on a ClearCase converter; when it is ready, it will be announced on the TFS Migration blog at *http://blogs.msdn.com/tfs_migration*

Component Software has created a converter that is compatible with VSS, GNU RCS, CS-RCS, GNU CVS, and Subversion (SVN).

Additional Resources

- For more information about TFS version control extensibility, see "Walkthru: The Version Control Object Model" at *http://msdn2.microsoft.com/en-us/library/bb187335(VS.80).aspx*
- For more information about the Component Software converter, see *http://www.componentsoftware.com/Products/Converter/*

Project/Workspace Management

- **How should I organize my team projects?**
- **How should I manage dependencies between projects?**
- **What is a workspace?**
- **How do I use workspaces to isolate a developer?**
- **What are the proven practices for workspace mapping?**
- **When should I create a new team project versus a new branch?**
- **How should I manage source code that is shared across multiple projects?**
- **How should I manage binaries that are shared across multiple projects?**
- **How should I organize my source tree?**

How should I organize my team projects?

Team projects are intended to represent the largest unit of work possible in your organization. Most often this will be a product under development.

Consider one of the following strategies for managing team projects:

- Create one project per application.
- Create one project per release.

Create one project per application

If you want to carry forward not only source code but also work items and other TFS assets between releases, consider using one project per application. When you use a single project for multiple versions of the application, all of the TFS assets are carried forward automatically for you for the next release. When you are ready to release a new version of your application, you can create a branch within the project to represent the release and isolate that code.

The following are reasons not to use one project per application:

- Releases in parallel are forced to share work item schemas, check in policies, and process guidance.
- Reporting is more difficult; because reports default to the entire project, you must add filtering by release.
- If you have hundreds of applications, each in its own project, you will run up against TFS performance and scale limits.
- You will accumulate 'baggage' over multiple releases. The easiest way to eliminate this baggage is to create a new team project and then branch code you want to carry forward into that project.

Create one project per release

If you want each release to start fresh without carrying forward work items and other TFS assets, consider using one project per release. When you use a new project for each release, you can modify work item schemas, workflow, check-in policies, and other assets without impacting the old release. This can be especially useful if the old release will be maintained by a separate team, such as a sustained engineering team who may have a different process and workflow than your main development team.

The following are reasons not to use one project per release:

- While it is very easy to move the source code from one project to another, it is difficult to move work items and other TFS assets from one project to another. Work items can only be copied one at a time to another project, if you want to copy sets of work items you'll need to write your own utility.
- If you have hundreds of applications and releases, each in its own project, you'll hit Team Foundation Server performance and scale limits.

Keep the following considerations in mind when choosing your strategy:

- Choose a structure that will suit your purposes in the long term, because restructuring existing team projects is difficult.
- Source can be easily shared among team projects as follows:
  - Branch source from one project to another.
  - Map source from another project into your workspace.

- Team Foundation Server can scale to ~500 projects by using the Microsoft Solution Framework (MSF) for Agile Development (MSF Agile) process template, or 250 projects using the MSF for CMMI® (MSF CMMI) process template. If you create your own process or customize an existing template, keep in mind that work item schemas have the largest impact on server scalability. A complex schema will result in a server capable of supporting fewer projects.

Additional Resources

- For more information about using team projects, see "When to use Team Projects" at *http://blogs.msdn.com/ericlee/archive/2006/08/09/when-to-use-team-projects.aspx*

How should I manage dependencies between projects?

If you need to reference an external assembly that is not built as part of your Visual Studio solution, such as a third-party assembly for which you only have the binary dynamic-link library (DLL), you have the following three choices:

- You can store the external assembly as a binary resource as part of your project. This works well if you plan to maintain the dependency for other projects that might want to reference it, or if yours is the only project that relies on this dependency.
- You can reference an assembly on your build server by using either a virtual drive letter or a Universal Naming Convention (UNC) path.
- You can store the set of external assemblies in a folder in a shared team project. This approach works well if there are many projects that want to reference this shared dependency and your project is not the clear owner of it.
  - If you want to receive immediate updates to the binary when it is changed, you can create a workspace mapping for this team project to your local computer. You can set a file reference to the assembly within your local file structure.
  - If you want to control the integration schedule for this dependency, you can create a branch from the shared project into your project and then merge whenever you are ready to pick up changes.

In general, you should avoid dependencies that cross team projects, and instead try to have all the related/dependent solutions/projects under the same team project. This reduces the need for build script customization. If you have a dependency, use project references to define the dependency. You should avoid file references because they are more difficult to manage.

Note: Project-to-project references are supported within a solution. Also note that a project file (csproj, vjsproj, vcproj, vbproj, etc) can be included by multiple solutions (sln files), so a project can be shared by multiple separate solutions.

Additional Resources

- For more information about project references, see "Project References" at *http://msdn2.microsoft.com/en-us/library/ez524kew(VS.80).aspx*
- For more information about branching, see "How to: Branch Files and Folders" at *http://msdn2.microsoft.com/en-us/library/ms181425(VS.80).aspx*
- For more information about workspaces, see *http://msdn2.microsoft.com/en-us/library/ms181383(VS.80).aspx*

What is a workspace?

A *workspace* is a client-side copy of the files and folders on the TFS version control server. Local pending changes are isolated within your workspace until you check these changes into the server as an atomic unit (referred to as a changeset). A single workspace can contain references to multiple team projects. You can use multiple workspaces to isolate files or versions for your use only.

Note: Workspaces are created per machine, per user account. Therefore, you can have different workspace definitions for each computer you use. Also, you can have multiple workspaces on a single computer by using multiple user accounts to log onto the computer.

Additional Resources

- For more information about workspaces, see *http://msdn2.microsoft.com/en-us/library/ms181383(VS.80).aspx*

How do I use workspaces to isolate the work of a developer?

As a developer, you can create two workspaces: one containing references to files and folders being worked on by the rest of the team, and another containing files and folders that you want to isolate. You might want to isolate these files in order to evolve specific files in parallel with work that is happening elsewhere. For example, you can use this approach to work on risky pending changes, or to conduct a code review.

Additional Resources

- For more information about workspaces, see *http://msdn2.microsoft.com/en-us/library/ms181383(VS.80).aspx*

What are the proven practices for workspace mapping?

Workspace mapping is the means by which you map files and folders on the server to a location on your local hard drive.

Consider the following practices for creating workspace mappings:

- **Create mappings at the team project root level.** For new team projects, map your team project root ($/MyTeamProject) to a folder with the same name on your local drive; for example, C:\TeamProjects. Because mappings are recursive, your entire local folder structure is created automatically and will be exactly the same as the structure in source control.
- **Use a unique local folder path on shared computers.** Two users of a single computer cannot share the same workspace mapping. For example, you and a colleague cannot map the same team project ($/MyTeamProject) to the same folder on the local computer. Instead, create mappings beneath My Documents (although this leads to long location paths) or establish a team folder naming convention on the local computer (e.g., C:\TeamProjects\User1, C:\TeampProjects\User2 etc).
- **You may not need the entire tree.** To improve performance and reduce disk size requirements, only map the files you need for your development project. In general, you will only need the files and projects associated with the solution on which you will work.
- **Avoid using workspace mapping to support cross-project dependencies.** In general, you should avoid dependencies that cross team projects and try to have all the related/dependent solutions/projects under the same team project. This reduces the need for build script customization. If you have a dependency, use project references to define the dependency, or branch the dependency from a shared project into your project. You should avoid file references because they are more difficult to manage. The exception is when the dependent project is developed in parallel and you need to make real-time changes. In this case, you can consider using the workspace mapping. You can still consider branching to create a buffer of isolation if the dependent code is causing too many breaking changes.

Additional Resources

- For more information about creating a workspace, see "How to: Create a Workspace" at *http://msdn2.microsoft.com/en-us/library/ms181384(VS.80).aspx*
- For more information about editing a workspace, see "How to: Edit a Workspace" at *http://msdn2.microsoft.com/en-us/library/ms245466(VS.80).aspx*

When should I create a new Team Project versus a new Branch?

Create a branch if you want to isolate the code that developers are working on within a project while at the same time sharing all other TFS assets such as work items, process guidance, and reports.

Create a new team project if you want to use different TFS assets such as work items, process guidance, and reports. Also create a new team project if you want to carry forward your code without carrying forward any other TFS assets.

Additional Resources

- For more information about branching, see "How to: Branch Files and Folders" at *http://msdn2.microsoft.com/en-us/library/ms181425(VS.80).aspx*
- For more information about adding a new project, see "How to: Add a Project or Solution to Source Control" at *http://msdn2.microsoft.com/en-us/library/ms181373(VS.80).aspx*

How should I manage source code that is shared across multiple projects?

Managing shared source involves two decision points:

1. Where do you want to store the source?
2. How do you want your team to access the shared source?

The following options are available for storing the source:

- If the shared source is clearly owned by a particular team, store it in their team project.
- If the shared source has no clear ownership, create a team project specifically for the shared code.

If you want to use the source in another project, choose one of the following two options:

- If you need to stay in sync with shared code at all times, map the source from the shared location into the local workspace on the client machines.
- If you only need to stay in sync periodically, branch from the shared location into the consuming team project. Every time you perform a merge from the shared location to the consuming project, you will pick up latest source.

Whether you use workspace mapping or branching, use naming conventions that make it clear where the shared source location is located in your project; for example:

Main—Container for all assets you need in order to ship the product

- **Source**—Container for everything you need in order to build
  - **Code**—Container for source code
  - **Shared Code**—Container for source code that is shared from other projects
  - **Unit Tests**—Container for unit tests
  - **Lib**—Container for binary dependencies
- **Docs**—Container for documentation that will ship with the product
- **Installer**—Container for installer source code and binaries
- **Builds**—Container for team build scripts
- **Tests**—Container for test team test cases

Additional Resources

- For more information about project references, see "Project References" at *http://msdn2.microsoft.com/en-us/library/ez524kew(VS.80).aspx*
- For more information about branching, see "How to: Branch Files and Folders" at *http://msdn2.microsoft.com/en-us/library/ms181425(VS.80).aspx*
- For more information about workspaces, see *http://msdn2.microsoft.com/en-us/library/ms181383(VS.80).aspx_*

How should I manage binaries that are shared across multiple projects?

Managing shared binaries is similar to managing shared source you must decide where you want to store the binaries and how you want your team to access the binaries.

The following options are available for storing the binaries:

- If the shared binaries are clearly owned by a particular team, store it in their team project.
- If the shared binaries have no clear ownership, create a team project specifically for the shared binaries.

The following options are available for using the binaries in another project

- Shared binaries are usually updated only periodically. If this is the case for your project, branch from the shared location into the consuming team project. When the binaries change, you can execute a merge to get the latest version.
- If you need to stay in sync with the shared binaries at all times, map the source from the shared location into a local workspace on the client machines.

Whether you use workspace mapping or branching, use naming conventions that make it clear where the shared binary location is in your project; for example:

Main—Container for all assets you need in order to ship the product

- **Source**—Container for everything you need in order to build
  - **Code**—Container for source code
  - **Shared Code**—Container for source code that is shared from other projects
  - **Unit Tests**—Container for unit tests
  - **Lib**—Container for binary dependencies
- **Docs**—Container for documentation that will ship with the product
- **Installer**—Container for installer source code and binaries
- **Builds**—Container for team build scripts
- **Tests**—Container for test team test cases

Additional Resources

- For more information about project references, see "Project References" at *http://msdn2.microsoft.com/en-us/library/ez524kew(VS.80).aspx*
- For more information about branching, see "How to: Branch Files and Folders" at *http://msdn2.microsoft.com/en-us/library/ms181425(VS.80).aspx*
- For more information about workspaces, see *http://msdn2.microsoft.com/en-us/library/ms181383(VS.80).aspx*

How should I organize my source tree?

Your source tree structure consists of a combination of folder structure, file structure, and branch structure. Within your Main branch, the following folder and file structure has been proven to work for teams of various sizes:

Main—Container for all assets you need in order to ship the product

- **Source**—Container for everything you need in order to build
  - **Code**—Container for source code
  - **Shared Code**—Container for source code that is shared from other projects
  - **Unit Tests**—Container for unit tests
  - **Lib**—Container for binary dependencies
- **Docs**—Container for documentation that will ship with the product
- **Installer**—Container for installer source code and binaries
- **Builds**—Container for team build scripts
- **Tests**—Container for test team test cases

Any branches that you create off of Main will copy this folder and file structure into the new branch; for example:

Development—Development branch

- **Source**—Container for everything you need in order to build
  - **Code**—Container for source code
  - **Shared Code**—Container for source code that is shared from other projects
  - **Unit Tests**—Container for unit tests
  - **Lib**—Container for binary dependencies

Main—Integration branch

- **Source**—Container for everything you need in order to build
  - **Code**—Container for source code
  - **Shared Code**—Container for source code that is shared from other projects
  - **Unit Tests**—Container for unit tests
  - **Lib**—Container for binary dependencies
- **Docs**—Container for documentation that will ship with the product
- **Installer**—Container for installer source code and binaries
- **Builds**—Container for team build scripts
- **Tests**—Container for test team test cases

Additional Resources

- For more information about creating a workspace, see "How to: Create a Workspace" at *http://msdn2.microsoft.com/en-us/library/ms181384(VS.80).aspx*

Shelving

- **What is shelving?**
- **What is a shelveset?**
- **When would I typically use shelving?**
- **How do I use shelving to back up my work?**
- **Why would I want to unshelve a shelveset?**

What is shelving?

The process of shelving a change or set of changes (also known as creating a shelveset) allows you to store pending changes under source control without having to check in the changed files. This means that you benefit from having the files on the (backed up) server while ensuring that the potentially incomplete work on those files does not impact and break your regular builds.

Additional Resources

- For more information about shelving pending changes, see "How to: Shelve and Unshelve Pending Changes" at *http://msdn2.microsoft.com/en-us/library/ms181404(VS.80).aspx*

What is a shelveset?

A *shelveset* is a set of files that are saved but are not yet ready to be committed to source control. Files can be shelved in order to save pending changes to the workspace, or to be shared with other team members for feedback. You can also use shelved files to hand off partially completed work.

Additional Resources

- For more information about shelving pending changes, see "How to: Shelve and Unshelve Pending Changes" at *http://msdn2.microsoft.com/en-us/library/ms181404(VS.80).aspx*

When would I typically use shelving?

There are a number of common scenarios in which you would use shelving:

- You are midway through making changes to a set of source code when new, higher-priority work is allocated (for example, an emergency bug fix is required). At this point you need to go back to a stable version of the code but do not want to lose your changes. You can shelve your code and easily retrieve it later.
- You have not completed work at the end of the day but want to ensure that your current work is backed up on the server. By shelving your current changes, the changes are applied to the Team Foundation Server and can be retrieved by you (or others) on another day.
- You want to discuss or review your partially completed code with a remote team member. Rather than e-mailing the code, you can shelve it and then have your remote colleague retrieve the files from the shelf.
- You want to pass partially finished work to another developer for completion.

Additional Resources

- For more information about shelving pending changes, see "How to: Shelve and Unshelve Pending Changes" at *http://msdn2.microsoft.com/en-us/library/ms181404(VS.80).aspx*

How do I use shelving to back up my work?

If your work on one or more source files is not complete at the end of the working day, you can shelve your code to ensure that the source is uploaded to the server without checking in partially completed work.

Additional Resources

- For more information about shelving pending changes, see "How to: Shelve and Unshelve Pending Changes" at *http://msdn2.microsoft.com/en-us/library/ms181404(VS.80).aspx*

Why would I want to unshelve a shelveset?

You might unshelve a shelveset to:

- Resume work on a set of files that you backed up previously by using a shelveset.
- Integrate shelved pending changes into your work going forward.
- Review someone else's code.
- Pick up another developer's partially completed work.

Additional Resources

- For more information about unshelving pending changes, see "How to: Shelve and Unshelve Pending Changes" at *http://msdn2.microsoft.com/en-us/library/ms181404(VS.80).aspx*

Source Control Resources

- For more information about TFS Source Control, see "Team Foundation Source Control" at *http://msdn2.microsoft.com/en-us/library/ms181237(VS.80).aspx*

How To: Add a New Developer to Your Project in Visual Studio 2005 Team Foundation Server

Applies To

- Microsoft® Visual Studio® 2005 Team Foundation Server (TFS)
- Microsoft Visual Studio Team System
- Microsoft SQL Server™ Reporting Services

Summary

This How To article walks you through the process of adding a new developer to your team project in Team Foundation Server.

Contents

Objectives

- Allow a developer to access the team project
- Grant a developer Read and Contributor access to SharePoint
- Allow a developer to view and subscribe to reports

Overview

Whenever you add a new developer to a project, you need to grant the developer appropriate permissions to access your team foundation project and its associated SharePoint project site. The new developer's account must also have sufficient permissions with SQL Server Reporting Services to be able to view reports such as those presented by the team site portal.

Summary of Steps

- Step 1—Grant Access to the Team Project
- Step 2—Grant Access to the Microsoft Office SharePoint® project site
- Step 3—Grant Access to SQL Server Reporting Services

Step 1 — Grant Access to the Team Project

In this step you grant your new team member access to the Team Foundation Server.

► **To grant access to the team project**

1. Logon to Visual Studio with an account that is a member of the Team Foundation Administrators application group.
2. Add the required project to **Team Explorer** (if it is not already listed)
3. In **Team Explorer** right-click the team project, point to **Team Project Settings** and click **Group Membership**.
4. Select **Project\Contributors** and click **Properties** and then add the new developer's account to this group.

Note that membership in the Contributors group provides the typical set of permissions that a developer requires, including the ability to add, modify and delete items within the team project and perform builds.

Step 2 — Grant Access to the SharePoint Project Site

In this step you grant your new team member access to the SharePoint project site.

► **To grant access to the SharePoint project site**

1. Access the team project site with an account that is a member of the SharePoint Administrator site group.

   Note that the project site for a project named YourProject is located by default at http://server/sites/YourProject/default.aspx
2. Click **Site Settings**.
3. Under **Administration** title, Click **Manage Users**.
4. Click **Add Users**.

5. Enter the account name of the new developer's account in the form **domain\useraccount** of the new developer's account, select **Contributor** and then click **Next**.
6. Enter the developer's e-mail address in the address field, and optionally type a message to welcome them to the site.
7. Click **Finish**.

Note that membership in Contributors group allows the developer to view and add content to existing document libraries and lists. Membership in the Reader group, provides read only access to the site, it may be sufficient depending on the needs of the new developer.

Step 3 — Grant Access to SQL Server Reporting Services

In this step you grant your new team member access to SQL Report Services.

► **To grant access to SQL Server Reporting Services**

1. Logon to the SQL Server Reporting Services administration Web site at http://server/reports by using an administrator account. .
2. Click your team project name.
3. Click the **Properties** tab.
4. Click the **Security** tab.
5. Click **New Role Assignment**.
6. Enter your developer's Microsoft Windows® account name, select **Browser** and then click **OK**.

Note that membership in the Browser group enables the developer to view and subscribe to reports.

Additional Resources

- For a tutorial explaining how to work set permissions in SQL Server Reporting Services, see "Setting Permissions in Reporting Services" at *http://msdn2.microsoft.com/en-us/library/aa337491.aspx*
- For more information on security roles in the application-tier, see "Securing Reporting Services" at *http://msdn2.microsoft.com/en-us/library/ms157198.aspx*
- To view *SharePoint Administrators Guide* to "Managing Site and Group Permissions", see *http://www.microsoft.com/resources/documentation/wss/2/all/adminguide/en-us/stsf03.mspx?mfr=true*
- For more information on managing permissions in TFS see "Managing Permissions" at *http://msdn2.microsoft.com/en-us/library/ms253094(VS.80).aspx*

How To: Automatically Run Code Analysis with Team Build in Visual Studio Team Foundation Server

Applies To

- Microsoft® Visual Studio® 2005 Team Foundation Server (TFS)
- Microsoft Visual Studio Team System

Summary

This How To article walks you through the process of configuring Team Build to include code analysis as a build step. This will automatically run code analysis as part of your team build and will report the results of the analysis in the build results.

Contents

Objective

- Run code analysis as part of the build in order to validate code quality.

Overview

Visual Studio Team System Team Build allows you to define build types for your project that enable a build server to compile your application and make it available on a network share. You can turn on code analysis for the team build so that each build automatically performs code analysis and reports the results to the build results report page. This How To article walks you through the process of configuring Team Build to include code analysis as a build step.

Summary of Steps

- Step 1—Test the Build
- Step 2—Turn Code Analysis on for the Build
- Step 3—Test Code Analysis

Before You Begin

Before you can turn on code analysis for Team Build, you must ensure you have the following pre-requisites in place:

- Your Team Foundation user ID must have permission to administer a build. Ask you administrator if you are unsure of your user's allowed permissions.
- A team build must already exist for your project. You can check this by looking at Team Build in the Visual Studio Team Explorer.

Step 1 — Test the Build

Start by testing the team build to make sure there are no problems before you turn on code analysis. You can do this by performing the following steps:

1. In Visual Studio, open **Team Explorer** in Visual Studio.
2. Expand the node for your team project.
3. Expand the **Team Builds** node.
4. Right Click an existing team build and then select **Build Team Project**.
5. Ensure the build has completed successfully. If there are build breaks or the build is not able to complete, fix these errors before moving to the next step.

Step 2 — Turn On Code Analysis for the Build

Once you have verified that the build is working properly, you can turn on code analysis. Use the following steps to turn on code analysis:

1. Open **Source Control Explorer**.
2. In Source Control Explorer, expand your team project folder.
3. Expand the **TeamBuildTypes** folder.
4. Select the team build folder for which you want to turn on code analysis.
5. Check out **TFSBuild.proj** file from source control. You may need to perform a Get Latest Version operation on the folder first.
6. In Source Control Explorer, double click **TFSBuild.Proj** to open it.
7. If you want all projects to run code analysis, regardless of project settings, change the **<RunCodeAnalysis>** tag to **Always**.
8. If you want to run code analysis on each project based on project settings, change the **<RunCodeAnalysis>** tag to **Default**.
9. If you are using per-project settings and want to turn on code analysis for a project:
   a. Open the solution in Visual Studio.
   b. In Solution Explorer, right click on the project.
   c. Select **Properties**.
   d. Click on **Code Analysis.**
   e. Select the **Enable Code Analysis** check box.
   f. Check out the .csproj file for the project from source control.
   g. Save the file by clicking the **save** icon in toolbar while properties window is displayed.
   h. Check the .csproj file for the project back into source control.
10. Save TFSBuild.proj and check it back into source control.

Step 3 — Test Code Analysis

Once you have turned on code analysis for a team build, you can test to make sure it is working properly. Use the following steps to test code analysis for your build:

1. In Team Explorer, right click the build type and then click **Build Team Project**.
2. When the build has completed, click the link to the build log.

3. You should see some code analysis warnings at the end of the build log. The warning IDs will start with "CA", such as in the following examples:
   - MSBUILD: warning : CA2209 : Microsoft.Usage : No valid permission requests were found for assembly 'HelloWorldTest'. You should always specify the minimum security permissions using SecurityAction.RequestMinimum.
   - MSBUILD: warning : CA2210 : Microsoft.Design : Sign 'HelloWorldTest' with a strong name key.
   - MSBUILD: warning : CA1014 : Microsoft.Design : 'HelloWorldTest' should be marked with CLSCompliantAttribute and its value should be true.

Additional Resources

- For more information on code analysis tools, see "Guidelines for Using Code Analysis Tools" at *http://msdn2.microsoft.com/en-us/library/ms182023(VS.80).aspx*
- For more information on team builds, see "Overview of Team Foundation Build" at *http://msdn2.microsoft.com/en-us/library/ms181710(VS.80).aspx*

How To: Create a Custom Report for Visual Studio Team Foundation Server

Applies To

- Microsoft® Visual Studio® 2005 Team Foundation Server (TFS)
- Microsoft Visual Studio Team System
- Microsoft SQL Server™ Reporting Services

Summary

This How To article walks you through the process of creating a new custom report and then publishing it to the team reporting portal in Team Foundation Server.

Contents

- Objectives
- Overview
- Summary of Steps
- Before You Begin
- Step 1—Create a new Reporting Project
- Step 2—Create the data sources
- Step 3—Create a new report in your project
- Step 4—Modify the report
- Step 5—Deploy the report to your Team Foundation Server
- Step 6—Test the report
- Additional Resources

Objectives

- Learn how to create a reporting project in Visual Studio
- Learn how to create a new custom report in the reporting project
- Learn how to publish the new report to the report server

Overview

The reports that ship with VSTS are SQL Server Reporting Services reports. You can amend these reports or create your own custom reports by using the SQL Server 2005 Reporting Services Designer inside Visual Studio (Business Intelligence Development Studio), which ships with the SQL Server 2005 client tools. To create a custom report, you create a reporting project in Visual Studio, and then create data sources to connect to the TFS relational database and Online Analytical Processing (OLAP) database.

Summary of Steps

- Step 1—Create a new reporting project
- Step 2—Create the data sources
- Step 3—Create a new report in your project
- Step 4—Modify the report
- Step 5—Deploy the report to your Team Foundation Server
- Step 6—Test the report

Before You Begin

Before you can customize a report for Team Foundation Server, you must ensure you have the following prerequisites in place:

- You must have Business Intelligence Development Studio installed on the machine you will be using to customize the report. To test if it is installed, check Visual Studio to see if you have Business Intelligence Project type when you create a new project.
- Your user account must be a member of the Microsoft Analysis Server TfsWarehouseDataReaders security role on the data-tier server.
- Your user account must have administrator rights to the TFSWarehouse database on the data tier.
- Your user account must be a member of the SQL Server Reporting Services Publisher role on the application-tier server.

Step 1 — Create a new reporting project

Create a new reporting project so that you can add a new report to the project and customize it. Perform the following steps to create a new reporting project in Visual Studio:

1. In Visual Studio, click **File**, then click **New**, then click **Project**.
2. Select the **Business Intelligence Project** type.
3. Select the **Report Server Project** template.
4. Set your project's **Name** and **Location** and then click **OK**.

Step 2 — Create the data sources

In order to edit and publish the customized report, you need to add data sources for the Team Foundation Server data warehouse and OLAP cube. Once these data sources are added to the Visual Studio project the report can pull data from the server.

► To create the warehouse data source

1. In the **Visual Studio Solution Explorer**, right click **Shared Data Sources** and then click **Add New Data Source**.
2. On the **General** tab, enter **TfsReportDS** into the Name text box.
3. Select **Microsoft SQL Server** from the **Type** combo box.
4. Click the **Edit…** button.
5. Fill in your data tier server name.
6. Select the database **TFSWarehouse** database.
7. Click the **OK** button twice to add the data source.

► To create the OLAP data source

1. In **Solution Explorer**, right click **Shared Data Sources** and then click **Add New Data Source**.
2. On the **General** tab, enter **TfsOlapReportDS** into the **Name** text box.
3. Select **Microsoft SQL Server Analysis Services** from the **Type** combo box.
4. Click the **Edit…** button.
5. Fill in your data tier server name.
6. Select the database **TFSWarehouse** database.
7. Click the **OK** button twice to add the data source.

Step 3 — Create a new report in your project

Now that the data sources have been added to your project you can add a new report. Perform the following steps to add a new report to your project and customize it:

1. In **Solution Explorer**, right click **Reports** and then click **Add->New Item**...
2. Select the **Report** template.
3. Name the report and then click **OK**.

Step 4 — Modify the report

After you have added a report to the project, you can modify it as follows:

1. If the **Report Designer** doesn't open automatically, open the report for modification by double clicking it in the **Solution Explorer**.
2. Click the **Dataset** drop down and then select **<New Dataset...>**.
3. Name the dataset, for example TestDataSet.
4. Select **TFSOlapReportDS (shared)**.
5. Click **OK**.
6. Click the **...** button next to **Build** (just below the **Dataset** drop down list) and then select **Team System**.

You are now set up to modify report by dragging measures and dimensions from the **Dataset** tree into the **Query Pane** and **Filter Pane.** You can modify the report's layout by clicking the **Layout** tab. You can preview your report by clicking on the **Preview** tab.

Step 5 — Deploy the report to your Team Foundation Server

After you have modified the report, you can deploy it to your team project's reporting portal by performing the following steps:

1. In Solution Explorer, right click on the report project and then click **Properties**.
2. Ensure that **OverwriteDataSources** is set to **false**.
3. Modify **TargetDataSourceFolder** to reflect your team project name; for example: **TargetDataSourceFolder** = TestProject.
4. Modify **TargetReportFolder** to reflect your team project name; for example: **TargetDataSourceFolder** = TestProject.
5. Modify **TargetDataSourceFolder** to *http://<data-tier servername>/reportserver*. For example: **TargetDataSourceFolder** = http: / / tfsrtm / reportserver.
6. Click **OK**.
7. In Solution Explorer, right click on the rdl file and then click **Deploy**.
8. Watch the **Output Pane** to confirm successful completion.

Step 6 — Test the report

After you have published the report to your team project's report server you can test it to make sure it was successfully deployed:

1. In **Team Explorer** expand your team project node, right click **Reports** and then click **Show Report Site**.
2. In the report site, select the report you just created.
3. Verify that the report looks the way you expected.

Additional Resources

- For more tutorials explaining how to work with reporting projects, see "Reporting Services Tutorials" at *http://msdn2.microsoft.com/en-us/library/ms170246.aspx*
- To read the Microsoft MSDN® article on editing reports, see "How to: Edit Reports in Report Designer" at *http://msdn2.microsoft.com/en-us/library/ms244655(VS.80).aspx*
- For more information on security roles in the data-tier, see "Securing Access Through Analysis Services" at *http://msdn2.microsoft.com/en-us/library/ms174839.aspx*
- For more information on security roles in the application-tier, see "Securing Reporting Services" at *http://msdn2.microsoft.com/en-us/library/ms157198.aspx*

How To: Create a "Risk over Time" Report for Visual Studio Team Foundation Server

Applies To

- Microsoft® Visual Studio® 2005 Team Foundation Server (TFS)
- Microsoft Visual Studio Team System (VSTS)
- Microsoft SQL Server™ Reporting Services

Summary

This How To article walks you through the process of creating a new report that shows how **Risk** work items trend over time. The article then shows you how to publish it to the team reporting portal in TFS.

Contents

- Objectives
- Overview
- Summary of Steps
- Before You Begin
- Step 1—Create a New Reporting Project
- Step 2—Create the Data Sources
- Step 3—Create a New Report in Your Project
- Step 4—Modify the Report
- Step 5—Deploy the Report to your Team Foundation Server
- Step 6—Test the Report
- Additional Resources

Objectives

- Create a reporting project in Visual Studio.
- Create a new Risk over Time report in the reporting project.
- Publish the Risk over Time report to the report server.

Overview

The reports that ship with VSTS are SQL Server Reporting Services reports. You can amend these reports or create your own custom reports by using the SQL Server 2005 Reporting Services Designer inside Visual Studio (Business Intelligence Development Studio[BISD]), which ships with the SQL Server 2005 client tools. To create a custom report, you create a Report Project in Visual Studio and then create data sources to connect to the TFS relational database and Online Analytical Processing (OLAP) database. This How To article shows how to create a simple report from scratch - the Risk over Time report that identifies number of Risk work items over a given period of time.

Summary of Steps

- Step 1—Create a New Reporting Project
- Step 2—Create the Data Sources
- Step 3—Create a New Report in Your Project
- Step 4—Modify the Report
- Step 5—Deploy the Report to your Team Foundation Server
- Step 6—Test the Report

Before You Begin

Before you can customize a report for TFS, you must ensure you have the following prerequisites in place:

- You must have Business Intelligence Development Studio (BIDS) installed on the machine you will be using to customize the report. To verify whether BIDS is installed, check Visual Studio to see if you have the Business Intelligence Project type option when you create a new project.
- Your user account must be a member of the Microsoft Analysis Server TfsWarehouseDataReaders security role on the data-tier server.
- Your user account must have administrator rights to the TFSWarehouse database on the data tier.

- Your user account must be a member of the SQL Server Reporting Services Publisher role on the application-tier server.
- The project must contain Risk work items so that the report shows some data.

Step 1 — Create a New Reporting Project

In this initial step, you create a new reporting project so that you can add a new report to the project and then customize the report. Perform the following steps to create a new reporting project in Visual Studio:

1. Click **File**, then click **New**, and then click **Project**.
2. Select the **Business Intelligence Project** type.
3. Select the **Report Server Project** template.
4. Set your project's **Name** and **Location** and then click **OK**.

Step 2 — Create the Data Sources

In order to edit and publish the customized report you first need to add data sources for the TFS data warehouse and OLAP cube. Once these data sources are added to the Visual Studio project the report can pull data from the server.

► **To create the warehouse data source**

1. In the **Visual Studio Solution Explorer**, right-click **Shared Data Sources** and then click **Add New Data Source**.
2. On the **General** tab, in the **Name** text box, enter **TfsReportDS**.
3. Select **Microsoft SQL Server** from the **Type** combo box.
4. Click the **Edit**… button.
5. Fill in your data tier server name
6. Select the **TFSWarehouse** database.
7. Click the **OK** button twice to add the data source.

► **To create the OLAP data source**

1. In **Solution Explorer**, right-click **Shared Data Sources** and then click **Add New Data Source**.
2. On the **General** tab, in the **Name** text box, enter **TfsOlapReportDS**.
3. Select **Microsoft SQL Server Analysis Services** from the **Type** combo box.
4. Click the **Edit**… button.
5. Fill in your data tier server name.
6. Select the **TFSWarehouse** database.
7. Click the **OK** button twice to add the data source.

Step 3 — Create a New Report in Your Project

Now that the data sources have been added to your project you can add a new report. Perform the following steps to add a new report to your project and customize it:

1. In **Solution Explorer**, right-click **Reports** and then select **Add->New Item**...
2. Select the **Report** template.
3. Name the report and click **OK**.

Step 4 — Modify the Report

After you have added a report to the project you can modify the report as follows:

1. If the **Report Designer** doesn't open automatically, open the report for modification by double clicking it in the **Solution Explorer**.
2. Click the **Dataset** drop down and the select **<New Dataset...>**.
3. Name the dataset, example TestDataSet.
4. Select **TFSOlapReportDS (shared)** and then click **OK**.
5. Click the **...** button next to **Build** (just below the **Dataset** drop down list) and then select **Team System**.
6. In the **Dataset Tree**, expand **Measures**.
7. In the **Dataset Tree,** expand **Current Work Item**.
8. Drag **Current Work Item Count** into the main query window.
9. In the **Dataset Tree**, collapse **Measures**.
10. Scroll down to **Team Project** and drag it into the **Dimensions Grid**.
11. In the **Dimensions Grid**, click the **Filter Expression** cell and select your team project name. This filters the results to just your team project.
12. Expand the **Work Item** dimension in the **Dataset Tree**.
13. Drag **WorkItem.WorkItemType** from the **Dataset Tree** into the **Dimensions Grid**.

    You may see **System_WorkItemType** instead of **WorkItem.WorkItemType**, if this is the case it will still work, but it means you should apply SQL Server Service Pack 2.
14. Drag **WorkItem.WorkItemType** from the **Dataset Tree** into the main query window and drop it in front of the **work item count** column.

    You may see **System_WorkItemType** instead of **WorkItem.WorkItemType**, if this is the case it will still work, but it means you should apply SQL Server Service Pack 2.
15. In the **Dimensions Grid,** click the **Filter Expression** cell and then select the **Risk** type. This filters the results to include only Risk work item types.
16. In the **Dataset Tree,** expand the **Date** dimension.

17. Drag the **Date** dimension value into the main query window; dropping it in front of the **work item type** column.
18. Click the **Layout** tab.
19. Open the **Toolbox** window.
20. Drag the **Chart** item from the **Toolbox** to the layout grid.
21. Adjust the size of the chart to fit.
22. Right-click on the chart and then select **Chart Type Line Smooth Line**.
23. Open the **Datasets Pane**.
24. Expand your data set, for example, TestDataSet.
25. Highlight the graph so that the **Data**, **Series** and **Category** drop targets appear.
26. Drop **Current_Work_Item_Count** into the **Drop Data Fields Here** drop target box.
27. Drop **Work_Item_Type** into the **Drop Series Fields Here** drop target box.
28. Drop **Date** into the **Drop Category Fields Here** drop target box.
29. Right-click the graph and then select **Properties**.
30. Enter a title for your graph and then click **OK**.
31. Click the **Preview** tab to view what the report will look like.

Step 5 — Deploy the Report to your Team Foundation Server

After you've created the Risk over Time report, you can deploy it to your team project's reporting portal by performing the following steps:

1. In **Solution Explorer**, right-click on the report project and then click **Properties**.
2. Ensure that **OverwriteDataSources** is set to **false**.
3. Modify **TargetDataSourceFolder** to reflect your team project name; for example. **TargetDataSourceFolder** = TestProject.
4. Modify **TargetReportFolder** to reflect your team project name; for example: **TargetDataSourceFolder** = TestProject.
5. Modify **TargetDataSourceFolder** *to http://<data-tier servername>/reportserver*; for example: **TargetDataSourceFolder** = http: // tfsrtm / reportserver.
6. Click **OK**.
7. In **Solution Explorer**, right-click on the .rdl file and then click **Deploy**.
8. Observe the **Output Pane** to verify for successful completion.

Step 6 — Test the report

After you've published the report to your team project's report server you can test it to make sure it was successfully deployed:

1. In **Team Explorer** expand your team project node, right-click on **Reports** and then select **Show Report Site**.
2. On the report site, select the report you just created.
3. Verify that the report looks as you expected.

Additional Resources

- For more tutorials explaining how to work with reporting projects, see "Reporting Services Tutorials" at *http://msdn2.microsoft.com/en-us/library/ms170246.aspx*
- For the MSDN article on editing reports, see "How to: Edit Reports in Report Designer" at *http://msdn2.microsoft.com/en-us/library/ms244655(VS.80).aspx*
- For more information on security roles in the data-tier, see "Securing Access Through Analysis Services" at *http://msdn2.microsoft.com/en-us/library/ms174839.aspx*
- For more information on security roles in the application-tier, see "Securing Reporting Services" at *http://msdn2.microsoft.com/en-us/library/ms157198.aspx*

How To: Create Custom Check-in Policies in Visual Studio Team Foundation Server

Applies To

- Microsoft® Visual Studio® 2005 Team Foundation Server (TFS)
- Microsoft Visual Studio Team System

Summary

This How To article walks you through the process of creating, registering, and applying a custom check-in policy for TFS. Check-in polices allow you to run rules whenever a developer attempts to check-in a source file, in order to ensure that the source file being checked-in meets a specified set of criteria. As an example, this How To article uses a custom policy to enforce that check-in comments are supplied with all check-ins. To implement a custom check-in policy, you create a class that derives from **PolicyBase** and implements the **IPolicyDefinition** and **IPolicyEvaluation** interfaces. You register the policy assembly in the Microsoft Windows® registry and you apply the policy to your team project.

Contents

Objectives

- Learn what a custom check-in policy is.
- Learn how to create, register, and apply custom check-in policies.

Overview

Check-in policies enforce constraints whenever files are checked into source control. Team Foundation Server provides a number of out-of-box check-in policies including policies to check that unit tests have run and been passed, policies to perform static code analysis to ensure that code meets coding standards and .NET guidelines, and policies to check that work items are associated with check ins. The Microsoft Visual Studio 2005 Team Foundation Power Tool also provides a number of additional check-in policies. In this How To article, you will learn how to create, register, and apply a custom policy. The example policy ensures that developers supply check-in comments whenever they check in a file.

Before You Begin

Note that, to create a check-in policy, you must have the **Manipulate** security settings permission set to **Allow**.

Summary of Steps

- Step 1—Create and Build a Custom Policy Class
- Step 2—Register the Custom Policy in the Windows Registry
- Step 3—Apply the Custom Policy
- Step 4—Validate the Custom Policy

Step 1 — Create and Build a Custom Policy Class

In this initial step, you create a custom policy class by deriving from the **PolicyBase** base class in the **Microsoft.TeamFoundation.VersionControl.Client** namespace. By deriving from this base class, your class implements the **IPolicyDefinition** and **IPolicyEvaluation** interfaces. The example policy code below forces a developer to supply check-in comments whenever he or she checks in a source file.

1. Use Visual Studio to create a new Visual C#® class library project.
2. Add an assembly reference to **System.Windows.Forms.dll**. You use this assembly to display message boxes.

3. Add an assembly reference to **Microsoft.TeamFoundation.VersionControl.Client.dll**. By default, this is installed in the following folder:
4. \Program Files\Visual Studio 2005 Team Foundation Server\Tools
5. Replace your skeleton class code implementation with the following source. Note that the class derives from the **PolicyBase** base class and is marked as serializable.

```
using System;
using System.Windows.Forms;
using Microsoft.TeamFoundation.VersionControl.Client;

[Serializable]
public class CheckForCommentsPolicy : PolicyBase
{
    public override string Description
    {
        get { return "Remind users to add meaningful comments to their check-
ins"; }
    }

    // This is a string that is stored with the policy definition on the source
    // control server. If a user does not have the policy plug-in installed,
this string
    // is displayed.  You can use this to explain to the user how they should
            // install the policy plug-in.
    public override string InstallationInstructions
    {
        get { return "To install this policy, read InstallInstructions.txt."; }
    }

    // This string identifies the type of policy. It is displayed in the
 // policy list when you add a new policy to a Team Project.
    public override string Type
    {
        get { return "Check for Comments Policy"; }
    }

    // This string is a description of the type of policy. It is displayed
    // when you select the policy in the Add Check-in Policy dialog box.
    public override string TypeDescription
    {
        get { return "This policy will prompt the user to decide whether or not
they should be allowed to check in."; }
    }

    // This method is called by the policy framework when you create
    // a new check-in policy or edit an existing check-in policy.
    // You can use this to display a UI specific to this policy type
    // allowing the user to change the parameters of the policy.
    public override bool Edit(IPolicyEditArgs args)
    {
        // Do not need any custom configuration
        return true;
    }
```

```
    // This method performs the actual policy evaluation.
    // It is called by the policy framework at various points in time
    // when policy should be evaluated. In this example, the method
    // is invoked when various asyc events occur that may have
    // invalidated the current list of failures.
    public override PolicyFailure[] Evaluate()
    {
        string proposedComment = PendingCheckin.PendingChanges.Comment;
        if (String.IsNullOrEmpty(proposedComment))
        {
            return new PolicyFailure[] {
                new PolicyFailure("Please provide some comments about your
check-in", this) };
        }
        else
        {
            return new PolicyFailure[0];
        }
    }

    // This method is called if the user double-clicks on
    // a policy failure in the UI. In this case a message telling the user
    // to supply some comments is displayed.
    public override void Activate(PolicyFailure failure)
    {
        MessageBox.Show("Please provide comments for your check-in.", "How to
fix your policy failure");
    }

    // This method is called if the user presses F1 when a policy failure
    // is active in the UI. In this example, a message box is displayed.
    public override void DisplayHelp(PolicyFailure failure)
    {
        MessageBox.Show("This policy helps you to remember to add comments to
your check-ins.", "Prompt Policy Help");
    }
}
```

Step 2 — Register the Custom Policy in the Windows Registry

In this step, you add an entry to the Windows registry so that your policy appears in the **Add Check-in Policy** dialog box. Note that you must install the policy assembly on any computer that needs to reference the assembly. This includes the computer of the team project's administrator who needs to associate the policy with the team project and on all of your team members' computers where the policy is actually evaluated.

Important: The policy is evaluated on the client when a developer checks in a file.

1. Start Regedit.exe and locate the following key:

   HKEY_LOCAL_MACHINE\Software\Microsoft\VisualStudio\8.0\TeamFoundation\SourceControl\Checkin Policies

   The registered policies are listed in the right pane.
2. Right-click in the right-hand pane, point to **New,** and then click **String Value**.
3. Type the name of your custom policy dynamic link library (DLL), without the DLL extension; **CheckForCommentsPolicy** in the above example.

   Important: The new string name must match your DLL filename exactly, without the DLL extension.
4. Double-click the new string value and set its value to the fully qualified path and filename to the .dll containing your custom policy.

Step 3 — Apply the Custom Policy

In this step you add the custom policy to your team project. This ensures that the policy is evaluated each time a developer checks in a file to this team project.

1. In **Team Explorer**, right click your team project, point to **Team Project Settings** and then click **Source Control**.
2. Click the **Check-in Policy** tab and then click **Add**.
3. Select your custom **Check for Comments Policy** and click **OK** and then **OK** again.

The policy is now applied each time a developer checks a file into this team project.

Step 4 — Validate the Custom Policy

In this step, you check-in a source file to ensure that the custom policy works correctly.

1. Make a change to a source file and then check-in the file without supplying a check-in comment.
2. Verify that the check-in is prevented because the policy rule is not satisfied.
3. Add some comments and complete the check-in. With a supplied comment the check-in should work successfully and you will not see a policy failure notification.

Additional Resources

- To learn how to customize a check-in policy, see "Walkthrough: Customizing Check-in Policies and Notes" at *http://msdn2.microsoft.com/en-us/library/ms181281(VS.80).aspx*
- To see sample code that will disallow selected patterns on check-in, see "Check-in Policy to Disallow Certain Patterns" at *http://blogs.msdn.com/jmanning/archive/2006/02/02/523125.aspx*
- To see sample code that will enforce comments on check-in, see "Sample Check-in Policy: Make Sure the Comment Isn't Empty" at *http://blogs.msdn.com/jmanning/archive/2006/01/21/515858.aspx*
- To learn how to register a new check-in policy, see "I've Made a New Check-In Policy! How Do I Add It?" at *http://blogs.msdn.com/jmanning/archive/2006/02/07/526778.aspx*

How To: Create Your Source Tree in Visual Studio Team Foundation Server

Applies To

- Microsoft® Visual Studio® 2005 Team Foundation Server (TFS)
- Microsoft Visual Studio Team System

Summary

This How To article walks you through the process of creating a new source code tree structure in TFS. The purpose of this How To article is to familiarize you with the end-to-end steps required to create your source tree.

Contents

Objectives

- Learn how to create a new team project
- Learn how to create a workspace mapping
- Learn how to create a source tree in Team Foundation Server source control

Overview

Although you can quickly add a solution to source control by right-clicking your solution in Solution Explorer and then clicking **Add Solution To Source Control**, this option does not enable you to explicitly set up your source tree structure in source control. By explicitly defining your source tree structure in source control, you can arrange your source beneath top-level folders and use separate top-level folders to contain your main source base and your branched source base such as the branches you might use during development or to maintain production releases.

In this how to you will see the steps required to explicitly create a source control tree structure.

Summary of Steps

- Step 1—Create a new team project
- Step 2—Create a workspace mapping
- Step 3—Create your folder structure in Source Control
- Step 4—Add your source code to your source tree

Step 1 – Create a New Team Project

In this initial step, you create a new team project with default settings.

1. In **Team Explorer**, right-click your TFS server and click **New Team Project...**
2. In the **New Team Project** dialog box, type a project name such as **MyTeamProject1** and then click **Next**.
3. On the **Select a Process Template** page, leave the default **MSF for Agile Software Development - v4.0** and then click **Next**.
4. On the **Specify the Settings for the Project Portal** page, leave the team project portal name as **MyTeamProject1** enter a description for the team project portal and then click **Next**.
5. On the **Specify Source Control Settings** page, leave the default option **Create an empty source control folder** selected and then click **Next**.
6. Click **Finish** to create the project.

A new team project is created on your TFS server, using the selected process template with an empty source control node.

Step 2 – Create a Workspace Mapping

In this step you create a workspace mapping to define the mapping between the folder structure on the TFS server and client. You need to do this in order to create a source tree structure. First, the source tree structure is created in your workspace. You then need to perform a check-in to your TFS server.

You can create a workspace mapping in one of two ways:

- Set the workspace mapping explicitly
- Perform a get operation on your team project.

To set a workspace mapping explicitly

1. In Visual Studio, on the **File** menu, point to **Source Control** and then click **Workspaces**.
2. In the **Manage Workspaces** dialog box, select your computer name and then click **Edit**.
3. In the **Edit Workspace** dialog box, in the **Working folders** list, click **Click here to enter a new working folder**.
4. Click the ellipsis button, select your team project (for example **MyTeamProject1**), and then click **OK**.
5. Click the Local folder cell to display another ellipsis button.
6. Click the ellipsis button beneath **Local Folder** and then browse to and select the local folder on your development computer where you want to locate your team project workspace; for example C:\DevProjects\MyTeamProject1.
7. Click **OK** twice to close the **Edit Workspace** dialog box.
8. Click **OK** in response to the Microsoft Visual Studio message box that informs you than one or more working folders have changed.
9. Click **Close** to close the **Manage Workspaces** dialog box.

To perform a Get operation on your team project

1. In **Team Explorer**, expand your **MyTeamProject1** team project node.
2. Double-click **Source Control** beneath your team project.
3. In **Source Control Explorer**, right-click the root folder **MyTeamProject1** and then click **Get Latest Version**.
4. In the **Browse For Folder** dialog box select your local path (for example C:\DevProjects\MyTeamProject1) and then click **OK**. This maps the team project root folder within TFS to a local path on your computer.

Step 3 — Create Your Folder Structure in Source Control

In this step, depending on your strategy and project requirements you create a source control folder structure on your server. This should generally start with a /Main/Source folder structure, which enables you to subsequently create **Development** and **Releases** branches at the same level as **Main**. For example, the **Releases** folder would be used to contain branched code corresponding to the software releases that you are maintaining. The **Development** folder contains your isolated development branch.

/Main					
	/Source				
		/MyApp1			Contains MyApp1.sln
			/Source		Container folder
				/ClassLibrary1	Contains ClassLibrary1.csproj
				/MyApp1Web	Contains Default.aspx
			/UnitTests		Contains unit test projects
				/ClassLibrary1Tests	Test project for ClassLibrary1
				/MyApp1WebTests	Test project for MyApp1Web
/Build					Contains build output (binaries)
	/Docs				Contains design docs etc
	/TestCases				Contains test case documentation

/Development					
	/FeatureBranch1				
		/Source			
			/MyApp1		
				/Source	
					/MyApp1Web
					/ClassLibrary1
				/UnitTests	
					/ClassLibrary1Tests
					/MyApp1WebTests
	/FeatureBranch2				

/Releases

/Release1

/MyApp1

/Source

/ClassLibrary1

/MyApp1Web

/UnitTests

/ClassLibrary1Tests

/MyApp1WebTests

/Release 1.1

/Release 1.2

► **To create a folder structure on the server**

1. In **Team Explorer**, expand your **MyTeamProject1** team project node.
2. Double-click **Source Control** beneath your team project.
3. In **Source Control Explorer**, select the root node, right-click in the **Local Path:** pane, and then click **New Folder**.
4. Type the name **Main** and then press ENTER.
5. Create a **Source** folder beneath Main.
6. Repeat the previous steps to create any other root folders you might need including **Development** and **Releases** folders.
7. After you have created your tree structure, right-click the **MyTeamProject1** root node in **Source Control Explorer** and then click **Check-in Pending Changes**.
8. In the **Check In - Source Files – Workspace** dialog box, select the folders you need to check-in, add a comment, and then click **Check In**. This builds your local folder structure and adds the structure to TFS source control.

Step 4 — Add Your Source Code to Your Source Tree

In this step, you add source code from your local drive to your source control tree on the server. In this example, you create a new Web application and class library project and add these to source control.

► **To create a new Visual Studio solution file**

1. On the **File** menu, point to **New**, and then click **Project**.
2. Expand **Other Project Types** and then click **Visual Studio Solutions**
3. In the Templates pane, select **Blank Solution**.

4. Type **MyApp1** in the **Name** text box and C:\DevProjects\MyTeamProject1\Main\Source into the **Location** text box.
5. Click **OK**.

Visual Studio creates your new solution and places the solution (.sln) file in the C:\DevProjects\ MyTeamProject1\Main\Source\MyApp1 folder.

► **To add a new Web site to your solution**

1. In Solution Explorer, right-click your solution, point to **Add**, and then click **New Web Site**.
2. Select **ASP.NET Web Site** from the **Templates** list, **File System** as the **Location** and C:\DevProjects\MyTeamProject1\Main\Source\MyApp1\Source\MyApp1Web as the path.
3. Click **OK**. Visual Studio creates the Web site.

► **To add a new class library project to your solution**

1. In Solution Explorer, right-click your solution, point to **Add**, and then click **New Project**.
2. Select **Visual C#** from the **Project types** list, and **Class Library** from the **Templates** list.
3. Leave the name as **ClassLibrary1** and set the **Location** to C:\DevProjects\MyTeamProject1\Main\Source\MyApp1\Source.
4. Click **OK**.

Visual Studio creates the new project structure. Your local file structure should now look like the following:

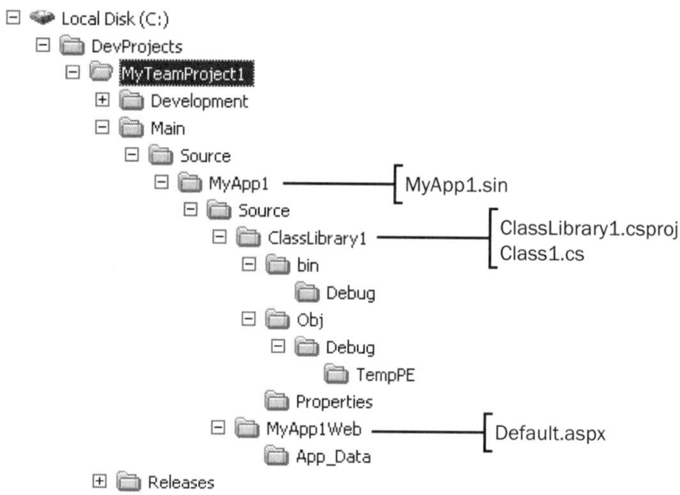

► **To add your solution to source control**

In Solution Explorer, right-click your solution and then click **Add Solution To Source Control** Your solution and two projects are added to Team Foundation Source Control.

Your source control tree structure now should look like the following:

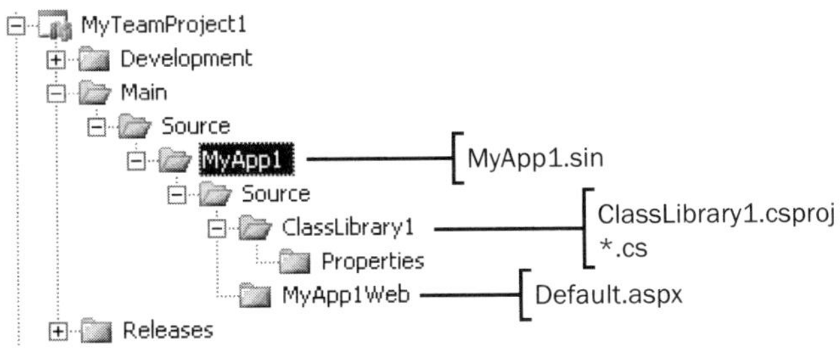

Additional Resources

- For more information on creating a workspace, see "How to: Create a Workspace" at *http://msdn2.microsoft.com/en-us/library/ms181384(VS.80).aspx*

How To: Customize a Process Template in Visual Studio Team Foundation Server

Applies To

- Microsoft® Visual Studio® 2005 Team Foundation Server (TFS)
- Microsoft Visual Studio Team System (VSTS)

Summary

This How To article walks you through the steps for modifying a process template in order to better suit your team's needs, and explains the tools that you use to do so. Process templates define the initial process settings for team projects. By customizing a process template, you can define:

- Security for team project access control.
- What templates are available on the Microsoft Office SharePoint® project portal.
- Presence of source code control check-in notes.
- Work item types and queries.
- Reports for monitoring project progress and health.
- Iterations and areas used for project organization.

Follow the steps in order to walk through the modification of a template, and then test the changes you made.

Content

- Objective
- Overview
- Summary of Steps
- Step 1—Install Process Editor
- Step 2—Choose the Process Template
- Step 3—Download the Process Template

- Step 4—Open the Process Template in Process Editor
- Step 5—Modify Work Item Types
- Step 6—Modify the Default Work Items
- Step 7—Modify and Manage Queries
- Step 8—Modify Areas and Iterations
- Step 9—Modify Groups and Permissions
- Step 10—Modify Source Control Settings
- Step 11—Modify the Project SharePoint Portal
- Step 12—Modify Reports
- Step 13—Upload the Modified Process Template
- Additional Resources

Objectives

- Learn what parts of a process template can be modified.
- Customize a process template by using the Process Editor tool.

Overview

Visual Studio Team System (VSTS) and Team Foundation Server (TFS) provide an integrated environment that supports most of the process activities involved in a software-development project. TFS implements life-cycle methodologies for team projects by using process templates. A *process template* is a set of Extensible Markup Language (XML) files that provides specifications for different artifacts and processes of a methodology. By modifying a process template, you can change the default work item types, security settings, source control settings, and reports that are set up when a new team project is created.

You can manually customize the XML files, or you can use the Process Editor tool available with the Team Foundation Server Power Tool. Using the Process Editor tool is the recommended method because it is a user interface (UI)–based tool, which makes customizing a process much easier and less error-prone compared to manual customization of XML files.

To modify a process template, you must first download the template you want to modify and then use the Process Editor to make necessary changes.

Summary of Steps

- Step 1—Install Process Editor
- Step 2—Choose the Process Template
- Step 3—Download the Process Template
- Step 4—Open the Process Template in Process Editor
- Step 5—Modify Work Item Types
- Step 6—Modify the Default Work Items
- Step 7—Modify and Manage Queries
- Step 8—Modify Areas and Iterations
- Step 9—Modify Groups and Permissions
- Step 10—Modify Source Control Settings
- Step 11—Modify the Project SharePoint Portal
- Step 12—Modify Reports
- Step 13—Upload the Modified Process Template

Step 1 — Install Process Editor

In this initial step, you will install the Process Editor tool, which provides a convenient UI–based method of viewing and customizing process templates. The Process Editor is part of the Team Foundation Server Power Tool, a set of enhancements, tools, and command-line utilities that improve the TFS user experience.

1. Install DSL Tools for Visual Studio 2005 before you run the Power Tool installer. This is a prerequisite for the Team System Process Editor. If you do not install DSL Tools, the Power Tool installer installs everything except the Process Editor. The DSL Tools download is available at *http://go.microsoft.com/fwlink/?LinkId=82410*
2. Download the Power Tool from: *http://www.microsoft.com/downloads/details.aspx?familyid=7324c3db-658d-441b-8522-689c557d0a79&displaylang=en*
3. Run through the default installation, and then verify that the Power Tool has been installed correctly with the Process Editor as follows:
   a. Click **Start** and then click **Programs**.
   b. Click **Microsoft Team Foundation Server Power**.

   If the Microsoft Visual Studio Team System Process Editor appears, this means the Process Editor has been installed correctly. If it does not appear, uninstall the Power Tool and then reinstall it according to the correct sequence as specified in the preceding steps.

Step 2 — Choose the Process Template

In this step, you choose the out-of-box template that most closely suits your own process. This reduces the number of changes required in order to adapt the template to your own team's process. TFS provides the following two templates out of the box:

- Microsoft Solution Framework (MSF) for Agile Software Development (MSF Agile)
- MSF for CMMI® Process Improvement (MSF CMMI)

Read the following details about these process templates to help make the correct choice.

MSF Agile

The MSF Agile process template is a lightweight process template for small, agile, or informal software projects on a rapid delivery schedule. This process template is based on scenarios and context-driven actions and is both project-centric and team member (people)–centric. You can use the MSF Agile process template in the following project scenarios:

- Your project does not include a documented process and does not rely on formal processes.
- You do not need to certify your process or prove compliance with process standards.
- Your project is of a short duration.
- Your project needs quick releases for the purpose of community/user feedback.

MSF CMMI

The MSF CMMI process template is designed for more mature software projects. This process template extends the MSF Agile process template by providing support for auditing, verification, and formal processes. You can use this process template in the following project scenarios:

- Your project involves a documented process, or you want to develop more formal processes.
- Predictability of releases is more important than flexibility.
- Your project is of a long duration.
- You have to certify your process or prove compliance with process standards.

Note: You are not confined to the default process templates. If you have installed other process templates from third parties, such as the Scrum process template, you can choose these templates as well.

Step 3 — Download the Process Template

In this step, you download the chosen process template to be adapted to your customized process.

1. In Visual Studio, click **Team** and then select **Team Foundation Server Settings**.
2. Click **Process Template Manager**.
3. In the **Process Template Manager** dialog box, select the process template you want to modify, and then click **Download**.
4. In the **Download Process Template** dialog box, select the folder location on your local drive where you want to save the template, and then click **Save**.

For instance, you can download the MSF CMMI process template to your desktop for use in the next step.

Step 4 – Open the Process Template in Process Editor

In this step, you load the downloaded process template into the Process Editor in order to modify various settings.

1. In Visual Studio, click the **Team** menu.
2. Click **Process Editor**, and then click **Open Process Template**.
3. In the **Open Process Template fileset** dialog box, navigate to the downloaded process template, and then click **Open** to open the ProcessTemplate.xml file inside Visual Studio.
4. Specify the **Name** of the methodology you are customizing.

For instance, you can specify 'My Template' as the new process template name.

Step 5 — Modify Work Item Types

In this step, you add new work items types that are specific to your process, or modify the default work item types.

► **To add new work item types**

1. In the Process Template Explorer, click **Work Item Tracking**.
2. In the right pane, click the **Type Definitions** tab.
3. To create a new work item, click **Add** in the toolbar in the right pane.
4. In the **New Work Item Type** dialog box, enter a name for the work item type, or select an existing work item type from the **Copy From** drop-down list.

   The new work item type will be created and will be available in the **Item List** on the **Type Definitions** tab in the right pane.
5. On the **File** menu, click **Save** to save your changes.

For example, you can create a new Bug type named 'My Bug,' copied from the Bug work item type.

You can now edit the work item type to modify its behavior.

► To edit a work item type

- If you want to add/remove attributes fields to/from the new work item type or an existing work item type, on the **Type Definitions** tab, right-click the work item type you want to edit, and then click **Open**.

  The selected work item type opens in a new Visual Studio window where you can add or remove the attributes you want.

► To add a new field to the work item

1. Click the **Fields** tab, and then click **Add** in the toolbar.
2. In the **Field Definition** dialog box, enter the details as specified below:
   a. **Name**—Type the name of the new field.
   b. **Type**—In the **Data type** the drop-down list, select the data type for this field.
   c. **RefName**—Enter a unique **Identifier** for the field in TFS. The identifier must have at least one period in the name; for example, Test.Test1.
   d. **Help Text**—Type the text that you want the user to see when he or she moves the pointer over the name of the field. Generally, this text provides a definition of the field's purpose.
   e. **Reportable**—Select the desired option in the **Reportable** drop-down list. This determines whether to make the data in this field available for TFS reports. The following options are available:
      i. **Dimension**—Use this for fields that have lists of valid values. Work Item Type and State are good examples of dimensions. The Dimension field can be used to filter reports.
      ii. **Detail**—This option is a good choice for unrestricted text fields because it lets you use them in reports. However, any reports that you build using these fields must use the relational database instead of the cube.
      iii. **Measure**—Measures are the numeric values in your reports. Each measure will appear in both the Current Work Item measure group and the Work Item History measure group.
   f. **Formula**—This drop-down list is shown only if you select **Measure** in the **Reportable** field. Examples of formula options include **sum**, **count**, and **avg**.
3. For any new field added to the work item type, you can constrain the values that the user can enter into a field. You can also constrain a field when the work item is in a particular state; and when the work item is making a particular transition. Perform the following steps to add constraints:
   a. Click the **Rules** tab and then click **New**.

b. In the **Select a rule type** dialog box, select a rule type. The most commonly used types are:

    i. **AllowedValues**—Use this rule type when you want to set a list of values that can be entered.

    ii. **DefaultValue**—Use this rule type when providing a starting value.

    iii. **Required**—Use this rule type when forcing the user to always supply a value.

    iv. **ValidUser**—Contains the name of a user on a project.

    The dialog box that appears allows you to set the rule's parameters.

c. Click **OK** twice to save the changes.

4. After you have added a field to a work item, you need to decide where and how the field needs to displayed. Perform the following steps to add a field to your work item layout:

    a. On the Work Item Type page, click the **Layout** tab.

    b. On the **Layout** tab, select the location in the Layout tree where you want the new field to appear.

    c. In the left pane, right-click the selected node and then select **New Control**.

    d. Add an appropriate label and then in the **FieldName** property of the control, use the Ref Name that was added for the field in the above steps.

    e. Click **Preview Form** to verify that the new control is properly positioned on work item form.

For example, you can add a new Security Impact field to the My Bug work item type you created previously, as follows:

1. Click the **Fields** tab, and then click **Add** in the toolbar.
2. In the **Field Definition** dialog box, enter the following information:
    a. **Name**—Security Impact
    b. **Type**—String
    c. **RefName**—MyBug.CustomField.1
    d. **Help Text**—Enter the security impact of this bug, from 1 – 5 where 1 represents the lowest impact and 5 the highest.
    e. **Reportable**—Set the value as **Dimension** so that it is possible to create a report that will show which bugs have security impact.
3. Click the **Rules** tab, and then click the **Add** button.
4. In the **Select a rule type** dialog box, select the **ALLOWEDVALUES** option and then click **OK**.
5. In the **ALLOWEDVALUES** dialog box, click **Add** button five times, each time adding a value from 1 to 5.

6. Click **OK**.
7. Click the **Layout** tab.
8. Add the new field to the Status group as follows:
   a. Under **Group – Status**, right-click the second **Column** node and then click **ew Control**.
   b. Set **FieldName** to **MyBug.CustomField.1**.
   c. Set **Label** to **S&ecurity Impact**.
   d. The '&' assigns the ampersand character as a hotkey for the field.
   e. Click **Preview Form** to ensure that the new field is in the right location.

   The new field has now been added to the custom work item type.

► To remove a field from a work item

Many times fields are referenced in queries, reports, etc. Rather than track down and remove all of these references, you can leave the fields in the system but remove them from the work item dialog layout so the user cannot set their values.

- Click the **Fields** tab, and then click **Delete** in the toolbar.

For example, you can remove one of the fields from the My Bug work item type you created previously, as shown below:

1. Click the **Layout** tab to display the form layout for My Bug.
2. On the **Layout** tab, in the tree, expand *TabPage Details Group Column Group Schedu le Column*, right click **Remaining &work,** and then click **Delete** to remove it from the layout.

You can add the field back into the layout at a future point because the field itself has not been deleted.

► To edit work item type workflow

After you have created a work item type and finalized the layout, the final step is to edit the work item type workflow. Workflow governs the states and transitions that are allowed throughout the life of a work item. Because you copied the work item from an existing type, the workflow was also copied. You now need to review the work item type workflow and decide how you want to modify it. Perform the following steps to modify the work item workflow:

1. Create states and transitions.
   a. Click the **Workflow** tab to open the Workflow window.
   b. To create a new state, drag a state from the WITDesigner toolbox into the Workflow window.
   c. To create a transition between two states, WITDesigner toolbox, click the **Transition Link**, click the starting state, and then click the ending state.

d. To indicate the initial state (that is, the state of a newly created work item), click the **Transition Link**, click a blank part of the diagram, and then click the initial state.
e. This creates a transition that has no source. There should only be one such transition on the diagram; if one already exists, you need to delete it.
f. To see a summary of the attributes of each state or transition, click the expand/collapse icon at the top right of the shape. In the list of fields in the summary, "+" marks a field that has a required rule; "-" marks a field that has an empty rule; and "*" marks a field that has other rules.
g. To edit the attributes of each state or transition, right-click the state heading, and then click **Open Details** or double-click the heading.

Note: If the WITDesigner toolbox is not visible, click Toolbox on the Visual Studio View menu.

2. Edit the rules governing a state as follows:
   a. Right-click the state heading and then click **Open Details**, or double-click the heading.
   b. This opens the **Workflow State Field Rules** dialog box. Each item in the list refers to a field of the work item type, and represents a set of rules governing that field while the work item is in this state.
   c. On the **Field Reference** tab, set the **RefName** to indicate the field you want to constrain while the work item is in this state. The drop-down list of available fields that you can set is located on the **Fields** tab of the work item type.
   d. On the **Rules** tab, click **New** to create a new rule, or click **Open** to edit an existing rule.
   e. The details provided in the dialog box on opening a rule vary depending on the type of rule.
   f. Click **OK** to complete your changes.
3. Edit a transition as follows:
   a. Right-click the transition heading and then click **Open Details** to open the **Workflow Transition** dialog box.
      - The **Transaction Detail** tab defines the **From** and **To** states of the transition. If this transition marks the initial state in which a new work item of this type is created, the **From** state is empty. These fields correspond to the links on the workflow diagram. The **For** and **Not** fields can contain the name of a user or group who can or cannot make the transition.
      - The **Reasons** tab defines the content allowed in the **Reason** field when the transition occurs. There should be at least one reason for every transition.

- The **Actions** tab defines the state transition actions necessary to automate transitions of work items at various points in their workflow. For example, a TFS version control system needs to support automatic transitions of work items at check-in time.
- The **Fields** tab defines rules constraining fields when the transition occurs.

b. Click **OK** to complete your changes.

Step 6 — Modify the Default Work Items

In this step, you add or remove the default work items that are created at the time of team project creation. These work items give a team working on a new project a head start by assigning default work items that should be completed to get the project up and running.

1. In the Process Template Explorer, click **Work Item Tracking**.
2. In the right pane, click the **Default Work Items** tab.
3. To create a new default work item type, click **Add** in the toolbar in the right pane.
4. In the **Choose Type** dialog box, select a work item type.
5. In the dialog box that opens, fill in the appropriate fields.
6. Click **OK**.

For example, you can remove the task **Setup: Migration of Source Code** by doing the following:

1. In the Process Template Explorer, click **Work Item Tracking**.
2. In the right pane, click the **Default Work Items** tab.
3. Select **Setup: Migration of Source Code**.
4. Click **Remove**.

The default task "Setup: Migration of Source Code" will no longer be created when this process template is used to create a new project.

Step 7 — Modify and Manage Queries

In this step, you modify, add, or remove the default queries created at the time of team project creation.

1. In the Process Template Explorer, click **Work Item Tracking**.
2. In the right pane, click the **Queries** tab.
3. To create a new query, click **Add** in the toolbar in the right pane.
4. In the **Query Reference** dialog box, enter the name of the new query.
5. Click **Edit Query Definition**.

6. Use the **Fields**, **Sorting**, and **Criteria** tabs in the **Query Edit** dialog box to define your query.
7. Click **OK**.

For example, you can create a new query to select all bugs that have the highest security impact by doing the following:

1. In the Process Template Explorer, click **Work Item Tracking**.
2. In the right pane, click the **Queries** tab.
3. Click **Add**.
4. Specify the **Name** as **Bugs with Security Impact**.
5. Click **Edit Query Definition**.
6. In the **Query Edit** dialog box, click the **Fields** tab, select all the relevant fields you want to display (including **MyBug.CustomField.1**) from the available columns, click the > button, to move them to the Selected Columns pane.

   If you do not see the custom field you have added, make sure that you have saved the ProcessTemplate.xml file and then try again.
7. Click the **Criteria** tab, leave the **And Or** column blank, and then in the **Field** column, select **MyBug.CustomField.1**. In the **Operator** column, select > and then in the **Value** column, type **"1"**
8. Be sure to add quotes around the value 1 because the field is a string data type. If you had selected integer or some other numeric type when creating the Security Impact field, the quotes would not be necessary.
9. Click **OK** twice.

This query ensures that all work items that have "MyBug.CustomField.1" set to a value greater than 1 will be displayed in the output of the query.

Note: The Process Editor does not provide comprehensive features for editing queries. It is better to edit and test queries in a running team project in Visual Studio than in a process template. You can then save the queries to files that can be imported into other projects or copied into process templates.

Step 8 — Modify Areas and Iterations

In this step, you set up the default iterations and areas that are available at the time of team project creation.

1. In the Process Template Explorer, click **Areas & Iterations**.
2. In the right pane, click the **Areas** or **Iterations** tab.
3. Use the toolbar in the right pane to add, remove, or move areas or iterations.

For example, you can add a few default areas to organize projects created by using this template as follows:

1. In the Process Template Explorer, click **Areas & Iterations**.
2. In the right pane, click the **Areas** tab.
3. Click the new button.
4. In the area name text field, type **UI**
5. Select **Area**, because you want the next area to be a child of the root area node.
6. Click the new button again.
7. In the area name text field, type **Back End**

Any new projects that use your process template will now automatically have a UI and Back End area defined for them.

Step 9 — Modify Groups and Permissions

In this step, you modify, remove, or add groups and their permissions that are available at the time of team project creation.

1. In the Process Template Explorer, click **Groups & Permissions**.
2. To create a new group, click **Add** in the toolbar in the right pane.
3. In the **Group** dialog box, enter the name of the new group and a brief description of what the members of the group can do, and then click **OK**.
4. In the top section of the right pane, select a group and then assign permissions to that group in the section below. You can select **Allow** or **Deny** or leave the permissions setting as **Unset**. An **Unset** permission is an implicit deny.

Step 10 — Modify Source Control Settings

In this step, you modify the source control settings for parallel edits and check-in edits.

1. In the Process Template Explorer, click **Source Control**.
2. In the right pane, click the **Checkout Settings** tab.
3. If you want to allow more than one person to edit a file at the same time, select the **Enable Multiple Checkout** check box.
4. In the right pane, click the **Checkin Notes** tab.
5. To create a new Checkin Note field, click **Add** in the toolbar in the right pane.
6. To edit an existing Checkin Note field, select the field and then click **Open**.

7. In the **Checkin Note** dialog box, make necessary changes.
8. Click **OK**.

Note: You cannot make any changes on the Permissions tab in this version of the Process Editor.

For example, you can require that all check-ins must have a check-in note by performing the following steps:

1. In the Process Template Explorer, click **Source Control**.
2. In the right pane, click the **Checkin Notes** tab.
3. Double-click each row, and then in the **Checkin Note** dialog box, select the **Required** check box.

All check-ins will now require a note.

Step 11 — Modify the Project SharePoint Portal

In this step, you modify the project SharePoint portal to display specific documents and process guidance.

1. In the Process Template Explorer, click **Portal**.
2. To create a new library, in the middle pane, right-click the **Portal** node and then click **New Document Library**.
3. In the **Document Library** dialog box, enter the name and description of the library.
4. Click **OK**.
5. Right-click a document library and then click **New Folder** to create a new folder.
6. In the **Folder Properties** dialog box, enter the name of the new folder.
7. Select a folder and then on the toolbar in the right pane, click **Add** to upload a new document.
8. In the **File Import** dialog box, browse to the file you want to upload.
9. The **Destination Folder** and **Share Point Folder** fields will be automatically populated. Leave the **Query Id** field unchanged.
10. Click **Import**.
11. To edit the properties of an existing document in the document library, select the document in the right pane, and then click **Open** on the toolbar.
12. In the **File Edit** dialog box, change the name of the file in the **Name** field. Do not change the other fields.
13. Click **OK**.

Step 12 — Modify Reports

In this step, you add or remove reports from the set of default reports created at the time of team project creation.

1. In the Process Template Explorer, click **Reports**.
2. On the toolbar, click **Add**.
3. In the **Report** dialog box, on the **Report Detail** tab, enter a name for the report.
4. Browse to the .rdl file you want to add in the **File Name** field.
5. Do not make any changes to the data on the **Properties** and **Parameters** tabs.
6. On the **DataSources** tab, enter the appropriate data sources. The default data sources for process templates shipped in TFS are /TfsOlapReportDS and /TfsReportDS.
7. Click **OK**.

For example, you can remove a report from the process template as follows:

1. In the Process Template Explorer, click **Reports**.
2. Select the **Load Test Detail** report and then click **Remove**.

The Load Test Detail report will no longer appear for projects created with this process template.

Step 13 — Upload the Modified Process Template

In this step, you upload the modified process template to TFS so that it will be available when the new team project is created.

1. In Visual Studio, click **Save** on the toolbar to save the ProjectTemplate.xml file.
2. Click **Team** and then select **Team Foundation Server Settings**.
3. Click **Process Template Manager**.
4. In the **Process Template Manager** dialog box, click **Upload**.
5. Browse to the local folder where the process template was downloaded and modified.
6. In the **Upload Process Template** dialog box, click **Upload**.
7. You should see the new process template listed in the **Process Templates:** list.
8. Click **Close**.

The customization process is now complete. The next time you create a new team project, the newly created process will be one of the options available when choosing the process templates.

To test the changes you made during the course of this How To article, first upload the My Test process template you created as follows:

1. Make sure that you have saved any process template XML files that are still open.
2. In Visual Studio, click **Team** and then select **Team Foundation Server Settings**.
3. Click **Process Template Manager**.
4. In the **Process Template Manager** dialog box, click **Upload**.
5. Browse to your desktop location where you downloaded and modified the My Test process template.
6. In the **Upload Process Template** dialog box, click **Upload**.
7. You should see the new process template listed in the **Process Templates:** list.
8. Click **Close**.

Next, create a new project based on this process template as follows:

1. Click **File** menu, click **New**, and then click **Team Project**.
2. Specify a name (for example, Test Project) and then click **Next**.
3. In the process template drop-down list, select **My Test**.
4. Click **Finish**.

Finally, review each area to see the changes you made by performing the following steps:

1. To view the new work item type:
   a. On the **Team** menu, click **Add Work Item**, and then click **My Bug** to create a new work item of the custom type you created.
   b. View the work item fields in the **Status** group box to see the **Security Impact** field that you added.
   c. Make sure that the field allows the adding of values only in the range of 1-5, add **5** as the value, and then save the work item.
2. To verify that the default work item you removed is no longer in the project:
   a. In Team Explorer, open your team project.
   b. Expand the Work Items folder.
   c. Expand the Team Queries folder.
   d. Double-click **All Work Items**.
   e. Review the default tasks to verify that the Setup: Migration of Source Code task does not exist.
3. To check the custom query you added:
   a. In Team Explorer, open your team project.
   b. Expand the Work Items folder.
   c. Expand the Team Queries folder.

   d. Double-click **Bugs with Security Impact**.
   e. Make sure that the bug you created above is displayed correctly.
4. To review the areas you added:
   a. Select a task from the **All Work Items** query you ran in the previous step.
   b. Click the **Area** drop-down list to view the two areas (**UI** and **Back End**) that you added to the template.
5. To ensure that the report you removed is no longer in the project:
   a. In Team Explorer, open your team project.
   b. Expand the Reports folder.
   c. Scan the list to verify that the **Load Test Detail** report has been removed.

Additional Resources

- For more information about process template customization, see "Process Template Customization Overview" at *http://msdn2.microsoft.com/en-us/library/ms194945(VS.80).aspx*
- To download the Team Foundation Power Tool, including the Process Template Editor, go to *http://msdn2.microsoft.com/en-us/vstudio/aa718351.aspx*
- For more information about customizing a process template using the Process Editor tool, see "Process Editor User Guide," available with the Process Editor Tool installation.

How To: Customize a Report in Visual Studio Team Foundation Server

Applies To

- Microsoft® Visual Studio® 2005 Team Foundation Server (TFS)
- Microsoft Visual Studio Team System (VSTS)
- Microsoft® SQL Server™ Reporting Services

Summary

This How To article walks you through the process of customizing an existing report and then publishing it to the reporting portal in TFS.

Contents

Objective

- Create a reporting project in Visual Studio.
- Customize an existing report to meet your needs.
- Publish the new report to the report server.

Overview

The reports that ship with VSTS are SQL Server Reporting Services reports. You can amend these reports or create your own custom reports by using the SQL Server 2005 Reporting Services Designer inside Visual Studio (Business Intelligence Development Studio), which ships with the SQL Server 2005 client tools.

Customizing a report allows you to add functionality to an existing report without having to build a new report from scratch. If a report you need is similar to one that already exists, you can customize the existing report in order to save time. To customize an existing report, it must be exported from the report server, added to an existing report project in Visual Studio, and then redeployed to the reporting portal after changes are made.

Summary of Steps

- Step 1—Create a New Reporting Project
- Step 2—Export the Report You Want to Customize
- Step 3—Create the Data Sources
- Step 4—Add the Report to Your Project
- Step 5—Modify the Report
- Step 6—Deploy the Report to Your Team Foundation Server
- Step 7—Test the Report

Before You Begin

Before you can customize a report for TFS, you must ensure you have the following prerequisites in place:

- You must have Business Intelligence Development Studio installed on the machine you will be using to customize the report. To verify that it is installed, check Visual Studio to see if the Business Intelligence Project type is available when you create a new project.
- Your user account must be a member of the Microsoft Analysis Server TfsWarehouseDataReaders security role on the data-tier server.

- Your user account must have administrator rights to the TFSWarehouse database on the data tier.
- Your user account must be a member of the SQL Server Reporting Services Publisher role on the application-tier server.

Step 1 — Create a New Reporting Project

In this initial step, you create a new reporting project so that you can add an existing report to the project and then customize it. Perform the following steps to create a new reporting project in Visual Studio:

1. Click **File**, click **New**, and then click **Project.**
2. Select the **Business Intelligence Project** type.
3. Select the **Report Server Project** template.
4. Set your project's **Name** and **Location** and then click **OK**.

Step 2 — Export the Report You Want to Customize

In this step, you export the report you want to customize from the project portal so you can import it into the new reporting project. Perform the following steps to export a report:

1. Right-click on your team project and then select **Show Project Portal**.
2. On the left side of the portal Web site, on the Quick Launch bar, click **Reports**.
3. Click the report you want to customize.
4. Click **Properties**.
5. Select **Edit**.
6. Save the report rdl file into the reporting project folder you created in Step 1.

Step 3 — Create the Data Sources

In order to edit and publish the customized report, you first need to add data sources for the TFS data warehouse and online analytical processing (OLAP) cube. After these data sources have been added to the Visual Studio project, the report can pull data from the server.

► **To create the warehouse data source**

1. In the Visual Studio Solution Explorer, right-click **Shared Data Sources** and then click **Add New Data Source**.
2. On the **General** tab, in the **Name** text box, enter **TfsReportDS**.
3. Select **Microsoft SQL Server** from the **Type** combo box.

4. Click the **Edit...** button.
5. Fill in your data tier server name.
6. Select the **TFSWarehouse** database.
7. Click **OK** button twice to add the data source.

► **To create the OLAP data source**

1. In Solution Explorer, right-click **Shared Data Sources** and then click **Add New Data Source**.
2. On the **General** tab, in the **Name** text box, enter **TfsOlapReportDS**.
3. Select **Microsoft SQL Server Analysis Services** from the **Type** combo box.
4. Click the **Edit...** button.
6. Select the **TFSWarehouse** database.
7. Click **OK** button twice to add the data source.

Step 4 — Add the Report to Your Project

Now that the data sources have been added to your project, you can add the report that you exported in Step 2:

1. In Solution Explorer, right-click **Reports**, click **Add**, and then click **Existing Item...**
2. Browse to the **rdl** file you exported in Step 2

Step 5 — Modify the Report

Now that you have added the report to your project you can make modifications in order to customize the report for your specific needs. To open the report for modification, double-click the report in the **Solution Explorer**. After you have opened the report you can make modifications such as:

- Modify query statements in the **Data Pane**.
- Drag new measures or members into the **Data Pane**.
- Modify the report layout in the **Layout Pane**.

Step 6 — Deploy the Report to Your Team Foundation Server

After you've made modifications to the report, you can deploy it to your team project's reporting portal by using the following steps:

1. In the **Solution Explorer**, right-click the report project and then click **Properties**.
2. Ensure **OverwriteDataSources** is set to **false**.

3. Modify **TargetDataSourceFolder** to reflect your team project name; for example: **TargetDataSourceFolder** = TestProject.
4. Modify **TargetReportFolder** to reflect your team project name; for example: **TargetDataSourceFolder** = TestProject.
5. Modify **TargetDataSourceFolder** *to http://<data-tier servername>/reportserver*; for example: **TargetDataSourceFolder** = http://tfsrtm/reportserver.
6. Click **OK.**
7. In the **Solution Explorer**, right-click on the rdl file and then click **Deploy.**
8. Observe the **Output Pane** to verify successful completion.

Step 7 — Test the Report

Now that you have successfully customized your report and deployed it to your TFS server, perform the following steps to test the report:

1. In **Team Explorer** expand you team project node, right-click on **Reports** and then click **Show Report Site.**
2. On the report site select the report you just deployed.
3. Verify that the report runs correctly.

Additional Resources

- For more tutorials explaining how to work with reporting projects, see "Reporting Services Tutorials" at *http://msdn2.microsoft.com/en-us/library/ms170246.aspx*
- For the Microsoft MSDN® article on editing reports, see "How to: Edit Reports in Report Designer" at *http://msdn2.microsoft.com/en-us/library/ms244655(VS.80).aspx*
- For more information on security roles in the data-tier, see "Securing Access Through Analysis Services" at *http://msdn2.microsoft.com/en-us/library/ms174839.aspx*
- For more information on security roles in the application tier, see "Securing Reporting Services" at *http://msdn2.microsoft.com/en-us/library/ms157198.aspx*

How To: Manage Projects in Visual Studio Team Foundation Server

Applies To

- Microsoft® Visual Studio® 2005 Team Foundation Server (TFS)
- Microsoft Visual Studio Team System (VSTS)

Summary

This How To article walks you through the process of initiating new software development projects by creating and configuring new team projects based on a selected template and shows you how to use TFS tools to manage, control and monitor the ongoing software development processes throughout the software development lifecycle.

Contents

Objective

- Learn how to create team projects in TFS
- Learn how to manage projects in TFS

Overview

Visual Studio Team System provides tools and reports to help project managers control and support the entire software development life cycle in a unified and centralized manner. By controlling the software process directly through VSTS and a centralized database shared by all team members, team communication is improved, and handoffs required between team members are automated. In addition using reports driven from the TFS data warehouse makes it much easier to monitor and track project progress.

This How To article walks you through the process of managing a team project from the first steps of creating and configuring a new project and then through the steps required to monitor the progress of an ongoing project.

Summary of Steps

- Step 1—Choose a Process Template
- Step 2—Create a Team Project
- Step 3—Create Security Groups (Optional)
- Step 4—Add Team Members in Team Foundation Server
- Step 5—Determine Your Iteration Cycle
- Step 6—Capture Your Project Scenarios in TFS
- Step 7—Identify the Scenarios for the Iteration
- Step 8—Define Your Quality of Service Requirements
- Step 9—Plan Your Iteration
- Step 10—Monitor Progress.

Before You Begin

Before you start creating a new team project, you should gather the following information:

- **The process you want to use for the project**. The process you want to use to manage your project determines the template you should select when creating a new team project. It also helps you evaluate the degree to which you should customize the supplied templates. If you favor an agile style of project execution, start by selecting the Microsoft Solutions Framework (MSF) for Agile Software Development (MSF Agile) template and then consider any customizations you might need.

- **The project name**. Give careful consideration to the naming convention that you use for the team projects you create. Make sure that your project names are sufficiently unique and use names that enable other people to easily find the project. Some organizations use project codes as part of their names, while others might use a combination of department and project title.
- **Source control structure**. Consider whether you need to start with an empty source control tree or whether your project should be based on existing source code. Evaluate an appropriate source control structure based on your code and branching needs. For more information, see "How To: Structure Your Source Control Folders in Visual Studio Team Foundation Server."

Step 1 — Choose a Process Template

Start by selecting your process template. Consider the process you would like to follow for your project and then examine the different features provided by each of the two templates supplied by TFS (see below). Features to evaluate include work item definitions (do they provide sufficient fields for your needs?), document templates, workflows, check in policies, and reports.

TFS provides following two process templates:

- **MSF for Agile Software Development (MSF Agile)**—This is a lightweight process for small and informal software projects. It is based on scenarios and context-driven actions and is both project-centric and team member (people)-centric.
- **MSF for CMMI® Process Improvement (MSF CMMI)**—This is designed for more mature software projects. It extends MSF Agile by providing support for auditing, verification, and formal processes. It relies on process and conformance to process and is organization-centric.

If required you can customize the supplied process templates to align them more closely with your processes. For more information about customizing the process templates see "How To: Customize a Process Template in Visual Studio Team Foundation Server".

The remainder of this How To article, assumes that you have selected the MSF Agile process template.

Step 2 — Create a Team Project

After you have selected the template you want to use, you are ready to create a new team project. To create a new team project:

1. Ensure that Visual Studio is connected to a TFS instance.
2. In **Team Explorer,** right click the server node and then click **New Team Project…**
3. On the first page of the New Project Creation Wizard, enter the name of your team project and then click **Next**.
4. On the **Select a Process Template** page, from the drop-down list, select the process template you chose in Step 1. For this example, choose the **MSF for Agile Software Development –v4.0** process template and then click **Next**.
5. On the **Specify the Settings for the Project Portal** page, enter the name and description for the team project portal and then click **Next**.
6. The name you supply here is used to build the Microsoft Windows SharePoint® Services Web site for your project portal.
7. On the **Specify Source Control Settings** page, select **Create an empty source control folder** and then click **Next**.
8. On the **Confirm Team Project Settings** page, review the settings and then click **Finish**.

This creates a team project on the TFS server based on the MSF Agile process template.

Step 3 — Create Security Groups (Optional)

When you create a project in TFS, four default groups are created for that project regardless of your choice of process template. By default, each of these groups has a predefined set of permissions that govern what members of those groups are authorized to do. The four groups are:

- Project Administrator
- Contributor
- Reader
- Build Services.

You can create security groups for your team project to better meet your organization's security requirements. Creating a security group is an efficient way to grant a specific set of permissions to a group of users on your team project. Make sure that you allow only the minimum permissions necessary for the group, and add only those users or groups who must belong to this new team project group.

To perform this procedure, you must be a member of the **Project Administrators** group although you do not need to be a Microsoft Windows® administrator.

1. In Team Explorer, select the team project for which you want to create a group.
2. On the **Team** menu, point to **Team Project Settings**, and then click **Group Membership**.
3. In the **Project Groups** dialog box, click **New**.
4. In the **Create New Team Foundation Server Group** dialog box, in the **Group name** box, type the name for the team project group.
5. In the **Description** box, type a description for the group.
6. Click **OK** and then **Close**.

After you have created a team project group, give the group the appropriate permissions, and add members to the group. By default, a team project group is created without any permission granted.

Step 4 — Add Team Members in Team Foundation Server

In this step, you identify the resources that will be working on the project and their roles, and then assign these team members to TFS. You can add users to existing team project groups or server-level groups. You must also add members to groups that you create. To perform this procedure, you must be a member of the **Team Foundation Administrators** group.

1. In Team Explorer, select your team project.
2. On the **Team** menu, point to **Team Project Settings**, and then click **Group Membership**

   -Or-
3. To add users to a server-level group, point to **Team Foundation Server Settings**, and then click **Group Membership**.
4. In the **Project Groups** dialog box, select the group to which you want to add users, and then click **Properties**.
5. In the **Team Foundation Server Group Properties** dialog box, on the **Members** tab, under **Add member**, select **Windows User or Group**.
6. Click **Add**.
7. In the **Select Users or Groups** dialog box, under **Enter the object names to select**, enter the domain name and alias of the users you want to add in the following format:

   domain\username

   To add more than one user at a time, separate the entries with a semicolon (;).
8. Click **OK** twice and then click **Close**.

Step 5 — Determine Your Iteration Cycle

Iterations are fixed-length chunks of periods in which you plan, schedule, and perform work. All components of the software development lifecycle - from requirements definition through analysis, design, development, coding, and testing - are grouped into these iterations, which typically last anywhere from 2 to 6 weeks.

In this step you determine the iteration cycle for your project. The important points to keep in mind while determining the iteration cycle are:

- The iteration cycle should be long enough to get substantial work done, and should cover at least a few scenarios
- The iteration cycle should be short enough to be flexible to accommodate changes and changing priorities.

The length of your iteration cycle will depend upon the size and complexity of your project. In practice, two-week iteration cycle works for most projects.

Step 6 — Capture Your Project Scenarios in TFS

In this step, you capture your project scenarios in TFS so that you can plan better execution of your project and track its progress.

1. Create a project back log (PBL) document from inputs provided by various stake holders, including customers, business analysts, end users and product managers. The PBL is generally a Microsoft Office Word document designed mainly to capture requirements.
2. Use the PBL as input and scope out various scenarios for your project.
3. You can create all the scenarios at the start of the first iteration or you can create scenarios as you move through iterations. To gain a complete picture of your project and to help track progress, you are recommended that you capture all your scenarios upfront.

► **To create a scenario in a project that uses the MSF Agile process template**

1. In **Team Explorer,** expand the project node and then right-click on the **Work Items** folder.
2. Point to **Add Work Item** and then click **Scenario.**
3. On the **New Scenario** page, enter the details for the Scenario.
4. Save your new scenario.
5. Repeat the preceding steps for all scenarios that you have identified for the project.

Step 7 — Identify the Scenarios for the Iteration

In this step, you identify the scenarios to be worked on during a specific iteration. You repeat this step for each iteration cycle.

1. Identify the scenarios to be worked on during a specific iteration, based on inputs from the project stakeholders and your feature priorities.
2. Assign these scenarios to the iteration

► **To retrieve work items and assign them to a specific iteration**

1. Expand the **Work Items** folder, expand the **Team Queries** folder, and then double-click the **All Scenarios** query to display all the scenarios in your project.
2. Double-click the scenario you want to work on in the current iteration.
3. Change the **Iteration** to the current iteration path and then click the save icon.
4. Repeat the preceding steps for all identified scenarios.

Step 8 — Define Your Quality of Service Requirements

In this step, you define your Quality of Service (QoS) requirements for each of the scenarios to be worked on during the iteration cycle. You repeat this step for each iteration cycle. This helps define the acceptance criteria for the scenario. The inputs for the QoS requirements come from project goals and requirements and specification documentation, if available.

1. Right-click on the **Work Items** folder of your project, and point to **Add Work Item,** and then click **Quality of Service Requirements**.
2. In the **New Quality of Service Requirements** page, add the following details
   a. Set the **Type** to an appropriate value such as Performance, Scalability, Stress or Security.
   b. Set the **Iteration** to the current iteration cycle.
   c. From the **Links** tab, link the QoS to a specific scenario, for easier traceability.
3. Save the new QoS requirement.
4. Create one QoS requirements for each discipline or type of quality requirements, bearing in mind that each scenario can have multiple QoS requirements.
5. Make sure you create QoS requirements for all of the scenarios in a specific iteration cycle.

Important: You can break down the QoS requirements into test tasks later.

Step 9 — Plan Your Iteration

In this step you plan for the iteration by breaking down the scenarios, QoS requirements, and other work items into tasks, estimating effort for each task and assigning the tasks to the relevant team members. You repeat this step for each iteration cycle.

Developer Tasks

1. Break down the chosen scenarios into developer stories:
2. Subdivide the developer stories into developer tasks.
3. Capture developer tasks in TFS as task work items.
   a. In Team Explorer, under your project node, right-click the **Work Items** folder, point to **Add Work Item** and then click **Task**.
   b. In the **New Task** page, add the following details:
      i. Set Discipline to Development.
      ii. Set Iteration to the current iteration cycle.
      iii. On the Links tab link the task to the specific scenario for easier traceability.
      iv. On the New Task Page, along with the description you can capture the acceptance criteria for the task, which can determine if the task is completed successfully.
      v. Set the Assigned to field to the developer who will be working on the task.
   c. Save the new task.
   d. Repeat the above steps for all the identified tasks.
4. Repeat the above steps for all the identified scenarios for the iteration.

Test Tasks

1. Break down the QoS requirements for the identified scenario into test cases.
2. Divide the test cases into test tasks, these test tasks are captured in TFS as task work items.
   a. In Team Explorer, under your project node, right-click the **Work Items** folder, point to **Add Work Item** and then click **Task**.
   b. In the **New Task** page, add the following details:
      i. Set Discipline to Test.
      ii. Set Iteration to the current iteration cycle.
      iii. On the Links tab link the task to the specific QoS requirements for easier traceability.

iv. On the New Task page, along with the description you can capture the acceptance criteria for the task, which can determine if the task is completed successfully.

v. Set the Assigned to field to the tester who will be working on the task.

c. Save the new task.

d. Repeat the above steps for all the identified tasks.

3. Repeat the above steps for all the QoS requirements for the iteration.

Others

1. Capture any relevant tasks for the iteration for other disciplines – such as Architecture, Release Management, Project Management and Requirements - which needs to be tracked.
2. Link each of these tasks to the appropriate scenario for easier traceability.

For large projects that contain a huge number of work items, you can use the Microsoft Office Excel® integration feature to create work items in an Excel spread sheet and then upload it to TFS. For more information see "Working with Work Item Lists in Microsoft Excel" at *http://msdn2.microsoft.com/en-us/library/ms181694(VS.80).aspx*

For large projects that contain a large number of resources, you can use the integration feature in Microsoft Office Project to track the work items and balance task assignment. For more information see "Working with Work Items in Microsoft Project" at *http://msdn2.microsoft.com/en-us/library/ms244368(VS.80).aspx*

Step 10 — Monitor Progress

Each process template includes a set of reports that you can use to track project status and health. Below are the default reports that you can use to monitor progress:

Bugs

The bug related reports enable you to see the kind of bugs being generated and fixed and to spot trends. The following bug related reports are available:

- **Bugs by Priority**. Are the correct bugs being found? This report shows you the rate of high priority bugs found vs. low priority. This report is both of the supplied process templates.
- **Bug Rates**. How effectively are bugs being found, fixed and closed? This report shows trends over time for new bugs, bug backlogs, and bug resolution. This report is available in both of the supplied process templates.

Release Management

Release management reports enable you to judge how close your software is to being fit for release. The following release management reports are available:

- **Actual Quality versus Planned Velocity**. How many scenarios can be completed before quality is unacceptable? This report presents the relationship, for each iteration, of estimated size to overall quality. This report is available in both process templates.
- **Builds**. What is the quality of a build? This report provides a list of available builds including build quality and other detailed information. This report is available in MSF for CMMI Process Improvement.
- **Quality Indicators**. What is the quality of the software? This report collects test results, bugs code coverage and code churn into a single report to track project health. This report is available in MSF Agile and MSF CMMI.
- **Velocity**. How quickly is the team completing work? This report shows how quickly the team is completing planned work and show rates of change from day to day. This report is available in MSF Agile and MSF CMMI.
- **Scenario Details**. What scenarios are we building the application against? This report provides information on each scenario including completion status, risks and testing progress.

Testing

Testing reports enable you to monitor the effectiveness and progress of your testing. The following test reports are available:

- **Regressions**. What tests passed at one point but are now failing? This report shows a list of all the tests that passed previously and now are failing. This report is available in MSF CMMI.
- **Requirements Test History**. How well tested are my scenarios and requirements? This report shows the progress of testing against defined scenarios and requirements. This report is available in MSF CMMI.
- **Test Failure Without Active Bug**. Are there bugs to track every known defect? This report shows any tests that have failed and are not associated with an open bug. This report is available in MSF CMMI.
- **Test Passing With Open Bug**. Is the bug list up to date and consistent with application quality? This report shows stale bugs for which tests are now passing. This report is available in MSF CMMI.
- **Load Test Summary**. What are the results of load testing on application performance? This report shows test results for load testing on your application. This report is available in MSF Agile.

Work Items

Work item reports enable you to assess the current state of your project and current project progress. The following work item reports are available.

- **Open Issues and Blocked Work Items Trend**. How many open issues remain? This report shows the remaining open issues as well as the trend toward resolving them. This report is available in MSF CMMI.
- **Reactivations**. How many work items are being reactivated? This report shows work items that have been resolved or closed prematurely. This report is available in MSF Agile and MSF CMMI.
- **Related Work Items**. What work items are dependent on other work items? This report shows a list of work items that are linked to other work items so you trace dependencies. This report is available in MSF CMMI.
- **Remaining Work**. How much work is left to be done and when will it be completed? This report shows work remaining, resolved and closed over time. Projecting remaining work trends forward can enable you to predict the point at which you will be code complete. This report is available in MSF Agile and MSF CMMI.
- **Triage**. What work items need to be triaged? This report shows every work item that is still in the proposed state. This report is available in MSF CMMI.
- **Unplanned Work**. How much unplanned work is there? This report charts total work versus remaining work and distinguishes planned from unplanned. This report is available in MSF Agile and MSF CMMI.
- **Work Items**. What are the active work items? This report lists every active work item. This report is available in MSF CMMI.
- **Work Items by Owner**. How much work is assigned to each member of the team? This report shows work items per team member. This report is available in MSF CMMI.
- **Work Items by State**. How many active, resolved and closed work items are there? This report lists work items organized by state. This report is available in MSF CMMI.

Area and Iteration Consideration

Keep in mind the following key considerations related to areas and iterations

- Areas are used to organize work in your team project, for example, you could organize your project work into areas such as a UI area, an Application area, and a Database area. You can assign scenarios and work items to the specific areas. Areas are used to group work items for queries and reports. You can start with a single root-level area and later as your project matures you can create areas once you need them.

- Iterations are used to define how many times the team will repeat a particular set of major activities (such as planning, development and testing) during the course of application development. Iterations are used to group work items and therefore impact work item creation, work item queries, and reporting.

Additional Resources

- For more information on using Microsoft Office Excel spreadsheets with work items, see "Working with Work Item Lists in Microsoft Excel" at *http://msdn2.microsoft.com/en-us/library/ms181694(VS.80).aspx*
- For more information on using Microsoft Office Project to track work items and balance task assignment, see "Working with Work Items in Microsoft Project" at *http://msdn2.microsoft.com/en-us/library/ms244368(VS.80).aspx*

How To: Migrate Source Code to Team Foundation Server from Visual Source Safe

Applies To

- Microsoft® Visual Studio® 2005 Team Foundation Server (TFS)
- Microsoft Visual SourceSafe® (VSS)

Summary

This How To article walks you through the process of migrating version-controlled source code from VSS to TFS by using the VSS converter tool. This tool allows you to migrate files, folders, version history, labels, and user information from a VSS database to a TFS source control database. Prior to migrating your source you need to back up and prepare your VSS source database.

Contents

Objectives

- Learn how to analyze VSS projects and prepare for migration
- Migrate VSS projects to TFS

Overview

Team Foundation Server provides tools to help you migrate existing source maintained in a Visual Source Safe (VSS) database to TFS source control. TFS provides a VSSConverter tool that allows you to migrate files, folders, version history, labels, and user information. Using the VSSConverter tool is a two-stage process; first you use the tool to analyze your existing VSS database to identify potential problems, and then you use it to actually perform the migration.

By following the steps outlined in this How To article, you should be able to successfully migrate your existing source code. The main issues that you are likely to encounter are due to some differences in the way TFS handles version control in comparison to VSS. For example, because TFS does not support sharing of files, shared files are migrated by copying the version of the file at the time sharing began to a destination folder. Also, because branching in VSS uses sharing, the migration of a branched file results in the file being copied to the destination folder in TFS source control. As TFS does not support pinning, to help you locate items in TFS source control that were previously pinned in your VSS database, the VSSConverter tool labels any file that was pinned with the "PINNED" label.

Before You Begin

To successfully perform the steps outlined in this How To article:

- You must be logged in with an account that is a member of the Team Foundation Administrators group.
- You must have the VSS 2005 client installed on the computer on which the converter is running. The converter stops with a warning if you are running an earlier version of VSS. You should also make sure that you use the VSS 2005 client **Analyze** command in the event that this command is able to detect issues that previous versions were not. The VSS database does not need to be a native VSS 2005 database.
- You must have Microsoft SQL Server™ 2005 Express Edition installed and enabled on the computer on which the converter is running. The converter tool uses the local SQL Server instance as a temporary database during the conversion. SQL Server Express Edition is installed by default with Visual Studio 2005.

- Make sure you gather your TFS domain name and the list of TFS user names as defined in your Microsoft Active Directory®.
- Make sure you have your VSS administrator user name and password and your TFS project administrator username and password.

Summary of Steps

- Step 1—Back Up Your VSS Database
- Step 2—Analyze Your VSS Database to Resolve Data Integrity Issues
- Step 3—Analyze Your Projects in VSS
- Step 4—Prepare to Migrate Your Projects
- Step 5—Migrate Your Projects

Step 1 — Back Up Your VSS Database

Prior to performing a migration, start by creating a backup copy of the VSS database you want to migrate.

1. Ask all users to check in their files and then log off the VSS database. Ask the users to close both the Visual Studio Integrated Development Environment (IDE) and VSS Explorer.

   Important: Checked-out files are not migrated to TFS.

2. Check that no one is currently logged into the database.
3. Make sure that no analyze jobs are scheduled to run against the database.
4. Copy the following folders (located beneath your VSS install directory) to your backup location:

   \DATA

   \Temp

   \USERS

5. Copy the following files to your backup location:

   User.txt

   Srcsafe.ini

   By default, you can find these files in the following folder: \Program Files\Microsoft Visual Studio\VSS

Step 2 — Analyze Your VSS Database to Resolve Data Integrity Issues

In this step, you use the Visual SourceSafe Analyze utility to locate and fix data integrity issues in the database.

1. Open a Command prompt and run Analyze.exe to search for database corruption or database errors. Use the following command:

   analyze "<sourcesafe data directory>"

   Use the **-I** option for unattended execution. This command reports potential problems.

2. If there are permissions problems, "unable to checkout files" errors, "losing checkout status" errors, or any other errors that refer to the Status.dat file or to the Rights.dat file, run the Ddconv.exe program or the Ddconvw.exe program. These programs update a VSS database from an older format to the current format. By default, these programs are installed in the \Admin subdirectory.

Step 3 — Analyze Your Projects in VSS

In this step, you determine which projects you want to migrate and then run the TFS command-line tool VSSConverter.exe to analyze the VSS database for any potential issues that might cause migration problems.

1. Create an Extensible Markup Language (XML) settings file (named for example, ConversionSettings.xml) as follows:

```
<?xml version="1.0" encoding="utf-8"?>
 <SourceControlConverter>
    <ConverterSpecificSetting>
      <Source name="VSS">
            <VSSDatabase name="c:\VSSDatabase">
            </VSSDatabase>
      </Source>
      <ProjectMap>
        <Project Source="$/MyFirstProject"></Project>
        <Project Source="$/MySecondProject"></Project>
      </ProjectMap>
    </ConverterSpecificSetting>
 </SourceControlConverter>
```

   In the above example, **MyFirstProject** and **MySecondProject** represent the names of the project folders in VSS that you want to migrate. To migrate an entire VSS database, use **<Project Source="$/"></Project>**.

2. Run VSSConverter.exe passing in the **Analyze** switch, from a Visual Studio command prompt to analyze your projects:

   VSSConverter Analyze ConversionSettings.xml

   When prompted, enter the Visual SourceSafe administrator password.

3. Examine the output report and identify any conversion errors. The conversion tool creates an output report named VSSAnalysisReport.xml.
4. Map VSS users to TFS users. The VSSConverter tool creates a UserMap.xml file that contains a list of all VSS users who performed at least one operation on the VSS database. Edit the UserMap.xml file and add your associated TFS usernames (Windows accounts). You must specify user names including the domain (MyDomain\MyUserName). The following example shows a Usermap.xml files that contains the VSS user accounts in the **From** attribute and the associated TFS usernames in the **To** attribute.

```
<?xml version="1.0" encoding="utf-8" ?>
<UserMappings xmlns:xsi="http://www.w3.org/2001/XMLSchema-instance" xmlns:
xsd="http://www.w3.org/2001/XMLSchema">
  <!--
    This file is automatically created by VSS Converter. You can optionally use
the file to map
    a VSS user to a Team Foundation user. For example, <UserMap From="Jane"
To="MyDomain\Janep"></UserMap>
    This mapping causes all actions logged by VSS user "Jane" to be changed to
Team
    Foundation user "MyDomain\Janep" during migration.
  -->
  <UserMap From="ADMIN" To="Contoso\Administrator" />
  <UserMap From="Dave" To="Contoso\DaveM" />
  <UserMap From="Chris" To="Contoso\ChrisP" />
  <UserMap From="John" To="Contoso\JohnR" />
</UserMappings>
```

Step 4 — Prepare to Migrate Your Projects

In this step, you use the VSSConverter.exe tool to migrate your VSS projects.

1. Modify the ConversionSettings.xml file created in Step 3 adding a new **<Settings>** element containing a **<TeamFoundationServer>** element as shown here:

```
<SourceControlConverter>
   <ConverterSpecificSetting>
   ...
   </ConverterSpecificSetting>
   <Settings>
     <TeamFoundationServer name="YourTFSServerName"
                          port="PortNumber"
                          protocol="http">
     </TeamFoundationServer>
        </Settings>
....
      </SourceControlConverter>
```

Add the <Settings> element directly after </ConverterSpecificSettings> as a child element of <SourceControlConverter>.

2. Modify the ConversionSettings.xml file you created adding **Destination** attributes to the **<Project>** elements as shown below. Set the value of the **Destination** attributes to the folder location in your TFS Team project to which you want to migrate your files.

```
<?xml version="1.0" encoding="utf-8"?>
 <SourceControlConverter>
   <ConverterSpecificSetting>
      <Source name="VSS">
          <VSSDatabase name="c:\VSSDatabase">
          </VSSDatabase>
      </Source>
      <ProjectMap>
        <Project Source="$/MyFirstProject"
                 Destination="$/MyTeam_ProjectOne">
        </Project>
        <Project Source="$/MySecondProject"
                 Destination="$/MyTeam_ProjectTwo">
        </Project>
      </ProjectMap>
   </ConverterSpecificSetting>
   <Settings>
     <TeamFoundationServer name="YourTFSServerName"
                           port="PortNumber"
                           protocol="http">
     </TeamFoundationServer>
   </Settings>
 </SourceControlConverter>
```

In the **<ProjectMap>** section, for each VSS folder that you are migrating, replace **MyFirstProject** with the source VSS folders and replace **MyTeam_ProjectOne** with the destination folders in TFS source control. Include a **<Project>** entry for all the folders that you want to migrate.

Step 5 — Migrate Your Projects

Copy your VSS database to a local folder such as C:\VSSDatabases on the computer on which you want to run analysis and migration. Although you can migrate a VSS database to a shared folder on a remote computer, the migration takes much longer to finish.

1. At the command prompt, type the following:

   VSSConverter Migrate Conversionsettings.xml

2. Enter **Y** to confirm the migration. When prompted, enter the password for the Visual SourceSafe admin user.

Additional Considerations

If you used, sharing, branching or pinning in VSS you should be aware of the following issues.

- **Sharing**. Team Foundation Server does not support sharing of files. Shared files are migrated by copying the version of the file at the time sharing began to a destination folder. Any subsequent changes made to the shared file are replicated to both the shared and the original copies.
- **Branching**. Because branching in VSS uses sharing, the migration of a branched file results in the file being copied to the destination folder in TFS source control. After the branch event, the changes to any branch are migrated to the respective copy in TFS source control.
- **Pinning**. Team Foundation Server does not support pinning. To help you locate items in Team Foundation source control that were once pinned in the VSS database, the VSSConverter tool labels any file that was pinned with the "PINNED" label.

For optimum performance (especially important for large VSS databases), run the conversion on your TFS server computer.

Additional Resources

- For more information on how to prepare for migration, see *http://msdn2.microsoft.com/en-us/library/ms181246(en-us,vs.80).aspx*
- For more information on how to perform the migration, see *http://msdn2.microsoft.com/en-us/library/ms181247(VS.80).aspx*
- For more information on the limitations of the Visual SourceSafe converter, see *http://msdn2.microsoft.com/en-us/library/ms252491(VS.80).aspx*
- For more information about the VSS Analyze tool, see *http://msdn2.microsoft.com/en-us/library/ysxsfw4x.aspx.*
- For more information about the VSSConverter migrate command, see *http://msdn2.microsoft.com/en-us/library/ms400685(VS.80).aspx*

How To: Perform a Baseless Merge in Visual Studio Team Foundation Server

Applies To

- Microsoft® Visual Studio® 2005 Team Foundation Server (TFS)
- Microsoft Visual Studio Team System (VSTS)

Summary

This How To article walks you through the process of merging files from two branches that are not related to one another. The process of merging items that are not directly branched from each other is called a *baseless merge*. To perform a baseless merge, you must use the **Tf merge** command. You cannot perform a baseless merge operation from Visual Studio.

Contents

Objectives

- Learn how to decide if a baseless merge is necessary
- Perform a baseless merge and resolve merge conflicts

Overview

The process of merging items that are not directly branched from each other is called a *baseless merge*. For example, you might want to merge a change between two release branches, which are siblings of each other, without merging up to the parent branch. You can only perform a baseless merge by using the **Tf merge** command. You cannot perform a baseless merge from within the Visual Studio IDE.

When you perform a baseless merge, TFS does not have any information about the relationship of the files in the branches. For example, if you have renamed a file, this will be viewed as a deleted file and a new file will be added in the branch. For this reason you have to perform more manual conflict resolutions than when you perform a normal merge. However, you only have to perform this conflict resolution once. After you have performed the baseless merge, TFS records merge history and establishes a relationship between the folders and files.

Summary of Steps

- Step 1—Evaluate Whether a Baseless Merge Is Needed
- Step 2—Perform a Baseless Merge Using Tf.exe
- Step 3—Resolve Merge Conflicts
- Step 4—Check-In the Merged Changes

Step 1 — Evaluate Whether a Baseless Merge Is Needed

In this step, you evaluate the branches and items to be merged to determine if you need to do a baseless merge or whether a regular merge will work.

If you are the owner/administrator of your team project, you will know the relationships between the branches or items. From Visual Studio, you can only merge the branches or items that have a parent-child relationship. If your project contains branches or items that do not have this relationship, you require to perform baseless merge.

If you are not aware of all the relationships between the branches or items, you can evaluate whether you need to use a baseless merge as follows.

1. Open Source Code Explorer.
2. Right-click the branched folder and then click Merge.
3. In the Source Control Merge Wizard dialog box, click the Target branch drop-down list.

   If you do not see an entry for the branch you want to merge, this indicates that no merge relationship exists between these branches. In this case you must perform a baseless merge.

Step 2 — Perform a Baseless Merge Using Tf.exe

In this step, you use the TFS command line tool **Tf.exe** to perform a baseless merge.

► To perform a baseless merge

1. Set the Workspace for both branches by performing a "Get Latest" operation on the branches to be merged:
   a. Open Source Code Explorer.
   b. Right-click the folder for the first branch to be merged, and click Get Latest Version.
   c. Repeat the previous step for the second branch to be merged.

   Note that if no workspace is mapped, Visual Studio prompts you to select a folder on your local drive.
2. Open a Visual Studio command window.
3. Run the following Tf.exe command from the command line:

   Tf merge /baseless <<source path>> <<target path>> /recursive

   Example

   Tf merge /baseless c:\data\proj1 c:\data proj2 /recursive

   If you need to merge specific versions of the code changes, you can use the version switch with Tf.exe as follows:

   tf merge /baseless <<source path>> <<target path>> / recursive /version:<<from Changeset>>~<<to Changeset>>

   Example

   tf merge /baseless c:\data\proj1 c:\data\proj2 /recursive /version:C123~C125

Step 3 — Resolve Merge Conflicts

In this step, you resolve conflicts that might occur when performing a baseless merge. After you run the Tf.exe command, it displays a **Resolve Conflicts** dialog box with a list of the files that have conflicts.

1. Select each file and click **Resolve**.
2. In the **Resolve version conflict** dialog box:
   - If there are no content changes, select the **Keep changes in the target branch** resolution option and then click **OK**.
   - If there are content changes, select the **Merge changes in merge tool** resolution option, and then click **OK**.
3. In the merge tool, click the conflict regions in the upper pane or type in the lower pane to apply changes for each conflicting line.
4. After you have applied changes for all of the conflicts, click **OK** in the merge tool.
5. After all the conflicts have been resolved, click **Close**.

Step 4 — Check-in the Merged Changes

In this step, you check-in the baseless merged changes

1. Open **Source Code Explorer**.
2. Right-click the target folder in which you have merged the changes and click **Check-in pending changes**.
3. In the **Check-In Source Files** dialog box, ensure that all the files to be checked in are selected.
4. Click **Check In**.

Additional Resources

- To learn how to merge files and folders, see "How to: Merge Files and Folders" at *http://msdn2.microsoft.com/en-us/library/ms181428(VS.80).aspx*
- To learn more about baseless merge, see the /baseless option in "Merge Command" at *http://msdn2.microsoft.com/en-us/library/bd6dxhfy(VS.80).aspx*

How To: Set Up a Continuous Integration Build in Visual Studio Team Foundation Server

Applies To

- Microsoft® Visual Studio® 2005 Team Foundation Server (TFS)
- Microsoft Visual Studio Team System (VSTS)

Summary

Although Visual Studio 2005 Team Foundation Server does not provide a Continuous Integration (CI) solution out of box, it does provide a framework on which you can build your own CI build solution. This How To article walks you through the process of setting up a CI build with TFS by using the solution provided by the VSTS team. This solution installs a Web service running under the account that has access to the TFS server. When you register the Web service for the **CheckinEvent** event, the Web service will initiate a team build whenever a check-in occurs.

Contents

Objectives

- Learn what a Continuous Integration build is
- Create a CI build by using **TFSBuild** and the VSTS team's CI solution.

Overview

An important mechanism for improving code quality is to give developers continuous feedback regarding the quality of the check-ins they make. This is especially important for check-in that causes a build break resulting in compilation errors. The earlier the developer receives feedback, the sooner they can fix any errors in the code, thus unblocking other developers/testers and improving all team members' productivity.

This is where the Continuous Integration build type—the process of creating builds whenever a developer checks code into source control—becomes valuable. The Continuous Integration build provides quick feedback to developers, who can also configure their CI builds with quality gates to ensure further improvement in your build quality.

Summary of Steps

- Step 1—Create and Test your Build
- Step 2—Install the Continuous Integration Solution
- Step 3—Configure the Continuous Integration Solution
- Step 4—Register for the CheckinEvent Event
- Step 5—Test the Continuous Integration Build
- Step 6—Set Up E-mail Alerts

Before You Begin

Make sure the account that runs your build service has, Start a build = Allow, permission in Team Foundation Server.

Step 1 — Create and Test your Build

In this initial step, you create a test build and make sure it works from within the Visual Studio Integrated Development Environment (IDE). If the team build does not work, you should fix it before moving on to the next step.

1. Create a Microsoft Windows® Form project that you can use for testing the build.
2. Build the project and make sure that it is working correctly.

3. Check your project into source control.
4. Create a team build as follows:
   a. In Team Explorer, right-click **Team Builds**, and then click **New Team Build Type**.
   b. Complete the self-explanatory **Team Build Type Creation Wizard**.
5. Verify that the team build is working by performing the following steps:
   a. In Team Explorer, double-click the Team Build Project you just created.
   b. On the **Build** menu of the Visual Studio instance, click **Build Team Project** *<<Your Team Build Name>>*.
   c. Confirm that the correct build type is selected and then click **Build**.
6. Review the build output and make sure that no errors occurred in the build process.

Important: Make sure your build services account (TFSService) has Full Control permission to the shared folder for the drops, as specified in **Team Build Type Wizard**.

Step 2 — Install the Continuous Integration Solution

In this step, you install the solution provided by VSTS team for setting up the CI build. Detailed information about the solution is available at *http://msdn2.microsoft.com/en-us/library/ms364045(VS.80).aspx*

1. Install the solution on your TFS server from following location *http://download.microsoft.com/download/6/5/e/65e300ce-22fc-4988-97de-0e81d3de2482/ci.msi*
2. On the second page of the installer wizard, ensure that the "**Team Foundation Server**" site is selected.

Setup creates a virtual directory beneath the root of the application-tier server for TFS. This should be an Internet Information Services (IIS) Web site named Team Foundation Server on port 8080.

Step 3 — Configure the Continuous Integration Solution

In this step, you will configure the CI settings to specify the project to be built and the build machine and team build type to be used.

1. Perform the followings steps to ensure that the virtual root runs in the "TfsAppPool" application pool:
   a. Open IIS Manager by clicking **Start**, click **Administrative Tools**, and then select **IIS Manager**.
   b. Under the **Web Sites,** expand the **Team Foundation Server** Web site.

   c. Right-click on the **CI Web Application** and make sure that **Application Pool** is set to **TfsAppPool**.

2. Configure Continuous Integration settings as follows:
   a. Open the **CI Web Application** Web.config file located at C:\Program Files\Microsoft Visual Studio 2005 Team Foundation Server\Web Services\CI\
   b. Set the following properties by adding a new key under the **<appsettings>** node:
      - **TeamFoundationServer**—the URL for the application tier, in the format http://machine:8080.
      - **TeamProject**—the team project for which you want to enable CI
      - **BuildType**—the build type to be used while creating CI builds. Typically, this is configured for builds only. You can also add a basic level of testing and static analysis.
      - **Build Machine**—an optional parameter, use this to override the default build machine specified in the build type.

   The following is an example of the configuration settings:

```
....

<add key="1" value="TeamServer=http://TFSRTM:8080;TeamProjectName=Advent
ureWorks;BuildType=Test Build"/>

....
```

Step 4 — Register for the CheckinEvent Event

In this step, you register for the **CheckinEvent** event by using the **bisubscribe** tool available with TFS.

1. Open a command prompt and navigate to the following location C:\Program Files\Microsoft Visual Studio 2005 Team Foundation Server\TF Setup\
2. Run the following command

   Bissubscribe /eventType CheckinEvent /address http://TFSRTM:8080/ci/notify.asmx /deliveryType Soap /domain http://TFSRTM:8080
3. If you get any errors, or if you want to confirm that you have registered correctly, do the following:
   a. Open Microsoft SQL Server™ Management Studio.
   b. Open the **tfsIntegration** database.
   c. Open the **tbl_subscription** table.

   The table has entries for all events that have already been subscribed; you should be able to find the entry for CI solution subscribed to the CheckinEvent event. If required, you can unsubscribe any registered event, by simply deleting the entry from the table.

Step 5 — Test the Continuous Integration Build

In this step, you verify that the CI build is working correctly.

1. Open the Windows Forms Application that was created in Step 1.
2. Make some nominal changes to the code. Be careful to ensure that the changes will not break the build.
3. Check-in the code changes you made.
4. If you have access to the build machine, open Task Manager and look at the machine's CPU usage; it should increase soon after the check-in to indicate that a build is occurring. If you look at the process list, you should see msbuild, csc, and/or aspnet_compiler using up CPU cycles, indicating that the build is in progress.
5. Give the build time to run and then in the **Team Explorer,** double-click on **All Build Types** and look for the build after it completes.

Troubleshooting

In case the build does not show up in the build list, you can troubleshoot the problem as follows:

1. Make sure that the event is subscribed correctly. For more information, see sub-step 3 of Step 4 above.
2. Make sure that the CI Web Application's Web.config is configured correctly, for more information, see Step 3 above.
3. Make sure that the CI Web application is running in the right context and that it has access to the TFS server.
4. If you have followed the preceding troubleshooting steps but the build still fails you can debug the CI Web application as follows:
   a. Create a new Web site project.
   b. Select to add an existing Web site to this new project.
   c. Click the local IIS button and then select the CI Web Application from the list.
   d. Open **notify.cs** and set a breakpoint on the **Notify** method.
   e. Press F5 to start debugging.
   f. Make changes to the Windows Forms test application and then check the code into source control.
      - If the breakpoint is not hit, the event is not being captured; try subscribing again.
      - If the breakpoint is hit, debug further.
      - Ensure that script debugging is enabled in Microsoft Internet Explorer. On tools menu select **Internet Options** and then click the **Advanced** tab, here make sure the **Disable Script Debugging (Internet Explorer)** option is unchecked.

Step 6 — Set Up E-mail Alerts

In this step you will set up an e-mail alert to be sent upon build completion, so that all concerned parties are informed.

1. In the Team Explorer, right-click the relevant team project.
2. Select **Project Alerts**.
3. Select the **A build completes** option and enter the e-mail address(es) for notification.

Additional Resources

- For more information on how to use the Visual Studio Team System CI solution, see "Continuous Integration Using Team Foundation Build" at *http://msdn2.microsoft.com/en-us/library/ms364045(VS.80).aspx*
- To download the Visual Studio Team System CI solution installer, go to *http://download.microsoft.com/download/6/5/e/65e300ce-22fc-4988-97de-0e81d3de2482/ci.msi*
- For more information on Agile Development and Continuous Integration in Team Foundation Server, see "Extend Team Foundation Server To Enable Continuous Integration" at *http://msdn.microsoft.com/msdnmag/issues/06/03/TeamSystem/default.aspx*

How To: Set Up a Scheduled Build in Visual Studio Team Foundation Server

Applies To

- Microsoft® Visual Studio® 2005 Team Foundation Server (TFS)
- Microsoft Visual Studio Team System (VSTS)

Summary

Although Visual Studio 2005 Team Foundation Server does not provide scheduled builds out of the box, you can use the **TFSBuild** command to implement your own scheduled builds. This How To article walks you through the process of setting up a scheduled build by using the **TFSBuild** command and the Microsoft Windows® Task Scheduler.

Contents

Objectives

- Learn what a scheduled build is.
- Create a scheduled build by using the **TFSBuild** command utility and the Windows Task Scheduler.

Overview

It is highly important that a project development team to generate regular builds in order to get timely feedback from a test team as well as other stake holders. This can be achieved through the use of scheduled builds. You can choose to schedule your build on a nightly, weekly, biweekly, or on any other regular schedule depending upon your project scope and requirements.

Although the Team Build feature in TFS does not have support scheduled builds out of box, it does provide a **TFSBuild** command line utility that enables you to initiate team builds from the command line. You can use any scheduler, such as the Windows Task Scheduler, to run the **TFSBuild** command utility in order to start builds at regular intervals.

Summary of Steps

- Step 1—Create and Test Your Build
- Step 2—Create the TFSBuild Command Line
- Step 3—Test the TFSBuild Command Line
- Step 4—Create a Batch File
- Step 5—Test the Batch File
- Step 6—Add a Scheduled Task
- Step 7—Test the Scheduled Task

Before You Begin

Make sure the account that runs your build service is assigned Start a build = Allow permission in TFS.

Step 1 — Create and Test Your build

In this step, you create a test build and make sure the team-build works from within Visual Studio Integrated Development Environment (IDE). If the build does not work, you should fix it before moving on to the next step.

1. Create a Microsoft Windows® Form project that you can use for testing the build.

2. Build the project and make sure that it is working correctly.
3. Check your project into source control.
4. Create a team build as follows:
   a. In Team Explorer, right-click **Team Builds**, and then click **New Team Build Type**.
   b. Complete the self-explanatory **Team Build Type Creation Wizard**.
5. Perform the following steps to verify that the team build is working:
   a. In Team Explorer, double-click the Team Build Project you just created.
   b. On the **Build** menu of the Visual Studio instance, click **Build Team Project** ***<<Your Team Build Name>>***.
   c. Confirm that the correct build type is selected and the click **Build**.
6. Review the build output and make sure that there are no errors in the build process.

Important: Make sure that your build services account (TFSService) has Full Control permission to the shared folder for the drops, as specified in the **Team Build Type Wizard**.

Step 2 — Create the TFSBuild Command Line

In this step, you create a command for the **TFSBuild** utility for the purpose of starting a build.

1. As the TFSBuild command utility needs a number of parameters in order to start a build, you first need to determine the parameters to be used, as follows.
   a. **Team Foundation Server**—The TFS URL where the solutions being built are checked in.
   b. **Team Project**—The name of the team project which you want to build.
   c. **Build Type**—The build type that you created using the Build Type Wizard in Step 1.
   d. **Build Machine**—The name of the build server that you want to use for building your project. This is an optional parameter; by default, it uses the build server specified in the team build type.
   e. **Build Directory**—The path to the directory where the build occurs. This is an optional parameter, by default, it uses the path specified in the team build type.
2. Create the build command as follows:

```
TfsBuild start <<TeamFoundationServer>> <<TeamProject>> <<BuildTypeName>>
```

If you plan to override the build machine name and build directory path specified while creating the build type, the command would then be as follows:

```
TfsBuild start <<TeamFoundationServer>> <<TeamProject>> <<BuildTypeName>>
/m:<<MachineName>> /d:<<BuildDirectory>>
```

Step 3 — Test the TFSBuild Command Line

In this step, you test that the TFSBuild command is working correctly.

1. Open the Visual Studio command prompt.
2. Type the **TfsBuild** command that you created in Step 2.
3. Review the output to make sure that no errors occurred and that the build was created successfully.

Step 4 — Create a Batch File

In this step, you create a batch file that will be used for scheduling the builds.

1. Open Microsoft Notepad and type following command; please note that the full path to the TFSBuild.exe file is specified so that it can run from Windows command prompt. The following is an example of the command:

   ```
   "C:\Program Files\Microsoft Visual Studio 8\Common7\IDE\TFSBuild" start
   <<TeamFoundationServer>> <<TeamProject>> <<BuildTypeName>>
   ```

   If you override the build machine and build directory path, the command in the batch file would be as follows:

   ```
   "C:\Program Files\Microsoft Visual Studio 8\Common7\IDE\TFSBuild"
   start <<TeamFoundationServer>> <<TeamProject>> <<BuildTypeName>> /
   m:<<BuildMachineName>> /d:<<BuildDirectoryPath>>
   ```

2. Save the file as a batch file; for example, batchbuild.bat.
3. Place the file in a build scripts folder in TFS server source control, for example **Main\Scripts**.

Step 5 — Test the batch file

In this step, you verify that the batch file you created works correctly.

1. Open a Windows command prompt.

   Note: Do not open a Visual Studio command prompt; by default the Windows scheduler will run the batch file in a Windows command prompt.

2. Start the batch file on the command line.
3. Ensure that the build works correctly without any errors.

Step 6 — Add a Scheduled Task

In this step, you add a schedule task for running the build command at regular intervals as required by your project.

1. Click **Start** and then click **Control Panel**.
2. Select the **Scheduled Tasks** option and then click **Add Scheduled Tasks**.
3. In the **Scheduled Task Wizard** click **Next**.
4. Click **Browse** and select the batch file you created in Step 4, then click **Next**.
5. On this page, type the name of the task and select the frequency at which you want to run the tasks – for example, **Daily** and then click **Next**.
6. Configure the **Start time** and **Start date** and then click **Next**.
7. Enter user name and password of an account with Start a build permissions and click **Next**.
8. Then click **Finish**.

Step 7 — Test the Scheduled Task

In this step, you verify that the scheduled task is running at the right time and that the build work properly.

1. Wait for the time at which the scheduled task should execute.

   -or-

   Click **Start** and then click **Control Panel,** then select **Scheduled Tasks** option, from the list right click on your scheduled task and select **Run**.
2. A command prompt should appear and your build should start.
3. If you do not have access to the build machine at the time the task should execute, you can check back later and see if a build has completed:
   a. In **Team Explorer** double-click **All Build Types**.
   b. View the list of builds to see if a build is completed at the time you scheduled.

Additional Resources

For more information on configuring a scheduled build, see "How to: Configure a Scheduled Build (Command Line)" at
http://msdn2.microsoft.com/en-us/library/ms181727(VS.80).aspx

How To: Structure ASP.NET Applications in Visual Studio Team Foundation Server

Applies To

- Microsoft® Visual Studio® 2005 Team Foundation Server (TFS)
- Microsoft Visual Studio Team System (VSTS)
- ASP.NET applications

Summary

This How To article walks you through the process of organizing and structuring your ASP.NET Web applications for Team Foundation Server. This article explains an appropriate source tree structure to use within TFS source control.

Contents

Objectives

- Learn how to structure an ASP.NET application in TFS source control.
- Learn about an appropriate tree structure to use in TFS source control.

Overview

This How To article shows you how to build a source control folder structure that is appropriate for ASP.NET Web applications. Because ASP.NET Web projects often include additional class libraries, a structure is required to accommodate these as well. Folders in which to maintain your ASP.NET Web projects are located beneath a **/Main/Source** top-level structure in source control. This structure enables you to easily use additional **Development** and **Releases** folders if you need to create branches for isolated development and for release maintenance. For more information about creating this top-level folder structure, see "How To: Structure Your Source Control Folders in Visual Studio Team Foundation Server"

Summary of Steps

- Step 1—Create Local Folders for Your Web Project
- Step 2—Create a Blank Solution
- Step 3—Add a Web Site to Your Solution
- Step 4—Add a Class Library (Optional)
- Step 5—Check Your Solution Structure
- Step 6—Check Your Local Folder Structure
- Step 7—Add Your Solution to Source Control

Step 1 — Create Local Folders for Your Web Project

In this step, you create an appropriate local folder structure for your Web project on your development computer. To ensure a consistent approach for your team development, and to keep team projects well organized on your development computer, you should keep your entire development source from all of the team projects you are working on grouped together beneath a single root folder such as C:\DevProjects.

Create a top level folder such as C:\DevProjects.

Step 2 — Create a Blank Solution

To create an ASP.NET Web Application, start by explicitly creating a Visual Studio Solution (.sln) file and then add your Web site and any supplementary projects you might need, such as class libraries. In the following steps, you create your solutions beneath a top level C:\DevProjects folder

1. On the **File** menu, point to **New** and then click **Project**.
2. Expand **Other Project Types** and select **Visual Studio Solutions**.
3. Select **Blank Solution**.
4. Name your solution **MyWebAppSln**.
5. Set the **Location** to C:\DevProjects and then click **OK**.

This creates a C:\DevProjects\MyWebAppSln folder. Visual Studio adds the solution (.sln) file and solution user options (.suo) file to this folder. Note that only the .sln file is subsequently added to source control in Step 7.

Step 3 — Add a Web Site to Your Solution

In this step, you add an ASP.NET Web site to your solution. The way you do this varies slightly depending on whether you are creating a new file system–based Web site that uses the Visual Studio development Web server or a Hyper Text Transfer Protocol (HTTP) Web site that uses Internet Information Services (IIS).

File System

► **To add a file system–based Web project to your solution**

1. In **Solution Explorer**, right-click **Solution MyWebAppSln**, point to **Add**, and then click **New Web Site**.
2. In the **Add New Web Site** dialog box, leave the **Location** as **File System**, and the **Language** as **Visual C#**.
3. Set the Location directory to C:\DevProjects\MyWebAppSln\Source\MyWebAppWeb.
4. Click **OK** to close the **Add New Web Site** dialog box.

   Note that the "Web" suffix is used in this example to clearly denote the folder as a Web site root folder.

HTTP

To create an HTTP-based ASP.NET Web site that uses IIS, start by explicitly creating your virtual directory so that your Web site directory ends up in your defined location rather than beneath \inetpub\wwwroot.

► **To create your Web site's virtual directory**

1. Use Windows Explorer to browse to C:\DevProjects\MyWebAppSln\Source.
2. Create a new folder beneath this location named **MyWebAppWeb**.
3. Right-click **MyWebAppWeb** and then click **Sharing and Security**.
4. Click the **Web Sharing** tab.
5. Click **Share this folder**.
6. Leave the **Alias** as **MyWebAppWeb**, leave the default **Access permissions** and **Application permissions,** and then click **OK**.
7. Click **OK** twice.

► **To add your Web site to your solution**

1. In **Solution Explorer**, right-click **Solution MyWebAppSln**, point to **Add**, and then click **New Web Site**.
2. In the **Add New Web Site** dialog box, set the **Location** to **HTTP** and leave the **Language** as **Visual C#**.
3. Set the **Location URL** to **http://localhost/MyWebAppWeb**.
4. Click **OK** to close the **Add New Web Site** dialog box.

Visual Studio adds your Default.aspx, Default.aspx.cs files to the C:\DevProjects\MyWebAppSln\Source\MyWebAppWeb folder and creates **Bin** and **App_Data** child folders.

Step 4 — Add a Class Library (Optional)

If your Web application requires additional class libraries, add them as follows:

1. In **Solution Explorer**, right-click your **MyWebAppSln** solution, point to **Add,** and then click **New Project**.
2. Select **Visual C#** as the project type and **Class Library** as the template.
3. Type the name **ClassLibrary**, set the **Location** to C:\DevProjects\MyWebAppSln\Source, and then click **OK**.

All new projects are added beneath the **Source** folder.

Step 5 — Check Your Solution Structure

Use Solution Explorer to verify your solution structure. It should resemble the following:

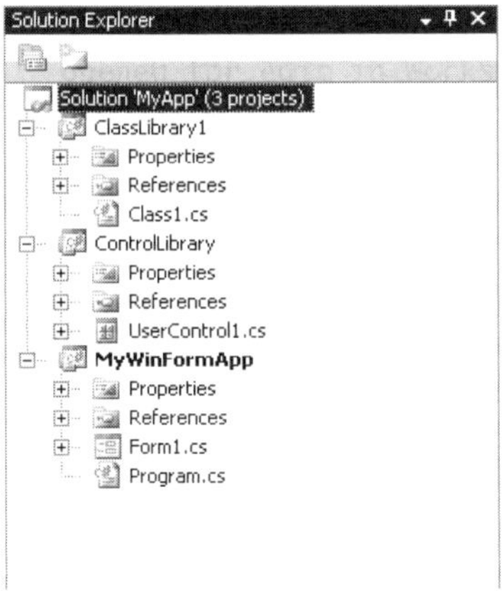

Step 6 — Check your Local Folder Structure

Use Windows Explorer to verify your local folder structure. It should resemble the following:

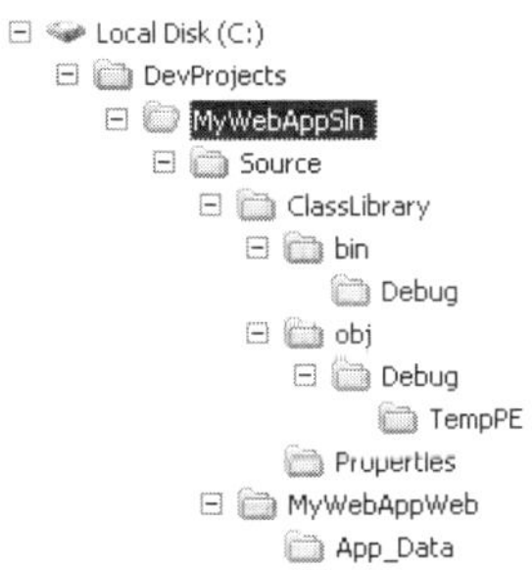

Step 7 — Add Your Solution to Source Control

In this step, you add your solution to TFS source control.

1. Right-click your solution and then click **Add Solution to Source Control**.
2. In the **Add Solution MyWebAppSln to Source Control** dialog box, select your team project
3. In the dialog box, click **Make New Folder**, and then name the new folder **Main**

4. Select the newly created **Main** folder and then click **Make New Folder**, name the new folder **Source**.
5. Select the newly created **Source** folder and then click **OK**.
6. Check your source control folder structure by clicking **Source Control** within **Team Explorer**. It should resemble the following:

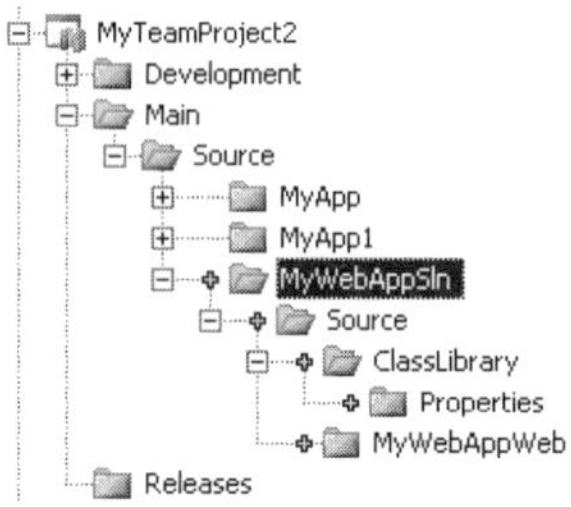

7. At this point you can view pending changes and check your solution source files into the server. To do so, on the **View Menu**, point to **Other Windows** and then click **Pending Changes**. Select your project and the source files to be checked-in, supply a check-in comment and then click **Check In**.

Shared Code Considerations

For ASP.NET Web applications that reference shared source code, you can consider the following two main options:

- Reference the code from a shared location
- Branch the shared code

Reference the Code from a Shared Location

With this approach, you map the source from a shared location such as another team project into the workspace on your development computer. This creates a configuration that unifies the shared source from the shared location and your project code on your development computer.

The advantage of this approach is that any changes to the shared source are picked up every time you retrieve the latest version of the source into your workspace. For example consider a team project named Common that contains the shared source. To reference the code from this location, you would map both team projects to a common path location on your development computer. For example:

- C:\DevProjects\MyWebAppSln\
- C:\DevProjects\SharedCommon\

The following workspace mappings are used:

Source Control Folder	Local Folder
$/MyTeamProject1/Main/Source/MyWebAppApp	C:\DevProjects\MyWebAppSln
$/MyTeamProject2/Main/Source/Common	C:\DevProjects\Common

For more information see "Working with multiple team projects in Team Build" at *http://blogs.msdn.com/manishagarwal/archive/2005/12/22/506635.aspx*

Branch the Shared Code

With this approach, you branch the shared code from the common team project into your team project. This also creates a configuration that unifies the source from the shared location and your project.

The difference with this approach is that the shared source changes are picked up as part of a merge process between the branches. This makes the decision to pick up changes in the shared source much more explicit. You decide when to perform a merge to pick up latest changes.

For example consider the team project named **Common** that contains shared source. To branch the code from this location:

1. In **Source Control Explorer**, right-click the root folder of the **Common** team project.
2. Click **Branch...**
3. In the **Branch** dialog box, set the **Target:** to the root folder of the $/MyTeamProject1/Main/Source/ team project and then click **OK**.
4. After the branch operation has completed do not forget to check-in the branched source code.

Additional Resources

- For more information on creating a workspace, see "How to: Create a Workspace" at *http://msdn2.microsoft.com/en-us/library/ms181384(VS.80).aspx*
- For more information on referencing assemblies in different team projects, see "Working with multiple team projects in Team Build" at *http://blogs.msdn.com/manishagarwal/archive/2005/12/22/506635.aspx*

How To: Structure Windows Applications in Visual Studio Team Foundation Server

Applies To

- Microsoft® Visual Studio® Team Foundation Server (TFS)
- Microsoft Visual Studio Team System (VSTS)
- Microsoft Windows® Form Applications

Summary

This How To article walks you through the process of organizing and structuring your Windows Form applications for Team Foundation Server. The article explains an appropriate source tree structure to use within TFS source control.

Contents

Objectives

- Learn how to structure a Windows Forms application in TFS source control.
- Learn about an appropriate tree structure to use within TFS source control.

Overview

This How To article shows you how to build a source control folder structure that is appropriate for Windows Forms applications. Because Windows Forms projects often include additional class and control libraries, a structure is required to accommodate these as well. Folders in which to maintain your Windows Forms projects are located beneath a **/Main/Source** top-level structure. This enables you to easily use additional **Development** and **Releases** folders if you need to create branches for isolated development and for release maintenance. For more information about creating this top level folder structure, see "How To: Structure Your Source Control Folders in Visual Studio team Foundation Server."

Summary of Steps

- Step 1—Create Local Folders for Your Windows Forms Project
- Step 2—Create a Blank Solution
- Step 3—Add a Windows Forms Project to Your Solution
- Step 4—Add a Control Library (Optional)
- Step 5—Add a Class Library (Optional)
- Step 6—Check Your Solution Structure
- Step 7—Check Your Local Folder Structure
- Step 8—Add Your Solution to Source Control

Step 1 — Create Local Folders for Your Windows Forms Project

In this step, you create an appropriate local folder structure for your Windows Forms project on your development computer. To ensure a consistent approach for your team development and to keep team projects well organized on your development computer, you should keep your entire development source from all of the team projects you are working on grouped together beneath a single root folder such as C:\DevProjects.

Create a top-level folder such as C:\DevProjects.

Step 2 — Create a Blank Solution

To create a Windows Forms application, start by explicitly creating a Visual Studio Solution (.sln) file and then add your Windows Forms project and any supplementary projects you might need, such as class or control libraries. In the following steps, you create your solutions beneath a top-level C:\DevProjects directory.

1. On the **File** menu, point to **New** and then click **Project**.
2. Expand **Other Project Types** and then select **Visual Studio Solutions**.
3. Select **Blank Solution**.
4. Name your solution **MyApp**.
5. Set the **Location** to C:\DevProjects and then click **OK**.

This creates a C:\DevProjects\MyApp folder. Visual Studio adds the solution (.sln) file and solution user options (.suo) file to this folder. Note that only the .sln file is subsequently added to source control in Step 8.

Step 3 — Add a Windows Forms Project to Your Solution

In this step, you add a new Windows Forms project to your solution.

1. In **Solution Explorer**, right-click **Solution MyApp**, point to **Add**, and then click **New Project....**
2. In the **Add New Project** dialog box, select **Visual C#** as the project type and **Windows Application** as the template.
3. Set the **Location** to C:\DevProjects\MyApp\Source directory.
4. Name your project as **MyWinFormApp**.
5. Click **OK** to close the **Add New Project** dialog box and add your project.

Step 4 — Add a Control Library (Optional)

If your Windows Forms application requires additional control libraries, add them as follows:

1. In **Solution Explorer**, right-click your solution, point to **Add**, and then click **New Project...**
2. In the **Add New Project** dialog box, select **Visual C#** as the project type and **Windows Control Library** as the template.
3. Set the **Location** to C:\DevProjects\MyApp\Source directory.
4. Name your Windows Control Library as **ControlLibrary**.
5. Click **OK** to close the **Add New Project** dialog box.

Step 5 — Add a Class Library (Optional)

If your Windows Forms application requires additional class library projects, add them as follows:

1. In **Solution Explorer**, right-click your solution, point to **Add**, and then click **New Project…**.
2. In the **Add New Project** dialog box, select **Visual C#** as the project type and **Class Library** as the template.
3. Set the **Location** to C:\DevProjects\MyApp\Source directory.
4. Name your Windows Class Library as **ClassLibrary1**.
5. Click **OK** to close the **Add New Project** dialog box.

Step 6 — Check Your Solution Structure

Use Solution Explorer to verify your solution structure. It should resemble the following:

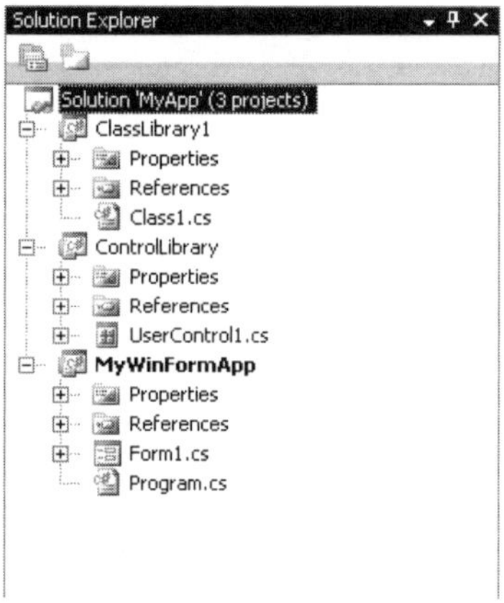

Step 7 — Check Your Local Folder Structure

Use Windows Explorer to verify your local folder structure. It should resemble the following:

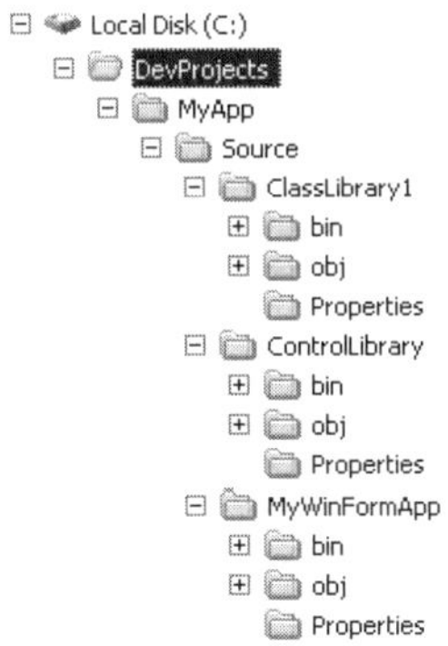

Step 8 — Add Your Solution to Source Control

In this step, you add your solution containing your Windows Form project, optional class libraries, and control libraries to TFS source control.

1. Right-click **MyApp** and then click **Add Solution to Source Control**.
2. In the **Add Solution MyApp to Source Control** dialog box, choose your team project.
3. In the dialog box, click **Make New Folder** and then name the new folder as **Main**.
4. Select the newly created **Main** folder, click **Make New Folder**, and then name the new folder as **Source**.
5. Select the newly created **Source** folder and then click **OK**.
6. Check your source control folder structure by double clicking **Source Control** within the Team Explorer. This displays **Source Control Explorer**. Your structure should resemble the following:

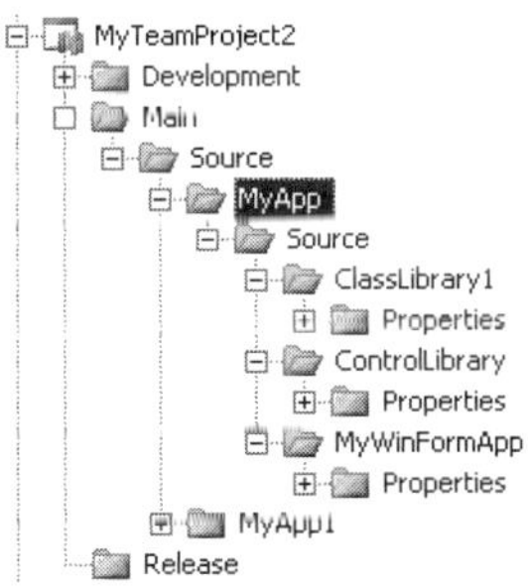

7. At this point you can view pending changes and check your source files into the server. To do so, on the **View Menu**, point to **Other Windows** and then click **Pending Changes**. Select your project and the source files to be checked-in, supply a check-in comment, and then click **Check In**.

Shared Code Considerations

For Windows Forms applications that reference shared source code, you can consider the following two main options:

- Reference the code from a shared location
- Branch the shared code

Reference the Code from a Shared Location

With this approach, you map the source from a shared location such as another team project into the workspace on your development computer. This creates a configuration that unifies the shared source from the shared location with your project code on your development computer.

The advantage of this approach is that any changes to the shared source are picked up every time you retrieve the latest version of the source into your workspace. For example consider a team project named Common that contains the shared source. To reference the code from this location, you map both team projects to a common path location on your development computer. For example:

- C:\MyProjects\MyApp\
- C:\MyProjects\SharedCommon\

The following workspace mappings are used:

Source Control Folder	Local Folder
$/MyTeamProject1/Main/Source/MyApp	C:\DevProjects\MyApp
$/MyTeamProject2/Main/Source/Common	C:\DevProjects\Common

For more information, see "Working with multiple team projects in Team Build" at *http://blogs.msdn.com/manishagarwal/archive/2005/12/22/506635.aspx*

Branch the Shared Code

With this approach, you branch the shared code from the common team project into your team project. This also creates a configuration that unifies the source from the shared location and your project.

The difference with this approach is that the shared source changes are picked up as part of a merge process between the branches. This makes the decision to pick up changes in the shared source much more explicit. You decide when to perform a merge to pick up latest changes.

For example consider the team project named **Common** that contains shared source. To branch the code from this location:

1. In **Source Control Explorer**, right-click the root folder of the **Common** team project.
2. Click **Branch...**
3. In the **Branch** dialog box, set the **Target:** to the root folder of the $/MyTeamProject1/Main/Source/ team project, and then click **OK**.
4. After the branch operation has completed, do not forget to check-in the branched source code.

Additional Resources

- For more information on creating a workspace, see "How to: Create a Workspace" at *http://msdn2.microsoft.com/en-us/library/ms181384(VS.80).aspx*
- For more information on referencing assemblies in different team projects, see "Working with multiple team projects in Team Build" at *http://blogs.msdn.com/manishagarwal/archive/2005/12/22/506635.aspx*

How To: Structure Your Source Control Folders in Team Foundation Server

Applies To

- Microsoft® Visual Studio® 2005 Team Foundation Server (TFS)
- Microsoft Visual Studio Team System (VSTS)

Summary

This How To article walks you through the process of structuring your folders in TFS. The recommendations in this article were created using lessons learned in practice by Microsoft teams as well as Microsoft customers in the field. The folder structure presented here is a starting point; more important than the structure is the rationale behind it. Use the rationale to help evaluate an appropriate folder structure and folder-naming convention for your own scenario.

Contents

Objectives

- Learn how to create a workspace mapping.
- Learn how to structure and name your source control folders.
- Learn how branching effects your source structure.

Overview

This How To article shows you how to build an appropriate source control folder structure that you can use with most common project types. The folder structure presented in this article uses three top level folders:

- **Main**. This is the main root folder that acts as a container folder for your main source tree, together with accompanying project artifacts such as design documentation, scripts, and test cases. The **Main** folder also contains your Visual Studio Solution (.sln) files.
- **Development**. This is an optional root-level folder that you can use if you need to create isolation for features or teams development. This folder is created by branching from **Main**.
- **Releases**. This is an optional root-level folder for released builds that you need to isolate; for example for ongoing maintenance of a particular release.

The folder structure presented in this article is summarized here:

```
/Main                                   Can contain solution (.sln) files
                                              for solutions that span projects
/Source
            /MyApp1                     Contains MyApp1.sln file
                  /Source                     Contain folder for all source
                        /ClassLibrary1  Contains ClassLibrary1.csproj
                        /MyApp1Web      Contains Default.aspx
/Build                                  Contains build output (binaries)
      /Docs                             Contains product docs etc
      /Tests                            Container for tests
```

/Development

/FeatureBranch1

/Source

/MyApp1

/Source

/MyApp1Web

/ClassLibrary1

/FeatureBranch2

/**Releases**

/Release1

/Source

/MyApp1

/Source

/MyApp1Web

/ClassLibrary1

/Release 1.1

/Release 1.2

Remember that this folder structure is only a starting point with a suggested set of folder names. More important than the structure and naming convention is the rationale behind them and the purposes of the different folders. For more information about the rationale behind this structure, see Chapter 5, "Defining Your Branching and Merging Strategy."

Summary of Steps

- Step 1—Create a Workspace Mapping
- Step 2—Create Your **Main** Folder
- Step 3—Create Folders for Your Project Artifacts
- Step 4—Add Your Solution to Your Source Tree
- Step 5—Create a Branched **Development** Folder for Isolation (Optional)
- Step 6—Create a **Releases** Folder for Release Builds Isolation (Optional)

Step 1 — Create a Workspace Mapping

In this initial step you create a workspace mapping to define the mapping between the folder structure on the TFS server and client. You need to do this so that you can create a source tree structure. You first create the source tree structure in your workspace and then perform a check-in to your TFS server.

You can create a workspace mapping in one of two ways:

- Set the workspace mapping explicitly.
- Perform a Get operation on your team project.

► To set a workspace mapping explicitly

1. In Visual Studio, on the **File** menu, point to **Source Control** and then click **Workspaces**.
2. In the **Manage Workspaces** dialog box, select your computer name and then click **Edit**.
3. In the **Edit Workspace** dialog box, in the **Working folders** list, click **Click here to enter a new working folder**.
4. Click the ellipsis (**...**) button, select your team project (for example **MyTeamProject1**), and then click **OK**.
5. Click the local folder cell to display another ellipsis button.
6. Click the ellipsis button beneath **Local Folder** and then browse to and select the local folder on your development computer where you want to locate your team project; for example, C:\DevProjects\MyTeamProject1.
7. Click **OK** twice to close the **Edit Workspace** dialog box.
8. Click **OK** in response to the Microsoft Visual Studio message box that informs you than one or more working folders have changed.
9. Click **Close** to close the **Manage Workspaces** dialog box.

► To perform a Get operation on your team project

1. In **Team Explorer**, expand your team project node; for example, **MyTeamProject1**.
2. Double-click **Source Control** beneath your team project.
3. In **Source Control Explorer**, right-click the root folder **MyTeamProject1** and then click **Get Latest Version**.
4. In the **Browse For Folder** dialog box, select your local path (for example, C:\DevProjects\MyTeamProject1) and then click **OK**. This maps the team project root folder within TFS to a local path on your computer.

Step 2 — Create Your Main Folder

In this step, you create a new root folder named **Main** in your Team Project source control. You use the **Main** folder as a root-level container folder for your source and other project artifacts. You can also use the **Main** folder to store any Visual Studio solution (.sln) files that span multiple projects. Solution files are also maintained in their own application folders lower in the tree structure.

► **To create a Main folder**

1. In Team Explorer, expand your team project and then double-click **Source Control**.
2. In Source Control Explorer, select your Team Project root folder.
3. Right-click in the right-hand pane and then click **New Folder**.
4. Type **Main** and then press ENTER.

Step 3 — Create Folders for Your Project Artifacts

In this step, you create folders beneath **Main** to hold your main source code tree and accompanying artifacts such as builds, documentation, script files and tests as shown below:

/Main

/Build

/Docs

/Source

/Tests

► **To create folders for your project assets**

1. Expand your team project and then in the left pane of Source Control Explorer, select the **Main** folder.
2. Right-click in the right pane, click **New Folder**, type **Build** and then press ENTER.
3. Repeat step 2 to create the remaining folders beneath **Main**.

Step 4 — Add Your Solution to Your Source Tree

In this step, you add your Visual Studio solution (.sln), project (.vsproj, .vbproj) and source files to your source tree in TFS source control.

Because you have mapped your root node to C:\DevProjects\MyTeamProject1 in Step 1, make sure the client folder structure and project structure are synchronized. Your solution (.sln) file should be at the following location:

C:\DevProjects\MyTeamProject1\Main\Source\MyApp1

The actual project-related files for MyApp1Web and ClassLibrary1 components should be at the following location:

C:\DevProjects\MyTeamProject1\Main\Source\MyApp1\Source

► To add the solution to your source tree

1. Open your solution in Visual Studio.
2. In Solution Explorer, right-click your solution and then click **Add Solution to Source Control**.
3. Because you have already established a workspace mapping in Step 1, the solution is added at this point.
4. Make sure that the correct **Local Workspace** is selected. This should be the same workspace that you used while creating your folder structure in TFS source control.
5. Click **OK** to add your solution to source control.

You source control folder structure should resemble the following:

/Main

/Source

/MyApp1

/Source

/MyApp1Web

/ClassLibrary1

/Build

/Docs

/Tests

For more information about how to setup an appropriate client-side folder structure, see:

- How To: Structure Windows Applications in Visual Studio Team Foundation Server.
- How To; Structure ASP.NET Applications in Visual Studio Team Foundation Server.

Creating a Folder Structure When a Project Has Unit Tests

If your project also includes unit tests, consider creating the following folder structure to store your unit tests separate from your main source folder:

/Main

/Source

/MyApp1

/Source

/MyApp1Web

/ClassLibrary1

/UnitTests

/Build

/Docs

/Tests

Step 5 — Create a Branched Development Folder for Isolation (Optional)

If you need to isolate for features or teams, consider creating a **Development** folder by branching from the **Main** folder. Note that if you do so, you must check any pending changes before you can branch.

► **To create a branched Development folder**

1. Create a root level **Development** folder (as a sibling of **Main**).
2. Create a sub folder named **FeatureBranch1**.
3. Select the $/TeamProject/Main/Source folder, right-click the folder, and then click **Branch**.

   Note: If **Branch** is grayed out, make sure you have checked in any pending changes.

4. In the **Branch** dialog box, click **Browse**, select MyTeamProject/Development/FeatureBranch1, and then click **OK**.
5. Click **OK** to create the branch.
6. Check-in your pending changes to push them to the server.

Your new folder structure in source control should resemble the following example:

```
/Development
    /FeatureBranch1
        /Source
            /MyApp1
                /Source
                    /MyApp1Web
                    /ClassLibrary1
    /FeatureBranch2
/Main
    /Source
        /MyApp1
            /Source
                /MyApp1Web
                /ClassLibrary1
    /Build
    /Docs
    /Source
    /Tests
```

Step 6 — Create a Releases Folder for Release Builds Isolation (Optional)

If you need to perform maintenance on a previously released build, while continuing development, consider isolating the maintenance work by creating a **Releases** folder. Beneath this folder you can create multiple sub folders, one per release.

► **To create a branched Releases folder**

1. Create a root-level **Releases** folder (as a sibling of **Main** and **Development**).
2. Create a sub folder named **Release1**.
3. Select the $/TeamProject/Development/Source folder, right-click the folder and then click **Branch**.

> **Note:** If **Branch** is grayed out, make sure you have checked in any pending changes.

4. In the **Branch** dialog box, click **Browse** select $/TeamProject/Maintenance/Release1, and then click **OK**.
5. In the **Branch from version** section, in the **By** list box, click **Label** and enter a label name in the **Label** text box. To find a label, click the browse button with the ellipses (**...**) next to the **Label** text box.
6. Click **OK** to create the branch.

Your new folder structure in source control should resemble the following example one shown here.

/Main

- /Source
  - /MyApp1
    - /Source
      - /MyApp1Web
      - /ClassLibrary1
- /Build
- /Docs
- /Source
- /Tests

/Releases

/Release1

- /Source
  - /MyApp1
    - /Source
      - /MyApp1Web
      - /ClassLibrary1

/Release 1.1

/Release 1.2

Additional Considerations

Keep in mind the following key considerations when structuring your source control folders in TFS:

- Do not branch unless you need to. You can label releases and branch at a later time if you need isolation.
- The above folder structure is ideally suited to scenarios where your project consists of one Visual Studio solution (.sln) file containing all of your project files. In this scenario, the **Main** folder contains the .sln file and you have one subfolder for each project file (.vsproj, .vbproj). In the above example project folders are represented by MyApp1, MyApp2 etc. You can also use the above approach for a single project file; for example, if you use a single project, with no solution file.
- For multiple-solution scenarios, you can locate multiple .sln files in the **Main** folder.

Additional Resources

- For more information on creating a workspace, see "How To: Create a Workspace" at *http://msdn2.microsoft.com/en-us/library/ms181384(VS.80).aspx*

Team Foundation Server Resources

Contents

patterns & practices

For more information on patterns and practices, refer to the Microsoft patterns & practices home page at *http://msdn.microsoft.com/practices/*

CodePlex Sites

- Team Foundation Branching Guidance at *http://www.codeplex.com/BranchingGuidance*
- Guidance Explorer at *http://www.codeplex.com/guidanceExplorer*
- Team Foundation Server Guide at *http://www.codeplex.com/TFSGuide*
- Team Foundation Server Guidance at *http://www.codeplex.com/VSTSGuidance*

Team Foundation Related Web Sites

- Team Foundation Server Team Center at *http://msdn2.microsoft.com/en-us/teamsystem/aa718934.aspx*
- Team Foundation Server FAQ at *http://msdn2.microsoft.com/en-us/teamsystem/aa718916.aspx*
- Team System Videos and Presentations at *http://msdn2.microsoft.com/en-us/teamsystem/aa718837.aspx*
- Team Foundation Server MSDN Documentation at *http://msdn2.microsoft.com/en-us/library/ms181232(vs.80).aspx*
- Download the Team Foundation Server Installation Guide at *http://go.microsoft.com/fwlink/?linkid=40042*

Partners and Service Providers

- Partner catalog at *http://catalog.vsipmembers.com/catalog/*
- Teamprise cross platform support at *http://www.teamprise.com/*
- Scrum support from Conchango at *http://www.conchango.com/Web/Public/Content/Home.aspx*
- ComponentSoftware source control migration at *http://www.componentsoftware.com/Products/converter/index.htm*
- Requirements management from Borland at *http://www.borland.com/*
- Business Process Modeling from RavenFlow at *http://www.n8systems.com/*

Forums

MSDN Forums listing can be found here:
http://forums.microsoft.com/MSDN/default.aspx?ForumGroupID=5&SiteID=1

Forum	Address
Team Foundation Server - General	http://forums.microsoft.com/MSDN/ShowForum.aspx?ForumID=22&SiteID=1
Team Foundation Server - Setup	http://forums.microsoft.com/MSDN/ShowForum.aspx?ForumID=68&SiteID=1
Team Foundation Server - Administration	http://forums.microsoft.com/MSDN/ShowForum.aspx?ForumID=477&SiteID=1
Team Foundation Server - Build Automation	http://forums.microsoft.com/MSDN/ShowForum.aspx?ForumID=481&SiteID=1
Team Foundation Server - Power Toys	http://forums.microsoft.com/MSDN/ShowForum.aspx?ForumID=930&SiteID=1
Team Foundation Server - Process Templates	http://forums.microsoft.com/MSDN/ShowForum.aspx?ForumID=482&SiteID=1
Team Foundation Server - Reporting & Warehouse	http://forums.microsoft.com/MSDN/ShowForum.aspx?ForumID=480&SiteID=1
Team Foundation Server - Team System Web Access	http://forums.microsoft.com/MSDN/ShowForum.aspx?ForumID=1466&SiteID=1
Team Foundation Server - Version Control	http://forums.microsoft.com/MSDN/ShowForum.aspx?ForumID=478&SiteID=1
Team Foundation Server - Work Item Tracking	http://forums.microsoft.com/MSDN/ShowForum.aspx?ForumID=479&SiteID=1

Microsoft Team Foundation Blogs

- Ask Burton *http://blogs.msdn.com/askburton/*
- Brian Harry *http://blogs.msdn.com/bharry/*
- Buck Hodges *http://blogs.msdn.com/buckh/*
- James Manning *http://blogs.msdn.com/jmanning/*
- Rob Caron *http://blogs.msdn.com/robcaron/*
- Team Foundation Blog at *http://blogs.msdn.com/team_foundation*

Service Packs

- Visual Studio 2005 SP1 at *http://msdn2.microsoft.com/en-gb/vstudio/bb265237.aspx*
- Microsoft® Visual Studio® 2005 Team Foundation Server Service Pack 1 at *http://www.microsoft.com/downloads/details.aspx?FamilyId=A9AB638C-04D2-4AEE-8AE8-9F00DD454AB8*
- Visual Studio 2005 Service Pack 1 Update for Windows Vista at *http://www.microsoft.com/downloads/details.aspx?FamilyID=90e2942d-3ad1-4873-a2ee-4acc0aace5b6&displaylang=en*
- SQL Server 2005 Service Pack 2 at *http://technet.microsoft.com/en-us/sqlserver/bb426877.aspx*

Training

A listing of training companies can be found here: *http://msdn2.microsoft.com/en-us/teamsystem/aa718793.aspx*

- Developmentor at *http://www.develop.com/*
- Pluralsight at *http://www.pluralsight.com*
- Notion Solutions at *http://www.notionsolutions.com*

Index

M

N

O

P

U

V

W

X